Language and Learning
The Home and School Years

THIRD EDITION

Terry Piper
BRITISH COLUMBIA OPEN UNIVERSITY
BURNABY, BRITISH COLUMBIA

Merrill
Prentice Hall

Upper Saddle River, New Jersey
Columbus, Ohio

Library of Congress Cataloging-in-Publication Data

Piper, Terry.
    Language and learning : the home and school years / Terry Piper.—3rd ed.
        p. cm.
    Includes bibliographical references and index.
    ISBN 0-13-060794-0 (pbk.)
    1. Children—Language. 2. Language arts. 3. Language acquisition. 4. Linguistics. 5.
Home and school. I. Title.
LB1139.L3 P53 2003
372.6—dc21

                                                                2002070939

Vice President and Publisher: Jeffery W. Johnston
Editor: Linda Ashe Montgomery
Editorial Assistant: Evelyn Olson
Production Editor: Linda Hillis Bayma
Production Coordination and Text Design: Tiffany Kuehn, Carlisle Publishers Services
Design Coordinator: Diane C. Lorenzo
Cover Designer: Jason Moore
Cover Image: Copyright © 1998-2001 EyeWire, Inc. All rights reserved.
Production Manager: Laura Messerly
Director of Marketing: Ann Castel Davis
Marketing Manager: Krista Groshong
Marketing Coordinator: Tyra Cooper

This book was set in Berling Roman by Carlisle Communications, Ltd. It was printed and bound by Maple-Vail
Book Manufacturing Group. The cover was printed by Phoenix Color Corp.

Pearson Education Ltd.
Pearson Education Australia Pty. Limited
Pearson Education Singapore Ptd. Ltd.
Pearson Education North Asia Ltd.
Pearson Education Canada, Ltd.
Pearson Educación de Mexico, S.A. de C.V.
Pearson Education—Japan
Pearson Education Malaysia Pte. Ltd.
Pearson Education, *Upper Saddle River, New Jersey*

10 9 8 7 6 5 4 3 2 1
ISBN: 0-13-060794-0

This book is dedicated to my mother,

Grace Ruth Ridpath,

whose own experience of language learning was nothing short
of awe-inspiring. Learning about her early years growing up
with non-hearing parents aroused my interest in language learning
and what became a lifelong passion and profession.

This one's for you, Mom!

Preface

This is a book about children and their learning. It is also a book about teachers for teachers. It traces children's language learning from birth through the school years, paying special attention to what is often a disjunctive experience between the home and school years. Children learn to speak, and often to read, at home under a variety of conditions. When they get to school, their experience, while not entirely homogenous from school to school or teacher to teacher, is often less variable, less diverse than it was at home. This book takes a practical look at the differences between language at home and language at school and offers ways of thinking productively about those differences.

This book is not a linguistics text, although it provides a rudimentary introduction to the various subdisciplines that linguistics entails, certainly enough for a teacher or prospective teacher to be comfortable with the basic concepts. Neither is it a methods text. It doesn't teach teachers how to teach. What it does is provide them with enough theory and sufficient examples of good and bad practice to guide them in making their own pedagogical decisions. It is not a book specifically dedicated to the needs of non-native speakers of English, yet it addresses the needs of those children at great length, taking the position that their needs and their experiences may not be quite as foreign as we sometimes believe. This is, in short, a book about language learning for the teachers of all children.

There are many similarities between this edition and the second edition; those will be apparent. There are also differences, reflecting the changes in the educational landscape over the past few years and a broadening of my own interest in language learning. In order to strengthen our knowledge and understanding about the phenomenon of language learning, I have incorporated the experiences of a wider variety of language learners—Kenny with Asperger syndrome (Chapter 7) and Grace, the hearing child of deaf parents (Chapter 4). Their stories enrich our understanding and appreciation not only for children's accomplishments but also for the teachers who take on the responsibility for their education. I have also added a number of references and resources and augmented the exercises and activities at the end of each chapter in order to make the book as user-friendly and as interactive as possible. New to this edition is a glossary of terms. This book celebrates, as did the earlier editions, the lives, the language, and the learning of children and their teachers.

ACKNOWLEDGMENTS

Writing is a lonely activity and yet, paradoxically, is possible only with the support of a lot of other people. I am very grateful for the work done by my research assistants over the years: Chris Grant and Kim Rebane for the first edition, Colleen Hickey and Susan George for the second edition, and Peter Christensen for the current edition. Many capable women, labeled "secretaries" and in reality able assistants, helped with formatting and protected my schedule and me from too many intrusions so that I could complete the book. For the current edition, they include Emily Tjimos at York University and Laureen Dailey at the British Columbia Open University, and I would like to thank them. I would also like to thank the York University Faculty of Education. Because they value scholarship and cultural diversity so highly, they served as a continual source of inspiration. The Office of the Vice-President Academic at York supported my efforts with an internal research grant without which I could not have completed the book. Finally, I would like to thank my family and friends who put up with my absence from the dinner or breakfast table, who ate take-out too often, and who didn't even complain when I overcooked the Christmas goose because I was upstairs working on the bibliography.

I would also like to extend my thanks to the reviewers of the third edition manuscript: Wendy Chambers, Georgia Southern University; Robert G. Collier, Western Illinois University; Hee-Won Kang, Sonoma State University; Edythe H. Schwartz, California State University; and Margaret Waters, Brooklyn College.

Brief Contents

Contents

Chapter Three / Learning the First Language   63

Chapter Four / Stories of First Language Learners   85

Chapter Ten / Schooling and Language Growth   **253**

CHAPTER ONE

Language Is Uniquely Human

Language belongs exclusively to human beings. I know that in writing such a blunt statement I run the risk of offending animal lovers, some of whom are convinced that their pet dog (cat, pig, hedgehog) speaks more sense than some of their relatives. If this is true, then it is more a comment on their kinfolk's conversational skills than on the pet's linguistic abilities. If language *were* simply a means of communication, then a reasonable argument might be made for its existence in other species. We all know, after all, about the "language" of dolphins or how bees communicate with each other about the location of pollen. We can likely tell stories about a household pet with a particularly impressive way of communicating its needs, danger, or joy. I even knew a professor of linguistics who was convinced that plants could communicate. But with all due respect to our near and not-so-near relatives in the animal kingdom, language is uniquely human and has been understood to be so since Aristotle.

It is tempting to claim that what sets human language apart from other forms of animal communication is speech. Certainly, the diversity of vocalization that characterizes human speech is probably unique in the animal kingdom. As we shall see later, however, language is possible without speech, and so its distinctiveness must rest elsewhere, in other attributes. One strong contender is the sheer complexity of human language. It has an inter-complexity, with nearly 40,000 known languages in current use on the planet. Each of these possesses an intra-complexity with multiple layers of sound, word formation, sentence structure, meaning, and rules for social use. Throughout the book, we will examine both kinds of complexity and what they mean to child learners. But to claim the uniqueness of language on the basis of complexity is a somewhat spurious quantitative argument. It is both spurious and dangerous, for it might take us down the ethnocentric road of evaluating languages on

1

the basis of some apparent difference in complexity, claiming, for example, that a language with more words is more complex (and thus more language-like and somehow better) than a language with fewer words. This kind of reasoning is patently foolish, of course, and there is no need to resort to it to bolster the claim that language belongs exclusively to humans.

Besides complexity, human language has many attributes, but for purposes of comparison with animal communication, three are definitive. First, language has **semanticity**. It conveys meaning through its capacity to represent ideas, objects, and events with symbols. Second, human language is **productive**. Speakers can understand and produce utterances they have never heard before, and they can also create new utterances by recombining elements they already know. In other words, in acquiring a language, speakers acquire the ability to generate new and unique utterances, with no limit on the number of original utterances they can create. Third, human language, as opposed to other communication systems, has the capacity of **displacement**, meaning that it can be used to create messages that are not tied to the immediate environment. Many animals have the ability to communicate in some limited ways. Bees, for example, use the "waggle dance" to tell other bees the direction and approximate distance to the nectar they have discovered. The information is contained in the movements of the bees' dance. A westward movement tells the other bees to move west; a "round dance" consisting of alternating circles to the left and right indicates that the source of nectar is near, and tail-wagging tells them that it is further away. Dancing bees don't lie about the direction or distance to the flowers, and presumably, the "listeners" don't misunderstand. Neither do dancing bees, nor the bees in their audience, comment on the quality of the nectar or hazardous flying conditions. They do not introduce any other topic of conversation or wander off topic. They communicate a particular kind of information that all bees understand. Their message is **iconic**, meaning that it looks like what it is conveying, and it is always located within the context of nectar-gathering. While it has limited semanticity, it does not meet the criteria of productivity and displacement.

Many animals have communication systems. Whales, dolphins, sticklebacks, gibbons, and meadowlarks (not to mention the family dog) have also been found to possess intricate ways of communicating. But none meets the three basic criteria that define human language. Not even chimpanzees, far closer to humans on the evolutionary scale, have more than an extremely rudimentary capacity for symbolic representation. Human language, however, can communicate about subjects and objects and events that are situated in the distant or near past, the present, or the future, or that do not occur at any time or any place at all. They can do so because human language is tied to human thought.

LANGUAGE AND COGNITION

Since Aristotelian times, poets and philosophers, physicists and psychologists—most of humankind, in fact—have recognized that there is a relationship between language and thought. The precise nature of that relationship has been the subject of some lively debate for hundreds of years. Aristotle's view, widely adopted in the centuries since, was that language was a medium through which to communicate thought. That view assumes a high degree of correspondence between linguistic structures and cognitive structures. At the very least, "if language is to serve as a useful tool for communication, the different categories of elements in language must reflect the categories used in thinking" (Whitney, 1998, p. 115). There is little agreement, however, on just how close the correspondence between linguistic and cognitive structures might be and thus on how closely language development parallels or is predicted by cognitive development.

During the 20th century, intellectuals in many different disciplines speculated on how coincidental language and cognition might be. There was little agreement. Philosopher Bertrand Russell saw the relationship as somewhat negative, considering language a "veil of confusion that hides the cognitive essentials" (Levinson, 1997, p. 1). The Russian psychologist Lev Vygotsky (1962) held, for example, that language and thought are separate but closely related processes, developing independently in children initially and then somewhat in tandem as children begin to use the internal voice while thinking. Albert Einstein (1954), a physicist, believed that an individual's mental development and conceptualization were greatly dependent on language, concluding that people who speak the same language share, to some degree, the same mentality. In a trivial sense, this must be true. As we have seen and will see later, language is at least partly culturally determined and so its speakers do share certain perceptions and concepts. Moreover, there is evidence that language influences what its speakers see. As early as 1932, psychologists studying human memory discovered that people's memory for a picture could be influenced by the label for the picture. More recently, Loftus and Palmer discovered that people estimated the speed of two cars in a filmed traffic accident differently according to how the question to them was phrased. Those asked "How fast were the cars going when they were hit?" judged the cars to be going slower than those asked "How fast were the cars going when they smashed into each other?" The verb *smashed* apparently influenced their perception of speed or at least their reporting and probably their memory since their later memory for what they saw may be affected by the wording of the leading question (Loftus & Palmer, 1974; Loftus, Miller & Burns, 1978, cited in Whitney, 1998, p. 128).

There are, however, compelling arguments against a much stronger interpretation of the notion of a "shared mentality" based on a shared language, and many of these will become apparent in the coming pages. As we consider the Sapir-Whorf hypothesis that linguistic differences between languages are directly reflective of cognitive differences between their speakers, we shall see that the relationship between language and thought cannot possibly be this simple.

Not even those scholars whose work touched most directly on matters of language and mind, the linguists and psycholinguists, could agree on the nature of the relationship between language and thought,. Many, however, were influenced by Chomsky's argument "that language functions as a mental organ separate from the rest of cognition" (Whitney, 1998, p. 116). In *Language and Mind* (1968), Chomsky argues that the linguistic and general cognitive systems exchange information but that the operating system of each is separate and unique. We shall revisit this and other perspectives on the relationship between language and cognition throughout the book, especially in Chapter 9, but whatever theoretical stance one might take on the strength or character of the link between language and cognition, there is little disagreement that the relationship exists, and that it sets human language apart from animal communication.

Clearly, as we examine language and cognition in the very practical setting of the school, we see that language forms the foundation for thinking about and learning math, science, social studies, and, to varying degrees, the fine arts. Children's talk "goes far to shape what they learn" (Barnes, 1995, p. 2). Language is unique as a school subject because it *can* be a rather fascinating subject of study, but it is also a prerequisite for the study of all other subjects. Language is the foundation to thinking about and learning math, science, or social studies, and in this respect it is special. Language plays a central role in children's learning because it is a partner to those central mental processes of perception, comprehension, attention, memory, and that somewhat amorphous activity we call thinking. I am not exaggerating to claim, in fact, that children's success in school depends, to a very large degree, on their facility with the four modes of language—listening, speaking, reading, and writing.

The converse is not true, of course: Although language is needed to study other subjects, children do not require prior facility with math, science, or any other subject area before they can learn language. There are prerequisites, of course, cognitive as well as social, and we will examine these more closely in Chapters 4 and 6, but it is obviously and significantly true that children need not be conversant with theories of mathematics or even know how to count before they learn the language of counting. Rather, they learn basic counting concepts *as they learn* the language for counting. This is true of much of children's learning—the concepts and the language required to talk about them are learned simultaneously.

When children begin school, they have already begun the lifelong task of acquiring language. This is a true of the other subjects in the curriculum in only a very rudimentary sense. More significantly, they have acquired their language without being taught. Children learn a great deal about the world without being formally taught by others, but they are able to do so in large part because they ask questions, they hear people talking, and, eventually, they read about their world and others' experience of it. In short, they rely on language for their learning. This cognitive basis of language makes it unique, whether it is a discrete subject in the school curriculum or, more appropriately, integrated into a seamless web of learning.

When I talk about how language is linked to cognition, I refer not only to oral language but to reading. Dickinson, Wolf, and Stotsky observe that "Reading represents one of the most interesting and cognitively complex systems and, as such, has a great deal to teach us about cognition in general" (1989, p. 231). Children's reading and writing are, in a very real sense, extensions of their oral language. They bring their life experiences, shaped first by oral language, to the task of learning to read and write, so that learning is also cognitively driven. Another sense in which written language is linked with cognition is in children's learning of it. In learning to read and to write, they are active participants. Indeed, we have known for some time that children in first and second grade are capable of assuming responsibility for their own learning to read and write (e.g., see Hansen, 1983). We have also come to view reading and writing, like oral language, as essentially processes of the interactive construction of meaning (Tierney & Pearson, 1984, p. 68). Once they have learned to read and write, children can use the written language in much the same way as they use oral language—to shape, store, and recall experience. Reading is one of our most important ways of increasing our experience. For those of us who love to read, "Some of our best memories never happened" (with apologies to Frank Zappa).

In Chapters 8, 9, and 10, I will talk more about the role language plays in learning, first outside the school as children (unencumbered by the formal requirements of schooling) learn to use language in a variety of social contexts, and then as they encounter literacy and other less contextualized language demands of schooling.

The link between language and cognition, important and fascinating though it may be, is not the only attribute of language that makes it special and of interest to teachers. I have identified five other features of language and language use that are especially important to our understanding of the importance and uniqueness of language in children's lives.

LANGUAGE IS NATURAL

I recall a doctoral examination many years ago in which much of the candidate's time was spent defending this simple assertion. One of the examiners, a science educator, took exception to this statement, claiming that certain biological processes such as cell mitosis are natural, but language is not. Because an infant is not born talking but has to learn language, language is a learned behavior, and while not necessarily *un*natural, it was not natural in the sense that biological processes are. Much to the delight of the doctoral student, the ensuing and lively debate took much the attention off her. Nevertheless, Chomsky and others would argue that language *is* natural precisely because the human infant is born with such a strong predisposition to acquire it, with all the right biological tools that are uniquely suited to linguistic learning. What the doctoral student meant is that children's learning of language is part of their nature in ways that no other human learning is. For example, language is learned by all children with normal or near-normal mental and physical abilities, and it is learned very early in their lives when those abilities are far from fully developed.

Similarly, the fact that no active intervention is required argues for the naturalness of language. In fact, most of us who have watched our own children grow are very grateful that we were not charged with the task of teaching them their native language. Even the finest teachers among us would likely fail, such is the enormity of the task and the magnitude of their accomplishment at so young an age. Many theorists have speculated, in fact, that children possess innate mechanisms that give them a head start on the task of language learning; that to talk of their "learning" language makes no more sense than to talk of a tulip bulb learning to become a tulip. Children are born with the biological potential to acquire human language and will overcome great handicaps to do so.

Evidence gathered in Nicaragua provides very strong support for the claim that language is instinctive. Rutgers University linguist Judy Shepard-Kegl discovered a group of deaf children in that country in 1985 who were in the process of developing a sign language of their own. The language is now so well developed that a dictionary of the signs is about to be published. According to newspaper reports in *The Globe and Mail* (Canada) and the *Daily Telegraph* (Britain), the researcher did not publish her findings in the early years for fear that someone would go to Nicaragua and try to teach the children American Sign Language— "help" they apparently did not need. The naturalness of language is a subject that we will explore in greater depth in Chapter 6.

An especially interesting question does arise, however, with regard to written language. Specifically, educators and theorists have debated for several decades whether written language is as natural as oral language. Smith (1984), Goodman (1984), and others have argued that it is, contending, for instance, that preschool children "know how to learn to read and write because written language presents them with problems similar to those they solve with spoken language" (Smith, 1984, p. 143). There is an obvious counterargument, though: Whatever similarities may exist between written and spoken language, the simple fact remains that most children do not learn to read and write without instruction. Still, it would be a mistake to focus on what may turn out to be a minor difference when research is beginning to point to the correspondence between the ways oral and written language are acquired.

Even before they come to school, children know a great deal about reading and writing and, especially, about the nature of literacy itself. They have a good idea about why people read books and the stories to be found in them, about why people write, and most have some general idea about the correspondence between squiggles on paper and meaning. Before they come to school, they have spent time drawing and labeling pictures (even though the adult reader might not know what the label says), marking on pavements and walls, newspapers and magazines. Hand a child a crayon or chalk on the first day of school and chances are good that she will know what to do with it. Children come to school wanting to write. Donald Graves claims that these early marks, undecipherable to teachers and parents, proclaim "I am" (1983, p. 1).

It would appear, then, that acquiring language—oral and written—is part of children's nature. The stories of Helen Keller and of a girl named Genie who managed to acquire her first language at the age of 13.5 after nearly 12 years spent in isolation, speak to the intensity of the human drive to acquire language. Language is so very much a part of human nature that the most interesting thing about language acquisition may be the *failure* to acquire it.

Later, in Chapters 4 and 7, we will meet children who learned language under a variety of different circumstances. Some overcame major biological or environmental deficits to acquire language, and in doing so, offered a unique testament to the overwhelming human motivation to communicate.

This emphasis on the naturalness of language should not be read as permission to ignore language in the school curriculum. Rather, it should be read as a challenge to design language programs in school that build upon children's real experience of learning and using language and to integrate oral and written language across all subjects in the curriculum.

LANGUAGE IS CULTURALLY BOUND

It seems perfectly obvious that a language would somehow be shaped to meet the needs of the speakers who use it. The fact that Inuit has more words for snow than English and that Arabic has more words for camel (than either language!) are often cited as evidence for language being more than casually linked to culture. In the British Isles, where English originated as in most places where it is now spoken, there is relatively little need to talk in great detail about snow—other than its presence or absence, amounts, and how soon it is likely to be removed. Similarly, when English speakers do need to cross deserts, they are more likely to pile into a Hummer than to climb onto a camel, and we have little need to talk about them except in biology classes or with the travel agent in planning exotic trips to the Middle East or Africa. When the conversation does turn to camels, we muddle along with the words we have, talking about one-hump and two-hump camels or, if we are only recently graduated from our biology classes, Arabian (or dromedary) and Bactrian camels.

The evidence from snow and camels notwithstanding, the exact nature of the relationship between language and culture is not as obvious as it appears to be. One of the best known hypotheses about the relationship is the Sapir-Whorf hypothesis, also known as the Whorfian hypothesis. Briefly, this hypothesis maintains that language and culture are inextricable from one another. In its strongest form, it states that:

> We dissect nature along lines laid down by our native languages. The categories and types that we isolate from the world of phenomena we do not find there because they stare every observer in the face; on the contrary, the world is presented in a kaliedoscopic flux of impressions which has to be organized by our minds—and this means largely by the linguistic systems in our minds. (Carroll, 1956, pp. 213–214)

This hypothesis is intriguing in its implications because it suggests that we are never free to observe anything "objectively." It implies that human beings cannot view any physical evidence freely, outside the constraints imposed by the language they speak. If this, or any substantially similar version of the hypothesis, were true, we could certainly understand the potential for communication breakdown in any multilingual situation. In Chapter 11, we take a closer look at the minefields of intercultural communication and why they exist.

The relationship between language and culture is important not only in thinking about intercultural communication. The relationship is important to consider from a monolingual perspective as well. In fact, we can find within any language community examples that are very similar to the *snow* and *camel* examples given previously. In English, for instance, we have a great many synonyms for talking about many subjects, yet only speakers who are interested in or familiar with the subject will have the experiences that give them the detailed vocabulary to talk about it. A decage ago, there were few people on the planet who knew (or cared) what a *URL* was. Outside the computer industry, most people still believe that *java* refers to coffee. The Internet has spawned an entire linguistic subculture found usually in chat rooms and cyber cafes. Any parent or teacher who is unfamiliar with the medium, or who still uses "real" English to communicate on it, will be hard pressed to do any meaningful eavesdropping. The following excerpt comes from an exchange between my 13-year-old niece and a friend:

	Translation
A: RUOK	Are you okay?
B: Roger that. But WRT BF SITD	Yes. But with regard to [my] boyfriend. [I'm] still in the dark.
A: WIBNI he just said, like, N/P	Wouldn't it be nice if he just said, like, no problem?
B: IAMY	In a million years.
A: WTH?	What the hell?
B: YABA	Yet another bloody acronym.
A: Roger that. Means what?	Yes. What does it mean?
B: In a million years.	
A: Cool. TTYL TPTB making me go AFK.	Cool. Talk to you later. The powers that be [are] making me go away from [the] keyboard.
B: L8R.	Later.

Although the traditionalists among us have difficulty in accepting that this is language at all, to those who use it, it communicates their message meaningfully. It is difficult to see much correspondence between this form of communication and the language that Swinburne used in his "March: An Ode":

Ere frost-flower and snow-blossom faded and fell,
and the splendour of winter had passed out of sight,
The ways of the woodlands were fairer and stranger
than dreams that fulfil us in sleep with delight;
The breath of the mouths of the winds had hardened on tree-tops
and branches that glittered and swayed
Such wonders and glories of blossomlike snow or of frost
that outlightens all flowers till it fade
That the sea was not lovelier than here was the land,
nor the night than the day, nor the day than the night,

Nor the winter sublimer with storm than the spring:
such mirth had the madness and might in thee made,

March, master of winds, bright minstrel and marshal of storms
that enkindle the season they smite.

But, to the users, each serves its function. The two samples are very different, but the point here is that language exists to meet the communicative needs of the speakers, and it would be very odd indeed if it were unable to meet those needs. The second sample, beautiful though it may be, would suit the needs of my niece and her friend in this instance no better than their acronym-filled communique would serve Swinburne's needs.

Children learn very young that "…the language we speak identifies us as members of a particular group. Members of different clubs, of different communities, do not speak in the same way. Our own particular language is an emblem of all our cultural ties" (Smith, 1988, p. 6). Children acquire their first language within their society of language users—that ever-widening circle that begins with the immediate family. They learn language in order to become a part of that society, and their learning entails a variety of social functions of language. For instance, they learn greetings, leave-takings, apologies, and excuses, and the only way they can do so is within the context of use. They hear people around them greeting and leaving each other and making apologies and excuses for their behavior, and they observe the conditions under which these activities take place and the bodily gestures that accompany the language. Children acquire not only the language of their community but the customs and values as well, and these customs and values vary somewhat among groups who speak the same language.

There is mounting evidence that culture plays an equally important role in the acquisition of literacy. Stressing that "literacy learning is influenced by one's language and cultural background," Strickland recommends the use of literature that reflects a wide variety of cultures, especially the children's own (1994, pp. 332–333). Her view is supported by research evidence. The work of Schieffelin and Cochran-Smith, for instance, suggests that children's interest in print emerges from a particular cultural orientation in which literacy is assumed. Children are socialized to be literate. Reporting on their study of nursery school children's early experiences with print, they observed that:

> …in cultures where adult-child dialogue is characteristic of language learning, children's caregivers initially accept almost any response as the child's part in a conversation…. These actions provide some insight into the way the nursery school children were acquiring literacy. Adults initially played all the parts in literacy events, completely producing and comprehending print for the children and behaving as if the children themselves intended for print to be used in particular ways and as if the children themselves were using the print. Little by little…the nursery school children took over the various roles in literacy events and need less and less help from adult intermediaries. (1984, p. 8)

The culture in which a child grows has a profound influence on language development, particularly written language. Children learn to read and write when they are socialized in a literate environment. Not all children are so fortunate. While most children develop normal oral language in almost any kind of environment, the absence of a literate culture in the preschool environment may have a negative impact on a child's success in learning to read and write in school. This is a topic of considerable importance that will receive fuller treatment in Chapter 10.

LANGUAGE HAS MANY VARIETIES

No one knows exactly how many different languages are spoken by how many people in the world today. A number of factors make it very hard to judge. First, the number of languages is decreasing. A hundred years ago, there were several hundred North American Indian languages that no longer exist. Other continents have experienced similar losses. Second, the population of the planet is growing, and third, migration is increasing. Finally, the technological revolution has put television and the Internet into homes all over the globe and given people the opportunity, and often the necessity, to learn new languages. Given all these factors, it is not surprising more people than ever speak English. In fact, according to the *Cambridge Factfinder* (1993), more people speak English than any other language in the world today—not as a first language, but as either a first or additional language. Therefore, it is not surprising that the number of non-white, non-English speaking children in North American classrooms continues to grow.

It is highly unlikely that a teacher will know all of the languages spoken by all the children he or she will encounter during a career. In the university in which I work, we have students representing 175 different languages, and most of these students are not foreign students but first- second-, or third-generation immigrants. Although we have some gifted linguists among our faculty, I know of no one who speaks more than 4 or 5 of those languages. Thirty years ago, when I first taught English as a Second Language (ESL), the first question most people asked me was how many languages I spoke. They were always disappointed when I replied, "one." It is not necessary for an ESL teacher or any other teacher to speak the native language of the children in her classes. What is important is to understand that languages can have very different structures from English, that the cultures they reflect and represent will also differ in significant ways, and that the child comes to school equipped with both.

As interesting as it is, language variation is not restricted to those differences that exist between distinct languages. A significant amount of variation exists among speakers of a given language, much of it because language changes and the distance between communities that existed hundreds of years ago led to the development of distinct dialects. Even in the information age, these differences remain, and even to the untrained ear, there is a distinctive sound to Scots English, Australian English, and the English spoken in Alabama.

The reality of geographical dialects was illustrated for me several years ago shortly after I moved to Newfoundland, an island province of Canada in the North Atlantic ocean. English is the only language of the island and has been since John

Cabot landed here 500 years ago. It is not, however, a variety of English that came easily to me despite my nomadic ways that have taken me from Missouri to New Hampshire, Alberta, British Columbia, and Nova Scotia before landing on this easternmost of Canada's provinces. During my first months, I was stopped as I hurried through the corridors late to the University's founder's day ceremony. A colleague stopped me and asked, "Who's after dying?" The befuddled look on my face must have led him to believe that I was "stunned" (a Newfoundland word meaning 'slow-witted'), and so he elaborated, "The flag's at half-mast." Then I understood that he was asking me who had died. I responded that no one had died, or at least not recently, but that it was founder's day. He then understood that the flag was at half-mast in honor of the dead of World War I, in whose honor the university had been founded. Many distinctive words and syntactic constructions set Newfoundland English apart from its cousins on the mainland, some of which are much closer to its British cousins. I puzzled over how a child might lose a cuff, as his mother claimed, before I understood that a *cuff* is a mitten in Newfoundland—not to be confused with a *duff*, which is a kind of cake or steamed pudding.

My experience in Newfoundland reminds us that language variation is sometimes marked by geographical bounds. That is not always the case, however. Within a geographical region, groups of people are sometimes identified by the language they speak. We may pretend that North America is a society without the social classes that characterize Great Britain, and certainly there is a less predictable relationship between social groups and language in North America than in the British Isles. Nevertheless, there are marked differences among the dialects spoken, for example, by Francophone children on the Port au Port peninsula in Newfoundland, Puerto Rican children in southern Florida, Mexican children in New Mexico, Sarcee children in Alberta, and African-American children throughout North America. These differences are caused not by where the children live but by the social and ethnic groups to which they belong. It is essential that teachers learn not to accept society's ill-informed judgments about linguistic diversity and, particularly, not to generalize them to judgments about the ability or the potential of the children whose language differs from their own. As Dorothy Strickland put it, "Competence isn't tied to a particular language, dialect, or culture" (1994, p. 333). Language, ethnicity, and culture are topics that take up a great deal of space in the professional literature of teaching today. Rightly so. Throughout the remainder of this book, I will revisit these issues from a variety of perspectives.

Most dialect differences are neutralized in the written language. In other words, if there is a standard dialect of English, it is probably best represented by the written forms. But across languages, there is a great deal of variability in writing systems. The two basic categories are systems that show a clear relationship between sounds and graphic symbols (phonological systems) and systems that do not show a relationship (nonphonological systems). Most of the languages of the world are represented by phonological systems. These include both syllabic and alphabetic systems. The smallest unit in syllabic writing systems is the syllable. Japanese *kana* and Cherokee have syllabic writing systems. The smallest unit in alphabetic systems is the letter, but languages vary in the degree of predictability between the letter and the sound. Spanish, for instance, has a very regular correspondence between sound and symbol. But any bilingual Spanish speaker will tell us that English does not. How could we possibly explain the spelling of *tough* if it did? Modern nonphonological writing systems are mostly logographic. In these, the graphemes represent words. Chinese and Japanese *kanjii* script are some of the better known of these languages.

Children who have been born and attended school in non-English-speaking countries have probably learned a different language and a different writing system. Even another alphabetic system may be based on a different script. Cyrillic (used for Russian), Arabic, and Greek are good examples. If education is to be universally accessible and equally effective for *all* children, then teachers must understand the cultural and linguistic diversity of their students and plan and act accordingly.

We know, for example, that the dialect and language differences that influence children's speech also influence their comprehension of what they hear and read. This is not an insignificant point for teachers, who must keep in mind that such differences reflect, in part, differences in experience and world view that lead, in turn, to interpretations that may differ from those of the teacher or other children in the class from the dominant culture. Later in the book, in Chapters 4, 5, and 10, we will return to the subject of the child who speaks a language other than English.

LANGUAGE HAS STRUCTURE

Obviously, we cannot base a claim for the uniqueness of language on the fact that it has structure. Almost everything in our lives is structured in some way. Language structure is special, however, because it is so very complex, and despite the complexity, children manage to learn it at a very young age. Language structure has always been of special interest, not only to linguists but to average language users. Many of the latter seem to be preoccupied with finding out what among competing forms is the *correct* form, not understanding that what they are really talking about is a standard—mostly written—versus a dialectical variation. Here in Newfoundland, *saw* as the past tense of *see* is rarely heard in the spoken language, even among educated speakers. Visitors to the island may conclude that their hosts are using an incorrect form, but if they listen more closely they will discover that this rich dialect has its own structure that differs in other important ways from the standard written form. In speech, they favor, for example, a past tense that has its roots in Irish English and is rarely heard on the North American continent. The earlier example, "Who's after dyin'?" illustrates this form as do sentences such as "It's after snowing 10 inches last night" or "He's after buying lottery tickets for 20 years." Nothing is *incorrect* about any of these sentences, but my Newfoundland-born colleagues at the

University told me that any English teacher worthy of the name devoted her career to eradicating such forms from the language—unsuccessfully, as it turned out, and happily, I think, for the language is richer for having such variation. This anecdote should tell us something about teaching. Provide a good model of standard English and opportunities to learn it, but respect the linguistic heritage that children bring to the classroom.

While we may remember school grammar lessons as tedious and boring, most of us will admit to a certain curiosity about the structural peculiarities of the language we speak. But language structure is also important from another perspective. It helps us appreciate the enormity of children's accomplishments in acquiring language. Language is systematic in a myriad of ways. It consists of sounds that are strung together to make words that are strung together to make sentences that are, in turn, strung together to form discourse—not that this is what we do in normal language production. The point is that no human language allows this stringing together to be done in random fashion. Laws govern the ways in which elements at every level can be combined. In English, for example, we cannot combine the sounds /m/ and /b/ in that order unless there is a syllable boundary between them. Swahili, however, permits this combination, leading more than one Swahili speaker to conclude that the correct syllable division for *hamburger* is *ha/mburger.* Nor in English can we combine words in random order. Try it and note the looks of confusion on the faces of your listeners.

Somehow children in the first 5 years of life must figure out enough about these structures to make sense of what they hear. The fact that language seems so complex to the adult, whether linguist or person-on-the-street, and yet seems so easily learned is something that makes language truly unique. By the time children come to school, they have mastered much of the structure of their first language (and sometimes another), and it is the task of the school to extend this understanding to new uses. As teachers, we are likely to underestimate the importance of our task. Because children's language accomplishments have been so very impressive thus for, we tend to assume that they can understand the highly abstract language of the school when, in fact, they do not. How many young children correctly interpret the opening lines of "The Star–Spangled Banner?" How many children have any idea what *pledge* or *allegiance* mean or what they are promising when they utter them in the pledge to the American flag? Canadian children are equally bewildered by their own national anthem even though the language is more contemporary. More importantly, how many teachers think about and take the time to explain things to children in language they can understand? Stories about children's interpretations of the language they hear can be very revealing of the mismatch that frequently occurs between what is said and what children understand.

After reading my story (in the first edition of this book) about Maria, a child who came home from Sunday School with a picture she had drawn of a teddy bear with very strange-looking eyes, several people confessed that they were in junior high school before they realized that there was no hymn titled "Jesus the Cross-eyed Bear."

Another story from that edition, illustrative of the assumptions children sometimes make about adult language, bears (oops!) repeating in its entirety:

> Three brothers, 6, 8, and 9 years old, were sitting on the floor playing cards. Several times during the play, I heard them say "I'm going to drop one card" or "I'm going to drop two." In every way, the rules of the game they were playing seemed to mirror those of poker. Finally, I asked what they were playing.
>
> **Paul:** *Drop poker.*
> **Me:** *Is that the same as "draw poker?"*
> **P:** *I don't know that game.*
> **M:** *Why is it called "drop poker?"*
> **P:** *(Shrugging) Cause you drop the cards you don't want, I guess.*

In the example of the cross-eyed bear, the child's interpretation is structurally correct and is far more consistent with her own experience than is the intended meaning. In the second example, Paul's interpretation is also structurally sound. He has assumed that the *p* that begins the word *poker* also ends the previous word. This kind of boundary confusion is perfectly normal in continuous speech because we do not, as we sometimes think we do, pause or leave any space between words. This interpretation was accepted by the children since to *drop* cards made more sense than to *draw* cards, especially if they knew only the most obvious meaning of *draw*.

While it is not important for elementary school teachers to know the structure of English in the detail that a linguist does, they should understand the relationship between form and meaning, to what degree and how children have come to master that relationship before starting school, and how to build on their understanding so that it will serve not only their linguistic needs but their other learning needs as well.

One of the ways in which the school extends children's understanding of language structure is in teaching them to read and write. But written language shares only some of the structural properties of oral language, and one of the jobs of schooling is to teach, or to help children to discover, those new structures. Many children come to school knowing a great deal about the structure of text—most know, for instance, how stories are organized—but they still have much to learn about creating that structure in their own writing. We will return to a discussion of language structure in Chapter 2.

LANGUAGE AND THE CHILD: AN EXAMPLE

The title of this chapter implies the question "Why is language special?" In the next few pages, I attempt to answer that question by describing some of the ways in which language is set apart from other subjects in the school curriculum. The question might be better answered, however, from a more personal perspective. Sensible decisions about curriculum and teaching are impossible to make on the basis of theories and descriptions about language. We have to consider the significance of language in the life of the child. After all, as we saw earlier, language is natural and the child needs neither the school nor the teacher to learn it and function in it. In this section, we will consider further why language is special in the life of the child.

Lucy

A few years ago, when I was conducting research in a kindergarten in a small community in coastal British Columbia, I met a young Portuguese-speaking child who taught me a great deal about the role language plays in children's learning. About half the children in the kindergarten arrived in September knowing little or no English. Lucy was one of these children, and she caught my attention right away. Every day, she was brought to school and then taken home again either by her mother or by her friend Jenny's mother. In the brief greetings and leave-takings, both girls and their mothers spoke only in Portuguese. I learned from the ESL consultant, who visited the homes of the ESL children, that Lucy's family had been in Canada for only a few months and spoke no English at all. I expected, therefore, that Lucy and Jenny would speak Portuguese at school, at least when talking to each other.

I was wrong. During the first month of school, I never once heard them speaking Portuguese. Actually, I heard Jenny say very little at all, not surprising since she knew no English. But Lucy was a different story! Not knowing English didn't even slow her down. She chattered away, using the few words she acquired each day in a variety of ways. To an adult English speaker's ears, Lucy made many mistakes. She didn't bother with past tense endings or with the third-person singular marking on verbs. She had no time for plural suffixes either. She was too busy learning the words that matter to bother with the frills of grammatical niceties, and she made those words do double and triple duty. Initially, she used *teacher* to refer to any adult, and then she used it to refer only to her teacher (assuming, perhaps, that it was a unique name). Eventually she sorted out the appropriate referents, but in the meantime she managed to communicate very effectively. Her few verbs, *be* and a couple of action verbs (*go* and *get* were predictable favorites of this active child), were used in whatever way she needed them.

All the time she was busily acquiring English, Lucy "made do" with the language she had at her disposal, but her language grew impressively, with notable changes taking place almost daily. Early in October, Lucy's mother gave birth to a baby boy. On Halloween, I had the following conversation with Lucy about her new brother:

> **Lucy:** *He cry. All the time cry.*
> **Me:** *Who cries?*
> **L:** *My baby.*
> **M:** *Oh, right. Your new brother.*
> **L:** *Yeah. All the time he cry.*
> **M:** *What do you do?*
> **L:** *I pat him. Hims back. (She pats her own back.)*
> **M:** *Does that help?*
> **L:** *(She nods.) He can't talk.*
> **M:** *No, not yet. But he lets you know when he wants something, doesn't he?*

> **L:** *(Doesn't seem to understand.)*
> **M:** *Can you tell when he's hungry?*
> **L:** *Yeah. He cry.*
> **M:** *Right. That's his way of talking right now, isn't it?*
> **L:** *Yeah. I not cry.*
> **M:** *No, you know how to talk, don't you? Lucy, how many languages do you speak?*
> **L:** *(Looks puzzled.)*
> **M:** *How many different languages do you know?*
> **L:** *One!*
> **M:** *Which one?*
> **L:** *Mine!*

My last two questions to Lucy were silly ones to ask a 5-year-old child simply because answering them required her to think about language as an object apart from herself. Gradually children acquire what we call *metalinguistic awareness* (the ability to think about language as language), but she had not done so at this point. Much of what goes on in classrooms demands metalinguistic thinking that is even more sophisticated than in this example. Most 5-year-olds just beginning kindergarten are limited in their capacity to think in this way. Lucy's answer makes it clear that using language is much higher on her agenda than talking about it. And so it should be. Even if she had spoken seven languages in addition to English and Portuguese (and perhaps she did!), her answer would have been the same. To her, language was part of her thinking, something so much a part of her that it could not be objectified and counted.

Lucy's answer also provided a clue as to why she never spoke Portuguese in school. One of the things children learn very quickly is to shift registers in different situations. In other words, they learn very early that the language of the playground may have to be modified for the classroom and yet again for the home. Children make these adjustments in register quite easily, and that seems to be precisely what Lucy was doing as she shifted from Portuguese to English and back to Portuguese again. The languages were no more different to Lucy than the different registers of English used by a native English-speaking child moving from "Gimme the ball" to "Would you please pass the potatoes?"

From this brief dialogue, we see once again how natural is the business of acquiring language. We also see how central a role a child plays in the process. Lucy is by no means a blank sheet on which some adult imprints language. In the uttering of only 17 different words, Lucy has demonstrated that she knows a great deal about English and its use.

Lucy's Utterances Were Unique

Although it is true that Lucy must have previously heard the 17 distinct words she used here, it is unlikely that she had ever heard them combined in exactly the same way. In fact, given the absence of grammatical markings in her language, it is extremely unlikely that she had heard exactly the same sentences uttered before. Lucy combined the words to create the meaning she wanted to make at that particular time, meaning that was relevant to the conversation she was having with me.

If we compare Lucy's sentences to those an adult native speaker would use, we see that Lucy's are different. Forms such as *hims* are considered to be developmental forms (rather than errors) and are noteworthy for several reasons. First of all, the presence of **developmental forms** makes it clear that for Lucy, what she says is more important than how she says it. In this dialogue, as in all her language use, Lucy does not concern herself with grammatically perfect utterances. As far as she is concerned, although most likely she is unaware of it, she is constructing her utterances in response to the situation, that is, to communicate with me about her baby brother. This centrality of meaning and communication in children's language acquisition is a topic to which we will return throughout this book.

Second, Lucy was not taught such forms as *hims*, and it is unlikely that she ever heard them. She created them based on her observation of other forms in the language. In this case, she had correctly worked out that English nouns and many pronouns require an *-s* ending for the possessive form. She had not yet worked out the details of the pronominal system that would prevent *hims*. Lucy was constructing her own language rules based on the observations she had made. In other words, she was not parroting back fully formed utterances she had heard before. She was creating them anew to meet the communication need before her. To do so, she had to have created her own set of "rules" for using English, a task requiring her to hypothesize about the structure and meaning of the language around her, test her hypotheses, and either discard or modify those found faulty. While there is little doubt that hypothesizing is one way in which children come to recreate the full set of linguistic rules that govern language, there is also little doubt that an hypothesis-testing model is inadequate to explain all the learning they do. In Chapter 6, we will look at hypothesis-testing and some alternative language learning strategies.

In the brief dialogue with Lucy, I did not correct her "hims" nor her "he not cry." This is not unusual behavior for an adult talking with a child. Research tells us that parents and teachers rarely correct children's language unless there is an error in content. Research also tells us that correcting either grammar or pronunciation is a futile act. Numerous anecdotes attest to children's resistance to such correction, one of the most famous of which provided by Berko and Brown (1960), came to be known as the *fis* **phenomenon**:

> One of us, for instance, spoke to a child who called his inflated plastic fish a fis. In imitation of the child's pronunciation, the observer said: "This is your fis?" "No," said the child, "my fis." He continued to reject the adult's imitation until he was told "That is your fish." "Yes," he said, "my fis." (Berko & Brown 1960, p. 531, quoted in Reich, 1986, p. 58)

If Lucy had referred to her baby brother as her *sister*, then I might have corrected her, but for the same reasons that she did not understand the questions I asked her *about* language, she would not have responded to the correction of the grammatical *forms* of her language.

One other point should be made about developmental forms. It is tempting to think about the mismatches between children's and adults' language forms as deficits or flaws in children's language. To do so, however, implies a particular view of language learning, one that is at odds with much of the evidence we now have about child language acquisition. According to this view, the task of children in language acquisition is to mimic adult production, coming progressively closer to adult forms. This view considers the child's system as a lesser variant of the adult's, and in doing so, ignores the systematic integrity of the child's *own* system, obscures the facts about that system, and minimizes the child's accomplishment. The enormity of this accomplishment and the conditions under which it occurs are topics for discussion in Chapters 3 through 7.

Lucy Understood the Language Spoken to Her

In the brief dialogue, I used a total of 68 words, 45 *different* words, and a variety of sentence types. In addition to the statements, I asked Lucy nine questions of three different structural types, five of which required more than *yes* or *no* responses. Of the four that did require *yes* or *no*, two were tag questions, meaning that there was a question tagged onto the end of a statement, and I merely required confirmation. The remaining two also required yes/no answers, but they also asked for information. Even when Lucy failed to understand the question, it is clear that it was not the structure of the question that was problematic but the meaning. She understood far more words than she produced or was able to produce. This is an important observation about language learning: children are almost always able to understand more than they are able to produce, but the reverse is never true.

When we consider all that is involved in comprehension, we begin to appreciate what the child has accomplished. Lucy had to recognize the incoming sounds as speech, segment the unbroken stream into potentially meaningful units, work out the structure that would give those units meaning, and interpret that within her understanding of my intent within the context of our conversation. The comprehension she exhibited during the brief exchange was in itself an impressive psycholinguistic feat.

Lucy's Language Was Situationally Appropriate and Showed Cultural Awareness

I said previously that Lucy responded appropriately to my questions. Not only did she give the linguistically expected response, but a socially accepted one appropriate to the conversation as well. Consider an example: Lucy nodded in response to my question "Does that help?" and introduced a new but related topic into the discourse with "He can't talk." This may seem trivial, but given that she had been in contact with English speakers for only a few weeks and considering the range of inappropriate responses she might have given, it is a noteworthy demonstration of her linguistic competence. This aspect of linguistic competence dealing with the appropriateness of utterances is often overlooked in the literature on language acquisition, but much rides on children's acquiring it.

Lucy's Pronunciation Was Clear and Accurate

Because I did not transcribe the session phonetically, the reader cannot judge the quality of her pronunciation. Each session I had with Lucy was tape recorded, however, and the recording of this dialogue revealed very little of what we commonly call a "foreign accent." In 8 short weeks, Lucy had effectively mastered the sound system of English, a system that is appreciably different from that of her native Portuguese. In doing so, she accomplished something that most adult learners never do. This accomplishment is partly cognitive, partly linguistic (because there is an underlying system or "grammar" to the sound system as well as to the sentence), but it is also a physiological feat. Of course, Lucy did not begin as an infant would. She had already mastered the sounds of Portuguese. However, English has different sounds, requiring different kinds of articulatory control, and these she mastered in a very short time.

Lucy's Second Language Acquisition Strongly Resembled First Language Acquisition

This is not to say that Lucy's speech was in any way infantile, and certainly the rate of acquisition was much faster than it would be in an infant. This speed can be attributed not only to her age and more advanced cognitive ability but to the simple fact that she had already learned one language. She merely had to engage the "mechanism" again. There is abundant evidence that first and second language strongly resemble one another, so much in fact, that much of the next several chapters is devoted to drawing parallels.

The case for the similarity between first and second language will be made later in this book, and it will be made on theoretical as well as practical grounds. Here, however, it is useful to consider the most obvious reasons for the similarity between Lucy's second language acquisition and her first. Perhaps the most conspicuous reason is the language learning environment. Many linguists who study second language acquisition believe that there is a difference in kind between second language learning in an informal environment and in a structured environment such as an ESL class. Although Lucy did acquire her language in school, the environment of the kindergarten did not constitute the kind of formal, structured language "class" that we think of when we think of formal environments. It may well be the case that, especially for young learners, the less contrived the language learning environment, the easier the task of learning. The fact that Lucy learned so rapidly and that she apparently experienced little crossover or interference from her native Portuguese suggest that the informal, talk-centered atmosphere of the kindergarten class comprised as friendly an environment for acquiring a second language as the home did for acquiring her first language.

Lucy's teacher organized a kindergarten classroom that was demonstrably friendly to second language learners. She did not believe in structured language lessons but took her cue from observations of children acquiring their first language and provided a rich environment for language to grow. Drawing on her knowledge of cognitive development in young children, she provided concrete materials and experiences for them to think and talk about, but she also allowed them to share their own experiences. The language in the sample dialogue was not, thus, a result of repetition drills or of vocabulary lessons with flash cards. It was made possible because Lucy spent many hours in a classroom where there was much to do and to talk about, where the teacher nourished the natural functions of language in each child's life.

In Chapters 8 and 9, we look at the uses to which children put language and how they acquire those uses. Then, in Chapters 10, 11, and 12, we return to the issue of language in the school and examine how some teachers have created healthy environments for language growth. We will also visit a second-grade class where children from eight different countries talk and learn together.

IF LANGUAGE IS SO NATURAL, WHAT IS THERE TO TEACH?

The dominant theme of this chapter so far has been the uniqueness of language, the major argument being that it forms a natural part of human existence in a way that no other subject in the school curriculum does. If that is the case, one might wonder, then why bother to teach it? Or, more precisely, what exactly is there to teach? One answer to the first question is that we should not teach it. Certainly if what is meant by *teaching* language is to sit children in rows and drill language structures and spelling lists into their heads, it *would* be better not to teach language. If, on the other hand, by teaching language we mean creating an environment that is sensitive to the demands children place on language and to their use of language as a medium for their other language, then it is of utmost importance in the primary/elementary curriculum.

One of the most significant demands, of course, is cognitive. Oral and written language enable almost all other learning that children do through their school years and, indeed, in life. We will see in the remainder of this book that this is so. Even, or *especially*, in the computer age, schools are text places. Whether they are reading books from the class library or material that has been downloaded from the Internet, children must have a high degree of literacy to succeed in school. That literacy depends to a large degree, as we shall also see, on the child's having established a solid foundation of oral language. In an article on speech problems and the danger of ignoring them in the mistaken belief that a child with early language problems may be "the strong silent type," Gary Fowlie (1996) made this stark observation:

> I do know that Johnny's going to need all of his strength to survive in a school system where the best indicator of his academic success at 18 is how good his language skills are when he walks in the door at age 5. (p. A22)

This observation offers the best answer to the question raised in the heading to this section. Language deserves special attention precisely because it *is* natural and because it is essential to school success. Giving language a prominent place in the school day permits teachers to exploit the naturalness of language to the child's benefit. In other words, since language learning comes more easily to children than any other kind of learning, and since language is the foundation for success in other learning, it makes good sense to ensure that the foundation is solid and strong.

The Remainder of the Book

In the preceding pages, I have given the very briefest introduction to the issues that are raised and discussed throughout the text. My bias is clear. I hope my goals are also obvious. They are simply to help teachers and potential teachers to understand more about how the children we meet in our classrooms acquire language before they come to us and to understand how to build on that early experience to create a school environment in which every child has an equal opportunity to succeed.

The first seven chapters look at language acquisition, both first and second as well as extraordinary. Chapters 8 through 11 consist of a close examination of what happens and what *should happen* to children's language in school. The final chapter of the book takes us on a visit to a school in Atlantic Canada—a school that embodies many of the ideals set forth earlier. From that visit, we are able to extract a set of concluding principles or guidelines for making learning a positive experience for all our children.

For Further Study

1. The author claims that animal communication differs from human language in three fundamental ways. Can you think of other similarities or differences?

2. The author refers to Lucy's *hims* as a "developmental form." Why distinguish between developmental forms and errors? Would it ever be appropriate to call a child's form that differed from an adult form an *error*?

3. Some mathematicians claim that mathematics is a *pure language*. In what ways does it qualify as a language, according to the author's definition of language, and how does it differ from human language?

4. What other instances of the *fis* phenomenon have you witnessed, and what did they reveal about language acquisition?

5. The author writes "Children are almost always able to understand more than they are able to produce, but the reverse is never true." Why can the reverse never be true? Why is this an important observation (for teachers, especially) about language acquisition?

For Further Reading

August, D. & Kenji, H. (Eds.). (1998). *Educating language-minority children*. Washington, DC: National Academy Press.

Baker, C. (2000). *A parents' and teachers' guide to bilingualism*. Boston, MA: Multilingual Matters.

Chen, G. & Starosta, W. (1998). *Foundations of intercultural communication*. Boston, MA: Allyn and Bacon. (See Chapter 4, Language and Culture.)

Pinker, S. (2000). *How the mind creates language.* New York: Harper Perennial.

Tabors, P. (1997). *One child, two languages: A guide for preschool educators of children learning english as a second language.* Baltimore, MD: Paul H. Brookes Publishing Co.

Whitney, P. (1998). *The psychology of language.* Boston, MA: Houghton-Mifflin. (See Chapter 4, Theories of the Language-Thought Relationship.)

CHAPTER TWO

The Study and Structure
of Language

People are fascinated by language. Humans are nothing if not self-absorbed, and what could be more fascinating as an object of study than this intimate yet observable facet of our humanity? Language is as compelling a subject for scholars as it is for everyone else, and they study it for many different purposes. Poets study it or, more accurately, push the boundaries of its use in exploring the human experience. Psychologists study it to gain insights into human understandings and behaviors. In between are novelists and biographers, journalists and playwrights, anthropologists, sociologists, psychiatrists, educators, and, among many others, linguists of various ilk. Even criminologists and profilers are becoming applied linguists toward very specific ends.

For every aspect of language we might identify, there is someone interested in studying it. The number of perspectives on language study grows steadily as it becomes more and more specialized. Ten years ago, for example, few, if any, people studied the effects of e-mail and chat room correspondence on the written language. Today, there are a number of researchers including rhetoricians and sociologists examining the impact of the computer age on the written language. To some, it is an educational problem or even crisis, but to others it is merely language *change-as-it-happens* or history in the making. Many teachers and parents worry about the effects of word processors' spell-check programs on children's ability to spell. The advent of e-mail, chat rooms, and message boards is also changing the written language, as seen in the example in Chapter 1. The forms invite short communications, fragments instead of sentences, sentences rather than paragraphs, and alternate ways of writing words. It is too soon, however, to know what the effect will be on other modes of written communication. The computer age has also led to rapid additions to the English language. Only time will tell whether terms such as *addon, plugin, backward compatibility*, or *chunky floppy* will earn a permanent place in dictionaries of the English language or will be made as rapidly obsolete as the machines that spawned them. The speed of exchange made possible by the computer is also having a profound impact on language usage. Traditional conventions of punctuation and expression are being replaced by new conventions, some of the most noticeable of which are the abbreviations. BRB, OMG, and TPTB all have meaning to participants in chat rooms or "discussants" on discussion boards. Even *room* has taken on a new meaning in the virtual world. In all likelihood, a generation from now, we will have to revisit first language acquisition to learn what effect being on-line has had on first-(and subsequent) language learners in much the same way that researchers 30 and 40 years ago studied the effects of television on oral and written language development.

In describing some of the more current directions language study has taken, I am by no means implying that all enquiries of a more traditional nature have been answered. On the contrary, despite all the scholarly attention language has received over the past few centuries, we still know relatively little about language processes or about individual languages, and no one runs any risk of running out of questions or data to study—even if they eschew the computer revolution.

This chapter is about some of the people who study language, about the structure of language, and about language change over time. It is, in brief, a broad overview of the discipline called **linguistics**. It is by no means exhaustive; it is only the briefest of introductions to an area of study that has fascinated us for centuries and will, no doubt, continue to do so as long as we remain on the planet.

THE STUDY OF LANGUAGE

Foundational to the work of all linguists is a rational, accurate description of language structure. Descriptive and theoretical linguists provide insights into the structure of language and in doing so advance our understanding of children's language acquisition as well as our understanding of how they comprehend, speak, read, and write. By giving us a clearer picture of the structure—or possible structures—of language, these linguists bring us some appreciation of the enormity of the task. Because there are competing descriptions within any one language, they also provide alternative bases from which to try to understand language learning.

Traditional descriptive linguists have contributed directly to language teaching practice. Traditional phonics instruction, for instance, is based not only on the observation that there is some degree of correlation between sound and symbol but on basic concepts from phonemics as well. Though English presents certain problems for phonics instruction, because the sounds of English do not correspond exactly to its spelling, this is hardly the fault of the linguists who have clarified our understanding of what correspondence does exist. Whatever we might think about the appropriateness of phonics, we cannot deny that our understanding of sound-symbol corre-spondence is largely attributable to the work of this group of linguists. (We will re-turn to a fuller description of phones and phonemes later in this chapter.)

Theoretical linguists are also concerned with philosophical issues such as the essence of language, the relationship between language and formal logic, and the ex-istence and nature of universal properties of language. While their field of enquiry might seem further removed from the day-to-day realities of teaching practice, we must not undervalue their contribution to our work. Noam Chomsky (1975), for ex-ample, taught us that language and language behavior were rule-governed and that we could learn a great deal about children's understanding of the rules by observing the language they produced. A descriptive and theoretical linguist, historian, and philosopher, Chomsky was arguably the first of the true psycholinguists.

Although the label of their discipline is somewhat daunting, psycholinguists probably speak more directly to the language concerns of educators than any other type of linguist, with the possible exception of historical linguists, whose work we will consider separately at the end of the chapter. Unlike theoretical/descriptive and historical linguists, whose data come mainly from printed language that occurred sometime in the past, psycholinguists mostly work with oral language in the present. They are more interested in the people and processes that create the data. Psy-cholinguists study **psycholinguistics**, the three processes that comprise human lan-guage *behavior*—language acquisition, comprehension, and production.

Psycholinguists have increased our understanding of how these processes work, and in doing so have had a significant impact on language teaching practice. In fact, among the ranks of psycholinguists today can be found a great many educators. Among them are those who study the reading process. Recognizing that reading in-volves an interaction between reader and text was a major change from earlier be-liefs about the nature of reading and methods of teaching it. In the past, the identification of sounds and words dominated the teaching of reading, a practice that had a limited psycholinguistic basis itself because it assumed that the reader made mental connections between the printed symbol and the language sound. It was a far cry, however, from the kind of active cognitive processing assumed by more recent educators and psycholinguists who have given the child more mental "work" to do in the business of learning to read.

Psycholinguists also study the relationship between children's language devel-opment and their general cognitive growth, an issue that is foundational to educa-tional theory and practice. It is to be expected, then, that psycholinguistics is the branch of linguistics that does most to inform our teaching practice and why one might assert that good teachers are also linguists.

Since psychology is a science of the mind, it would be reasonable to expect that psycholinguistics would include the study of the relationship between language and brain functions. There was a time when this was so, when some psycholinguists did venture into brain study, but the major work in this area today is now done by neu-rolinguists. **Neurolinguistics** is the study of brain structure, how it influences lan-guage learning and processing, and how damage to the brain affects language learning, production, and comprehension.

There are two broad avenues of enquiry that have demonstrated some potential for informing language education. Brain maturation studies try to discover how brain development relates to language development. Studies of neurological bimodality study the differences between the two hemispheres of the brain and how those differences contribute to the learning of the first or a subsequent language. Usually, the hemispheres being studied are the left and the right. Some Canadian researchers have postulated, however, that the distinction between the front and back of the brain has as much or more potential for understanding linguistic and behavioral differences as left/right hemisphericity. While our knowledge about brain functioning is not sufficiently sophisticated that we can rely on it to dictate sound teaching practice, I am convinced that as we learn more about neural maturation and hemispheric differentiation we will eventually find the basis for a closer correspondence between the human "hardware" and the educational "software."

Psycholinguists and neurolinguists both work at the level of the individual. Although they may use large populations for their studies, they are primarily concerned with the process of language learning or use within the individual. The relationship between speakers or the broader contexts in which language is learned and used is not of particular interest to them. The study of language in relation to social factors such as age, sex, ethnic origin, social class, and educational level is called **sociolinguistics**. These are factors that educators must take into account in all their educational activities. Sociolinguists might study some of the same general issues as psycholinguists and neurolinguists, but they would do so from a community perspective. All three, for example, might be interested in bilingualism. A psycholinguist might ask how bilinguals process their two languages, what cognitive strategies are involved, or whether they are the same for the two languages. A neurolinguist would wonder about the physical effects of bilingualism—whether or not there is a measurable difference in the brains or in the cerebral functioning of bilinguals. A sociolinguist would likely be more concerned with how the community of language users influence the individual's language learning or use, or about the linguistic indicators of socioeconomic class.

Another area of overlap between sociolinguists and psycholinguists is **discourse analysis**. From the psycholinguist's perspective, the goal is to discover what cognitive processes we use to understand spoken or written text. For the sociolinguist, the relevant questions might be the conversational differences between men and women or between doctor and patient. There is, in fact, an entire domain of research known as unequal power discourse that studies speech events during trials, doctor-patient encounters, and in classrooms.

An important area of research undertaken by sociolinguists (and by applied linguists) is the interaction that takes place between mother, or other caretaker, and child. From sociolinguistic studies we have learned, for example, that many aspects of mother-child interaction and maternal expectations are culturally determined (Harris, 1985). Freedman (1979) observed, for instance, differences in the ways aboriginal and Anglo mothers attracted the attention of their infants. These, together with studies showing differences in the way native children interact with adults, constitute a major contribution to educational practice.

It is the job of educators to discover the pedagogical uses to which research findings of sociolinguists (as well as other linguists) might be put. In this, we are helped by *applied linguists*, some of whom also happen to be educators, often ESL teachers. **Applied linguistics** is the subdiscipline of linguistics that is concerned with real-world language use. Some scholars who consider themselves applied linguists are concerned with foreign language learning and teaching. Others study the role of language in practical problems such as lexicography, translation, and speech pathology. Still others, sometimes called educational linguists, are concerned with aspects of language research that have broad application in education. Literacy, for example, is a primary concern of educational linguists. They interpret scholarship in psycholinguistics, neurolinguistics, developmental psychology, and educational theory in their attempts to explain how children learn to read and write. Their aim is not to tell teachers how to teach language but to interpret the latest theories and findings of quality research in such a way that it is useful to teachers. How to teach, and to a large degree WHAT to teach, remain the prerogative of teachers and teachers of teachers who study children, classroom interactions, approaches, methods, and techniques of instruction in the classroom environment.

LANGUAGE STRUCTURE

There are many reasons for studying language structure, but the most compelling for teachers is to understand what children actually accomplish in acquiring language. Here we will examine five aspects of language structure and talk briefly about their importance to teaching. They are phonology, the study of the sound system; morphology, the structure of words; syntax, the structure of sentences; semantics, the structure of meaning; and pragmatics, the study of language as it is used in actual communication.

For purposes of description, it is useful to compartmentalize language in this way. It might even be useful for analyzing children's language data for the purpose of better understanding language acquisition. If this is the case, however, it is not because such segmentation mirrors children's experience of learning language—in fact, it is quite alien to children's experience. Children do not learn the sound system before attempting to put words together or master a large vocabulary before attempting sentences, nor do they learn the sound system one unit at a time in isolation from others or distinct from words. In fact, because their focus is on meaning and not on structure, they are scarcely concerned at all with structure. But our purposes here are different, and to understand anything at all about the complex structure underlying English it is useful to separate it into these five levels. One caveat is necessary. This is not a text on linguistics, so this is the barest of introductions to a topic about which thousands of volumes have been written. At the end of this chapter you will find a reference list for further reading, but I am hopeful that this brief introduction to language structure will provide a useful overview and generate sufficient interest for further reading. We begin with the sound system.

Phonology: The Sound System

Broadly speaking, phonology is concerned with both **phonetics,** or the articulatory and acoustic properties of speech sounds, and **phonology,** or the somewhat abstract system of rules that govern how those sounds are produced and combined. If we think about the sound system from the perspective of children acquiring language, the question is, quite simply, what has to be learned? Broadly, children must come to understand and produce the sounds necessary for communicating meaning in their language. At the onset of speech, it is unlikely that their attention is commanded by any unit smaller than the word or the syllable; there is, in fact, evidence that children, before they learn to read, find phonetic segmentation difficult. Eventually, of course, children learn to distinguish among all the individual speech sounds—the consonants and vowels of their language—a task they prepare for throughout the babbling period but one which is more complicated than it seems. Every speaker a child encounters utters each sound a little differently from every other and a little differently in some words than in others. Children must figure out which sounds are distinctive and which are not—in other words, which differences in sound signal a changed meaning. They also have to learn that a great deal of the variation between the speech sounds they hear can be safely ignored. An example of the latter is the different pronunciations of -*ing* at the ends of words. Speakers of several dialects of English regularly pronounce -*ing* as /in'/ while other speakers produce the standard form. Yet both mean the same thing, and children learn to ignore this non-distinctive difference. Similarly, there are a great many variations in the quality of word-final *r*, as in *far, fear,* and *fur*, but children eventually learn to recognize that the sound that ends the different words is the same, as far as English speakers are concerned, even though the different vowels before each *r* render them acoustically quite different.

As they learn to speak, children do not learn individual sounds and they do not combine sounds in syllables and words, although that may seem to be the effect of their learning. They do not learn to pronounce /p/ and /l/ and eventually combine them to produce /pl/, which is eventually combined with vowels to produce words such as *play* and *plum*. Even their early difficulty with pronouncing the cluster /pl/ is not a problem with "combining" sounds, not from the child's perspective. To the child, the unit is a single one. It is simply hard to produce, just as the /th/ sound is hard to produce. Thinking or talking about children's learning to combine sounds is an adult linguist's perspective on what is done because in terms of describing the sound system, that is what is easiest to do. The evidence, now well-established, portrays children learning first the larger units, either the syllable or the rhyme (discussed later). Eventually they learn finer segmentation but mostly as a result of learning to read.

Another aspect of the sound system that children come to master is the stress and intonation patterns of their language, a skill that they began preparing for in the crib. If a child is Chinese, the task is very different than it is for an English-speaking child, but for both, learning the meaning conveyed by these more subtle cues is an essential part of language learning. In the next few pages, I offer the briefest introduction to the English sound system, concentrating on those units that are central to understanding children's acquisition of both the spoken and written language.

Minimal Pairs and Phonemes

English has many pairs of words that differ from each other by only one sound. These are called **minimal pairs**, and they tell us which sounds are distinctive. For example, we know from the following list of words that the consonants /p, b, g/ are distinctive because substituting one for the other changes the word meaning. For the same reason, we know that the two vowels, /i, a/ are distinctive sounds.

pill	pall
bill	ball
gill	gall
hill	hall
fill	fall

On the other hand, each consonant and vowel sound has several possible and permissible pronunciations. We articulate the /g/ in *gill*, for example, just a little differently from the /g/ in *gall*. In the first, the tongue touches the roof of the mouth near the hard palate while in the second, the tongue touches the roof of the mouth further back, near the soft palate or velum. Substituting the exact /g/ sound in *gill* for the one in *gall* will result in a distorted pronunciation that will sound strange to the native speaker but will not change the meaning. To demonstrate that this is true, start to form the first sound in *gill* but stop the articulation, holding the tongue in its exact place and continue, producing *gall* instead.

For every distinctive sound in the language, there are many permissible articulations, but all articulations of each are distinct from all articulations of any other sound. These distinctive sounds of a language are called **phonemes**. Linguists indicate them with slashes (//), and every language has a different set. Phonemes can be classified into two broad categories, **consonants** and **vowels**. A third and smaller category of sounds resembles both consonants and vowels, called **semivowels**. Linguists would correctly point out that people do not actually speak in phonemes. Rather, each phoneme serves as a categorical name for the group of sounds speakers use and recognize as the same. Actual speech sounds are described in terms of *phones*, and each phoneme is made up of many different phones, all of which would be identified by native speakers as the same sound despite the many variations among them. To give an example, there is a great deal of acoustic variation (as any ESL learner will tell us) among the actual pronunciation of /l/ in each of the following words:

lip

low

flap

mall

mill

Figure 2.1 The Resonators of the Human Vocal Apparatus

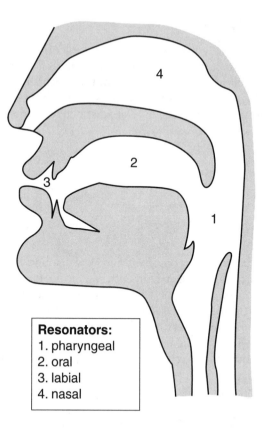

Resonators:
1. pharyngeal
2. oral
3. labial
4. nasal

And yet, native speakers will readily identify the first sound in *lip* and *low*, the second sound in *flap*, and the final sound in *mall* and *mill* as the same sound. For convenience here, and because the literature on reading uses the term, I will use *phoneme* to refer to individual sounds.

Individual speech sounds are described according to how the airstream is modified to produce them. During speech, as air moves from the lungs through the mouth or nose, it is modified in a number of ways to produce different sounds. In the articulation of consonants, the airstream is either partially or totally blocked in the mouth. In the production of vowels, the air from the lungs is not blocked at all, but the shape of the mouth gives each vowel its characteristic sound. Semivowels, as their name suggests, resemble vowels and are produced with only very slight interference. Figure 2.1 shows a schematic representation of the principal resonators that affect the quality of speech sounds. These are the nasal, oral, and pharyngeal cavities. The lips are also included because they can alter the shape of the oral cavity, but also because they can be used to resonate, as in the production of /m/.

In producing consonants, the airstream coming from the lungs is obstructed to some degree, and this obstruction may occur anywhere in the oral cavity. One other alteration to the airstream is made by the vocal folds in the larynx. If the folds vibrate, as they do with the articulation of /z/ and /m/, for example, the sound is **voiced**. If they do not, as in /s/ and /f/, the sound is voiceless. The consonants of English can be distinguished from one another, then, on the basis of three modifications to the airstream—the place in the oral cavity where air is impeded, the manner in which it is impeded, and voicing.

Vowels are very different from consonants. To begin with, because the airstream is not impeded, they are highly resonant and, in almost all languages of the world, all vowels are voiced. Vowels are easier to hear, and it is easier to distinguish between them. A common example demonstrates that this is true. If you must give your name over the phone, you may have to spell it because it is hard to hear the difference, for instance, between /b/ and /d/ or between /f/ and /p/. So if your name is *Bonnie*, it may sound like *Donny* on the phone, and even if you spell it, you will have to say something like "Brava oxen niner niner," although the "oxen" isn't really necessary since /o/ is a vowel and easily distinguished.

The particular quality of each vowel is achieved by changing the shape of the oral resonator. Vowel quality depends on which part of the tongue is raised—front, central, or back—and on how far the tongue is raised—high, mid, or low. High front vowels are those in which the front part of the tongue is raised almost to the roof in the mouth, as in the vowel sounds in *cheap* and *chip*. To distinguish these two vowels, another feature is required. This feature refers to the amount of muscular tension in the vocal tract, principally the lower jaw. Vowels produced with a relatively greater degree of movement and with greater tension are called tense vowels and those produced with less movement and less tension are called lax vowels. This is a particularly salient distinction for elementary teachers because it corresponds roughly to the categories of long vowel and short vowel used in phonics. The short (or lax) vowels are produced with comparatively little movement or tension and include the vowels in *bit, blood, put, bat, bought*, and *father*. Long vowels are those produced with greater movement and muscular tension and include the vowels in *beep, brood, bake*, and *boat*. Also in the category of long vowels are the *diphthongs* in *boy, bite*, and *bout*. Diphthongs are treated like single vowels, but they are really two vowel sounds produced with one gliding into the other. Because they are produced with a gliding motion of the tongue, diphthongs are tense. My description of vowels is based on the "standard" of the mid-East-coast United States and much of eastern Canada. Throughout the English-speaking world, and even in these areas, however, there may be variations from these descriptions. The vowel /e/, for instance, is diphthongized in much of North America to /e^1/, meaning that in the pronunciation of *bait*, there will be a slight raising of the lower jaw just before the articulation of the final consonant.

Semivowels are produced with only very slight interference of the airstream in the oral tract. These sounds are, in fact, more like vowels in their articulation, but in English they function like consonants. They include the initial sounds in *wax* and *yaks*. The first of these is very similar to a /u/ and the second to an /i/. To illustrate, try saying /wæks/ followed by /uæks/ and then /yæks/ followed by /iæks/.

Syllables

The consonants, vowels, and semivowels are not the only units of the sound system. Another important one is the **syllable**, a unit which people intuitively recognize. There are even writing systems based on syllables. English syllables are, however, rather difficult to define formally or even to identify consistently. Does *chocolate*, for example, have two syllables or three? The answer depends on at least two variables—the dialect the individual speaks and how carefully he or she pronounces the word. In what is called *citation form*, meaning that the word is spoken clearly in isolation from other words, it will have three syllables in many dialects. In spoken discourse (e.g., in the sentence *We're out of chocolate ice cream, but we may have pistachio*), it is more likely to have only two syllables. Interestingly, two different dictionaries gave the syllabification of the word as *choc•o•late* but the pronunciation as /chawkhlit/. Only one, the *Cambridge English Dictionary*, gave both the two- and three-syllable pronunciations.

English has a number of different kinds of syllables. A syllable can be composed of a single vowel and no consonants (remember, we are talking about sound, not writing), or a vowel with one or more consonants on either side (*car, scar, scars* are all single-syllable words). English permits up to three consonants before the vowel (e.g., *strip*) and up to four following the vowel (*texts*—pronounced /teksts/).

Although syllable structure is somewhat awkward to describe, evidence is growing that children cope well with syllables at an early age. In recent years, researchers have come a long way in their understanding of how children learn the structure of syllables. In order to make sense of children's accomplishments in acquiring syllable structure, Demuth and Fee (1995) postulated a universal structure for syllables. Greatly simplified, it is this:

- The basic structure of a syllable has two parts, an onset consisting of an optional coda consonant or consonant cluster and a rhyme.
- The rhyme has a nuclear vowel and may have a coda, which may be a consonant or consonants or another vowel (as in a diphthong or a long vowel).
- Each unit that forms the rhyme is called a mora, which is a unit of time.

Schematically, syllables are structured as follows:

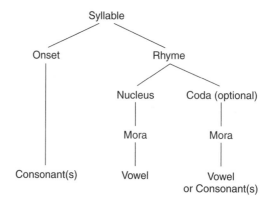

The second vowel of the rhyme is realized either as the second part of a diphthong (as in *buy*) or as a long vowel (as in *bee*). Thus, the word (and syllable) *plant* consists of the onset *pl-* and the rhyme *-ant*. Similarly, *die* consists of the onset *d* and the rhyme *ie*. They may be represented schematically as:

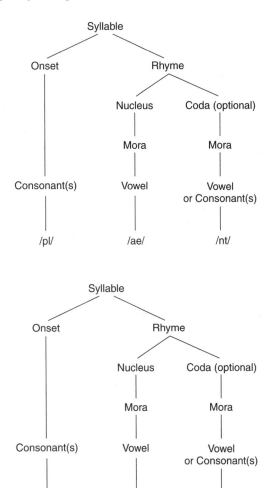

Syllable structures vary, of course, from language to language, and these differences pose certain problems for second–language learners. In Mandarin, for example, syllables normally consist of a consonant followed by a vowel. The only consonants permitted at the end of a syllable are nasals. When Mandarin speakers learn English, they frequently "drop" or fail to produce the consonants at the ends of words such as *cat*, *dog*, and *rob* but produce words such as *can*, *sing*, and *rum* correctly. These errors occur as a result of their applying the syllable structure rules of their language to English.

Much of language is more difficult to describe than it is to learn or to use. Such is the case with syllable structure. While an accurate description of the syllable is fairly complex, there is evidence that onsets and rhymes are psychologically valid even to very young children. Preschool children, for example, are generally good at rhyming. They can produce *rub, grub, club, sub, flub, hub* (and perhaps some made-up syllables) in a rhyming game. Goswami (1993) and other researchers (cf. Bowey & Francis, 1991; Kirtley, Bryant, MacLean & Bradley, 1989; Treiman, 1985) have provided a great deal of evidence that when children come to school they already have phonological knowledge about onsets and rhymes. They are not so good, however, at phonemic analysis—telling how many different "sounds" in *grub, club,* or *rub* or choosing the "odd" member of a set of sounds when the unit of sound is smaller than an onset or a rhyme. Children who have learned to read are better at this level of phonemic analysis, suggesting that it may be a product of learning to read rather than a prerequisite. This is important and a subject to which I will return in Chapter 3.

Phonological Processes

The task of learning the individual sounds and the syllable structure of a language is a complex one, and it is made more so by the fact that the actual pronunciation of speech sounds varies under different conditions. For example, we may pronounce a vowel one way when it is stressed and another when it is not. Whether the vowel is stressed depends, in part, on the prefixes or suffixes present. The process by which a vowel sound becomes neutralized to schwa when it loses its stress is called vowel reduction. This process occurs with certain words when they change their part of speech (their grammatical role in a sentence). Consider these pairs of words:

receive (v.)	reception (n.)
conceive (v.)	conception (n.)
cleave (v.)	cleft (adj.)
bereave (v.)	bereft (adj.)
sustain (v.)	sustenance (n.)

Notice that in each pair the same syllable is stressed, but when the part of speech changes, the quality of the vowel changes. This process is called vowel alternation and is very common in English. We see it in the conjugation of certain irregular, or strong, verbs:

leave left left	break broke broken
lose lost lost	sink sank sunk
ring rang rung	sing sang sung
write wrote written	bite bit bitten

Although vowel quality changes are more predominant, consonant sounds may also be reduced in various ways. One way is illustrated in the pairs just listed. Notice the alternation between /v/ and /p/. The other environment in which consonants may be reduced is in continuous speech. This is a type of reduction of which native speakers are usually not aware. It can cause non-native speakers to sound "foreign" because they do not reduce consonants in the same way. In the sentence,

Alma and Fred will have the dog groomed next week

unless the speaker is articulating very precisely, the final *t* in *next*, normally pronounced /nekst/ in citation form, will be left out. A similar process occurs in the pronunciation of *dog groomed*. Here, because the final consonant of *dog* is the same as the first consonant of *groomed*, speakers will often reduce the two sounds to a single /g/. This is one of several types of **assimilation**, or the changing of one speech sound to become more like another sound in its immediate environment. If the speaker is from parts of Britain or New England, he or she may also introduce an /r/ sound between *Alma* and *and* (producing something akin to "almarand"). This is a kind of dissimilation, the opposite of assimilation, and apparently occurs to break up two similar or identical sounds. Although both assimilation and dissimilation are natural processes, the first to reduce and somewhat simplify the stream of speech, it is curious that the processes occur in different contexts in different dialects.

The Sound System and Literacy

There is a great deal of speculation about the relationship between children's phonological awareness and their later ability to read and write. Certainly, in the broadest sense, it is true that in learning to read and write most children have learned to manipulate speech sounds in print. It is, however, possible to learn to read without having mastered the sound system of a language at all. As many who have acquired a "reading knowledge" of a foreign language will attest, it is possible to make the direct link from print to meaning without having much idea at all of how the language sounds when spoken. Children who are profoundly deaf also learn to read without the benefit of phonological association. There is evidence that even children with normal hearing initially approach literacy as a distinct task from oral language. For a child, learning to write may be more similar to learning to draw than learning to speak (i.e., another form of visual representation). However, for most children, reading and writing will eventually entail at least some mapping between print and the sounds of speech. It requires, however, a giant leap in reasoning to reach any conclusions about the nature of the phonological awareness they need in advance.

Some researchers and educators *define* phonological awareness as a child's "ability to reflect upon and manipulate components of spoken words" (Snowling, Hulme, Smith, & Thomas, 1994, p. 161). This definition is of a metalinguistic ability (the child's ability to think about language) rather than a linguistic ability (the child's ability to use language) and still begs the question of what kind of knowledge is required. What seems to be the case is that while there is a relationship between early phonological awareness and learning to read, that awareness does not necessarily mean the ability to identify and manipulate individual phonemes. Rather, there is growing evidence that early sensitivity to rhyme is the determining factor in learning to read. Wimmer, Landerl, & Schneider (1994) found, for example, that children's ability to identify rhymes, as measured before the onset of reading instruction, was a predictor of their ability to read at the end of third-grade. Their ability to isolate onsets, on the other hand, was significantly correlated, albeit barely, with their ability to read at the end of first-grade but had lost all predictive power by the end of third-grade. This is an interesting finding when one considers the relative importance of vowels and consonants in speech and writing. In speech, vowels are easier to hear and to differentiate than consonants. In writing, however, the vowel is somewhat less important. Consider, for example, the following sentences, written entirely without vowels:

Th bldng n th crnr ws trn dwn lst wk
Bth brd nd grm rctd thr wddng vws n frnt f mnstr

Even though there is some uncertainty (e.g., whether the article "a" might appear before "minister" in the second sentence), it doesn't take long to decode either sentence. Consider, in contrast, the same two sentences written with vowels only:

E uii o e oe a o o a ee
O I a oo eie ei ei o I o o iie

Given our knowledge of the language, we can predict the vowels from the pattern of the consonants. We cannot, of course, do the reverse because, while vowels carry much acoustic information, they are not so important in the written language, with one major exception, and that is "citation" form or lists of words. In word lists, for example, where there is no context for decoding the word, the vowel could be very important. In isolation, *pat*, *pet*, *pit*, *pot*, and *put* would be indistinguishable from one another without the vowel. But in context, the vowel is less important:

Mthr bght th dg fd t th pt str
Pls dnt pt th glss n th tbl

It is unlikely that anyone would confuse *pet* with *pat* in these two sentences, even without the vowels.

What is most important about the findings of Wimmer et al. is their compatibility with the findings of other researchers that the ability to segment by phoneme is a consequence of, rather than a prerequisite to, reading, though it may be necessary to learning to spell (Bradley & Bryant, 1983; Goswami & Bryant, 1990; Snowling et al., 1994). Goswami and Bryant (1990) have demonstrated that preschoolers' performance on rhyme and alliteration tasks predicts their later ability to read. They have argued rather convincingly that at the earliest stage of learning to read children need to be able to discriminate onsets and rhymes. While some researchers still insist that the ability to isolate and manipulate individual sounds (i.e., phonemes) is what is required of children, the emerging consensus is that the salient units are onsets and rhymes.

Studies of children learning to read English after first learning to read a nonalphabetic language are useful in determining the effect of prior learning on alphabetic decoding. Comparing British children with children from Hong Kong, Huang and Hanley (1995), found that British children had more difficulty in deleting the first phoneme from an initial consonant cluster (i.e., *s-* from *sp-*) than did children from Hong Kong. In contrast, the British children found it easier to isolate the *s-* from *sit* and to perform similar tasks than the Chinese children. It would seem that English-speaking children viewed the initial consonant cluster, common in English phonology, as an integral unit while the Chinese children remained true to their phonology (that does not have consonant clusters). More important, however, was the finding that phonological awareness contributed only to the reading of an alphabetic language. This is important because most of the studies use correlation methodology, and this methodology has an inherent weakness in interpretation. Specifically, even though the relationship between rhyming and alliterative ability on the one hand and reading ability on the other has been demonstrated through correlation, it is always possible that another undetected variable is influencing both phonological awareness and reading ability. If that were the case, as Huang and Hanley point out, this undetected variable should cause an equally strong relationship between phonological awareness and the reading of a non-alphabetic language. Since this is not the case, they argue, there is good reason to believe that "phonological awareness is a primary cause of differences in reading ability amongst children who read an alphabetic script" (1995, p. 92).

Most children acquire the sound system quite easily despite its complexity. When reading and writing become part of children's language awareness, the sound system gets more confusing because the sound-symbol correspondence is not always predictable. If it were predictable, we would be able to abide by the old "one symbol for each sound and one sound for each symbol" idealized rule of correspondence between oral and written language.

One of the glaring irregularities in English writing is related to that strange phenomenon known as the "silent letter." The silent letter is primarily a reading rather than a writing concept. In other words, the issue of the silent letter first arises when we are decoding printed text into sound units, and it might be tempting to try to rid the language of such culprits. It is fairly easy to demonstrate, however, that many letters that are silent in one form of a word make plenty of noise in another. Consider the following pairs:

sign   signature
autumn   autumnal

column	columnar
bomb	bombard
resign	resignation

The pronunciation of the words in the second column would suggest that if we changed the English writing system to make it strictly *funetik*, we might well complicate it instead, since the relationship between such pairs of words would be far less obvious. Other kinds of silent letters exist, of course, for less obvious reasons. Many phonics rules are intended to make sense of the silent letters in very common words. "When two vowels go walking, the first one does the talking" tells the beginning reader that the first vowel of a digraph "says its name" while the second is silent, thus telling a child who encounters words such as *beak, leaf, braid,* or *boat* how the vowel is pronounced. The concept is virtually useless when it comes to trying to figure out the spelling of these words. We are still faced, for instance, with many choices for *beak*, including *beek, beke, beik,* or *beeke* as well as the correct one.

Stress and Intonation

Another important aspect of the English sound system is the prosody, or the stress and intonation patterns, of the language. Stress refers to the force with which a syllable is articulated. When stress serves to distinguish the otherwise identical in-VALid from INvalid, for example, it is said to be distinctive. It is also predictable to a certain degree in that there are very general rules that tell us which syllable of a word to stress. For example, for two-syllable words ending in three consonants (words such as *deduct, resent, result, adapt,* and *report*), stress usually falls on the second syllable. In contrast, two-syllable words ending in a single consonant (such as *exit, cancel, festive*) are stressed on the first syllable. The rule is, however, more complicated than that. Consider, for example, *erase, refrain, align,* and *remove*. Stress on these words is on the second syllable despite their single final consonant (once the reader has figured out that the *g* in *align* is silent). This is because the vowel is tense (or long).

Unfortunately, this "rule" for assigning stress to two-syllable words is complicated further by the existence of many noun-verb pairs in English, which are identical but for their stress. Unlike the example of inVALid/INvalid, these pairs are related in meaning. They include words such as:

NOUN	**VERB**
PERfume	perFUME
TORment	torMENT
CONvict	conVICT
REcord (REHcord)	reCORD
SUBject	subJECT

The rules for assigning stress to words in English are complex, and they have many exceptions. It is unlikely, however, that children learning the language have to be concerned with learning the rules. The pronunciation of the word includes its stress placement, and it is likely that this is part of what we call lexical learning. In other words, the matter of learning individual words is NOT a matter of learning a rule that will apply widely (as is learning to pluralize, for example), but of simply learning the phonetic configuration which identifies that word as unique from all others. Stress is part of that configuration and presents no particular problem to children. Not, that is, until the child begins to read. When faced with the task of matching up the words on the printed page with the words stored in their memories, children are introduced to the systematicity of stress. Similarly, in trying to "sound out" an unfamiliar word, children begin to come to terms with stress assignment rules.

Intonation refers to the pattern of stress and rising and falling pitch that occur in connected speech. Intonation can also be used for special purposes such as emphasis. Consider, for example, the different meanings that result from the shift of stress in the following sentence:

> WHAT are you doing here? (It looks pretty strange to me!)
>
> What ARE you doing here? (You should be somewhere else!)
>
> What are YOU doing here? (I was expecting Arnold.)
>
> What are you DOING here? (Whatever it is, you shouldn't be doing it!)
>
> What are you doing HERE? (Instead of Bagdad!)

This use of stress is called contrastive stress, and it is used to give emphasis to a particular part of the sentence. Another intonation feature which conveys meaning is pitch. Rising pitch is normally used at the end of a question and is also used to signal uncertainty or doubt in statements or single-word utterances.

The Sounds of Other Languages

The sound systems of the world's languages vary greatly. Some have a large number of distinct sounds while others have very few. Some Polynesian languages, for example, have as few as 11 or 12 segments, including both consonants and vowels. There is a language, Xu, in the Khoisan family, on the other hand, with 141 different segments, 24 of which are vowels.

Another way in which sound systems vary is in the particular consonants and vowels which occur. Most languages have between 5 and 7 vowels, a fact which may surprise English speakers since English and many of its relatives have from 10 to 15. Some languages distinguish nasal vowels (resonance in both the oral and the nasal cavity) from oral vowels, but in general, it is the consonants that give learners more difficulty.

Speakers of other languages sometimes complain that English has especially troublesome consonants. Certainly English has some relatively rare consonants, including the /th/ sound. Speakers of German, French, and a host of other languages experience difficulty with these sounds, which are also difficult for very young children just gaining control of their articulators. On the other hand, most English speakers would find the clicks found in Zulu difficult, although they are quite capable of making very similar sounds when starting horses or clucking disapproval.

It isn't only the individual sounds that distinguish the sound systems of languages. In more than half the languages of the world, it is possible to change the meaning of a word simply by changing the pitch at which it is articulated. These languages are called *tone languages*, and there are a number of possible tones and combinations of tones ranging from 2 to 6. In Mandarin, which has 4 tones, the word *mai* can mean either "to buy" or "to sell," depending on the tone. *Mai*, meaning to buy, is articulated with falling-rising tone while *mai*, meaning to sell, is articulated with falling tone. In general, speakers of tone languages have less difficulty in learning non-tone languages than speakers of non-tone languages have in learning tone languages.

The job of learning the sound system is a formidable one for both non-native and native learners. Learners must acquire motor control of the articulators as well as all the cognitive aspects of phonology. Neither children nor second language learners learn the sound system in isolation. They learn it as part of the process of learning words and larger communication units. One of the central of these is the morpheme.

Morphology: The Structure of Words

If we were to ask people who have not studied language structure what the smallest meaning-carrying unit is, most would probably say that it is the word. The word is, after all, the smallest unit that can normally stand alone in speech or in writing. It is not the word, however, but the **morpheme** that is the smallest unit of meaning. Some morphemes happen to be words—*cat*, *banana*, and *trigger* are all words consisting of a single morpheme (i.e., they stand alone and cannot be reduced further without loss of meaning). These are free or free-standing morphemes. They can have other morphemes added to them, but they can also be used alone. Other morphemes may be equally meaningful but cannot stand alone as words. {Bio-}, {semi-}, and {-logy} are examples of non-word morphemes and are called **bound morphemes** because to function in the language they must "bind" themselves to another morpheme. Bound morphemes include morphemes such as {bio-} (meaning "life"), {phot-} (meaning "light"), and {anti-} (meaning "against") and have meaning just as words do, but these must be attached to another morpheme to be used.

There are other ways of classifying morphemes. When children learn that a *dusty road* is a road layered with dust, they have learned a **derivational morpheme**. The addition of the morpheme {-y} to words such as *dust, rust, might, trust*, and *dirt* to form *dusty, rusty, mighty, trusty*, and *dirty* is highly productive in the sense that it is widely used in English to change nouns to adjectives. There is not a great deal of meaning carried by this morpheme; it serves principally to change the part of speech. Although most derivational processes are highly productive, they can be problematic for first or second language learners. The same {-y} sound, for example, that can change a noun to an adjective turns the adjective *full* into the adverb *fully*. The {-er} that turns the verbs *teach, write, play,* and *sing* into *teacher, writer, player,* and *singer* takes a different form in *actor* and still another in *lawyer*. It also sounds just like the morpheme that turns *cold* and *bold* to *colder* and *bolder*. This latter morpheme, however, is an **inflectional morpheme**.

Inflectional morphemes, like derivational morphemes, serve more as grammatical indicators than as meaning bearers. Inflectional morphemes include the plural suffix, the past tense suffix, the possessive suffix, the third person plural suffix, {-ing} and the present perfect form, as well as the comparative and superlative forms, {-er} and {-est}. Learning the grammatical inflections is an important aspect of morphological learning. When they learn a new noun, children do not have to be told what the plural form is. Assuming that the word takes a regular plural ending, they can figure out the correct form because they already know how nouns are pluralized in English. Nor do they have to wonder about the past tense of a new verb; knowledge of the inflectional system tells them exactly how it is formed. There are irregular plural forms, such as *women* and *children*, and irregular past tense forms such as *bought* and *rode*, but learning the regular inflections gives children a head start on the business of word learning.

Another important aspect of what children learn about English morphology is how words combine to form **compounds**. At first blush, the process seems simple enough. *Milk* and *man* combine to form *milkman*, the man who brings the milk (ignoring for the moment that the person may be a woman). Except to the native speaker, however, this relationship may not be at all obvious. A *snowman* is NOT a man who brings snow but a man who is made of snow. We would not be too pleased, either, if the garbage man were to deliver garbage instead of take it away. A doorman, on the other hand, does not deliver nor remove doors; neither is he made of them. Words in English combine in myriad ways to form new words, but the meanings of combined forms are not nearly as predictable as we might assume.

English, in fact, abounds with words that don't always mean what they should. An **idiom** is an expression whose meaning cannot be worked out from its individual parts, and the learning of idiomatic expressions is a major challenge for both children and for non-native learners. *Hit the road* is a good example. Knowing every possible meaning of each component of the phrase is of little value in making sense of the expression. Understanding this idiom requires, essentially, understanding the idiomatic use of the word *hit*. An idiomatic expression such as *to wear one's heart on one's sleeve* cannot be interpreted in the same way. There is no alternate meaning to a single word that will decode the message. Non-native speakers find learning the idioms of English one of the greatest challenges in the task of language learning. Learning the appropriate use of idioms requires knowledge not only of word meanings but of how sentences are structured.

Syntax: The Structure of Sentences

Most native speakers consider the basic unit of expression to be the sentence despite the fact that they frequently do not speak in complete sentences. They believe they do, and they recognize the sentence as the means by which they make themselves understood. The study of how morphemes combine to form sentences is called **syntax**. Notice that I wrote morphemes and not words. This may seem somewhat confusing since I said earlier that morphemes combine to form words and am now talking about how they combine to form sentences. While it is the case that the word is an important constituent of the sentence, it is also true that in order to understand how grammatical sentences are formed, it is necessary to examine the behavior of smaller units. Consider the following example:

> Julian lies.
> Ivy lies.
>
> Julian lies.
> Julian lied.

It would be impossible to describe the difference between the first pair of sentences in the same way as the second. What differentiates the first pair of sentences is a single word, the subject or agent of the verb. What differentiates the second pair of sentences is a unit smaller than a word, a morpheme that changes the tense of the verb from present to past tense. In both pairs, there is a meaning difference, but the meaning changes in each pair in fundamentally different ways.

What children must learn in order to understand and produce sentences they have never heard before is a great deal of knowledge about how sentences are formed. If that language is English, they must acquire two kinds of knowledge, the order in which words are put together to form sentences and the relationships that exist among the different constitutents, for in sentences, not all words have the same magnitude of importance. Linear order is an obvious aspect of sentence organization in English. Rearranging the words in an English sentence can have amusing, confusing, or even disastrous results. There is, after all, a significant difference in meaning between *baby eats goldfish* and *goldfish eats baby*. Less obvious but equally important is hierarchical structure, which refers to the ways in which the morphemes in a sentence are organized into coherent groupings or units that are themselves organized into larger groupings or units. These units are referred to as constituents of a sentence. In the sentence *Barnaby found a mud puddle under the deck*, we can see that there are a number of groups of words that have meaning. We can also see that not all sequences of words make up sentence constituents. For example, most native speakers would agree that *found a mud puddle under the deck* has some meaning of its own and, more significantly, contributes to the meaning of the sentence in a coherent way. Specifically, it tells us what Barnaby (our white poodle) did; it is the predicate of the sentence.

We can further divide the predicate into constituents. Native speakers would likely agree that the next two major constituents are *found a mud puddle* and *under the deck*, even though they might not be able to explain why this is the case. They could even break these two constituents down further if asked.

What is it about these groupings that marks them as constituents? First of all, they DO have some meaning of and on their own and could serve as answers to questions. To the question, *Who found a mud puddle under the deck?* one might well answer *Barnaby*. Or to the question *Where did Barnaby find a mud puddle?* One would likely respond not with the entire sentence but *under the deck*. In contrast, it is difficult to imagine the question to which *mud puddle under* might be the answer, although those words appear in that order in the sentence.

A second way in which we know that these are true constituents is that parenthetical expressions can be used between them. We might say, for instance, *Barnaby, after many hours of looking, found a mud puddle under the deck*, or *Barnaby found a mud puddle, which had been thrown there and left last summer by my absent-minded cousin Shirley, under the deck*. Conversely, the sequence *Barnaby found a, I was surprised to see, mud puddle under the deck* would be highly unlikely in English. In general, we cannot insert parenthetical comments WITHIN grammatical constituents.

A third attribute of constituents is that often they can be replaced with a single word. For example, in answer to the question *Who found a mud puddle under the deck?* We could answer with the full sentence, although we would be more likely to answer *Barnaby*. We could also say *Barnaby did*. In this case, *did* stands in for the entire predicate. Constituents, then, are more than just words or words in sequence. They are meaningful units which are hierarchically arranged in the sense that a single constituent may be part of a larger constituent, which may in turn be part of a still larger constituent.

Returning to the full sentence, we can see that *deck* is a constituent of the larger unit *under the deck*, which is a constituent of *mud puddle under the deck*, etc. We could demonstrate this and the other hierarchical relationships in the sentence with brackets:

[[Barnaby][found a mud puddle under the deck]]

[[Barnaby][[found][a mud puddle under the deck]]]

[[Barnaby][[found][[a mud puddle][under the deck]]]]

[[Barnaby][[found][[[a][mud puddle]][[under][the deck]]]]]

[[Barnaby][[found][[[a][mud puddle]][[under][[the][deck]]]]]]

This is one way of representing constituent structure, but it does not convey the hierarchical relationship in an easily discernible way. Most linguists today use the tree diagram to show the linear as well as the hierarchical structure of sentence elements. In the tree diagram, each constituent of the sentence forms a branch. The simplified tree diagram in Figure 2.2 conveys exactly the same information as the brackets.

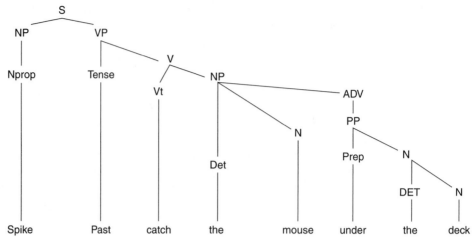

Figure 2.2   Tree Diagram of *Barnaby Found a Mud Puddle Under the Deck*

Ambiguity

Tree diagrams are especially useful for demonstrating the different constituent structures of ambiguous sentences (i.e., sentences which share a common shape, or sequence of words, but have two or more distinct meanings). The sentence *Mad dogs and Englishmen go out in the noonday sun*, for example, has two interpretations. In one, both dogs and Englishmen are mad and in the second, only dogs are mad (although both go out in the noonday sun).

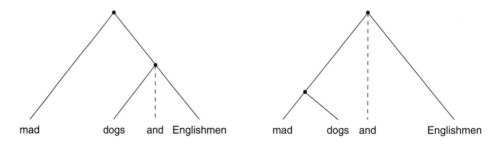

Sentences that are syntactically ambiguous look the same but have two (or more) different meanings.

Sentences that are syntactic paraphrases of one another share certain properties: They are comprised of the same main lexical items; they have essentially the same meaning; other sentences of the same structure can be paraphrased in exactly the same way. Consider, for example, the following sentences:

The soothsayer made the prediction.

The prediction was made by the soothsayer.

What the soothsayer made was a prediction.

It was a prediction that the soothsayer made.

Each of these sentences has a different form, but they all have the same principal words—*soothsayer, made,* and *prediction.* They all express the meaning that a soothsayer made a prediction, and they are all related to each other in such a way that every other sentence with the same structure can be transformed in the same ways.

Brokers buy stocks.

Stocks are bought by brokers.

What brokers typically buy are stocks.

It is stocks that brokers buy.

All these sentences have the same basic, or underlying, structure which may be represented as:

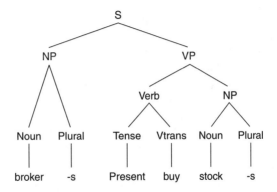

It is not sufficient that the syntax of English demonstrate the common underlying structure for these kinds of sentences. It must also demonstrate how that common structure can be transformed in so many ways without changing the core meaning. Ambiguity and paraphrase, then, impose two very different demands on a syntactic description. Ambiguity requires that the syntax account for the fact that two superficially identical sentences may have very different constituent structures. Paraphrase, on the other hand, requires the syntax to account for the fact that a number of superficially different sentences may have a common constituent structure. But the demands do not stop there. Certain sentences are related to each other in systematic ways but involve changes in meaning. Questions and negatives are good examples of these kinds of sentences. The systematic relationship between affirmative declarative sentences and various kinds of questions is easy to see:

1. Uncle Harry wrote the book in prison.
2. Did Uncle Harry write the book in prison?
3. Who wrote the book in prison?

4. What did Uncle Harry write in prison?

5. Where did Uncle Harry write the book?

Certain regularities can be seen among all four questions. The question word is always at the front of the sentence whether the question requires a yes/no answer, as in 2, or specific information, as in 3, 4, and 5. Notice that in 2, the past tense of *do* has been inserted at the beginning of the sentence because English word order does not permit *Write the book in prison...?* although middle English did allow such a form. In modern English, a verb cannot begin a question unless it is a form of *be*, *have*, or *do*. Likewise, in 4 and 5, *did* has been added just after the question word. This addition is not required in 3 because the question word replaces the subject noun phrase (Uncle Harry) and the verb *wrote* is already near the beginning of the sentence and does not have to be moved. The same regular pattern occurs throughout the language.

The relationship between affirmative sentences and negatives is systematic in a similar way. The following sets of sentences demonstrate the regularity:

6. The jury acquitted Uncle Harry on appeal.

7. The jury didn't acquit Uncle Harry on appeal.

8. Uncle Harry's books sold well.

9. Uncle Harry's books didn't sell well.

10. Aunt Maud is angry with Uncle Harry.

11. Aunt Maud isn't angry with Uncle Harry.

12. Uncle Harry has many original ideas.

13. Uncle Harry hasn't many original ideas.

14. Uncle Harry doesn't have many original ideas.

Once again, a form of *do* is required to "support" the negative in sentences without *be* and may be used in sentences with *have* (some dialects require it). We can see, then, that both questions and negatives are related to affirmative statements in a regular and predictable way. These kinds of systematicity must also be reflected in a complete description of English sentences. This might be accomplished in a number of ways, but the most efficient is through a two-level system of grammar such as the one proposed by Noam Chomsky (1965) and refined by linguists and teachers over the past 25 years.

Transformational-Generative Grammar (TG)

One of Chomsky's major goals in conceiving his bilevel grammar was to account for sentences that appeared to have the same structure but in fact had different underlying meanings. He used the sentences *John is eager to please* and *John is easy to please* to demonstrate that sentences that appear to be structurally identical, may in fact, have radically different constituent structures. His aim was to provide a way of analyzing sentence structure that accounted for these divergent underlying structures. One level of structure was intended as a way of representing the meaning. This was the underlying structure of the sentence, which he called the generative component or base component.

The base component consists of a set of phrase structure rules that are intended as general statements about how the most basic or core sentence patterns of a particular language are constructed. They consist of statements such as *A sentence consists of a noun phrase and a verb phrase* and *A noun phrase consists of an optional article and a noun which may be singular or plural*. Linguists use a notational system that simplifies the writing of phrase structure rules and would represent these two as:

S ----➤ NP + VP
NP ----➤ (Det) + N + (Plural)

Using this notational convention, ( ) indicates optionality (i.e., elements that may occur in some constituents but not others). The phrase structure rules serve as "directions" for constructing the trees we saw earlier, more properly called *phrase markers*. The structure that results from applying the phrase structure rules is called a *deep structure*.

An example will be useful in understanding how the second level of grammar operates. Let's consider two of the syntactic paraphrases from an earlier example:

Uncle Harry wrote the book in prison.
The book was written by Uncle Harry in prison.

Because they are syntactic paraphrases, they have the same deep structure, but although the surface structure of the first sentence will look essentially the same as its deep structure, the second will differ dramatically.

To transform the deep structure into the surface structure shown in Figure 2.3, a number of changes must occur. Briefly, they are:

1. Reverse the order of the subject and object noun phrases
2. Add *by*
3. Add a form of the verb *to be*
4. Add the past participial ending to the main verb

The transformational component of the grammar makes these alterations to the deep structure and produces the passive form of the sentence. Transformational rules add, delete, and move sentence elements, but although they may result in slight meaning changes, they do not change the core meaning of the sentence. The structure that results from applying all relevant transformational rules is called the *surface structure*.

Figure 2.3
Surface Structure of
*The Book Was Writ-
ten by Uncle Harry
in Prison*

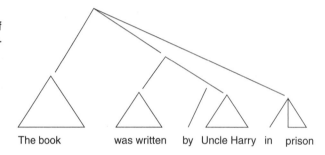

Recursion

A complete syntactic description of a language should account for all possible sentences in the language. This is no minor undertaking since it is theoretically possible to string any number of elements together to form compound, complex, and compound complex sentences. Stringing noun phrases together forms compound subjects or objects:

> Barnaby chased the weasel.
> Barnaby and Spike chased the weasel.
> Barnaby, Spike, and Binky chased the weasel.
> Barnaby and Spike chased the weasel and caught the toad.
> Barnaby and Binky chased the weasel, caught the toad, and spent Tuesday at the pound.

We can also conjoin complete sentences:

> Barnaby ate his kibble, and Spike ate the squid.
> Barnaby ate his kibble, and Spike ate the squid, but Binky stayed on her diet.

In theory, using conjunctions such as *and, or,* and *but,* it would be possible to conjoin subjects, predicates, and complete sentences indefinitely. In this way, the number of possible sentences in English would be infinite, but conjunction is only one way of creating new sentences. Another way is to embed one sentence within another, and English has several ways of doing this. Consider the following sentences:

> The streetcar runs along King Street.
> The streetcar stops on my corner.

Assuming that *streetcar* in each sentence refers to the same vehicle, we can combine these two sentences by embedding one within the other:

The streetcar that runs along King Street stops on my corner.

We could embed still another sentence:

The streetcar that runs along King Street, which is three blocks south of Queen Street, stops on my corner.

And another:

The streetcar that runs along King Street, which is three blocks south of Queen Street, stops on my corner, which is not normally busy.

There are other ways of embedding sentences within sentences. English has an entire class of verbs, in fact, which take sentences as their objects. Verbs such as *know, believe, imagine, deny*, and *claim* take sentences, frequently beginning with *that*, as objects. For example, in the sentences *The Senator denies that he lied to the Senate* and *Sheila claimed that the Senator lied to everyone*, the object of the verb is a complete sentence. *He lied to the Senate* is the object of *denies* in the first sentence and *the Senator lied to everyone* is the object of *claimed* in the second. The fact that English sentences can be embedded within other sentences is another reason why the number of possible sentences is infinite. This being the case, we can easily see that an adequate syntactic description of English must include a mechanism for describing **recursion**. Otherwise, we would have to generate an infinite number of rules to account for an infinite number of sentences.

A complete syntax of English is beyond the scope of this book. The purpose here has been to introduce the notions of linearity, hierarchical structure, sentence constituents, ambiguity, syntactic paraphrase, and recursion as well as to give a broad indication of the types of rules linguists use to represent the role each plays in English sentences.

Morphemes, Sentences, and Other Languages

One of the principal ways in which languages differ is in their rules for combining morphemes into words. In English, we are able to combine a number of morphemes in a single word, and these morphemes may impart either grammatical or lexical meaning. The word *dialogues*, for example, consists of three morphemes—{dia-} meaning "two," {logue} meaning "to speak" and {-s}, indicating that the noun is plural. Some languages are far more ambitious in the number of morphemes that can be combined in a single word. In fact, languages such as Japanese, Turkish, Finish, and many North American languages are classified as *agglutinating languages* meaning that words are made up of long sequences of morphemes with each expressing a particular grammatical function or meaning. The *Learning Practical Turkish* website provides a number of examples and explains how the words are constructed. For example, the word *evdekiler*, meaning "the people in the house," is explained as follows:

Take the simple noun *ev* meaning "house." Then add the suffix *de* meaning "in," which gives *evde*; "in the house."

Next glue on *ki* to convey "that" and you have *evdeki*; "in that house."

Finally, you finish off your creation with *ler* to express "the people" (literally, "the ones") and you have *evdekiler*, "the people in that house" or more simply, "the people in the house." (adapted from Learning Practical Turkish, http://abone.superonline.com/~user0001/difficulties-of-turkish—agglutination.html)

In contrast, in inflecting languages, a single word may represent several grammatical categories and in isolating languages each word consists of only one word element.

Mandarin is primarily an isolating language, meaning that there are no endings on words, and word order is used to show the relationships among words in a sentence. The sentence *We sold the horses to the teacher* would be rendered in Mandarin: *wo men ba ma mai gei lao shi le*:

wo	1st person pronoun
men	plural
ba	object indicator
ma	*horse*
mai	*sell*
gei	benefactive case marker
lao	*venerated*
shi	*master*
le	past tense marker

Between the two extremes of agglutinating and isolating langugages are the *inflecting* or *synthetic* languages such as Greek, Latin, and Arabic. In these languages, grammatical relationships are expressed by changing the structure of words. As the name suggests, this is most often accomplished by using inflectional endings. The Latin word *amo* conveys, literally, "I love," but also that the verb is in the present tense, active, and indicative.

Although languages are typically classified into one of the three categories, most are, in fact, combinations of all three types. English is one of the world's languages that resists clear categorization. It is, for example, an isolating language (its dependence on word order is a major clue), but it also has examples of inflection. The plural form of nouns (*bird, birds; mouse, mice*), the third person singular in the present tense (*I, you, we, they write; he writes, she writes*), the past tense (*play, played; sing, sang*), participials (*wring, wringing*), and comparatives (*dull, duller, dullest*) are all formed by inflection. It is also agglutinating in the sense that it can build words out of several morphemes (such as *nonreturnable, humanitarianism,* and *neurolinguistically*).

Whichever language a child learns to speak, the learning will entail the ability to understand and to produce novel sentences. Children learning to speak English must learn how morphemes are agglutinated, how the inflectional system works, and the rules for sequencing words into meaningful sentences. However difficult the task may seem, however, it would be much more difficult if not for the systematicity of these processes. However difficult they may seem, it is much easier to learn a set of generalizations, together with the myriad exceptions, than to try to memorize a store of prepared sentences. The ability to generate a new utterance at will and to understand whatever utterances one hears lies at the heart of language acquisition and use. No amount of learning about sentence structure will be sufficient, however, to the task of making and understanding meaning.

Semantics and Pragmatics: The Study of Meaning

It is, of course, impossible to talk about meaning independent of other levels of linguistic description. It is also impossible to study meaning without reference to real-world objects and events or without consideration of how people use language. In fact, this is the business of semantics, or more accurately, semiotics. Technically, semiotics refers to the study of meaning in its broadest sense. Many theorists consider semiotics to consist of three categories or divisions of study: syntax, the study of the relationship between linguistic signs; **semantics,** the study of the relationship between linguistic signs and the real world; and **pragmatics,** the study of the relationship between linguistic signs and language users. To illustrate the difference, consider the sentence:

Will those people who did not receive this message, please respond? From a syntactic perspective, there is nothing wrong with the sentence; every word has meaning and the words are properly sequenced and violate no syntactic rules. And yet, from a semantic perspective, the utterance expresses a real-world impossibility. It is not nonsensical in the way that Chomsky's famous *Green ideas sleep furiously* is, but both sentences violate semantic rules while being perfectly formed syntactically. The sentence, of relatively little interest to syntacticians and semanticists, however, might be grist for the pragmatist's mill. Concerned with the relationship between speakers and utterances, a pragmatic analysis might focus on the intended message, the state of mind of the speaker or writer, the likelihood that the impossibility of complying with the message might escape a significant number of readers, or even the societal conditions that have created so many "poor" readers.

We have already examined the syntactic level of linguistic meaning. In this section, we will consider semantics and pragmatics.

Semantics

Semantics refers broadly to the study of meaning as it resides in language. Of course, it is impossible to study ANY aspect of language without considering meaning, but in linguistics, semantics is concerned with word meanings, with meaning that results from combining words in various ways, and with how language represents real-world meaning. The study of semantics is particularly fascinating, then, because in talking about semantics we are talking about how people represent reality. Although language must have standard conventions in order for people to use it to communicate, standardization is a nebulous notion when the subject is how people view and represent reality. To a significant degree, reality is defined by individual and cultural experience—meaning categories of a language are specific to that language and the culture it represents, but there is also dramatic variation within languages and even within dialects. It sometimes comes as a shock to a monolingual to discover that speakers of other languages may not share the same reality. As an example, speakers of English have relatively few words for the fluid chemists identify as H_2O. If it happens to be falling from the sky we call it *rain*, but otherwise we make do with *water* whether it is in a bathtub, an ocean, or a glass with ice. The Japanese language, in contrast, differentiates between hot water (*oyu*) and cold water (*mizu*), and it is impossible to talk of water without specifying which is intended. Clearly this distinction has, or had at some time, particular significance for Japanese speakers.

In Central Alaskan Yupik, a language spoken by approximately 13,000 aboriginal Alaskans, there are about 15 distinct words for snow, including words describing snow particles as they fall, words describing the characteristics of fallen snow, and words describing meteorlogical events. Certainly, the number of different words for *snow* in various aboriginal languages of Alaska and northern Canada has often been cited as evidence in the case that language is culturally determined. But is English so very different? We have *flurries, flakes, hail,* and *sleet* to describe snow particles as they fall; we have *frost, dusting, powder,* and *hardpack* to describe snow that has fallen; and we have *snowfall, snowstorm,* and *blizzard* to describe meteorlogical events. We also have *avalanche, packed powder, granular,* and *ice-pack.* This is not to say that English and Yupik or Inuit or any other Eskimo language mark the same distinctions where snow is concerned. The point is that in a large part of the English-speaking world, we have a need to mark certain distinctions concerning snow and these distinctions differ from locale to locale and from context to context. Although all the words listed previously exist in the English language, for those living in the Arizona desert or in Florida, some of them might be known only from movies.

Colors offer especially rich distinctions among languages, in large part because they offer direct evidence of differences in perception. English has the distinction between *red* and *pink,* pink being the color red to which sufficient white has been added to change the English speaker's perception of the color. Blue, however, is blue whether it be navy, sky, powder, or baby. In Russian, the exact opposite holds true. *Blue* and *light blue* are expressed by two distinct words, as different as *red* and *pink,* but for the Russian speaker, adding white to red results only in light red. The significance of colors is also culturally dependent, of course. The color pink is associated with feminity in North American English-speaking cultures, but that is less true of light red in Russian culture.

While to a large degree, word meanings are culturally agreed upon, as they must be for people to communicate, there are subtle differences in the meanings words hold for individual speakers of a language. These differences are largely a function of experience. An English-German bilingual once explained to me that the English word *lap* had little meaning for her beyond the dictionary definition (the front of a sitting person, from waist to knees). The German equivalent, *schoss,* on the other hand included memories of being held and cuddled by her German grandmother. She also explained that her reading of the Biblical "bosom of God" had only literal meaning for her, but the German translation, which replaced *bosom* with *schoss*, conveyed a very special message.

There are subtle distinctions between the way Canadian English speakers use the word *quite* and the way American speakers use it. For Americans, it is most commonly used to mean wholly, completely, or to an extreme. An essay that is *quite good* in American English is very good or even extremely good. In Canadian English, on the other hand, an essay that is quite good will more likely be viewed as having some notable problems. The essay may not be bad; it's just that *quite* denotes more reservation or qualification in Canadian and British English than in American English. In this context, for many speakers, *quite* means "somewhat" or "to some extent."

These cultural and individual variables have contributed to the frustration that linguists experience in trying to formalize semantics in the same way as they have formalized phonology, morphology, and syntax. But there are other reasons why semantics resists precise formalization. Chief among these is that meaning resides in so many places—in words, sentences, and in larger discourse units and in all of them at once, so semanticists must deal with all levels of linguistic structure in formulating theories of how meaning is made and shared. Nevertheless, some linguists have attempted to describe the structure of meaning independently. Working under the assumption that semantics and syntax are distinct language components that can be described independently of one another, they have developed models that are called *interpretive*. Other linguists believe that the distinction between syntax and semantics is artificial, and that a description of the two language components must be integrated. Their work has led to *generative* theories and to *case grammar*. Both these theories hold that syntax is determined by semantics and that it is impossible to consider syntactic structures independent of meaning. While their arguments are compelling, they are beyond the scope of this text.

A certain amount of meaning in a language resides in the components and structure of the language—in words and sentences—somewhat independent of particular speakers and hearers in particular contexts. Another aspect of meaning is communicative meaning, and it resides in social situations and in the relationship between particular speakers and hearers. The study of this communicative meaning is commonly called pragmatics.

Pragmatics

Pragmatics refers to the use of language for real communication in real time and encompasses almost any aspect of human society that involves language. Pragmatics is concerned, for example, with the language of power relationships, gender differences in language use, and how language is used to manipulate thought (e.g., in advertising or propaganda). To study and talk about linguistic pragmatics, thus, is to study and talk about the myriad of meanings that human beings make and transmit among themselves.

Although they are not as formalized, there are rules or conventions of pragmatics (i.e., that govern language use in a variety of situations). Bolinger lists a total of four such conventions that account for the meaning differences conveyed by minor variations in word order, but there are many others. In the section on syntax, we saw that when sentences are related to one another in systematic ways, they are called syntactic paraphrases. But in actual language use, they are seldom true paraphrases at all. Bolinger (1980, p. 29) points out that English has conventions for arranging sentence elements to signal meaning. These are not grammar rules but usage conventions, and they include, for instance, the following "rule":

> …When a modifier goes before a noun, it characterizes the noun, says something about the way the noun 'really is'. When it follows, the 'really is' quality is neutralized. *The corner house* is the house that belongs on the corner; *the house on the corner* could be one in the process of being moved, perhaps parked there overnight. *The people ready were picked up* refers to a temporary state of readiness; *The ready people were picked up* sounds strange because it implies that 'being ready' is something you have with you as part of your nature, not just a temporary condition. Sometimes the same adjective can be used both ways: the only handy tool and the only tool handy. (Bolinger, 1980, p. 29)

Certainly it is possible to get by in English without any conscious awareness of conventions of this type, but in order to become effective speakers and writers, we do learn and follow these subtle rules even though they are rarely taught. Children must acquire them and it is a lifelong process to do so, as many college and university English professors will attest. Yet another aspect of learning the pragmatics of language is learning how to manipulate the language for specific purposes. English abounds in opportunities for doing so. It has been pointed out repeatedly that there are many more pejorative words in the language for talking about females than for talking about males. A more subtle form of linguistic sexism is **semantic derogation**, or the process by which words referring to women are demeaned or acquire sexual connotations. Compare the following:

Charley is Rose's master.

Rose is Charley's mistress.

As Wareing points out, this use of master suggests that Charley is Rose's boss or that he has power over her (and let's assume for purposes of illustration that Rose is not a dog). The relationship suggested by the second is more than opposite; it illustrates a rather common occurrence in the language, namely that "words for women often end up referring to women in a sexual capacity" (1999a, p. 70). Throughout the language are examples of language that diminishes females. For example, words such as *steward, actor,* and *tiger,* may be used to refer to a steward, an actor, or a tiger whether they be male or female. The words *stewardess, actress,* and *tigress,* on the other hand, can only refer to females. In linguistic terms, the first group are known as unmarked terms while the second, with their *-ess* suffixes, are known as marked terms. In English, it is not at all unusual for unmarked terms to be used for males and for the marked terms to be used for females. Fortunately, the use of the marked form is disappearing from North American English, but there is a more insidious form of discrimination present in some usage. Consider the following:

Lady surgeon

Male nurse

Female engineer

The very fact that the noun modifier identifies the sex of the noun referent suggests that surgeons and engineers are supposed to be male and nurses female. These are underlying assumptions that influence society's beliefs and the career choices made by both men and women. The effect of this distinction is to mark the terms for female as somehow different from the "norm."

It is not only in the lexicon of a language that sexism is found. It occurs in discourse; for example, in the following example from Bolinger:

> If a woman driver makes a bad maneuver, a man may be heard to say *What does that woman think she's doing!* with *woman* lengthened and pronounced with a rise-fall-rise intonation—which makes it an expression of disregard. A similar use of *man* would be taken as an emphatic way of expressing the emotion of the whole sentence, not as a reflection of the man's sex. (1980, p. 93)

The assymetries in language tend to favor males over females, to diminish women but not men. This is not to say that men cannot be the subject of sexist language because, of course, they can. However, the very words of the language do not carry the burden of negative connotation that they do for females.

Unfortunately, the language of the school does relatively little to offset the pervasive effects of linguistic bias. The stories and books they read emphasize sex roles and the language uses masculine pronouns and other male terms with far greater frequency than female terms. As Bolinger observes,

> …when adults write for one another, they refer to young people as *children*, almost as often as they call them *boys* and *girls*. When writing books and stories for children, however, adults use the gender words *boy* and *girl* twice as often as the neutral words *child* and *children*…. (Bolinger, 1980, p. 93)

Bolinger goes on to cite studies showing that in schoolbooks the ratio of use of *he/him* to *she/her* was almost 4 to 1 (Graham, 1975) and that the same disproportion occurs in the 200 million achievement tests commonly given in U.S. schools (Tittle, 1973). While the feminist revolution may have had some impact on the language of books, it takes only a cursory look at the books on the shelves of any elementary school to see that the bias has by no means been eliminated. We do not yet know the impact of this particular form of bias on children's performance; given that girls now outperform boys on most measures in school year, it is difficult to assess the impact on either boys or girls. But it is difficult to believe that there is no effect; indeed the effect may be manifest in more subtle and more dangerous ways in the society.

To understand why, it is useful to think about the broader matter of language and power, or more specifically, the question of how language and power are related. As Shân Wareing points out, "power is often demonstrated through language; it is also actually achieved or 'done' through language" (1999b, p. 11). This is true in both public and private domains. For example, politicians create and exert power not only in what they say but through the language of law. Parents and teachers demonstrate and exert power over children in the language they use. It is, in fact, the way that parents and teachers talk to children that establishes the power relationship. Establishing and maintaining power, of course, involves one person or group manipulating others.

A more subtle but probably equally dangerous form of manipulation comes in the language of commercial advertising. Bolinger's delightful sentence, "We reduced the size because we didn't want to increase the price" (1980, p. 58) is an example of the kind of doublespeak to which we are exposed daily. Because they are to some degree innocent believers in the voices of authority, children are more prone to commercial manipulation than are adults, though, obviously the target of Bolinger's example was the adult population. I am not sure which is more alarming, the fact that advertisers *believed* that such a slogan would be effective or the likelihood that for some of the population, it probably was.

All of these areas—language and gender, language and power, language and advertising—are topics of inquiry encompassed by linguistic pragmatics. Other areas include language and the media, language and class, language and age, and language and racism. At the heart of all these areas is the power of language to transform and to enlighten and to wound and to destroy. Children learn very early the fallacy of the playground taunt "Sticks and stones may break my bones but words will never hurt me." Part of their lifetime language learning is not only to realize but to take responsibility for the fact that words do indeed wound—to learn, in other words, the paradox that oral language is at once ephemeral and permanent. Words find their targets and inflict their wounds, and while the wounds may heal, the act which inflicted them cannot be undone—words remain alive in memory. Counselors and educators alike now recognize that while verbal abuse may not be life-threatening in the same way as extreme physical abuse, it can do extreme damage to children, damage that may take a lifetime to heal if it heals at all.

LANGUAGE CHANGE

When I was an undergraduate student in the English Department at the University of New Hampshire, I took in my last semester a course entitled *The History of English*. It was the most demanding and difficult course that I had taken in the English department, but it is the one that whetted my appetite for linguistics. Those of us enrolled in that course began to get some idea about the work done by historical linguists who trace changes in language over time and help us to understand the origins of modern-day peculiarities of our language. What they study is various and fascinating, but it is also relevant. It is relevant because understanding the dynamic nature of language leads us to new understandings about the relationship between language change and language variation. It also helps us to better understand meaning relationships that exist among certain words and for understanding usage and grammatical conventions that may seem peculiar even within a system that is arbitrary, because in historical terms, it often is not arbitrary. Consider the greatly maligned *ain't*. Viewed as incorrect by legions and generations of English teachers, editors, and parents, *ain't* has, in fact, a noble history. It is merely a variant of *am't*, a contracted form of *am not*. Fans of Dorothy L. Sayers mysteries will recall the erudite and educated Lord Peter Wimsy using *ain't* routinely. As Alistair Cooke explained to U.S. audiences at the time that PBS broadcast the mysteries starring Ian Carmichael, the term was an affectation used by the upper British classes during the first third of the 20th century, and Lord Peter was merely being true to his "class." It is unfortunate that *ain't* has such a bad reputation since it would be very useful and more regular (thus making it easier for ESL learners) to have the following:

He/she is.	He/she's not.	He/she isn't.
You are.	You're not.	You aren't.
I am.	I'm not.	I ain't (or am't).

The technically correct *am I not* is, in common usage, more usually *aren't I* as in *I'm in your way, aren't I?* Indeed, *I'm in your way am I not?* might be deemed to have a slightly different meaning.

There are many irregularities in English for which the only explanation is historical change. There is no rational explanation for the regular past tense of *go*, for instance, unless we look several centuries back into our language's history. We find thus that there was once a verb *wend* that meant about the same thing as *go* and which is still used in certain expressions. The conjugation of *go* and *wend* somehow collapsed into a single one, retaining *go* and *gone* from *to go* and *went* from to *wend*.

By looking at English from an historical perspective, linguists help us to understand why certain words that rhymed in Shakespeare no longer rhyme today. Throughout Shakespeare, *where* and *were* are treated as exact rhymes—in fact, it is Shakespeare's rhymes which that give linguists some of their strongest evidence for how English words were pronounced during the early modern period of the language. Consider, for example, the following examples, the final two lines from five of Shakespeare's sonnets:

1. *O, him she stores, to show what wealth she had*
   In days long since, before these last so bad. (LXVII)
2. *For we, which now behold these present days,*
   Have eyes to wonder, but lack tongues to praise. (CV)
3. *If some suspect of ill mask'd not thy show,*
   Then thou alone kingdoms of hearts shouldst owe. (LXX)
4. *For I am sham'd by that which I bring forth,*
   And so should you, to love things nothing worth. (LXXII)
5. *Therefore, like her, I sometimes hold my tongue,*
   Because I would not dull you with my song. (CII)

While it is possible that Shakespeare was having an off day when he wrote the last two sonnets, it is more likely that his rhymes were as exact as those in the first three examples, but changes in pronunciation in the centuries since his writing have differentiated them.

The kinds of questions that historical linguists try to answer in their research may seem to be of little direct relevance for modern language teachers. Issues such as which sounds might have existed in a language before it was written down, for example, or why the /th/ sound is relatively rare in the languages of the world, seem far removed from the life of a 7-year-old child. However, we also have historical linguists to thank for much of what we now understand about English spelling (although, unfortunately, we can't blame them for it!). What seems at times a chaotic and random system makes a great deal more sense when we understand that current English spelling is a product of its history. Consider, for example, the spelling of *thumb*, which makes no sense synchronically. It does make sense, though, when we know the history of the word. In Old English, it was a two syllable word, *thuma*. Through a natural phonological process, a /b/ came to be inserted between the /m/ and the /a/ (remember the similarities between /m/ and /b/ as well as other words in the language such as *thimble* where /b/ follows /m/). When the final syllable was lost, there was no need for the /b/ and it dropped out of the pronunciation but remained in the spelling.

We are a little more tolerant of the spelling of words such as *autumn*, *hymn*, and *sign* when we consider the pronunciation of *autumnal*, *hymnal*, and *signal*. On the other hand, natural processes of language change may well eventually regularize forms for which there are is no significant morphological kinship by doing so. *Light*, *night*, and *right* come to mind. Certainly, advertising and the Internet are influencing spelling of the first two already. *Lite* and *nite* are taking over in certain domains, and there is no strong argument beyond tradition and a loss of etymological information for their not being spelled as *mite*, *rite*, and *site*. Of course, each of these has an *–ight* homophone, which in itself might constitute an argument for maintaining, although not a strong one since there are many words in the language (such as *invalid*) that have the same spelling and vastly different meanings. Moreover, English words have so many different meanings that having one form take on additional meanings that are usually clear from the context does not constitute a strong argument. In other words, if we were to lose the distinction between *rite* and *right*, *rite* would become the common spelling for all meanings of both, not an onerous burden, one that *right* almost carries now, taking up half a dictionary column.

A very brief look at that history reveals a language with a long and chequered history but one whose writing system was only standardized about 250 years ago. It is not possible to pinpoint a time when English was "born," but most scholars choose a date around 450 A.D. when the British Isles were invaded (as they were often in subsequent centuries), this time by three Northern European Germanic tribes, the Angles, Jutes, and Saxons. Not a highly civilized crowd, these invaders managed to meld their various languages or dialects into the language that was once called Anglo-Saxon until scholars changed their minds. Perhaps noticing that this appellation neglected the Jutes, who, being a particularly fierce tribe with possible descendants who would not be amused by the omission, scholars decided to call the language Old

English. What has survived from Old English into modern times are the words that were needed in their daily pursuits—principally farming, once they stopped warring among themselves long enough to plow a field and gather the eggs. Words such as *earth*, *tree*, *dirt*, and *sheep* all come from Old English as do most of the 100 or so most frequently used words in contemporary English.

About 150 years after these invasions, St. Augustine landed in Britain, bringing with him Christianity and Church Latin. The establishment of monasteries had a profound influence on language and culture in the British Isles, and some influence on the English language (but not very much). Learned monks did some writing in English, but for the most part, they wrote in Latin, and their efforts led to England's becoming a centre of learning and culture throughout Europe and the "publishing" capital of the world.

By the end of the millennium, Britain had survived the Viking invasion, which brought the Danish language to Britain, and had begun another renaissance led by Alfred the Great. This wise king encouraged the printing of books in the vernacular— Old English—and it is, in large part, because of his efforts that we know as much as we do about Old English.

The Middle English period began with yet another invasion, the Norman Conquest of 1066. The major linguistic effect of this invasion was the introduction of French. Although French was used mainly at court, a great number of words that we use today—approximately 40% of our vocabulary—were brought to the English language by William the Conqueror. Words for cuisine, for example, such as *beef* and *pork* (cf. French *boeuf* and *porc*) came to be used instead of the perfectly utilitarian *cow* and *pig* that the British would have used in earlier times. There remains today, incidentally, a certain snobbery attached to the use of French words *de cuisine* leading us to shun the perfectly descriptive *snail* in favor of *escargot* or *cake* in favor of *gateau* (in Britain), and don't even bother thinking about the English equivalent of *hors d'oeuvres* (although with the mangled pronunciation most of us inflict on the last term, the French might be excused for thinking it *is* English).

The Norman Conquest furthered Britain's claim as a cultural centre, and by the 14th century the demand for books was growing. When Caxton brought the printing press to England in 1476, the subject of how to spell English words became important. It had been a fairly flexible affair before that and after the introduction of the printing press remained so. The fact that the early printers emigrated to Britain from what is now the Netherlands and spoke Dutch did little to add precision to an already lax system. To complicate matters further, at the time that the printing press was introduced to Britain, the pronunciation of a great many English words was in flux as a result of what has come to be known as the Great Vowel Shift. Understanding how modern spelling came to represent the spoken language depends to some degree on knowing what happened in the development of English vowels. Moreover, if Bear, Templeton, Invernizzi, & Johnston (1996) are correct in asserting that children's learning of the spelling system parallels the historical development of spelling, then it is useful to look at the Great Vowel Shift a little more closely.

Sometime during the period of early Modern English, a change occurred in the pronunciation of the vowels that we typically characterize as *long*. As a result of the Great

Vowel Shift, words that had been pronounced with an /e/ sound as in modern *lake* came to be pronounced with an /i/ as in modern *leek*. *Sheep*, in middle English, would have sounded more like modern *shape* and today's *boot* would have sounded to the modern speaker like *boat*. This shift did not affect the pronunciation of short vowels such as the ones in *it*, *bet*, or *fat*. We can begin to understand certain vowel alternations better when we consider the simple fact of the Great Vowel Shift. Consider, for example, *sheep* and *shepherd*. We typically think of vowels as occurring in long/short pairs. The long vowel in modern day *sheep* is represented as /i/. It's corresponding short vowel is the vowel in *sit*, which linguists represent as /I/. In Middle English, however, the vowel in *sheep* would have been /e/ (as in *shape*), the short version of which *is* the same vowel as is still found in *shepherd*. The language is replete with examples of alternations that would have been quite regular in middle English but are no longer so today. The alternation between the vowels in *bite* and *bit* provides another good example. In Middle English, the sound that today is the diphthong /ai/ would have been /i/ as in modern *beet*. The Great Vowel Shift changed the long high vowels /i/ and /u/ into the diphthongs /ai/ (as in *bite*) and /au/ (as in *cow*). The corresponding short vowels were unaffected so that the alternation between long and short vowels in these words is not the natural one it once was. Shakespeare's seeming indifference to spelling can thus be explained. He was writing at a time when the pronunciation of the language was going through a major change, it was printed by foreign printers who doubtless imposed some of their own pronunciations, and most of the population of Britain was still illiterate.

It was not until the modern English period and the publication of Samuel Johnson's *Dictionary of the English Language* in 1755 that English spelling was standardized. And since then, although the pronunciation of the language has gone through some major changes, the spelling has remained more or less constant. There are some exceptions, such as the American spellings of *favour*, *honour*, *colour*, etc., but these had nothing to do with regularizing sound-symbol correspondence.

We owe far more to Shakespeare, of course, for his contribution to the richness of the English language. He introduced a number of fresh expressions into the language that are commonplace today. Bernard Levin, in his entertaining *Some Thoughts on the Impact of Shakespeare on Our Language* points out dozens including, *it's Greek to me*, *high time*, *clear out*, *bag and baggage*, and other commonly used expressions. Of course, historical linguists share their interest in Shakespeare's language with a legion of scholars devoted exclusively to the study of Shakespearean language.

Even though the facts of language change interest some young children, most teachers would not use the information in this way but to inform their own understanding. Knowing that English is much more regular and predictable than it first seems makes us less likely to treat it as a puzzle without a solution.

CONCLUSION

In this chapter, we have seen that language interests people for a variety of reasons and that scholars study language from a variety of perspectives. We have also seen that their seemingly arcane or esoteric scholarship may provide valuable insights for educators. And yet, we have merely scratched the surface of this vast field that is linguistics or even of the study of language. The reader is invited to study further by considering the questions for discussion and by exploring the bibliographic sources listed at the end of this chapter.

For Further Study

1. The author claims that descriptive linguists advance our understanding of how children learn and use language by providing "a clearer picture of the structure—or *possible structures*—of language…" What does she mean by *possible structures*?

2. In Portia's famous "Quality of mercy" speech from the *Merchant of Venice*, Shakespeare wrote the following:

   The quality of mercy is not strain'd;
   It droppeth as the gentle rain from heaven
   Upon the place beneath: it is twice bless'd…

   What is the function of the apostrophe in *strain'd* and *bless'd*? Why is it no longer needed today?

   Why would an historical linguist insist on keeping the anachronistic forms when changing the words to *strained* and *blessed* would not alter the intended sound or meaning of the language?

3. The author explains how *went* came to be the past tense of *go*. Have you ever wondered about the strange conjugation of other common verbs such as *to be*? Try to find out what historical explanation there is for the diverse forms *be, am, was, were*.

4. The author implies that good teachers of young children are necessarily practising psycholinguists. Can you provide further evidence in support of this suggestion?

5. Much of neurolinguistic data comes from brain-damaged patients. Does this affect the use of the data for understanding normal language functioning?

6. The author describes consonant alternation between /v/ and /f/ in words such as "cleave" and "cleft." Can you find examples of other consonant pairs that alternate in such a predictable fashion?

7. Shakespeare is credited with first using the expression *one fell swoop* to mean "all at once." What is the meaning of *fell* in this expression and how is it related to the word *felon*? (Hint: See question 4!)

8. The author uses an example of an English-speaking child (Sarah) and an Asian child, both kindergarten age and both having difficulty with /l/ and /r/. Consider a third child, an Asian child of 11 or 12, having the same difficulty, and speculate about the degree to which the source of the problem in each is similar. See if your answer changes after reading Chapters 3 and 4.

9. What is *neurological bimodality*, and why is it an important notion for teachers?

10. The author says that a Chinese-speaking child learner and an English-speaking child learner face different tasks in learning the intonation of their languages. Why is this true? Does it mean that the task is easier for an English-speaking child? Why?

11. Pick out the pair in each of the following sets that does not belong and explain why. (Hint: This is a phonetics question, not a spelling problem.)

fix, fax	dimple, pimple	show, stow
mix, max	dump, pump	shine, sine
firm, farm	dare, pair	shine, sign
kitsch, catch	day, play	shell, sell

12. The author says that in most of the languages of the world, all vowels are voiced. Using the Internet, find at least three languages that have distinctive voiceless vowels (i.e., vowels that are distinguished from other sounds by virtue of being voiceless).

13. Draw syllable structure trees for each of the following words, creating a separate tree for each syllable.
    a. diet
    b. mustard
    c. cranial
    d. Phillip

For Further Reading

To delve more deeply into some of the topics covered in Chapter 2, see the following:

Websites

http:///www.takeourword.com
http://www.fun-with-words.com
http://dmoz.org/Science/Social_Sciences/Language_and_Linguistics/
http://linguistlist.org/
(And many others added daily.)

Books

Campbell, L. (1999). *Historical linguistics*. Cambridge, MA: MIT Press.

Coupland, N., & Jaworski, A. (Eds.). (1997). *Sociolinguistics: A reader and coursebook*. New York: St. Martin's Press.

Crane, S., & Lillo-Martin, D. (1999). *An introduction to linguistic theory and language acquisition*. Oxford: Blackwell.

Fromkin, V. (Ed.). (1999). *Linguistics: An introduction to linguistic theory*. Cambridge, MA: Polity Press.

Hudson, G. (1999). *Essential introductory linguistics*. Oxford: Blackwell.

Lightfoot, D. (1999). *The development of language: Acquisition, change and evolution*. Oxford: Blackwell.

CHAPTER THREE

Learning the First Language

Most of the children in the world speak more than one language before the end of their school years, a fact that may be strange to much of the English-speaking world where we tend to view bilingualism as something out of the ordinary. For many of the world's children, that second language is English, which is the reason more people in the world speak English than any other language. That is not to say that more people speak English as a first language, for this is not the case. But if we were to take a census of the world's population and have them list every language they speak and counted the result without regard for whether the language is native or not, English would win. Given that the world's largest national population (currently approaching 1.4 billion) speaks Chinese, this is an impressive statistic. The children many of us teach are, then, members of a minority if they speak only one language and members of the majority of world speakers who speak English.

Although some children grow up simultaneously learning more than one language, in this chapter and the next, we will be concerned primarily with children acquiring their first language. Many children will subsequently learn additional languages, but our focus here will be the first language learning experience. In this chapter, we begin with a description of the task, trying to come to terms with the enormity of the child's achievement in the first years of life. We will then examine the various environments in which children accomplish this task and conclude with speculation about how they actually do it in a section on theoretical perspectives. This chapter sets the stage for the stories, in Chapter 4, of three children acquiring their first language under very different circumstances.

THE TASK OF LANGUAGE LEARNING

The two previous chapters have given us some idea of the complexity of human language from which we can draw some conclusions about the nature and the enormity of children's linguistic achievements in the first 5 years. A naïve assumption might be that children's task is merely to parrot back what they have heard and that learning entails closer and closer approximation as they mimic adult sounds. This view, of course, is easily demonstrated to be false. Take, for instance, the following utterances:

> It tooks too long!
> Doggy bited my hand.

Young children utter sentences like this frequently despite the fact that they would never have heard them that way from the adults around them. Similarly, they are capable of making up words and sentences that are completely unique. If they had to wait around until some adult happened to speak the word or phrase needed to make the child's meaning, they would grow up linguistically poor indeed. No, there is no doubt that the task of language learning is, in large part, the task of learning the vastly complicated rule system on which language is built.

It is easy to see that language is systematic (or it would be virtually impossible to learn), and so understanding what children accomplish in language learning is in part understanding how they acquire the many systems (sound, morpheme, word, sentence) that form the foundation of language. From the child's perspective, however, language is communication, so we must also come to terms with how children learn to communicate meaning. They are not, after all, little linguists, puzzling over the structures and trying to ascertain the underlying systematicity. Rather, they are trying to figure out what means what and how to communicate what they want and need to communicate. Therefore, as we examine the task, it is important that we keep in mind the child's perspective as well as our own.

In learning language, children have to learn to make sense of the acoustic stream of speech sounds. If we think about hearing someone talk in a language we do not know, it's easy to understand the importance and the difficulty of this first task. There is not actually any "space" between words to help us figure out where the word boundaries are. There are a finite number of meaningfully distinct speech sounds, but many, many more variations of each sound that make it difficult to figure out which differences matter and which do not. For example, English speakers have at least three pronunciations of each of the voiceless stop consonants, /p, t, k/, but most people are not aware of the difference between the /p/ in pitch and the /p/ in stop. It's predictable and not relevant to native speakers, but children have no way of knowing this at the beginning and have to sort out whether the difference between these two articulations of /p/ is as important, for example, as the difference between /p/ and /b/. At the same time, they must learn to control their immature articulators to form the words in close approximation to the adult pronunciation. They are not allowed the luxury of learning just this, however, because they are simultaneously learning the rules for combining sounds into syllables, morphemes, and words; an enormous number of individual words; and the rules for combining them into meaningful sentences. At the same time, they are trying to work out the various communicative functions that language serves and how each one might be realized in different contexts. They have to learn how to participate in conversation with all its conventions for turn-taking, topic shifting, maintaining topic, meaning confirmation, etc. There is no doubt that the business of language learning is an enormous task, otherwise all of us would be multilingual.

Despite all the difficulties in learning language, children do it with astonishing speed and they waste little time getting on with it. Convincing research evidence indicates, for example, that in the first 3 months of life, newborns exhibit early signs of communicative interest and behavior. They are visibly interested in human faces, voices, and speech sounds, more so than in other objects and sounds. We have several decades of evidence that infants pay more attention to people than to objects, that they prefer human voices over other acoustically similar sounds, female voices over male voices, and their mother's voice over other female voices. Moreover, infants show a very early ability to identify relevant sound distinctions in their native language, some as subtle as the difference between /p/ and /b/ or /t/ and /d/ (Reddy, 1999, p. 35). It would seem that challenging as the task may be, children are well-equipped for it.

For non-hearing children, the task is slightly different but no less, and possibly more, complex. They have to decode and encode language visually rather than aurally and learn a different system for communication at the same time that they learn to cope in a hearing world where most of the people around them are communicating in another language. For all children, the first 5 years of life represent a stunning linguistic achievement. They grow from infants with amazing powers of linguistic perception but with little productive ability (beyond babbling and non-verbal signs) to school-aged children capable of producing complex sentences and sophisticated meanings. In the next chapter, we will see how three children progress through the complexities of language learning. For now, we will turn our attention to the issue of environment and its role in language learning.

THE ENVIRONMENTS IN WHICH CHILDREN LEARN LANGUAGE

Although there are documented cases of moderate to severe language delay resulting from environmental factors, those factors have been so extreme and the cases so few that we can conclude that children routinely learn language in many, many different settings. We can no more sketch a single best or an ideal environment for children to learn language than we can declare positively that in certain conditions they will not learn language. The well-documented case of Genie makes the point very well. In Los Angeles in 1970, a girl of 13 years and 9 months was discovered after having been kept in physical and social isolation from the age of 20 months. Genie had been kept in a small, closed room where she was physically punished for making any noise and was never spoken to. Her father and brother sometimes made barking noises at her, and her mother was forbidden all but minimal contact at meal times. The house had neither radio nor television. Not surprisingly, when she was found, Genie was in such traumatized condition that she required hospitalization for nearly a year until she was placed with a foster family.

Physicians who examined her during that time found no evidence of neurological disease or brain damage, although functionally the girl was severely retarded (McLaughlin, 1984, p. 51). It appeared that she was healthy apart from suffering the devastating effects of complete social isolation. Having been denied exposure to language from the age of 20 months, Genie could in no way be deemed to have experienced a "normal" language learning environment, and indeed, when she was discovered she had acquired virtually no language. Needless to say, linguists were very interested in Genie, and her language development has been carefully charted. Perhaps the most remarkable thing about Genie is that she has acquired any language proficiency at all, but she has; in fact, she has attained considerable proficiency in English. As might be expected, however, analysis of her development has revealed a number of abnormalities. The gap between her ability to produce and comprehend speech was found to be wider than normal, she had difficulty in acquiring certain syntactic skills, and her overall rate of development was abnormally slow (Curtiss, 1977). The point to be made here is that the change of environment was most likely the major factor in Genie's developing any language proficiency at all.

Genie is not the only child to grow up in social isolation. Crystal lists 48 such children either reared in the wild by animals or in isolation from human contact. Most of the reports of these children are sparse, and only a few contain any information about the children's language ability. According to Crystal, what information exists is clear: "None could speak at all, and most had no comprehension of speech. Most attempts to teach them to speak failed" (Crystal 1987, p. 289). And yet, children tolerate other conditions that would seem less than ideal and go on to speak, read, and write normally. The hearing children of non-hearing parents usually develop language normally (both sign language and spoken language) as do the non-hearing children of hearing parents. This is not to say that "minimal" contact is the desired amount.

While children do learn language under conditions that are far from ideal, it is nonetheless the case that their later success in school depends to a large degree on the language proficiency they have when they arrive there. What this means is that environment can play a major factor in the level of language proficiency that children attain. For example, children who have been exposed to language used in a variety of situations for many different functions will have less difficulty adjusting to the new linguistic culture of the school. This is just common sense, but it is common sense that has been validated by research and by the experience of many teachers.

Understanding the role that environment plays in children's language learning is important to planning for their success in school because we can partly re-create the conditions for success. But it is also important to try to understand *how* they learn language—to speculate about whether language learning is truly unique or whether it is related to other kinds of human learning. In either case, there are many unanswered questions about what actually happens in the minds of young children as they grow from non-verbal infants to talkative toddlers and then readers and writers of one or more languages.

HOW THEY DO IT: THEORETICAL PERSPECTIVES

We know a great deal, though by no means all, about what children have to learn; we know that environment plays an important role, interacting with whatever genetic predisposition children might bring to the task of language acquisition. What we do not know is how they do it. At the end of this chapter, indeed, of this book, we still will not know. It isn't that researchers, teachers, and parents have not tried to figure it out. Indeed, for much of human history, scholars have been fascinated by children's language learning. It's just that the question is far too complex—or rather, the human learner is too complex—and our tools for studying it too rudimentary. Yet, theory is important because it provides a framework and a language for discourse from which we can further our understandings of how children actually accomplish the task of language learning.

Theoreticians have been speculating for centuries about how children manage to accomplish all that they do at a time when they are cognitively immature. Although the problem is not "solved," we have advanced our understanding even since the first half of the 20th century when behaviorism was the received wisdom. In earlier editions of this book, I devoted several pages to the behaviorists. Here, I will use less space because, at the beginning of a new century, I believe that we have come far enough in our thinking to leave this theory behind except for considering its historical contribution to the present state and the ongoing development of linguistic theory.

In earlier editions of this book, I also wrote about four competing theories as distinct, though somewhat related, explanations of language acquisition. In recent years, however, I, along with other writers and researchers, have begun to rethink the matter of theory and the issues underlying theoretical differences of opinion. There are two principal questions, the answers to which situate theorists in one of four general camps. The first is whether some or most of language acquisition can be accounted for by children's biological endowment. Is there, in other words, an innate language acquisition mechanism that regulates or controls how and at what speed children acquire language? The second issue is whether language is a unique *kind* of human learning. In other words, are the cognitive resources devoted to language unique to language, or do children use the same cognitive resources for all, or even other non-language, learning? Linguists talk about this second issue in terms of *domain-specific* and *domain-general* theories of language acquisition. Domain-specific views would see language learning as a wholly unique human learning experience. Shortly, I will sketch the four general camps into which theorists fall along the two axes of nativism and domain specificity.

Before we look at competing theoretical stances, it is useful to think about how theorists go about constructing a theory of language acquisition. Some, mainly linguistic philosophers, read and think about language structure and what the child must achieve in learning it. They speculate about what must occur for children to master particular structures, construct theories, and debate with one another about how tenable one theory might be in comparison with another. This is a valuable exercise, but at some point, these theories must be tested against actual child language data. A "perfect" theory is not very useful, after all, if it fails to capture the realities of what children actually learn. In other words, if a theory predicts a particular order of acquisition—say, that children will learn "yes-no" questions before WH- questions—but we learn that, in fact, a significant number of children do not demonstrate that order—say, they learn WH- questions first or the two kinds of questions simultaneously—then the theory is of little value. Theory, then, must be built on or at least answerable to data.

But what kind of data? If we want to understand the totality of the language learning experience, we would have to study many children from birth through puberty, or at least, the first 5 years of life. Moreover, we would have to collect data so very carefully that we preserved its phonetic, morphological, and syntactic integrity and keep precise records of the conditions under which each utterance was made. These would be nearly ideal *longitudinal* data. They would also be virtually impossible to collect. Linguists often rely, then, on cross-sectional data, or those data acquired from studies of large numbers of children at different stages in their language development. Such designs can produce a large amount of data very quickly and can give a good indication of what a large number of children know or can do at a particular age. If researchers collect data on a large number of children aged 2, 4, and 6, for example, they may be able to discern a pattern in the acquisition of whatever structure or behavior they are studying. But because these data capture only a moment in time, they may yield different results from longitudinal data. Since a theory of language acquisition must account for *both* development and language behavior at any point in that development, it is important to have both kinds of data to work with.

In constructing theories of language acquisition, then, theoreticians have to rely on less-than-perfect sources. Fortunately, there has been no shortage. In the 20th century alone, a large amount of data was amassed. In the early years of that century, a French linguist named Ronjat (1913) studied and published reports of the bilingual development of his son. Other major contributors in the first half of the century included Leopold (1939, 1947, 1948, 1949a, 1949b), Jakobson (1941, 1968), and Velten (1943).

Even more data were collected in the second half of the century, particularly in the last three decades. Raw data, however, are of interest only to the researchers themselves. If research findings are to be applicable (i.e., useful to practitioners and especially to educators trying to understand and plan for children's continued language learning), acquisition data must be organized within the framework of a general theory. The relationship between research data and theory is actually very straightforward. The data provide the materials from which a theory can be constructed and against which it can be tested. A coherent theory must account for all the facts of language acquisition found in the mass of data, but as we have seen, these facts come from a complex of behaviors encompassed by human language. They come from phonology, morphology, syntax, semantics, and pragmatics; thus, it is not surprising that the task of constructing a general, comprehensive theory of language acquisition is a formidable one.

The task is complicated further by the fact that much of the data, gathered by different researchers under different conditions, seem contradictory in part because the findings emerge from a variety of research designs and, indeed, research questions. To date, then, there is no one theory capable of organizing the facts gleaned from data collected from a variety of sources, of generating and testing hypotheses based on those facts, and of reaching a coherent explanation of the acquisition process.

As researchers continue to speculate about the nature of the underlying processes, they work within or through particular theoretical approaches. These approaches both guide their inquiry and help them interpret their results. While there are a number of competing theories of child language acquisition that linguists and educators categorize in various ways—as behaviorist, linguistic, cognitive, or interactionist, for example—the difficulty with such categorizations is that too frequently theories do not fit neatly into the assigned category. As I mentioned earlier, a more useful approach is to situate discussion of language theory along two axes related to where a theorist stands on the question of nativism and on the cognitive specificity of language learning. To put it in terms of positive and negative positions on each question, we would have the following combinations:

A	B	C	D
+Innate	+ Innate	−Innate	−Innate
+Specific	−Specific	+ Specific	−Specific

Behaviorist theories hold that there is nothing unique about language learning, that *all* human behavior, including language, has its basis in physical processes and can only be studied in terms of those processes. It is, thus, an extreme example of Category D. The most radical of these theorists, linguists such as B. F. Skinner (1957), proposed an elaborate scheme of stimulus, reinforcement, and association, and attempted to account for the acquisition of syntax as well as word meaning. According to this view, children's attempts at language structures would be rewarded if they closely approximated the adult form, but those that did not would be punished. Then, as children grow more proficient, the adult modifies the practice of reinforcement, rewarding only those that fully conform to the adult standard.

Behaviorists contended, in summary, that infants begin as producers of random verbalizations. Adults hear those random verbalizations and positively reinforce the correct ones and punish, or at least fail to reward, the incorrect ones. Children, according to this view, become meaningful communicators through the simultaneous processes of classical conditioning, operant conditioning, and imitation, processes applied by others in their environment. This radical "Category D" stance has few adherents because the case against it is too strong. More precisely, it is at odds with the data in the following ways:

1. *Evidence of regression.*   An example of regression occurs when a child apparently loses the ability to pronounce correctly a word that was previously correct. In her study

of the acquisition of phonology, Lise Menn (1971) reported that the child Daniel's pronunciation of two words actually deteriorated. Where initially he had pronounced *down* as [dawn] and *stone* as [don], he subsequently began to pronounce *down* as [nawn] and *stone* as [non]. These changes occurred at a time when he was acquiring other nasal consonants in words such as *beans*, which he pronounced as [menz] and *dance*, which he pronounced as [naens]. It would take considerable contortion of behaviorist theory to account for this or other types of regression, yet parents and others who have observed young children closely know that regression is a common occurrence in their language learning.

2. *Children's ability to produce novel forms.*   The fact that children are able to produce combinations of words and pronunciations they have never heard before is beyond the scope of strict behaviorism to explain. It is true that the principles of imitation and analogy can account for some novel production, but they cannot be stretched to cover all. Consider, for example,

> **a.** Mikey gots no toys. [Mikey has no toys.]
>
> **b.** Want other one spoon, Daddy. [I want the other spoon, Daddy.]
>
> **c.** Me wants him all gone. [I want him to leave.]

These utterances are problematic for behaviorism on two grounds. First, children cannot imitate what, in all likelihood, they have not heard before. Second, it is difficult to imagine that any adult ever provided reinforcement for these forms. But then, this is the crux of another central difficulty with behaviorism, the fact that parents provide little feedback in matters of form.

3. *The absence of reinforcement.*   A classic example comes from Roger Brown (1973, quoted in McLaughlin) who found that parents rarely accept or reject a child's utterance on the grounds of form. In response to the child who uttered "Mikey gots no toys," her mother responded "That's not true, dear. Mikey has a clown, and a truck and lots of other toys." She responded to the truth value of the statement and not to its form. This is common practice with adults talking with children.

4. *Failure to respond to negative feedback.*   Children rarely respond to negative feedback about their linguistic forms. Even if parents try to turn children's attention to form and even if they succeed to some degree in getting them to mimic the correct form, children ignore the parent's teaching when left to their own devices. Furthermore, few parents try to interfere with infant pronunciations, being charmed instead by the baby talk, or perhaps understanding the futility of correction. Those who try usually find themselves frustrated as did the researchers who reported the *fis* phenomenon described in the previous chapter.

Actually, there is even more direct evidence against the role of reinforcement in language learning. Katherine Nelson (1973, quoted in Reich, 1986, p. 321) found that the children whose mothers practiced reinforcement developed more slowly than the children whose mothers rarely or never practiced reinforcement for form. If language learning depends upon reinforcement, and reinforcement does not occur, then learning cannot occur. But learning does occur in the absence of reinforcement. And so, if positive reinforcement of grammatical forms actually impedes language development, then we have even more reason to question the theory.

5. *The uniformity with which children around the world learn language.* If behaviorists were correct and language developed merely as a result of environmental shaping of an organism without any particular facility for language learning, then there would be a great deal of variation among language learners if for no other reason than there are variations among adults, their behaviors, and their expectations of their children. However, this is not the case because almost all children acquire language, and there is evidence that they do so in a manner that is remarkably consistent. Both Brown (1973) and Slobin (1979) have reported that at the two-word stage children across many different languages exhibit remarkably similar language learning behavior. They express essentially the same kinds of meaning and intent in highly similar utterances. Parents of young children know that they learn very early to say "no" as in ("no nap" or "no go") and to ask for more ("more juice" or "more cookie").

6. *The uniqueness of language to the human species.* The argument goes like this: If language learning were simply a matter of conditioning and imitation as described earlier, then it would be expected that animals other than humans could learn language. Before we can sensibly address the question of animal language, however, we need some clear definition of language. Otherwise, we do not know whether the "waggle dance" of bees and the courting calls of jackdaws qualify as language. Clearly, each is a communicative system of some sort, but does either constitute language?

Human language, most researchers argue, has characteristics not found in any other form of animal communication. Although they have produced several different lists of attributes that mark human language, most researchers would likely agree that language has three essential attributes: First, it is productive, meaning that speakers can understand and produce utterances they have never heard before and they can also create new utterances by recombining elements they already know. Second, language has the capacity to represent ideas, objects, and events with symbols. This property is termed semanticity. Third, true language has the capacity of displacement, meaning that it can be used to create messages that are not tied to the immediate environment. Bees and jackdaws both fall short of establishing these criteria.

Bees use the "waggle dance" to tell other bees the direction and approximate distance of the flowers that are filled with nectar. The information is contained in the movements of the bees' dance. A westward movement tells the other bees to move west, a "round dance" consisting of alternating circles to the left and right indicates that the source of nectar is near, and tail-wagging tells them that it is further away. Their message is iconic (it looks like what it is conveying), and it is always located within the context of nectar-gathering, and thus fails on criteria of productivity and displacement.

Jackdaws, relatives of the crow, have courting (or mating) calls, calls used when they fly away, and warning calls which they use before attacking any creature carrying a dangling black object. Like the dance of the bees, this communication system has meaning to its users and thus might be considered to have semanticity. But also like the dance of the bees, it is very strictly bound to the context of the present. It thus fails the criteria of displacement and productivity.

Bees and jackdaws are not the only animals that have communication systems. Whales, dolphins, sticklebacks (a small fish), gibbons, and meadowlarks have also been found to possess intricate ways of communicating, but none meets the three basic criteria that define human language. It might be argued, however, that it is unfair to compare communication systems of animals, which are such a great evolutionary distance from humans. Perhaps it is fairer to consider only the linguistic abilities of the other primates, and it is certainly easy to do so because a number of attempts have been made to study primate language.

Earlier in the 20th century, people attempted to teach chimpanzees to talk. These early attempts failed because chimpanzees do not have a vocal apparatus that compares with a human's. Later, researchers abandoned the notion of speech and concentrated on the symbolic nature of language, sign language in the case of Washoe, Moja, Pili (Gardner & Gardner, 1975), and Nim Chimpsky (Terrace, 1980), and a form of written language involving plastic tokens in the case of Sarah (Premack & Premack, 1983).

Results of these studies have shown that chimpanzees have a very limited capacity for symbolic representation. There does seem to be some evidence, although not overwhelming at this point, that chimpanzees can be taught to communicate and that the system they use for doing so has some degree of semanticity. There is serious doubt, however, about the chimps' capacity for productivity and displacement.

Working with a team of researchers, a psychologist named H. S. Terrace conducted a more controlled study of a chimpanzee they named Nim Chimpsky. At first, the experiment looked promising when, after just 4 months, Nim produced his first ASL (American Sign Language) sign. At the end of 4 years, however, the chimpanzee had learned at most 125 sounds, and some members of the research team believed the number of genuine signs learned was as few as 25. There was little evidence that he could combine the signs effectively because, although he did string some signs together, there was little evidence that the content of his signing became any more complex as the number of "words" to his sentences increased. In other words, he would produce *Play me*, meaning "Play with me" but also *Play me Nim* with exactly the same meaning (see Fromkin & Rodman, 1988, p. 393).

Terrace's team (1980) found, moreover, that most of the chimp's signing was prompted by his teacher; that is, he did not initiate conversation and Nim's utterances mostly consisted of elements in his teacher's prior utterances. This brings to mind the story of Clever Hans, the horse who could do arithmetic problems; it was found that the trainer was unconsciously signalling the correct number of pawing movements. The debate over whether other primates possess language has not, however, gone away. As I write this in the summer of 2001, hundreds of websites are devoted to the subject, fuelled in part by the work of researcher Sue Savage-Rumbaugh with bonobos (African pygmy chimpanzees). The accomplishments that the researcher claims for the bonobos are certainly open to alternative interpretations and are not, in themselves, sufficient to convince most researchers that non-human primates (NHPs) are capable of language. A slightly more compelling argument is physiological. The language center in humans is generally acknowledged to be within the left hemisphere, specifically the area around the sylvian fissure (the deep fold in the brain lying roughly parallel to and above a line from the outside corner of the eye to the middle of the ear). In nearly all humans, this region appears to be the operations center for both sign language and spoken language. Moreover, most linguists argue that there is special neural circuitry needed for language and that this developed in humans many millions of years ago.

Still, Paul Churchland argues that we cannot dismiss the possibility of NHP language so readily because the rules for putting sentences together might turn out to be less dependent on "hard wiring," than on learning. As humans, we have learned to learn over many thousands of years; other primates may simply be in the process of learning to learn.

There are significant differences between human language and that of even the closest primate. Perhaps the overarching one, however, is that the chimpanzees must be taught. They do not learn anything close to human language otherwise when, in contrast, the human child needs only normal exposure. The linguistic accomplishments of non-human primates have so far failed to mount any serious challenge to the position that language is uniquely human. Even Nim Chimpsky's trainer, Herbert Terrace, concluded that while a chimpanzee might learn to associate a hand sign with food, this was likely a matter of simple conditioning much like Pavlov's dogs learning to salivate when they heard a bell. "If a child did exactly what the best chimpanzee did, the child would be thought of as disturbed" (Reuters, 1998). For now, it is safe to say that humans alone have language, and this constitutes strong evidence for linguistic, or nativist, theories.

There are, however, theorists less radical than the behaviorists who occupy Category D as well; "researchers who argue that the development of language is dependent upon **domain-general** processes or representations, but that these domain-general processes or representations are acquired during the course of development" (Barrett, 1999, p. 23). What separates these theorists from the behaviorists is that they are essentially cognivitists who assume the active participation of children in their own learning. Let us go back and consider the other three categories, in turn.

The first category, A, includes those researchers who, like Chomsky, believe that children possess certain innate capacities or knowledge that is dedicated to the task of language learning. Some take the extreme view that children are able to learn grammatical structures only because they possess innate grammatical knowledge (see Pinker, 1994, for example). Some even contend that the learning of words is governed by innate mechanisms that limit the kinds of hypotheses that children can construct about the meanings of words. Theorists in this category are biased toward a view that the child's ability to learn language can be attributed to an innate capacity for language learning. This "dedicated" capacity, which Chomsky (1965) called the *Language Acquisition Device* (LAD), is what prepares the child to make sense of language and to discover its structure and meaning-making potential. How the LAD is actually constructed is the subject of heated debate among linguists. Some argue that it consists essentially of a set of linguistic universals, such things as the existence and possible functions of word order, word classes, and the existence and function of sentences. These universals serve to constrain the possible hypotheses children make about the structure of the language they hear. They also compensate for the "poverty of the stimulus," a phrase which refers to the Chomskyan claim that the language to which children are exposed is too limited in both quality and quantity for them to acquire the complex underlying rule systems without a leg up. Others contend that the LAD is weaker, simply endowing children not with specific universal structures on which to build language-specific rules but instead with a general set of procedures for figuring out how to learn language. Although this is a less rigorous interpretation of what a language acquisition device might be, it should be noted that the general procedures are *not* general cognitive procedures for making sense of the world but procedures dedicated to the task of making sense of language. Proponents of linguistically based theories of language acquisition would not deny the importance of the environment in language learning, but they would minimize its impact. Rather than seeing the environment as shaping a child's language development, they view its function largely as one of activating the innate, physiologically based system.

Most cognitivists, on the other hand, take the view that language learning is not fundamentally different from other human learning, but that it is reliant on innate (though not dedicated) mechanisms. Cognitivists belong to Category B. Cognitive theories of language consider language acquisition as part of children's more general cognitive development. There are many kinds of cognitive theory, but two are of particular interest to understanding language acquisition. The first are theories which postulate stages of cognitive development that have parallels in linguistic achievement. The second is based upon information processing theory and postulate no particular innate mechanism. In the following pages, we will look at Piaget's theory of cognitive development and, very briefly, at those of Luria and Bruner.

Piaget, of course, was a biologist with a particular interest in how humans acquire knowledge. His theory of cognition is general and not applied specifically to language acquisition and holds that language is an aspect of general cognitive development. Although it shares certain beliefs with both behaviorism and nativism, it differs fundamentally from both. Piagetian theory resembles nativism because it relies on the notion of innate structures that function globally in the development of thought. The difference between Chomskyan nativism and Piagetian nativism is the difference between Categories A and B identified previously: Chomsky postulates an innate device dedicated to language learning while Piaget believes in an interdependence of language and cognition, that language development has its foundation in the more fundamental development of cognition.

Evidence showing links between cognitive development and language structures would support Piaget's hypothesis. Crystal uses the example of the comparative. Before children can express a sentence such as *This car is bigger than that*, they must first have the conceptual ability to judge the relative sizes of two objects (Crystal, 1987, p. 234). There is research evidence to support the view that early language correlates with certain kinds of conceptual development. For example, a concept that children acquire early, during the sensori-motor stage, is object permanence. At about the same time, they also acquire *disappearance* words such as "allgone" (Bohannon & Warren-Leubecker, 1989, p. 200). On the other hand, it would seem that the concept of object permanence should be in place before the emergence of the first words that frequently label those objects, but this does not seem to be the case. What does seem to be the case is that the first words appear once children understand that other people may act as agents for actions (Bates, 1976).

The job of explaining language acquisition is made easier if theorists can assume that certain parts of the learning mechanism are innate. But what is the evidence? Essentially there are two types. One is research evidence on children's learning of structural rules, and the other relies on the argument that humans must possess innate linguistic capabilities. A number of studies strongly indicate that children learn grammatical rules. Slobin (1971) asserts, for example, that the basic organization of language emerges from the time children begin putting two words together. At this stage and very clearly by the time they begin to produce sentences longer than two words, children use principles of hierarchical structure to form their utterances. Moreover, early awareness of syntactic rules has been documented not only in children learning English but also in children learning a number of different languages (see, e.g., Braine, 1963 and 1976).

Many researchers have focused on the phenomenon of overgeneralization (or overregularization) as evidence for rule learning. When children who have previously produced forms such as *made* and *went* suddenly begin to produce *maked* and *goed* (which they are unlikely to have heard before), researchers take it as evidence that they are in the process of learning the regular past-tense rule. They have overgeneralized the application of their newly acquired rule to irregular (and previously learned) as well as regular verbs. The phenomenon of overgeneralization has been observed in children acquiring a great many different languages including Spanish, Japanese, Hebrew, Russian, Finnish, Turkish, and English.

Children's knowledge of rules has been studied not only in natural observations of children but in laboratory studies as well. One of the best known laboratory studies was devised by Jean Berko (1958) to investigate children's knowledge of plurals and other grammatical morphemes. She showed children pictures of creatures and objects which she gave nonsense labels and asked children to produce alternate forms. For example, she showed a picture of a fat, birdlike creature and gave the following prompt: *This is a wug. Now there is another one. There are two of them. There are two _____.* This procedure has undergone adaptation and been replicated many times. Although investigators have sometimes disagreed on the precise nature of the rules children acquired, most agree that the evidence strongly indicates that children's language is rule-governed.

The second type of argument in support of innatist theories is biological, and there are a number of observations that support the view that children are born with special biological equipment, which, when triggered, results in language acquisition. For example, a number of studies have shown that very young infants have the ability to perceive relatively fine acoustic distinctions in speech sounds and to respond differently to speech and non-speech sounds. The fact that they can do so at such a young age argues for an innate predisposition to language learning.

There also seems to be remarkable consistency in the order in which children acquire larger syntactic structures. There is evidence, for example, that children acquire *WH-* questions (those beginning with what, where, who, when, how, and why) in a particular order (Wootten, Merkin, Hood, & Bloom, 1979, cited in Tager-Flusberg, 1989). Slobin (1982) observed that young children from a number of different language backgrounds used Subject-Object word order regardless of the order used by adult speakers of the same language. This ability might be attributed to some sort of innate predisposition toward language, a component of the LAD which "knows" or "expects" that grammatical classes exist.

On the other hand, it is likely that children produce Subject-Object structures in response to particular semantic relationships they encounter in their lives. At the two- and three-word stage, most of the sentences that children produce have semantic agents as subjects. This fact gives children a leg up on working out more abstract syntactic relationships in more complex sentences (Tager-Flusberg, 1989, p. 143). The fact that children prefer Subject-Object order, then, does not necessarily argue for the existence of a language acquisition device; it may be evidence only for a generalized cognitive ability to figure things out, among them the fact that agents act upon objects. It is fortuitous for English-speaking children that their language happens to express these relationships in the same syntactic order as they initially express them.

A final argument for linguistic nativism (Categories A and B) takes the form of evidence for a biological critical period during which language must be acquired if it is ever to be acquired fully. Specifically, there seem to be certain periods of development during which a certain stimulus has to be present if young animals are to develop normal behavior. One case that is somewhat analogous to the human is that of the white-crowned sparrow. Reich (1986) relates Marler's (1970) observation that this bird learns its own song if and only if it hears the song during a critical period of its development. It does not acquire its song if raised in isolation, nor does it acquire the song of other birds even if exposed during the critical period. Apparently, the fact that it does not acquire the songs of other birds cannot be attributed to its inability to produce other songs since it can acquire any of a number of different dialects present among members of the species. Marler argues that these birds appear to be born with a template that rejects all but their own song, an argument which seems analogous to Chomsky's case for humans (Marler, 1977, cited in Reich, 1986, p. 291).

Wilder Penfield was the first to make the case for a critical period related to language (Penfield & Roberts, 1959). Penfield based his argument on observations that brain-damaged children have better recovery potential than adults with similar damage. The argument for a critical period was further advanced by Eric Lenneberg (1967), who asserted that all that is required for a child to acquire language between the ages of 2 and puberty is adequate exposure to language. He also relied on the experiences of brain-damaged children and adults, arguing that if adults experienced injury to the left hemisphere (LH), believed to be the dominant hemisphere for language processing, and failed to recover within a few months, they would never recover fully. Children, on the other hand, were capable of a complete recovery of language functions if the LH damage occurred when they were very young. Based largely on Basser's (1962) survey of the literature on hemispherectomies, Lenneberg went on to conclude that children experienced no speech disorders following surgery (except where aphasia had occurred before the operation) while adults experienced a variety of language disorders and were unable to recover language function fully.

Later, Krashen (1973) re-examined Basser's data and found that all the children who had their left hemispheres removed were under 5 years of age at the time of the operation. This fact suggested that if Lenneberg and Penfield were right about a critical period, that it must occur before the age of 5 and not 9, as Penfield suggested, or 13, as Lenneberg suggested. Yet it is the case that a great deal of language learning occurs after age 5 (and, indeed, some occurs after age 13), and so it would seem that a critical period for language acquisition might be critical only for the triggering of language acquisition. That is, a weakened version of the critical period hypothesis would claim that if language acquisition is to occur it must *begin* during a critical period.

But what if it does not? The case of Genie, described on pages 65 and 66, suggests that language learning *can* occur even when it is begun much later than the age of 5. If Genie had acquired no language, her case would have provided very strong evidence for Lenneberg's version of the critical period hypothesis. But despite the fact that she had a difficult time of it, Genie did acquire a great deal of language, particularly vocabulary, and she did so after the age of puberty. It would seem, then, that her accomplishment offers no clear evidence either for or against the critical period hypothesis (Nova, 1997).

Genie is not the only child to grow up in social isolation, but her case is the best documented. Of those others that are known (Crystal, 1987, lists 48), the data concerning their language learning are sparse but seem to suggest that both comprehension and speaking ability was virtually non-existent. More significantly, perhaps, most attempts to teach them to speak failed. The difficulty in considering these children as evidence in favor of a critical period is the confounding factor of profound social deprivation. In other words, in accounting for these children's failure to acquire language, it is impossible to separate the effects of growing up isolated from normal human society from possible biological effects.

On the matter of a critical period for language acquisition, then, the jury is still out. The evidence is controversial and the conclusions tentative. It does seem that a first language is harder to learn after puberty than before, but since no one would be acquiring a first language at this age except in abnormal circumstances, the importance of this fact is dubious. As we shall find later, however, a great deal of second language learning is accomplished by adults. It may be the case that language learning that occurs after puberty requires a different kind of cognitive activity than early language learning. It is impossible to tell, given our present state of knowledge, whether this difference is biologically or environmentally determined or both. The critical period question will undoubtedly remain an important one for researchers in neurology and linguistics for decades to come.

As appealing as innateness might be in acquisition theory, there are arguments against it. One such objection concerns negative linguistic evidence. Central to the nativist approach is the belief that children are not generally provided with negative linguistic evidence and that when they are, they tend to ignore it. This being the case, they must have an innate mechanism by which to discover the rules. Otherwise, the poverty of the stimulus with regard to positive and negative information about structure would make it impossible for them to learn the rules of language. If it were the case, however, that children received information about the acceptability of language structure, then the nativist's arguments about learnability would begin to crumble. In fact, a number of studies have suggested that children *do* receive such information.

While parents and other caregivers do not negatively reinforce, in the behaviorist sense, utterances that do not conform with adult structure, there is evidence that they react differently to poorly formed and well-formed utterances. Several studies have been reported suggesting that parents do not ignore the grammatical errors of their young children. They may not correct the error overtly, but they repeat sentences with errors less frequently than they repeat well-formed ones (Hirsh-Pashek, Treiman, & Schneiderman, 1984). When they do repeat poorly formed sentences, they usually rephrase them. Parents are more likely to expand their children's ungrammatical sentences and to question children when their previous utterance contains a grammatical error than when it is error-free (Demetras, Post, & Snow, 1986; Penner, 1987). Moreover, Bohannon and Stanowicz (1988) report that "children are more likely to imitate expansions and recasts than any other utterances" (cited in Bohannon & Warren-Leubecker, 1989, p. 198).

It would seem, then, that adults do provide negative information about language structure and that children respond to it. While a great deal more research must be done before we can speak with any clarity on the role of negative information in language acquisition, it certainly cannot be ruled out as a contributing factor. This being the case, one of the foundations of linguistic theories of acquisition is weakened.

Another argument against nativism concerns environment. For fairly obvious reasons, nativists have never considered environment, beyond some very basic level of exposure to human interaction, as playing a central role in language acquisition. Yet teachers know that environment plays a major role in children's language development during the school years. In the next chapter, we will see how one child struggled to learn language after the age of 5. His was not a case of social isolation but of linguistic deprivation to the degree that when he began school, he had very limited language exposure. Other research tells us that children whose only exposure to language is television acquire little speech (Bohannon & Warren-Leubecker, 1989, p. 199).

Those theorists who are more closely aligned with Category C "postulate that language development depends upon **domain-specific** processes or representations," but that these "are acquired or emerge during the course of development, rather than being innately prespecified" (Barrett, 1999a, p. 22). An entire group of theorists who call themselves social interactionists fall into this category. They assume that the course of language development is influenced by a myriad of factors—physical, linguistic, and social—and that these factors interact with one another, modify one another, and may produce different effects in different children. Essentially, social interactionists believe that human speech emerged, and its forms have their bases in the social role that language plays in human interaction. As children grow older, they begin to interact with adults in more mature ways. They are faced with more complex communication tasks, and adult caregivers help them meet these tasks by providing appropriate language. With more sophisticated language skills, children are able to engage in even more complex social interactions for which the caregivers provide language assistance, and the cycle continues.

Neither social interactionists nor behaviorists are innatists. Both believe that environment plays a central role in the growth of language, and both see parents as crucial to the process, but there is a major difference. Behaviorists tend to view children as passive vessels into which language is poured while social interactionists believe that children are active participants through their interaction with their parents. Social interactionists believe that language learning is unique, that it differs in kind from other behavior and other learning. They do not, however, focus on structure to the same degree that nativists do. Rather, they are interested in how structure helps the child function socially with language and thus learn more of it. They would also concede that children come to the task of language acquisition with some innate predisposition to succeed, but they would argue that the innate ability is less important than the social environment.

Social interactionists agree with cognitivists that language learning is a complex accomplishment that involves the child's active participation. They would also agree that children cannot acquire language until they have reached a certain level of cognitive maturity. On the other hand, they emphasize that "the environment is the place to look for the emergence of language" (Berko-Gleason, 1993, p. 274). Social interaction theory assumes that a child's acquisition of language is influenced by the interaction of a number of factors that are physical, linguistic, and social in nature. Because children differ in physical and cognitive abilities as well as in the social environment in which they live, this interaction may produce different effects in different children.

There are a great many advocates for the role of the environment in language acquisition. One of them was Vygotsky, a Soviet psychologist who died in 1934. While his work might rightly be considered in the section on cognitive theories of language acquisition, I have placed it in this section because of the emphasis he placed on the role played by interaction with the environment, particularly with older children and adults. He believed language to be a necessary stimulant for conceptual growth which, in turn, depends on interaction with people and objects in the environment. Adults and older children would, in this view, play a significant role in stimulating language learning.

This stimulation, he believed, should occur within the zone of proximal development, which Vygotsky defined as the distance between a child's actual level of development and the level at which she could function with adult assistance. This emphasis on the role of the adult, whether parent, teacher, or friend, in the child's conceptual and linguistic development sets Vygotsky apart from Piaget and puts him in line with current theorists who emphasize the mother's (or other caregiver's) contribution to the child's language learning.

In the past two decades, interest has grown in the part this input plays in the child's linguistic accomplishments, and one of the central findings has been that mothers' talk to their children is by no means as impoverished as some researchers and theorists assumed it to be. Despite the fact that some parents talk to their children differently from the way they talk to other adults, research has shown that the adaptations they make facilitate rather than hinder language learning. Even baby talk, the unusual vocal behavior that characterizes some adults' speech with infants, seems to help. Field and colleagues (1982) hypothesize that children learn to control their vocal apparatus by watching their mothers making the exaggerated speech sounds of baby talk. Other researchers postulate that the talk and play that occurs between parents and young children forms the basis for later patterns of turn-taking in conversations (Stern, Beebe, Jaffe, & Bennet, 1977).

The question that is of primary interest in language acquisition theory is how children acquire the ability to express their intentions or meanings in language. Interactionists believe that they do so through a process of negotiation with their mothers or principal caregivers. This negotiation occurs partly as a result of mothers treating children's speech, even if it is babbling, as meaningful and intentional. Gradually, as mothers persist in trying to make sense of children's speech, they also begin to negotiate meaning and intent with their children. It is easy to demonstrate how such negotiation takes place: Christopher, age 1;1, is sitting on the living room floor, barefoot, playing with his older brother Kerry (2;0) and their mother:

Chris: *Want du!*
Mum: *You want your shoes?*
C: *(He looks puzzled.) Du. Du.*
M: *(She looks around for something else he might be asking for and holds up a stuffed bear.) You want Gurgles?*
C: *No. Want du.*
M: *(To her other son.) Do you know what Chris wants?*
Kerry: *He want this. (He holds up the wooden car he is playing with.)*
C: *(Showing no interest in the car.) Du peez. (At this point, he gets up and starts toward the kitchen.)*
M: *Oh, you want juice!*
C: *Yeah. Du.*

Here, Chris's mother does not give up easily on understanding him. There is evidence that mothers of even younger children behave in a similar manner and may, in fact, teach the child language in what Golinkoff (1983) has called "conversational bouts." Certainly they actively teach children the social routines of greetings, leave-takings, and politeness. Whether they engage in any other active teaching and whether it does anything to facilitate language acquisition are questions yet to be answered, although we do know how little effect the teaching of structure usually has.

Halliday (1975) saw language acquisition as relying heavily on communicative interaction. Taking a functional view, he believed that the language structures necessary for realizing the various language functions are learned, along with the functions themselves, through learning to communicate. Obviously, the child does not do this alone. It seems, however, that environment may play a different kind of role in children's learning of grammar. Specifically, if we assume that children figure out which forms are grammatical from being consistently exposed to correct forms, then the language that children hear plays a significant role in the acquisition process. Parents play an important role in matching the language input to the appropriate level of cognitive and language development of their children. Speech to the very young is much simpler than it is to older children. For example, sentences spoken to young children are shorter and not as varied in structure as those presented to older children. It is probably not the case that adults consciously make such adjustments to their speech; what is more likely is that in their attempts to communicate with children, they unconsciously match their language to the appropriate cognitive and linguistic level for the child.

There is another way in which parents or other caregivers likely contribute to children's language acquisition, and that is by talking with them about and focusing their attention on things that are in the immediate environment. One of the central tasks in learning language is to match language with meaning, a task that parents facilitate by focusing their talk on whatever is holding the child's attention. If the child is chasing the family cat, the cat is what they all talk about. The child thus comes to understand what the word *cat* means.

It may also be the case, as Bohannon and Warren-Leubecker point out, that the same process may lead children to notice the difference between their own expressions and the more mature ones of the older speakers around them (1989, p. 190). Parents are more likely to expand and extend their children's imperfectly formed utterances, and it is possible that when an expanded, correct utterance immediately follows an immature one, children may just notice the difference and, gradually, make changes to approximate the adult form more closely. In this way, it may be the case that imitation *does* play a role in language acquisition, but social interactionists would see this role as qualitatively different and less central to overall language development than would behaviorists.

One of the interesting and compelling aspects of social interaction approaches is that they come down on neither side of the nature/nurture controversy. On the one hand, social interactionists admit to the likelihood that children possess an innate predisposition to learn language. On the other hand, they believe that while environment alone cannot account for the acquisition process, it serves as more than a trigger for acquisition. It serves, instead, to provide a rich source of data from which children form and test hypotheses about language structures. The relationship between language acquisition and social interaction is symbiotic: Social interaction provides essential experience with language, and language affords children opportunities for expanding their social interactions.

As intuitively reasonable as Category C approaches and social interaction approaches, in particular, may seem, they are by no means widely accepted. There are several counter-arguments, three of which are worth noting here. The first argument against social interaction challenges the role of caretaker speech. Some researchers claim that although caretaker speech may be simplified in comparison with speech to adults, it is by no means simple. In other words, the caretaker speech may be different and to some degree simpler, but it retains a great deal of linguistic complexity. Others point out that researchers have failed to show correlations between the simplified input language and the parallel forms that subsequently appear in the child's speech. Bohannon and Warren-Leubecker report studies (e.g., Hoff-Ginsburg, 1986; Newport, 1976) showing "the complexity of maternal speech addressed to the children to be unrelated to the children's language gains" (1989, p. 207).

A second argument against social interaction theory relates to caretaker speech. The assumption is that caretakers adjust their speech to provide input that is both comprehensible and useful to children in making and testing hypotheses about language structure. Even accepting that this may be true (and as we noted, it is not by any means universally accepted as such), it remains for theorists to specify just how such adaptations facilitate language acquisition. They have yet to do so.

Perhaps the most persuasive counter-argument concerns universality. As Susanna Pflaum has pointed out, if the dialogue between parent and child is the critical mechanism for language learning, then such dialogues would be found in the language learning of all children everywhere. A number of researchers have demonstrated that this is not the case. Heath (1983; 1986), Schieffelin and Ochs (1983), and others have described very different adult-child exchanges in different cultural groups. In one community studied by Heath, for example, it appears that baby talk does not exist, and if children wish to participate in the talk of the group, they have to interrupt to do so. In Chipewyan communities, parents do not expect their children to speak until sometime around the age of 5 (Scollon & Scollon, 1981). Nevertheless, these children and children in all cultural groups learn language.

We must remember in considering the case against social interaction that, because it is a relatively new theory, many of its explanations for acquisition phenomena have not been subjected to empirical verification. This also means that the argument against social interaction theory is speculative as well.

WHAT THEORY HAS TO SAY ABOUT LANGUAGE LEARNING AND ENVIRONMENT

The theories discussed in this chapter take different views on the contribution the child's environment makes to language acquisition. With the exception of the strict, or strong-position nativists, most agree that some kind of interaction is necessary but disagree about the degree or kind of interaction children need to acquire language. Research has not yet resolved the issue, and I would suggest three reasons why this is the case. The first, and most obvious, is that research is never neutral. The hypotheses with which investigators begin, the observations they make, and the methods they use are all biased by their theoretical perspectives. Research cannot be neutral. In a real sense, theory serves as the lens that we point at and through which we see research data. It would be expected, then, that research findings would be somewhat contradictory.

The second reason is methodological. Our tools for evaluating social interaction and its impact on language acquisition still need refining. Because they have not been extensively used yet and because their use has been mostly confined to studies of children in the majority culture in North America, they are still relatively clumsy and largely untested. The third reason is that we still have too few studies of interaction patterns in other languages and cultures—studies of the caliber of those conducted by Shirley Brice Heath, for example. Only when we understand how a variety of peoples interact with their children can we begin to understand how that interaction influences language acquisition.

Still, we must hold onto the fact that no research to date has suggested that interaction plays no role. Even Heath's finding, which cited earlier that baby talk does not exist in some communities, should not be taken to mean that *no* social interaction occurs. It means only that parent-child interaction as we know it in the dominant European culture does not exist in this community, yet the children learn language. It also suggests that we need to look further to try to understand social interaction patterns in other cultures before we can really assess the role they play in language acquisition.

CONCLUSION

In this chapter, we have taken a cursory look at what children accomplish when they learn language and the circumstances under which they do so. We've taken a closer look at the theoretical perspectives from which researchers try to figure out how they do so. None of these theories stands alone either in the position it takes—we have seen how certain beliefs are shared by different theories—nor in its ability to tell us how children acquire language—we have seen that there are cases to be made against each one. But we have also seen how two fundamental questions underlie all theories. The first is whether or not children are born with special equipment that gives them a head start in the business of language learning. The second is whether there is something unique about language learning as opposed to other kinds of human learning. Obviously, there is no agreement on either of these questions; theorists hold differing views. Indeed, if anyone could tell us with any certainty how children accomplish what they do in language learning, we would not need this lengthy description of theory, for we would have entered into the realm of fact.

Teachers and students of language are sometimes uncomfortable with the uncertainty inherent in theory. Faced with the reality of teaching children and all the decisions that entails, they prefer hard truths. Unfortunately, the hard truth is hard to come by in this field, and so for the time being we must settle for something less. Yet, we are not working entirely in the dark. We have the benefit of an abundance of quality data about children learning language, and we have the privilege and the ability to consider those data and the theories they either support or refute within our own observations and experiences as teachers of young children.

My own bias, based on my experience as a teacher, linguist, and researcher, is toward the social interactive view of language. I have witnessed the growth of oral and written language in children in schools—growth directly attributable to the interaction among children and between children and teachers. Nowhere is the importance of social interaction more obvious than in ESL children. Social interaction is, in brief, a theory through which we can usefully view children's language growth in the school years.

For Further Study

1. How would behaviorism account for the learning of words such as *juice, cookie, dog,* or *car?* How would it account for the learning of words such as *question, idea, think,* or *must?* What is the difference between these two groups of words?

2. Find other examples of "regression" in children's language learning.

3. Animal communication systems are arguably distinct from human language. There are also differences among the ways in which animals communicate. Generally, there are considered to be three categories. The first category includes those communication systems consisting of a finite number of calls. The second includes those that are "analogue" systems meaning that a number of characteristics can be varied to communicate information—the waggle dance of the bee described earlier is a good example. The third is thematic. In this category, which would include most bird songs, the animal repeatedly uses a theme with some variations. Find examples of each of these communication systems and explain how these set the system apart from human language.

4. According to work done by Slobin (1979) and by Block and Kessel (1980), children generally acquire the plural and the progressive marker, *-ing,* before morphemes such as the past-tense marker or the third-person singular marker. Why might this be true, and which theoretical position is most consistent with your explanation?

For Further Reading

Cook, G. (2000). *Language play, language learning.* Oxford: Oxford University Press.

Pinker, S. (1995). Language acquisition. In L.R. Gleitman & M. Lieberman (Eds.), *An invitation to cognitive science: Language* (Vol.1, 2nd ed., pp. 183–208). Cambridge, MA: MIT Press.

Whitehead, Marion R. (1999) *Supporting language and literacy development in the early years.* Buckingham, UK: Open University Press.

CHAPTER FOUR

Stories of First Language Learners

Although children the world over learn a first language and do so under a variety of conditions, those who acquire only one language before the end of their school years are in the minority. For many of the world's children, the second language they learn is English, which is the reason that more people in the world speak English than any other language. The children many of us teach are, then, members of a minority if they speak only one language and a member of the majority of world speakers who speak English.

This chapter, however, is about children who grow up monolingual. I have two examples. One, picked up from the previous editions, is Grace, a hearing child born of deaf parents. The second is Janet whose language development is described in far greater detail. Unfortunately, I was not able to gather comparable amounts of data about Grace because her story comes from memories reconstructed in adulthood. What is presented does, however, carry forward our understanding of language acquisition.

We meet Janet as an infant and trace her language growth through the school years. The account of Janet's language learning is based on actual observation, mine and her mother's, as well as sporadic written accounts her mother made in letters to me during Janet's first 6 years. Grace's story is the account of a woman who acquired English while living with deaf parents in depression-era southern Missouri. It is based largely on her own recollections of the experience captured in adulthood and is augmented by data collected by other researchers studying the language of hearing children of deaf parents.

Human learning is a lifelong enterprise. So, too, is language, for although we acquire our fundamental competencies very early in life, we continue to grow into language—increasing our vocabularies, ways of expression, and venturing into new forms and purposes for communication. For our purposes here, what is important is language learning in the school years and the earlier learning that has such a profound impact on those years. Our discussion begins with an overview of early language development so that we might more usefully compare the experiences of our two learners.

OVERVIEW OF DEVELOPMENT

Infancy

Typically, the study of children's linguistic development begins with the first words. There is some interest in babbling, but most of the language acquisition literature pays little attention to anything that might occur before the child utters the first word. When parents talk about their children, the question "Is she talking yet?" refers to the first word, but language learning begins much earlier. Nature does not, after all, simply choose a day as the day language learning begins, and the child thus starts to talk. Rather, language is a seamless experience that begins at birth or possibly before. In recent years we have come to realize that the first year or so of a baby's life are not idle ones by any means. Much of the infant's behavior during this period signifies cognitive processes that make the acquisition of language possible. It is a period during which we observe behavior that is precursory to true language development.

The Precursors to Language

Children before the age of approximately 1 year are not yet able to produce language as we traditionally think of it—as words or utterances with intentional meaning. They do, however, demonstrate a great deal of sensitivity to and awareness of language. We see in that first year behavior that appears to form the foundation for later language growth. This is not true linguistic behavior but precursory behavior. Somewhat paradoxically, it differs in kind from true language, and yet it is essential for the growth of true language.

There are two important differences between precursory linguistic behavior and true language. Although children during their first year perceive and produce sounds; learn about events, objects, and relationships; and interact with others in their environments, they do not use the conventions of language in doing so. In the first year of life, infant behavior is largely related to observable events. Crying when wet, hungry, or tired is common behavior in infants, and there is often a direct and observable relationship between the cry and the condition. This begins to change in the second year when a *conventional mapping relation*—or language—begins to occur. The events and situations are still observable, but there is a new and more sophisticated verbal interaction or response with them.

The second crucial difference between the first and second year of life has to do with intent. Before the age of approximately 1 year, the infant "reflects feelings and states more that it intends a representation of affect and changes in affect." In the second year, in contrast, the child begins to communicate intentionally (Bloom & Lahey, 1978, p. 71). We refer, therefore, to children's language learning in the first year as precursory—not to underestimate its importance, for it is vital—but to emphasize the difference between this and later learning.

At only a few days old, most infants respond to human voices, and by the time they are 2 to 4 months old, they respond to different tones of voice. Research has shown, too, that babies as young as 1 month are able not only to discriminate between speech and non-speech sounds but to discriminate between speech sounds as similar as /p/ and /b/ (Eimas, Siqueland, Juscyzk, & Vigorito, 1971). This early perceptual sensitivity to the sounds of language makes it possible for them to learn the relevant phonological distinctions they will need to understand and to form intentional utterances as they get older.

It is not at all clear, however, just how this early perceptual ability is related to their later learning, since children appear to lose their ability to make certain discriminations. Research has shown, for example, that while infants of 1 to 4 months are able to distinguish between voiced and voiceless pairs of consonants, 2-year-old children find it one of the most difficult distinctions to make in discrimination experiments (Garnica, 1973; Graham & House, 1971; Shvachkin, 1973).

At about the same time as they are manifesting these perceptual abilities, infants begin to vocalize. We know from numerous studies that the vocalizations of infants younger than 6 months or so are likely to be cooing sounds. In fact, spectrographic analysis has shown them to be quite unlike human speech sounds (Titone & Danesi, 1985, pp. 64–65). Nevertheless, cooing plays an important role in later development of speech by serving as a rehearsal of the tongue movements, which are necessary for the production of speech.

Even crying behavior provides important insight into language development. Mothers often report, and Janet's mother was no exception, that their infants use different cries for different purposes. If this is true, as seems likely, then we have evidence of precursory language use—purposefully using language for different functions. In adults, the practice is easy to observe. Even in very young children, we see evidence that they use a single word to serve a variety of purposes. They may stress it differently, lengthen the vowel, or vary the volume or accompanying gestures to make a single word (from the adult's perspective) serve a variety of purposes. The difference, of course, is intent. The older child clearly intends to signal different meanings, but there is no evidence to suggest such intent on the part of the infant.

Around the age of 5 months, most children begin to babble. First babbling may sound to adults like random noises, some of them (in English-speaking children) English-like, but others quite foreign. Gradually the noises will start to sound more like the target language. This similarity between the sounds the infant makes in babbling and the sounds of the language around her appears to be universal babbling behavior. It is evidence that the *input* language is having an effect—that children are attending to the sounds of language. During these early months, children may be highly inventive in their production and combination of speech sounds, and they seem to be busily learning the intonation of their language as well as training their articulators for producing the individual segments.

Apparently it is not uncommon for infants to babble differentially. Menn (1976, 1989) has pointed out that such behavior is common in the later stages of babbling when children typically demonstrate two different types. In the first, *sound play*, children appear to be vocalizing for its own sake, presumably for the sheer pleasure of making and listening to the sounds. There seems to be little connection between the sounds they produce in sound play and intentional communication. In *conversational babble*, on the other hand, children really sound like they are talking, even though the listener would be hard pressed to identify any of the words. As they engage in conversational babble, children use eye contact, gestures, and the intonation contours of normal speech—all the elements of conversation except meaningful words. "Conversational babble can clearly convey requests for aid, rejection of food or toys, desire to direct attention to ongoing events" (Menn, 1976, cited in Menn, 1989, p. 73). It is possible, of course, that to the child, the words *are* differentiated but that the immature articulators are as yet unable to distinguish them for adult listeners. Even in this early stage of development, we find not only the precursors to language structure but also the foreshadowing of meaningful language used for different purposes. Many interesting questions are raised here about the babbling sounds made by deaf children or by hearing children raised by non-hearing (and non-speaking) adults.

In discussing precursory language behavior, we have focused on the infant's awareness of the sound system. Obviously in babies who do not yet produce words, or who produce only a few single-word utterances, it is difficult to speculate about their awareness of syntax. Many researchers believe, however, that infants do exhibit precursory syntactic awareness. Bloom (1973) reports observing a 16-month-old child early in the two-word stage of speech. This child used an interpretable word, *wid*, in combination with other common words in the child's vocabulary. The unusual word always occurred in the second position, and it only occurred with certain of the child's words such as *Mama, Dada, more*, and *no*, but not with other frequently used words. The child's utterances also indicated her awareness of the stress patterns in English. Bloom interpreted the child's behavior as evidence "that she had learned something about word order—with /wid/, which was consistently in second position, and with the few words that appeared with /wid/, which were always in first position" (Bloom 1973, cited in Bloom & Lahey, 1978, p. 91).

The child Bloom observed, however, was 16 months old and arguably past the precursory period and into the stage of true language development. Evidence for syntactic awareness in children of around 1 year or younger is sketchy, but several researchers have made the claim that infants use intonational changes to signal the differences in meaning that will later be signaled by word order. Von Raffler Engel (1973) claimed, for example, "that her son used humming with 'sentence intonation' before he used words, using rising pitch for requests" (cited in Sachs, 1989, p. 45). Nakazina (1962) reported that infants 8-months of age imitated adult pitch contours, an observation that is consistent with those made by Janet's mother. Nevertheless, it is difficult to claim with any degree of certainty that such behavior is evidence of early syntactic awareness. It does, however, indicate a strong sensitivity to *language*, and whether it is sensitivity to phonology or syntax seems hardly to matter.

The Preschool Years

Sometime after their first birthday, most children begin to combine their growing inventory of single words into two-word utterances. This is the point at which most people think language learning has truly begun. While we have seen that it is in fact already underway, it is certainly true that the rate of learning seems to increase. By the time they begin school, most children are producing well-formed, simple and complex sentences expressing a variety of meanings and fulfilling a number of communicative functions. They have gone from pre-linguistic infants to fully participating members of their language community in 5 short years.

As children grow from infants to school-age, their worlds expand to include people other than family and frequent visitors and places other than their own homes. Their linguistic and communicative needs grow as well. This is the period during which children acquire near-adult phonology and the complex rules they need to express their desired meanings for the increasingly varied situations in which they find themselves. They go from babies who point and produce a single, sometimes unintelligible, word to children able to produce sentences such as "Shelly gots no bear like mine to play with" (Janet 5;2). While not quite perfectly formed, the sentence clearly and correctly expresses a number of propositions. More importantly, it is not grounded in the here and now. Neither her friend Shelly nor the bear was present; Janet was simply reporting to her mother about her visit to her friend's house.

The preschool years encompass a wide spectrum of language development. Because children vary so greatly in the ages at which they achieve certain linguistic milestones, researchers commonly describe stages of language development independent of age. A common way of doing so is by mean length of utterance (MLU), or the average number of morphemes a child produces in an utterance. This is the approach taken by Brown in his impressive two-volume work (1973) and by a number of researchers before and since. It has the advantage of making comparison among children easier. One of the children in Brown's study, for example, reached an MLU of 2.8 at 22 months while another reached it at 35 months (p. 55). Therefore, it was easier and more useful to discuss language development in terms of MLU rather than age. During the preschool years, Brown identified five stages of language development, from an MLU of 1.75 to an MLU of 4.0.

Other researchers, however, break down the preschool years differently. Ingram (1976) identifies three distinct subperiods of development during the preschool years. The first corresponds with the latter part of the period that Piaget calls the Sensori-Motor period. Linguistically, the child enters the period of one-word utterances and acquires a vocabulary of approximately 50 words. The second subperiod, lasting from approximately 1;6 to 4;6, he calls the period of Preconceptual Thought. This marks children's earliest symbolic behavior and results in their "pretend play"—an alphabet block becomes a table, a house, or even a car, for example. For children at this stage, language is grounded in the here and now of the immediate environment. It is also a period of rapid growth "during which the child progresses from putting two words together to the point around 3;6 to 4;0 when most simple sentences are well formed by adult standards" (Ingram, 1976, p. 13). At the same time, children experience a period of impressive phonological growth, for it is during this time of expanding vocabulary that children face the first real need for a phonological system.

The third subperiod begins around age 4 and continues to age 6 or 7. This is the period during which children begin to come to grips with reality and "to abandon the dominant use of symbolic play. Rather than modify reality through play, the child begins to use play to express reality" (Ingram, 1976, p. 13). Children begin to enter into social games at this time although they still may not understand that there are arbitrary conventions which govern these games. Any parent who has tried to explain the rules of turn-taking in tag to a 5-year-old who doesn't want to be "It" will understand very well the limitations on the child's ability to comprehend abstract rules.

In language, more complex sentence structures begin to appear. Verb complements (*Gurgles thinks that's silly!*) appear along with a few relative clause structures (*Shelly want the doll that's mine!*), but the chief way of combining propositions is conjunction. Thus, conjoined sentences such as *Shelly want the bear and she took it home and I want it back* account for most of the longer sentences children produce during this period. In the pages that follow, I have assumed Ingram's divisions and terminology, but for the sake of clarity, I have presented the time periods in shorter segments.

JANET: LANGUAGE LEARNER

While I maintain that Janet's experience is a typical one, some readers of the first edition pointed out that Janet's intact family with university-educated parents is hardly typical of children beginning school at the end of the 20th and beginning of the 21st centuries. Unfortunately, they may be right in pointing out that the educational level and the high degree of literacy in Janet's home put her in a minority of North American children. Nevertheless, I maintain that Janet's history is instructive. In the first place, data from Janet's experience are contextualized within experiences of other children and other studies. Second, there is a great deal of evidence that children's early oral language development runs a similar course whatever the educational level of the parents. Success in school is another matter, but that is a fact that I will confront directly. Third, we have to ask the question, which child's experience is typical? Each child has a unique learning experience. Whatever a child's environment might be, there will be some differences between that child's language development and that of any other child, even a child in the same family. The best a researcher can do is to present the most complete data that exists and within the analysis speculate about how much or little can be generalized to other children. Therefore, although Janet's experience will not serve as a map for all other experience of first language learning, it is not *atypical* and it *is* instructive.

The organization of this section is, for the most part, chronological. Each section covers a particular period of time—usually 6 months to 1 year, and is introduced by a general overview of the course of language development during that time. This broad sketch is followed by a description of Janet and her language learning during the same period. This, in turn, is followed by a more detailed description and discussion of the course of language acquisition in most children of the same age.

Janet was born in Dover, New Hampshire, in January of 1972. Most of the observations that follow are based on notes and transcripts of my own interaction with her and on her mother's diaries, kept in detail until Janet was 7 years old and then sporadically until she was 14. Janet's only sibling, her brother Matthew, was 21 months old when she was born. Their father was a research physicist and their mother a lecturer in the English department at a nearby university. Janet arrived 3 weeks before her expected date of arrival, on her mother's 26th birthday. She weighed exactly 6 pounds, and her mother's diary entries during her first 6 months tell of a fairly untroubled infant. Janet cried when hungry, and seemed to be hungry every 4 hours around the clock, but otherwise slept well. She was alert and a real charmer with big blue eyes and a winning smile. She was a responsive child, particularly to her mother and to the antics of her older brother. The family spoke only English, and that was the only language Janet was exposed to until the age of 18 months when she had an occasional Spanish-speaking babysitter.

Between Janet's second and third birthdays, her family moved to another state. There, living in a city of approximately 750,000, Janet attended a Montessori school from the time she was 3 until she began public kindergarten in the September before her fifth birthday. Following first the father's and then the mother's career, the family moved again when Janet was 9 and again when she was 13. Her schooling was thus interrupted several times, and although she experienced a brief troubled period during her early teens, she graduated from an International Baccalaureate program with very high marks. She completed a university degree in biology and is currently a medical student in a Canadian university. Although she was a science major, Janet took sufficient courses in English to qualify for a minor, and her professors often lamented that she was not an English major, such was her facility with and obvious interest in the language. That fascination with language began in infancy.

Janet as an Infant

When she was only a few weeks old, Janet seemed to respond to her mother's voice. Her mother's diary notes that Janet would usually stop crying when her mother made soothing noises. By 2 months, Janet would stop gurgling or crying and appear to be listening when her brother was in the room and talking. Janet demonstrated the abilities that all normal babies have in her responses to her mother's voice. During the first 2 months, most of the sounds she produced were cries, but she did sometimes gurgle and seem to "coo" or "shriek" with delight when something pleased her. From 6 weeks to 3 months, her cooing and shrieking behavior increased. Her mother also noted that Janet's cries became differentiated during this period, (i.e., her cry when she was wet or hungry differed from the late afternoon "fussy" cry which her mother attributed to fatigue or frustration).

One of the more interesting questions about Janet's language acquisition at this age is the role played by those around her. Specifically, what effect did Janet's mother and her younger brother have on her early phonological development? This is never an easy question to answer. Her mother's diary and my own research notes from Janet's first year mention a number of occasions on which Janet was heard to imitate her brother. He would make a request, for example, and Janet would "sing" the intonation pattern of his utterance. Later, when she began to produce words, she would often mimic a single word from one of Matthew's utterances. In one instance, he said, "Want to watch Big Bird," and Janet promptly piped up "Buh" (bird).

Gradually, as her babbling increased in frequency and in length, her phonology also improved. There is also evidence that her babbling became differentiated at around 8 months. Janet's mother notes in her diary that Janet sometimes seemed to be singing and just playing with sounds. This behavior occurred when she was lying in her crib, either at nap time or upon awaking in the morning. At other times, especially when she was sitting on the floor playing with her toys, Janet's stress and intonation would sound more "purposeful, almost as if she were giving orders sometimes" (Diaries).

Before her first birthday Janet had begun to show signs of moving from precursory language to true language acquisition. As mentioned earlier, the two main differences between precursory and later language acquisition have to do with the use of conventions and intent. Researchers have identified a number of behaviors that they believe indicate communicative intent. They include the increased use of eye contact during gesturing or vocalizing, the emergence of consistent sound patterns in vocalizations, appearing to wait for a response after vocalizing or gesturing, and persisting in attempts to communicate (Bates, 1979; Bruner, 1973; Harding & Golinkoff, 1979; Scoville, 1983, all cited in Sachs, 1989, p. 47).

Janet exhibited some of these characteristics. A month before her first birthday, she was sitting on her mother's lap while her mother read to her. They had just finished reading *Cat in the Hat*, and her mother started to put the book down. "No," insisted Janet, trying to retrieve the book. When she failed, she looked directly into her mother's eyes and said again: "No!" This simple exchange is evidence that Janet was becoming as a true language user—she knew what she wanted and she communicated it effectively.

Transition: First Words

By the time Janet was 8 months old, she was producing long strings of babbling, with intonation patterns that sounded very much like English conversation. When she began to produce her first words, a few days before her first birthday, she produced them not as part of her stream of babble but independently. That is, she continued to babble, particularly at night or nap-time when she was alone in her crib, but she also began to produce the occasional word in isolation.

After the "No!," which Janet produced in the previous example, and which she used a great deal for the next 2 years, the first word that Janet's mother believed to be intentional was *weo*. Janet was sitting on the floor watching her older brother play with his cars and trucks. When he rolled a large yellow dump truck toward her, Janet giggled and shouted *Weo*! *Weo*, or "wheel," was also her brother's word for wheels, cars, or anything that had wheels. She also encountered the word in the title of a favorite book, Dr. Seuss's *Bears on Wheels*. It was a single word, but it marked the beginning of a period of rapid and very impressive language learning.

Janet from 1;0 to 1;6

Within a few weeks of uttering her first word, *weo*, Janet added to her vocabulary *baba* ("bottle"), *mumum* ("mummy"), *gaga* ("Gurgles," the name of her stuffed bear) and *du* ("juice"). Interestingly, with the exception of *weo* and *du*, these words were of the reduplicated form common in the babbling of children between 6 months and 1 year of age.

First words have long interested researchers—who have recorded and categorized them in a number of languages. Although there is variation between cultures and, indeed, between children in the same culture, it seems to be universally true that children's first words identify or label particularly salient objects or people in their immediate environments. Broadly, these include family members or frequent visitors, food, actions, body parts, clothes, animals, toys, vehicles such as cars or trucks, and locations. Assigning children's early words to such categories requires, of course, that the researcher, or in the case of Janet, her mother the diarist, make judgments about the meanings and functions these words serve. These judgments are susceptible to bias in the sense that the adults' preconceptions about what the child intends may influence their reporting. For this reason, it is important to have as much contextual information as possible about the conditions under which these early words are produced.

The number of words in Janet's vocabulary increased dramatically after her first birthday. By the time she was 16 months old, her mother had recorded a total of 24 different words. Table 4.1 shows the words, a phonetic transcription, a "gloss" or meaning, and in some instances a brief note about the situation in which the word was uttered.

There are a number of ways of classifying Janet's first two dozen words. Most appear to be nouns for naming things in her immediate environment. Her use of verbs (*stop* and *go*), adjectives (*more* and *dirty*), and the negative indicates that her communicative ability was well in advance of the naming stage. From her mother's diary and my own incomplete observational notes made at the time, it would seem that Janet's early words were used largely in the presence of the named object (i.e., she used *gaga* when pointing to her bear and not in its absence). Even *go* was used in what seemed to be an observational sense (i.e., when she saw her father with his coat on preparing to leave, she said *go*). There was no indication that she was asking to go with him. The other action word, however, was used in an attempt to direct her brother's behavior, ordering Matthew to stop tugging on her blanket on one occasion. Similarly, *more* was used to demand more of almost anything she wanted, initially cookies or juice.

Table 4.1   Janet's First Words

Weo	/wio/	wheel	car, truck, bus, or anything with wheels
Baba	/baba/	bottle	bottle, milk, glass
Gaga	/gaga/	Gurgles	Janet's stuffed bear
Mumum	/mamamam/	Mummy	Janet's mother
Du	/du/	juice	juice of any kind, coffee, any liquid other than milk
No	/no/	no	negatives of all kinds
Dada	/dædæ/	Daddy	Janet's father or other adult males
Buh	/bə/	bird	Big Bird
Da	/dæ/	cat/dog	from *Cat in the Hat,* also used for neighbor's dog and for other Dr. Seuss books
Mo	/mo/	more	used also to indicate she didn't want an action to cease
Doe	/do/	go	
bop/ba	/bap/ba/	stop	used only when playing with Matthew
Dee	/di/	street	Sesame Street
Bubba	/bəbə/	bubbles/water	bubbles for her bath, water, ginger ale, soap
Wimu	/wimu/	window/door	
Du	/du/	shoe	
By	/bai/	pie/cake/pudding	
Da	/dæ/	Janet	
Guh	/gə/	cup	
Dye	/dai/	diaper	
didi	/didi/	dirty	
Kuku	/kuku/	cookie	
Du	/du/	Matthew	Janet's brother

These first 24 words also reveal a great deal about Janet's developing phonology. We see a number of instances of reduplication (a process by which a child reproduces a single syllable in a multisyllabic word, as in *dindin* for "dinner"). We also see instances of homophony, or two different words that sound the same, such as *du* for "shoe" and "juice." This homophony results from the child's simplification of the adult system. In this case, Janet substituted /d/, which she was able to produce, for both /s/ and /j/, which that she was still unable to produce. Such substitutions typified Janet's speech at this stage, and are very typical of children at this and the next stage of development.

Ingram points out, however, that development during this period differs in significant ways from later development. During the early part of this period, for example, the child uses words with shifting reference. A "bow-wow may refer to a dog one day, a horse another, or even a clock the next..." (Ingram, 1976, p. 12). We see this to be true of Janet in her use of *pie, cat, bubble,* and *window,* each expressing a number of meanings.

In comparison with the next stage of development, the child's sound system at this time is relatively primitive, consisting of a limited inventory of individual sounds and syllable types. Although there is a great deal of variability among English-speaking children, their early consonants tend to be alveolar and labial stops, particularly /b/. Ferguson and Garnica (1975) have pointed out that /w/ is also one of the earliest sounds acquired. Children at this stage of development may have as few as two vowels or as many as six, but /i/ (the vowel sound in *feet*) and /a/ (the sound in *tot*) are among the most frequent.

In Janet's speech of this period we find rather extensive vowel development with five vowels and a diphthong. Her consonants included both labial stops as well as /w/ and /m/. In addition to the alveolar stop /d/, she also produced the voiced velar stop /g/ and the alveolar nasal /n/, but only in the word *no*. In *window*, she substituted /m/, suggesting that /n/ was not yet fully established.

Although she did produce some CVC syllables, in her versions of *street* and *mummy*, and a vowel as the second syllable of *wheel*, she overwhelmingly preferred CV syllables at this stage. Ingram reports that this is the preferred syllable configuration for the first 50 words or so, but VC may be found as well. His child, Jennika, used a great many VC syllables, while Janet and the children studied by Menn and by Velten rarely did so. We see in Janet's speech another process characteristic of children in this stage. When she produced words of more than one syllable, she did so by duplicating the first syllable. **Reduplication** is a common phonological process in children under 2 years of age although not all children use the process and others use it to varying degrees.

Two other aspects of phonological development are noteworthy at this stage. Sometimes children appear to regress in their phonological development so that their early approximations of new words are closer to the adult forms than later attempts (Ferguson & Farwell, 1975). Leopold observed that his daughter Hildegard's attempts to pronounce the word *pretty* were better formed at 10 months than at 1;3 and even 1;10 (cited in Ingram, 1976, p. 21). Piper (1984a,b,c) reports a similar phenomenon in 5-year-old children acquiring English as a second language. At first blush, this may seem to be a strange occurrence, but perhaps not.

The explanation appears to be that at first the child is imitating and does not yet have a productive phonological system of her own. Later, as she attempts to come to terms with the *systematicity* of sound, she uses a number of regular processes to simplify the adult system and thus her pronunciation appears to deteriorate. We see in Janet's speech at this point only one exemplar of this process, her pronunciation of *stop*. She first produced /bap/ and then a few days later deleted the final consonant to produce /ba/. Admittedly, this is slim evidence for regression, and Ingram notes that it is not well documented in the research literature, but it is one that raises important questions about how the child creates an early phonological system.

A second noteworthy aspect of children's phonology at this stage concerns their selection of words. Ferguson and Farwell provide evidence suggesting that children select words that fall within their current phonological capabilities and avoid those that do not. One of the children they studied acquired words beginning with /b/ but no words beginning with /p/. Leopold's Hildegard exhibited apparent "avoidance" of the same sound, and although Smith (1973) does not mention it, his account of his son's phonology from age 2 shows only three words beginning with /p/ at the earliest stage but a great many more beginning with /b/. It would appear that many children consider sound patterns in choosing the words they acquire, or at least words that they produce since there is no evidence that they fail to understand words beginning with particular sounds.

Table 4.2   Janet's First Sentences

1. Weo go	/wio do/	wheel go	She is rolling a toy car
2. Buh dere	/bɔdɛ/	Bird there	
3. Tu no	/tuno/	Matthew, no.	A directive to Matthew to stop some action
4. Dada go	/dædæ do/	Daddy go	
5. Dada weo	/dædæ wio/	Daddy wheel	Her father's car
6. Goggie go	/gagi do/	Doggie go	
7. Su dode	/tu kod/	Shoe cold	Her mother has put a shoe on her that has been on the mud porch
8. No nap	/no næ/	No nap	
9. Tu weo	/tu wio/	Matthew's wheel	Matthew's car
10. Kiki dere	/kiki dɛ/	Kitty there	

Table 4.3   Janet's New Vocabulary at 1;10

Hi	/hai/
Byebye	/baɪbaɪ/
Up	/ də /
Down	/dæ/
Sock	/dak/ or /da/
Oscar	/aka/
Crayon	/ge/
Book	/bu/

In describing and discussing the first subperiod in the preschool years, we have focussed on the phonological system. This is true because at this stage it is the most visible of the child's language systems. This is not to say that the child knows nothing about word or sentence structure but only that it is not yet apparent to the observer. In the next 6 months, however, as Janet began to combine words, we are able to make interesting observations about her syntactic as well as her phonological development.

Janet from 1;6 to 2:0

The onset of this age period is marked by a rapid increase in vocabulary and by the child's combining of words into early sentences. According to her mother's diary, Janet added a new word or two each week and at 1;6 uttered her first two-word sentence, "No nap." Table 4.2 shows excerpts from her mother's diary when Janet was 1;10. Here we find both an expanded vocabulary and evidence of two-word sentences. From this sample we can see that Janet had added *go, there, doggie, cold, nap,* and *kitty* to her vocabulary. The diary recorded that she had also produced the words listed in Table 4.3. These new words brought her observed productive vocabulary at age 1;10 to 38 words.

Syntax and Semantic Relations

Once children begin to combine words, we can attempt to describe and to understand the rules governing their syntax. Researchers have shown a great deal of interest in the meanings conveyed by children in their two-word utterances. An obvious question that has arisen is the degree of universality in these early expressions. In other words, when they first begin to combine words, do children produce the same types of sentences? Apparently, there are similarities in the early meanings conveyed, but there is also a great deal of variation among individual children. Some of the more common meanings include:

An Agent performing an Action	Katie eat.
An Action affecting an Object	Kick ball.
An Object being given a location	Baby there.
A Person or Object being described	Katie cold.
	(Crystal, 1987, p. 243)

The danger in describing children's utterances in this way is that we cannot always be sure what meaning is intended. In the utterances just listed, for example, the child *could be* doing essentially the same thing in both the first and last sentences, namely describing some attribute of Katie. It may be only an adult's imposition of structure on the child's language to assume that a verb is used in one case and an adjective in the other.

Using the categories from Crystal's example, we see that Janet was conveying similar meanings:

An Agent performing an Action

An Action affecting an Object

An Object being given a location

A Person or Object being described

We also see additional meanings in these sentences. In sentences five and nine of Table 4.2 we see that she can express possession and, in sentences three and eight, negative intent. Janet appeared to be telling Matthew, in the third sentence, not to take her stuffed mouse, and in the eighth, she was telling her mother that she didn't want to take a nap. Not only was Janet able to create a number of meanings, we see even at this two-word stage clear evidence of early syntactic variety. In 10 utterances consisting of only 12 different words, Janet was effectively using six different sentence structures.

Although the first two-word utterances tend to consist of verb and object (or action and object), very shortly after two-word utterances appear, many children start using two-word noun phrases. The first expansion of the noun phrase usually occurs with the addition of an adjective (*bad doggie*) or a quantifier (*more juice*). After these come, more or less in order, the ordinals (*other spoon*), cardinals (*two bears*), the demonstratives (*this cookie*), possessives (*my hat*), and finally the articles (*a, an,* and *the*). All these may occur as early as age 2. By 2;6, children may produce noun phrases with two modifiers before the noun (*this old hat*) and by 3;0, their noun phrases may have three or even four prenominal modifiers.

Phonology

With the addition of new words, we also find changes in Janet's phonology. She had added to her inventory of sounds two consonants. One was /t/, which she now used instead of /d/ in *Matthew,* and the other was /h/ in *hi*. She also used a new vowel, /ɛ/ in *there*. Although she still showed an overwhelming preference for CV syllables, she did produce the occasional CVC syllable, as in *sock* and *cold*. In *sock,* however, the CVC syllable alternated with the CV syllable, suggesting that she hadn't fully "settled" on the CVC form. Indeed, we find a few weeks later that she had chosen /da/ as her pronunciation. We also see that she still uses reduplication as a strategy for producing two-syllable words such as /kiki/ (kitty) and /dada/ (daddy).

Janet from 2;0 to 3;0

Sometime around their second birthdays, many children begin to produce three- and four-word sentences. Obviously, once they begin to produce these longer utterances, more complicated syntax is needed to describe them. Children now begin to add questions and commands to the statements that characterized the two-word stage. Although children at this stage may be telegraphic in their tendency to omit grammatical morphemes such as the verb *to be* and the conjunctions, this tendency has largely disappeared by the time they are 3 years old.

Syntax

Two months before her second birthday, Janet produced her first three-word sentence, and by the time she was 2;0, they appeared regularly enough in her speech that her MLU was approximately 2.2. Considering that she still produced a number of single-word utterances, this MLU showed rapid development. When Janet was 2;6, her mother's diary included the list of sentences in Table 4.4.

Table 4.4 is not a complete list of Janet's three-word sentences at this age; it consists of those sentences for which phonetic or near-phonetic transcriptions were available. These were representative, however, of all the semantic relations recorded between 2;0 and 2;6.

The meanings expressed in these items included:

Agent Action Object (1, 2, 4, 5, 12)

Possessor Possession Locative (3)[*]

Possessor Possession Attribute (6,7)

Action Entity Attribute (8)

Table 4.4 Janet's Sentences at 2;6

1. Janet eat cookie.	/dæ i kuku/	2;3
2. Matthew eat cookie.	/tu i kuku/	2;3
3. Matthew cookie there.	/tukuku dɛ/	2;4
4. Mummy see kitty.	/məmi si kiki/	2;4
5. Daddy go wheel.	/dædæ go wio/	2;5
6. Matthew face dirty.	/tu ses dədi/	2;5
7. Daddy big wheel.	/dædæ bIk wio/	2.6
8. See big wheel.	/si bIk wio/	2;6
9. Want Matthew gum.	/wã tu kəm/	2;6
10. Mummy no go.	/məmi no go/	2;6
11. See doggie there.	/si dagi dɛ/	2;6
12. Daddy chase Matthew.	/dædæ ses tu/	2;6

Action Entity Locative (11)
Action Object Attribute (9)*
Negative Agent Action (10)*

Most of these relationships are typical of those found in children beginning to form three-word sentences. Except for those marked with *, all were identified by Brown (1973) as prevalent in the speech of children at this stage. Once children reach the three-word stage, it is possible to view their sentences as having hierarchical structure. The sentence *Daddy chase Matthew*, for example, would traditionally be viewed as having two major constituents with *chase* and *Matthew* forming the VP constituent. That is the adult's way of parsing the sentence, but what is the evidence that it is the child's? In other words, how do we know that the Action (*chase*) is more closely bonded to the Object (*Matthew*) than it is to the Agent (*Daddy*)? Martin Braine (1971b) has suggested one kind of evidence, the "build up," or expansions, the child sometimes makes.

Eat cookie. . . . Janet eat cookie.

Unfortunately, this is an isolated instance in Janet's language, and we do not know whether it is a common hierarchical structure. Another type of evidence could be sought in her two-word sentences. If it were the case that action and object were more closely bonded in her three-word utterances, it would likely also be the case that these were the predominant relationships in her two-word utterances. Returning to her two-word utterances, we find both agent-action and action-object bonding. This is consistent with research evidence showing that some children form stronger action-object bonds and others stronger agent-action bonds.

Table 4.5 Early Grammatical Morphemes

1. Matthew playing.	/tu pen/	2;6
2. Matthew's wheel.	/tus wio/	2;6
3. Janet's shoe.	/dæns su/	2;6
4. Janet's baby.	/dæns bebi/	2;7
5. Mummy's juice.	/mə mis du/	2;7
6. Shoes there.	/sus dɛ/	2;8
7. Shoe in bed.	/su In bɛt/	2;8
8. Gurgles in bed.	/gagas In bɛt/	2;8
9. See in window.	/si In wlno/	2;9
10. Got two book.	/ga tu bə/	2;9
11. Doggie got Gurgles.	/dagi ga gagas/	2;10
12. Matthew's shoe there.	/tuz su dɛ/	2;10
13. Matthew chasing doggie.	/tu sesIn dagi/	2;10
14. Sit on bed!	/sitɔn bɛt/	2;11
15. Gurgles jumping!	/gagas dəmpIn/	2;11

Another important dimension of syntactic development apparent in Janet's speech at this age was her use of pronouns. Although there are no pronouns in the language data reproduced in Table 4.4, Janet did begin to use pronouns during this year. Most children use *it, this,* and *that* before the personal pronouns, and Janet was no exception, using these pronouns before she was 2 years old. The personal pronouns, specifically *he, she, him* (sometimes *hims*) *I,* and *me* all appeared with some regularity in her speech by the time she was 2;8. Young children's learning of the first person pronouns is an especially impressive feat. As Perera (1984) points out, children hear themselves addressed as *you* yet must learn to address themselves as *I* or *me.* Parents don't always provide that much help, either, using names rather than pronouns in sentences such as *Mummy will put Lindsey to bed* (p. 104).

Grammatical Morphemes

Before the age of about 2;6, Janet's speech was usually devoid of grammatical frills. At about this time, however, she began to produce two grammatical inflections: The progressive form, *-ing* and the possessive inflection on nouns appeared on certain words. These first appeared, as shown in Table 4.5, in two-word sentences—but note that the number of *morphemes* in each utterance remains three.

The period during which children acquire the inflectional morphemes has been of considerable interest to researchers, and there is a rigorous protocol for determining that order (see Brown, 1973). When children are between 1;9 and 2;10, and the MLU is approximately 2.5, they typically add a few prepositions, principally *in* and *on,* an article or two, and perhaps the plural and possessive forms. Other grammatical morphemes follow as the child marks finer syntactic distinctions. These remaining morphemes are acquired during a time when the child is between approximately 2;0 and 4;0, and the mean length of utterance is between 2.0 and 2.5 (Brown, 1973, p. 271).

The earliest grammatical morphemes to appear in Janet's language were the progressive inflection on the verb and the possessive inflection on the noun. This is consistent with Brown's finding that two of his three subjects acquired the present progressive before any of the other inflectional morphemes. The possessive came higher in the acquisition order for Janet than would be predicted by Brown's study, but she was well within the age range during which they acquired the possessive. Following shortly were the plural, although *shoes* was the only form to appear for some time, and the prepositions *in* and *on*. It is interesting to note that in learning *in* Janet seems to have acquired not one but two prepositions. In sentences eight and nine in Table 4.5, we find her using two very different senses of *in*.

Phonology

Although certain infantile pronunciations remained, Janet rapidly added to her inventory of sounds. She maintained her earlier pronunciation of *Matthew, cookie,* and *kitty* but improved upon her *Mummy* and *doggie*. Notice that the second syllable of *Mummy* is no longer reduplicated and the initial consonant of *doggie* is now a /d/. While she was still unable to produce consonant clusters, such as the /pl/ in *playing*, we can see in Table 4.5 that she had added the individual sounds /k,s,o/ and stabilized her use of /n/, using it instead of /m/ in *window*, for example. Another kind of instability appeared, however, as she began her acquisition of the possessive. As she added to her inventory of individual sounds, Janet inevitably began to produce a greater variety of syllable shapes. In the language samples in Tables 4.4 and 4.5, CV syllables still dominate, but we also find CVC, VC, and even a CVCC syllable.

Researchers have investigated the order in which children add to their basic inventory of the previous stage, both in naturalistic case studies and in experimental studies. Despite variation among children, certain patterns of development seem to hold true. Vowels, for example, are acquired first and are most often fully in place by the time a child is 3 years old. Janet had acquired the full inventory of vowels by 2;3 although she did not always follow adult pronunciations. For example, she maintained her pronunciation of *kitty* as /kiki/ even though the vowel /I/ was in her inventory. She also continued to pronounce *cookie* as /kuku/ although she had used both /U/ and /I/ in other words.

Because vowels occur singly in syllables, an acquisition order is relatively easy to establish. For consonants, such an order is more difficult to describe because they may occur in sequences in syllables and in a great many configurations. Moreover, children do not acquire individual sounds but sequences of sounds. As might be expected, children generally acquire single consonants before clusters. Templin studied 480 children ranging in age from 3 to 8 years and found that by the age of 4, children have acquired most single consonants with the following exceptions: /t/ between vowel sounds (as in *eating*), the /ch/ sound, the /j/ sound between vowels (as in *budgie*), the /th/ sounds, /v/ and /z/ at the beginning and end of words, the middle consonant in *leisure*, and word-final /l/ and /s/ (Templin, 1957, cited in Ingram, 1976, pp. 26–27).

By 2;6, Janet had acquired /p, b, t, d, s, k, g, m, n, w / but not in all positions. She still showed a tendency to delete or devoice word final consonants, producing /ga/ for *got* and /bIk/ for *big*. She was still missing a number of single consonants, notably /n,c,j,r,l/, but she used words with these sounds nevertheless. She did so by substituting sounds she could manage and by simplifying sequences of sounds. Her pronunciation of *playing* as /pen/ illustrates: She substituted /n/ for /ŋ/ and reduced the initial cluster to a single /p/. This behavior highlights one of the most interesting aspects of phonological development at this stage, namely the appearance and gradual loss of certain regular processes.

At this age, children are not able to produce perfectly formed imitations of adult speech. Rather, they simplify adult sound sequences to those they can manage with their immature cognitive and articulatory abilities. They appear to apply a set of universal processes resembling those described in Chapter 2, but these are developmental and get left behind or suppressed as children become more proficient at producing adult forms. *Developmental processes* are of three basic types: *syllable simplification* (by reducing the number of consonants in a syllable), *assimilation* (making one sound more like another), and *substitution* (replacing a difficult sound with an easier one they have already mastered).

Because English syllables may consist of consonant sequences that are very difficult to pronounce, and because young children find CV syllables much easier to pronounce, there is a universal tendency to reduce syllables to the CV type (Grunwell, 1982; Stampe, 1979). For children learning English, this tendency may be realized in a variety of ways. A 2 year old who produces /du/ for *juice* or /ti/ for *cheese* is simplifying a CVC syllable to a CV syllable by deleting the final consonant. This is a very early process in children's speech and may not appear at all in some children. Grunwell reports that it has usually disappeared by the age of 3;0 or 3;3. Janet was still reducing some syllables to CV at 2;9 (/ga/ for *got*), but the process had disappeared by 3;0.

In the early months of language acquisition, children produce mainly one-syllable words but attempt many words of more than one syllable. Sometimes these early attempts involve deleting the unstressed syllable. Most of us have heard children pronounce *banana* as /nana/, but /ap/ for *apple* is also possible in the very young child (Grunwell, 1982, p.170). This process is called *weak syllable deletion*. Although this is an early process, we see a remnant of it in Janet's pronunciation of *Cinderella* as /sIndrɛlə/ at 4;0 (see Figure 4.2).

Simplifying the syllable shape is not the only way in which children simplify the adult phonological system. Through **assimilation**, or making one sound more like another, children effectively reduce the total inventory of sounds they have to produce. Although there are several types of assimilation possible in child speech, two are very common. In the first type, one consonant in a word affects the pronunciation of another. The following examples come from Janet's speech:

Janet's Form	Adult's Form
/gagi/	*doggie*
/kiki/	*kitty*

/ses/   *chase*

/dæns/   *Janet's*

In each of these words, the initial consonants become the same as or more similar to the following consonant in the word. Young children have, incidentally, a preference for voicing consonants that precede vowels (Ingram, 1976, p. 36), and this is also a kind of assimilation: Just about the only way of making a voiceless consonant more like a vowel without completely changing its character is to voice it. Janet, for example, pronounced /s/ as /d/ in *sock* and /k/ as /g/ in *clock*.

The third major type of phonological process by which children simplify the adult sound system is substitution. It is similar to assimilation, in which children substitute one sound for another, but with substitution processes the sound they substitute is not influenced by another in the immediate environment. This is not to say that substitution is random. Children behave in similar ways in replacing one sound for another. Ingram (1976) reports, for example, that the process of stopping, or replacing fricatives and affricates with stops, is common in both normal children and in those with phonological disabilities. This process accounts for Janet's pronunciation of *juice* as /du/, *jumping* as /dəmpIn/, and *sock* as /dak/. Notice that the stop is articulated in the same place as the fricative or affricate it replaces.

Fronting is another type of substitution process common in the speech of young children. The process is called fronting because of the apparent universal preference for consonants articulated near the front of the mouth. The most common realization of this process is the substitution of an alveolar consonant for a velar one, resulting in pronunciations such as the following:

Child's Form	Adult's Form	Source
/bæt/	*back*	Menn (1989)
/tæt/	*cat*	Menn (1989)
/tek/	*cake*	Hills (1914)

This was a process that Janet appeared to use only rarely and only when she was very young. Her pronunciation of *go* as [do] at 1;10 was the only reported incident of fronting. That it was not a process she generally favored is shown in Table 4.2. At the same time she was saying /do/ for *go* she was also correctly producing /k/ and /g/ in *cold*, *kitty*, and *doggie*. Other researchers have noted that although consonant fronting is a well-attested process in the speech of young children, it is also one that does not occur in all children. Smith (1973) conducted a careful, detailed study of his son's phonological development and found virtually no instances of fronting. In children who do exhibit the process, it usually disappears by the age of 2;6; Grunwell (1982) reports that velar consonants (the ones affected by fronting) are mastered by all normal children by the age of 3;3.

Most of the examples used so far in describing the more common simplification processes children use in mastering the sound system have involved a single process. In real speech, however, children frequently apply a number of phonological processes at once. Ingram (1976) has reported as many as seven processes operating in a single word, and certainly two, three, or four are common. In a child's pronunciation of *scratch* as *tat*, for example, we can see three processes operating. The initial consonant cluster is reduced to a single consonant, the /k/ sound in that cluster is fronted to a /t/, and the final affricate is replaced by a stop, /t/ (Grunwell, 1982, p. 182). In Janet's pronunciation of her own name as /dæ/ at 2;3 (Table 4.4), we see the substitution of an alveolar stop, /d/, for /j/ as well as weak syllable deletion.

Identifying the processes that link children's pronunciations with the corresponding adult pronunciations depends, to a large degree, on how well we *hear* children's speech. Of course, just as we hear a foreign language through the filter of our own language, we also hear children's speech through the filter of our adult perception. Even trained transcribers must exercise caution in transcribing children's speech. Using machine analysis, Macken and Barton (1980) demonstrated, for example, that some children who appeared to be using voiced stops at the beginnings of words where they should have used voiceless stops were actually attempting to produce the correct form. What this suggests is that children may be further along their path to phonological mastery than they seem to be, given what we hear as their pronunciations. This is a caution that we would do well to keep in mind as we view children's language data. We cannot help but view it from our adult bias, and in doing so, we run the real risk of underestimating their accomplishment.

Janet from 3;0 to 4;0

This was a year of impressive progress for Janet in all areas of language acquisition. She continued her learning of the inflectional and grammatical morphemes, and she continued to combine words into sentences that grew in length to seven and eight words. She gained control of the phonology of her language, leaving only a few minor distinctions unmarked. Two transcripts, one taken the day before her third birthday and the other a week or so after her fourth, provide a good indication of the magnitude of her progress.

Janet was making giant strides forward in pragmatics, syntax, morphemic structure, and phonology. These are apparent in comparing the conversations reported in Figures 4.1 and 4.2.

Pragmatics

During this stage, Janet became far more sophisticated and resourceful in her uses of language. In Figure 4.1, we see her clarifying her question when her mother doesn't understand. She was not yet able to say, "No, that's not what I meant," but she very deftly let her mother know that she wasn't asking about the next number in the sequence but about the color of the paper liner. In the year between the first and the second conversation, we find that Janet has become increasingly adept at using language for a variety of purposes. The child who used language largely to report and comment on the present has evolved into one who attempts to manipulate her

Janet is standing on a chair helping her mother bake cupcakes for Matthew to take to his kindergarten class.

Mother: You want to help?
Janet: Me help?
　　　/mi hɛlp/
M: Yes. You can put these in here. (The paper liners in the tins.)
J: Like this?
　　/laik dɪs/
M: Right. Can you count them?
J: Count. One, two, three . . . what this?
　　/kãut wən tu twi wa dɪs/
M: Four?
J: No. This one yellow. This one yellow, too. This one . . .
　　/no dɪs wən yɛwo dɪs wən yɛwo tu dɪs wən/
M: Oh, the color. That one's pink. You know pink.
J: Yeah. Pink. This one pink. Me taste?
　　/yɛ plŋk dɪs wən pɪŋk mi tes/
M: You want to taste? Just a minute while I get you a spoon . . . There. What do you think? Is it good?
J: (Nodding) Good. Mat?
　　/gʊd mæ/
M: Matt? Oh yes, these are for Matt to take to school.
J: Me too!
　　/mi tu/
M: You want to go to school?
J: (Laughing) No. I want this one. (Points to cupcake.)
　　/no ai wan dɪs wən/
M: Oh, you want a cupcake. Well, when they're baked, you can have one. Okay?
J: Okay. This one.
　　/okei dɪs wən/

Figure 4.1　Janet at 3;0

mother and then play with the situation and the language in her opening line of *Cinderjanet*. While Janet at age 3 still relied heavily on repetition of her mother's phrases, by age 4 she was initiating utterances without direct reliance on her mother's words or structures.

Syntax and Semantic Relations

Janet's syntactic development was no less remarkable. By the time they are 3 years old, most children take or have taken a giant grammatical leap forward as they begin to produce sentences with more than one clause. These clauses are still largely conjunctive (i.e., linked by *and*), and may run on and on. Janet was nearly

Matthew and Janet have been begging to stay up to watch a children's special on television. Matthew has conceded the battle and headed toward bed, but Janet continues to argue with her mother while getting dressed for bed.

Mother: Which gown do you want?
Janet: Don't want *any* gown!
       /dõt wãn Ini gawn/
M: Well, that's up to you, but you might get cold.
J: I don't care. (She sits down on her bed and sulks.)
   /ai dõt kɛr/
M: I see. Do you care which story I read?
J: Nope. I don't care. I want to watch Charlie Brown.
   /nop ai dõt kɛr ai wat tu wač čarli brawn/
M: I'm sorry, it's on too late. But you'll be able to see Charlie Brown another time. Don't forget, he's in the comics every Sunday.
J: I want to see him *now!*
   /ai wãt tu si hIm naw/
M: We're through talking about Charlie Brown, Janet. Now do you want me to read to you or not?
J: I'll read.
   /ail rid/
M: You'll read to me? What will you read?
J: How about Cinderella?
   /haw bawt sIndrɛlə/
M: That's a pretty hard one. Do you think you can read all of it?
J: (Defiantly *reading*) There was a mean wicked mother and she had a poor little girl named Cinderjanet.
   /ðɛr wəz ə min wIkId məðə ænd ši hæd ə po:r lIto gəro nemd sIndərjænIt/

Figure 4.2   Janet at 4;0

a textbook case when it came to conjunction. Her mother's diary records the following sentence at 3;6:

> Matt want my baby and I said he can't have her and he take Gurgles and I take his book about bears and he hit me.

Children of this age are also capable of producing sentences with subordinate clauses, principally with *because* ('coz), correctly:

> My baby cry coz she want me (Janet, 3;4)

and sometimes not:

> Spike bite me coz it hurt. (Kate, 2;9)

Janet at age 3;5
Mother: What happened here?
Janet: It broke.
M: All by itself?
J: What?
M: Was the glass broken all by itself?
J: No. I broke it.

Janet at age 3;6
Janet: Your car broken?
Daddy: Yes, it was hit in the parking lot at work.
J: Who hit it, Daddy?

Figure 4.3   Understanding of Passives

Before they can use constructions like these correctly, a great deal of grammatical knowledge is required. Similarly, as they begin to produce longer and longer utterances, greater syntactic sophistication will be required to prevent the kind of muddled tenses experienced by this child, age 3;9, reported by Crystal (1987, p. 243):

> If Father Christmas come down the chimney, and he will have presents when he came down, can I stay up to see him?

At age 3, Janet's utterances were from two to seven morphemes in length, and she had begun to produce negatives, declaratives, and questions. It is usual for children to begin to produce different types of sentences at about the same time as the grammatical morphemes begin to appear. We saw that Janet had begun to produce certain grammatical morphemes at 2;6, and the transcript from 3;0 shows her beginning to use questions and some negatives. We still see, however, evidence of telegraphic speech, typical of infancy or the earliest preschool period. When she said *Matt?* with rising intonation, she was letting the single word carry a very large semantic burden—one that her mother recognized in her subsequent expansion of Janet's question.

By her fourth birthday, Janet's utterances ranged from 2 to 16 morphemes in length and most of her sentences were well-formed. Certainly those reproduced in Figure 4.2 were nearly perfect. At the same age, and for several months previous, she had been producing a variety of syntactic forms including questions, negatives, negative questions, imperatives, and negative imperatives. There is no record of Janet's producing passive constructions during this time, although the following dialogues recorded when she was 3;5 and 3;6, respectively, show her quite capable of understanding at least some passive constructions (Figure 4.3).

This is not to say that Janet's syntactic development was complete. As seen in Figure 4.1, she still relied heavily on conjunction for linking related propositions rather than relative or reduced relative clauses. That is, she typically produced sentences such as *Matt took Gurgles and Gurgles had a sore ear and I told him not to!*

(3;11) and *I saw Daddy's car and it was broken 'coz the wheel was on the ground and now he's going to fix it* (4;0).

The semantic relations expressed in Janet's sentences at age 3 were no longer restricted to the seven simple ones of 6 months earlier. She was producing well-formed SVO sentences (*I want this one*) although she did not yet produce the copula (*to be*). A moment's reflection explains why this might be the case. With *I want this one*, Janet was making her wishes known. Arguably, she could have done so without the first person pronoun, but the verb, object (*one*), and even *this* were essential to her specifying, and getting, exactly what she wanted. The copula, *is*, in the sentence *This one yellow* is clearly expendable. It is entirely redundant for expressing the meaning she wished to express. This is to say that children cannot learn *all* the grammatical conventions of language at once, and so the order in which they *do* acquire them is to a large degree determined by the meaning they wish to make.

It is possible to make certain observations about Janet's learning of the grammatical morphemes. We saw earlier evidence that she had acquired or was well on her way to acquiring the progressive, the possessive, and the prepositions *on* and *in*. Before the age of 3, she had added the plural form and certain irregular past forms such as *broke, saw, ate,* and *took*. Sometime around age 3 she had added the demonstrative article, *this* (see Figure 4.1) but still produced sentences without the copula (*What this?*). In the next year, however, Janet added the contractible auxiliary (*I'll read*), the contractible negative (*Don't want any*), other prepositions including *about, with, under, over,* and *beside,* as well as the copula in both the present and past tenses. She even made a stab at a complex sequence of tenses reminiscent of Crystal's earlier example:

> When Daddy would come home if Matthew is not home from school is it
> . . . (at this point, she gave up and started again) When Daddy would come
> home and Matthew wouldn't come home, can I go with him to feed the
> horses? (4;2)

If we were to examine this excerpt for its errors or deviations from the correct adult form, we would do Janet a grave disservice. Even though neither sentence is perfect when compared with the adult model, both represent tremendous syntactic growth. In this short excerpt, we find Janet using auxiliary verbs, complement structures (*go with him to feed the horses*), and making an attempt to express conditional relationships. She has come a long way from the child who, only 18 months earlier, was producing mainly two-word sentences.

Vocabulary

Children at this age are also busily acquiring a great many new words, and in the process sometimes get a bit muddled:

Exasperated Mother: *Will you PLEASE behave?*
Christopher (age 3): *I AM being hayve!*

It is estimated that children of age 3 have a vocabulary of between 800 and 1,200 words, and by the time they are 4 years old, that total will have risen to between 1,500 and 1,900 words (Crystal, 1987, p. 232). Assuming the lower end of each estimate, this means that children learn approximately two new words every day during this year. Parents of 3- and 4-year-olds will not be surprised by these estimates. If language use contributes to language learning, as it undoubtedly does, then most children have plenty of opportunity to learn. German researchers have reported that children age 3;6 produce nearly 38,000 words during a 12-hour day (Crystal, 1987, p. 244).

Phonology

Janet's phonological development at age 4 was mostly complete. Only a few individual sounds gave her any difficulty. She sometimes substituted /d/ for the interdental sound in *this* or *there* but at other times produced it correctly, indicating that she had not yet fully gained control of the interdental. She also substituted /w/ for /l/ at times, but her mother's diary notes that she usually did this when she was playing with her dolls and was, perhaps, engaging in baby talk. We see in Figure 4.2 her pronunciation of *little* as /lIto/ and *girl* as /gəro/. This substitution of a vowel, usually /u/ or /o/, for a consonant, usually *l* or *r*, is called vocalization. It is common among younger children, but it is not known how frequently it occurs in 4-year-old children. This is true in part because the process results in a sound that is not greatly deviant, and most adults do not notice it (Grunwell, 1982, p. 171). The fact that Janet's vocalization appeared to be restricted to certain words (e.g., *girl*, *little*, and *wheel*), and did not influence *I'll* or *call*, suggests that it was attached to certain lexical items that she had learned early and was likely in the process of being lost. By the time she reached her fifth birthday, all traces of this process had been lost.

By the age of 4, Janet could produce most sequences of consonants and, thus, most syllable shapes. She would still occasionally omit or substitute a consonant in a three-consonant cluster such as *spring*, which she produced sometimes as /spwin/ and other times as /spin/ at 3;11. She also pronounced *scream* as /skwim/ until just before her fourth birthday.

Janet from 4;0 to 6;0

During these last 2 years in the preschool period, children develop remarkably in every way—physically, cognitively, and linguistically. The tentativeness of the word *toddler* no longer applies to these young children whose language is marked by major growth. The smaller "building blocks" of language are largely in place, and development during this period occurs largely in syntax and vocabulary.

Syntax

By the age of 4, and for the next year or two, children gradually solve some of the more complex grammatical puzzles of their language. At this stage, certain kinds

> Janet: Spook doesn't like this food.
> Mother: How do you know?
> J: Well, you gived—gaved it to her last night and she doesn't ate—
>   no, she didn't ate it.
> M: Oh, well I guess you're right. What should we do?
> J: Give her some different food that she likes.

Figure 4.4   Evidence of Rules in Progress

of overgeneralizations appear as they work out the details of their rules-in-process:

> Heidi gots too many.
>
> Kate didn't went.
>
> Mummy wented to gets Daddy.

That children of this age are capable of actively working on the rules is evidenced by Janet at 4;4 trying to tell her mother that Spook, the family cat, had not eaten her food (Figure 4.4).

The overgeneralizations in *gived* and *gaved* provide evidence that she was working on the regular past tense form. Her two self-corrections suggest that she was intentionally doing so and that her past tense and third person singular rules were still in progress (i.e., that she hasn't yet worked out the exclusiveness of the past tense and third person singular inflections). Crystal notes that this kind of "sorting out" of grammatical forms "is a particular feature of 4-year-old speech" (1987, p. 243), and Janet's mother's diary abounds with examples of such grammatical struggles. Sometimes during the sorting-out process, children revert to word order typical of an earlier age. Janet, for example, was heard at 4;4 to ask *Where goes Daddy's car?* But at the same time, she was producing syntactically sophisticated sentences such as the last one in Figure 4.4, in which she used an imperative and a well-formed relative clause.

Relative clause formation begins during the preschool years, chiefly as a way of specifying information about the sentential object. The sentence Janet uses to tell her mother what kind of food to feed the cat is a good example. In three separate studies, Menyuk (1971), Limber (1973), and Bloom, Lahey, Hood, Lifter, & Fiess (1980) found that preschool-aged children never use relative clauses to provide additional information about the subject noun (as in *The dog that bit me is in the garden*). This construction develops during the school years. But the researchers also found, however, that the total number of relative clauses actually produced by the children they studied was very small. This was also true of Janet, and the reason may be that children tend to avoid the relative construction because it *is* difficult.

Consider the sentence *The cat that ate the tuna is mine.* To create this sentence, the child has to figure out how to create two sentences and embed one somewhere

Table 4.6 Examples of Conjunctive *and*

1. I sawed Big Bird and he was talking to Cookie.	4;1
2. Mummy made cookies and I helped.	3;11
3. Matt come home from school and then he wented.	4;4
4. Daddy fixed his car and now it will go.	4;6
5. Spook didn't sleep with me and I'm mad at her.	4;7
6. Grammy was here and now she's not.	4;5

in the other without losing track of the first one. Assuming that the child has worked out the appropriate placement for the embedded sentence (relative clause), a decision dictated by the meaning, several other decisions need to be made. What is the appropriate relative pronoun? *That, which, who,* and possibly *whom* and *what* are all possible candidates to the child learner. Knowing which one to use requires a lot of sophisticated grammatical knowledge. Similarly, the choice of verb form has to be made. In this example, the choice is easy but adult speakers are often tangled up in tense puzzles with relative clauses, particularly those involving a choice between *who* and *whom.*

Another syntactic structure that begins to develop during this time is the passive, a construction relatively rare in oral speech. It is used mainly to emphasize the object of the sentence by making it the surface subject. In the speech of young children, the passive appears so infrequently that researchers find it impossible to study unless they deliberately try to elicit it in experimental situations (Tager-Flusberg, 1989, p. 153). Such experiments were not performed with Janet, and there was only one recorded instance of her producing a passive construction. At 4;9, she ran into the house to tell her mother that *Spook almost got hit by a car!* In this sentence, the agent was specified, but in general, young children produce more truncated passives, or sentences without agents, than full passives, or sentences with passives (Horgan, 1978).

We saw that Janet's preferred syntactic device for expressing longer utterances had been conjunction for some time. This preference continued between ages 4 and 5 when she continued to use *and* to link a variety of propositions. Table 4.6 shows examples of the conjoined sentences she used during this period.

As this table shows, the conjunction *and* can be used to express a number of different relationships between the two clauses. Researchers have identified at least four relationships marked by *and* in the speech of young children. They have also found that there is a largely invariant order in which they are acquired (Bloom et al., 1980, cited in Tager-Flusberg, 1989, p. 156). The earliest relationship expressed is simply additive. Sentences 1 and 2 in Table 4.6 illustrate this kind of relationship. The second *and* that children use expresses a relation of time between the two elements in sentences such as *Daddy gave me a dime and then I went to the store.* The third sentence in Table 4.6 is an example of this relationship. The fourth sentence may be an example of the same relationship, or it may be an example of the next one to develop, causality. The fifth sentence more clearly expresses a cause-effect relationship, and the sixth could be simply temporal or an example of a contrasting or adversative relationship, the final *and* to appear. Tager-Flusberg gives the example *Cause I was tired and now I'm not tired* (1989, p. 156), but Janet's intent was less clear.

Vocabulary

If Janet was typical of children her age, and there is no reason to suppose otherwise, her vocabulary during this year grew from approximately 1,500 words to over 2,000 (Crystal, 1987, p. 232). Her words also became more complex as she learned most of the remaining grammatical inflections and some of the derivational ones as well.

Phonology

By this time, children have acquired a reasonably effective sound system, although they will continue to refine it for a number of years. From 4;0 to 6;0, they discontinue the simplification processes described earlier and their pronunciation becomes more adult-like. As they learn to cope with longer words, that result in part from their increasing sophistication with inflectional and derivational morphemes, they will demonstrate that their language is still under construction. There are numerous examples of children's difficulty with longer words that show them relying on the same simplification processes. At 4;7, Janet announced to her friends that her mother worked at the *unibersity* and that her father was a *searching fizzlist*. Certain words continue to be problematic for most children until they begin school or even after. Ingram (1976) reports creative pronunciations of *thermometer* and *vegetables* for children up to 5;11 (p. 45). Janet's pronunciation of *vegetables* as /veǰ boz/ at 4;0 and /veǰ blz/ at 5;1 are both typical. There is no evidence that she had any difficulty with *thermometer,* either because she did not talk about thermometers much or, as the daughter of a "searching fizzlist," she had no trouble with the word *thermometer.*

THE SCHOOL YEARS

By the time children reach school, they are adept language users. They understand the functions and uses of language and have mastered most of its syntactic structures. They have acquired most of its individual sounds as well as most of its intonational features, therefore, their learning of the sound system during the next several years will be of the finer distinctions marked by intonation and stress. They will begin to understand irony, for example, and other kinds of subtle meaning changes signaled by intonational changes. The most remarkable linguistic achievement during the school years, however, will be the sound symbol correspondence necessary for reading. Partly through reading and partly through the broader experiences they will have in school, they will add daily to their already substantial vocabulary.

Pragmatics

As they grow older, children's social circles widen, placing greater demands on their language. Even in these days of daycare, nursery schools, and preschools, there is still something very special about going to school. For a variety of reasons, the on-set of formal schooling represents a new milestone in the acquisition of pragmat-ics. Not only does it present the child with new social and learning situations with which to cope, but it provides a great many new people and opportunities from which to learn.

When Janet, who did not go to preschool, went to kindergarten, she hurried home every day for the first few weeks with a "Did you know?" question. She excit-edly reported all the routines of the kindergarten, not realizing that what was new to her was known to the others in her family. She added the vocabulary of the school, words such as *recess, tardy, show-and-tell,* etc., and she gradually learned the rules of usage associated with the social structure of the school. Janet observed after her first encounter with the school principal, *She's sort of the boss and we have to be VERY quiet when she comes in.*

Learning the roles of the principal, vice-principal, one's teacher, other teachers, janitors, secretaries, older children, and all the people who populate the school also means learning the register of speech appropriate to each as well as the subjects one might talk with them about. Children who do not already know learn very quickly that there may be severe penalties for breaking sociolinguistic rules. Because she is a native speaker of English, Janet did not make the mistake of a non-English-speaking girl in her class by answering the teacher's *Would you please be quiet now?* with the seemingly reasonable *No, thank you, I don't want to.* Over the next several years, and to some degree for the rest of their lives, children will continue to learn the social rules governing language use.

To become competent language users, children must also learn the rules for ini-tiating and maintaining conversation. They eventually must learn, for instance, that they will likely get off on the wrong foot if they try *That wart on your nose sure is ugly* or *Have you thought about wearing a more flattering wig?* as an opening gambit. They have to learn that turning and walking away without comment from a conversation that has begun to bore them will have social ramifications. Conversational rules, if broken, can result in more severe communicative and social breakdowns than bro-ken phonological, morphological, or syntactic rules.

The school years are also the years during which children learn the subtle dif-ferences conveyed by syntactic paraphrases or *equivalents.* They learn that *The inva-sion was ordered by the president* imparts a slightly different message than *The president ordered the invasion* and that there are reasons why governments might choose the truncated form, *The invasion was ordered,* over either of the other ver-sions. They learn that they can paraphrase *The cat is black* by saying *The black cat,* but if they name the cat, the syntactic rule changes. Thus, *Spike is white* is all right, but *white Spike* sounds child-like. These are pragmatic rules that border on the syntactic, which brings us to the next major area of accomplishment.

Syntax

We have seen that by the time children begin school, they have mastered the basic syntactic structures of English. There is still a great deal to be learned, however, and

Grammy doesn't come always on Sunday.	5;2
Daddy won't go with me never!	4;4
Kick the ball over here!	4;6
Matthew and Daddy will come later?	5;8
Bears on Wheels isn't anywhere!	3;10
I did looked everywhere.	4;4

Figure 4.5   Adverbials in Janet's Speech

over the next several years, they will learn to understand and produce more complex sentences including those that serve specific functions in the language, such as the passive and cleft sentence. Although it is possible to consider this learning from a number of perspectives, here we will concentrate on two broad areas of syntactic change—the global clause structure of sentences and development within their two major constituents, the noun phrase and verb phrase.

Clause structure refers to the patterns that children use in constructing their sentences—Subject-Verb-Object, Subject-Verb-Object-Complement, etc. Research has shown that although children are able to understand and produce a wide range of clause patterns by age 6, they typically produce only a few. The predominant ones are transitive SVO sentences either with or without a sentence adverbial. They also produce a number of intransitive sentences, with and without adverbs, but other structures, such as sentences with two objects (*Matthew gave Spook the food* or *Grammy gave that book to me*) are less common.

Adverbs play an important role in young children's clause structure, and the use of adverbs has been widely studied. The kinds of adverbs children use appears to be established by age 6 and remains unchanged throughout the elementary school years. The proportion of adverbs denoting place, time, manner, and cause or condition is largely predictable from the order in which they were acquired—place and time first at about 2;6, followed closely by manner adverbials, and then those expressing cause or condition. What does change from the age of 6 until the age of 14 or so, is the number and placement of adverbs children use. According to Strickland (1962, reported in Perera, 1984, pp. 94–95), children not only use more adverbials as they grow older, they are more likely to "include an adverbial within the verb phrase, e.g. *have been always trying*"— behavior that is rare among 6-year-olds. (Perera, 1984, p. 94). While there were only sporadic entries in her mother's diary after Janet began school, an earlier entry shows her constructing a sentence of just this form. This and other samples of Janet's adverbial constructions appear in Figure 4.5

Perera mentions one final interesting change in clause structure during the school years. The structure is the recapitulatory pronoun in which the noun phrase is repeated when the grammar doesn't require it (e.g., *These students with five classes they shouldn't work*). It appears less frequently in children's language as they grow older. Cotton (1978) found that children between 7;9 and 9;9 use this construction in speech (it is far less common in writing) but use it less with age (Perera, 1984, pp. 96–97). There are a few recorded instances of Janet's using this construction:

Spook she threw up on the floor.   5;4

Matthew and Daddy they left me here.   5;6

That mean boy outside he hit Spook.   5;10

Mummy and me we went to see Grammy.   6;0

The changing structure of the noun phrase is another indication of maturing syntax. Researchers generally believe that the use of complex subject noun phrases is a mark of linguistic maturity. Loban pointed to the fact that the most capable of the 12-year-old children in his study produced eight times as many expanded noun phrases in subject position than did the less capable (Loban, 1963, cited in Perera, 1984, p. 100). Complex noun phrases such as *The little dog with the bow on its collar* are more commonly found in writing than in speech, both in children and adults. This fact suggests that complexity in the noun phrase *may* result from some aspect of schooling, either literacy or overt teaching practice, such as sentence-combining exercises or editing of written work.

Another interesting aspect of noun phrase development is the acquisition of articles. As most non-native learners of English will attest, the rules governing the use of English articles are complicated, and native speakers do not work out all the rules until age 8 or later. Rules such as the one requiring *an* before a word beginning with a vowel and the plural agreement rule for *this* and *these*, for example, may not be perfectly learned even by age 12. Janet appeared to have worked out both rules before age 12, but at age 7;5, she produced the following sentences:

Matt said that he wanted a apple.

This ones are almost dead.

Another common error that children continue to make until age 8 or, more rarely, 10 or 12, is to use an article denoting definite reference (i.e., *the* for something which is unspecified for the listener). Normally, for the article *the* to be used, the noun following it must have been previously introduced into the conversation or be clearly known to both speaker and listener. Hence, to say *The house was painted white* implies that both speaker and listener know WHICH house is under discussion. Children learn gradually during the school years that the use of *the* is restricted in this way. They also learn that the same restriction applies to *this*, *these*, and *those*, although colloquially, *this* is coming to be used as an indefinite determiner, as in *I was on the bus and I saw this man looking at me* (Janet 14;5). In this sentence, it is not at all clear that Janet had committed a reference error. It is more likely that she was using the language of her peer group, which permits the use of *this* with a non-specified noun.

Verb phrase expansion in English refers mainly to the use of auxiliary verbs. Children master certain auxiliary verbs early. *Is, can, will,* and *could* are acquired early (by about 2;6), largely in negatives and questions. Major (1974, cited in Perera, 1984, p. 110) demonstrated that by the age of 5, most children have acquired *can, could, will, would,* and *should,* but many will not acquire *shall, may, might,* and *ought to* until age 8 or later. By 7;5, Janet appeared to have acquired all the modal auxiliaries, but at 6;9, she produced the following:

> Mrs. Baker should might bring it to school.
>
> Matt will might let me ride his bike.

Other kinds of difficulties with the modals persist well into the teenage years in some children. Conditionals and the hypothetical past presented particular problems for Janet:

> If it would rain, the rain will get in under the tarp. 11;5
>
> Uncle Jack can't had left early or he'd be here by now. 11;0

In fact, many native speakers fail to master the modals fully. Sports figures and other celebrities whose careers and fame depend upon something other than their facility with language might well produce a sentence such as this one: *If I would have known in advance, I wouldn't have come.*

Morphophonology

During the early school years, children add the few remaining sounds to their phonetic inventories. By age 7, or 8 at the latest, they can reproduce the full range of English sounds. If words such as *thermometer* and *vegetables* still give them difficulty, it is because they have not mastered all sequences of sounds in all environments. The most interesting aspects of phonological development during the early school years is closely connected with morphological growth. For example, children begin to learn the rules for the plural, past tense, and other inflectional and derivational morphemes that are phonologically governed.

Although this learning continues well into the teens, children between 4 and 7 make major gains. They master two of the three plural forms (the syllabic form that follows words ending in sibilants is learned a little later) and at least the same two forms of the possessive morpheme. Interestingly, children at this stage are better at producing the correct possessive form of *boss* than they are at producing the plural, although they sound exactly the same. Obviously, children are learning something more than phonetic patterns.

When children reach the age of 6 or 7, a stage of rapid morphophonemic growth begins. This period lasts for 5 to 7 years and it is during this stage that children acquire many of the derivational morphemes. We saw in Chapter 2 that regular sound changes occur with the addition of certain derivational morphemes. For example, when we add {-ity} to *divine* to produce *divinity,* the pronunciation of the vowel in the root word changes. Vowel alternation is one of the many morphophonemic processes that children learn during this stage, and it is one that Moskowitz (1973) studied in children between 5 and 12 years old. Specifically, her study asked whether children have knowledge of the rules governing vowel alternation and at what age they are acquired. Using a method that required her subjects to add the suffix *-ity* to nonsense forms, she found that 5-year-olds have no knowledge of the vowel alternation rule. She also found evidence that the 7- to 12-year-olds knew the rule, and that information about the rule is attained gradually.

Another kind of morphophonemic information acquired during this stage is how stress is used to differentiate compound nouns from noun phrases in pairs such as *BLACKboard* (compound noun) and *black BOARD* (noun phrase). In a study to test their ability to discriminate between such pairs, Atkinson-King (1973) showed children from kindergarten to sixth grade paired pictures of blackboards and boards painted black, red socks and members of the Boston baseball team, etc. She found that the youngest children could detect a difference but could not correctly signal the difference in any consistent way (cited in Menn, 1989) even though they could accurately imitate each pair. Atkinson-King found that children develop their knowledge of this morphophonemic stress rule gradually from first grade to sixth grade.

By age 7, then, children have not yet completed their acquisition of phonology; they gradually learn more complex morphophonemic rules until age 12 or so. Around this age, they move into the final stage of phonological development. Ingram (1976) identifies this as the Spelling Stage. It is at this time that children master (or come close to mastering) the spelling of English, a process that has begun much earlier. Ingram links this stage with Piaget's period of formal operations (roughly 12 to 16 years) and with the stage at which the child:

> becomes capable of making intuitional reflections on … language. … Decisions of grammaticality can be made. In phonology, the child can also begin to decide what is a possible sound change and what is not.
>
> This probably also has an effect on spelling, which develops markedly during this period. (Ingram, 1976, p. 14)

Vocabulary

As they acquire the ability to understand and to use derivational morphemes, children's vocabularies show a dramatic improvement. Estimates of the vocabulary of an average school-aged child vary from approximately 2,500 different words (Crystal, 1987, p. 232) to as many as 8,000 (Gleason, 1989, p. 4). This variation is caused not only by a wide range of actual vocabulary size in children this age but by disagreement among researchers on what should be counted as a different word, or type. Does one, for example, count only root or base words or does one count all plurals, possessives, past tenses, etc. as separate words? Whatever the true figure, clearly children understand several times more words than they produce (Crystal, 1987, p. 232). The size of both receptive and productive vocabulary will increase dramatically over the next several years in large part as a result of learning to read.

Literacy

Literacy is, of course, the dominant language learning task children face after the age of 5 or 6. In a real sense, learning to read and write is like learning another language since it involves learning another symbolic system. It is made easier, of course, by the fact that children have learned oral language. Otherwise, the task of learning to read and write would be a great deal more difficult than it is.

Janet learned to read at some point before she began first grade. From the time she was born, she was surrounded by books, magazines, and newspapers. Her parents read to her long before they had any hope that she understood the words. We saw Janet at age 4 pretending to read *Cinderella*. Sometime in the next 2 years, the pretend reading gave way to real reading. Janet's mother tells the story of Matthew having to learn a short poem for the Christmas play at school. He brought the poem, which he had printed onto lined paper, home with him to study. She went into the family room to find Matthew reciting the poem and Janet following the written page. *No, Matt, it doesn't say that,* Janet said when Matthew made an error. *It says 'the snows LAY deep and white,' not WERE deep and white.* Janet's mother checked the script and found that Janet was right. Janet was one month short of her fifth birthday; Matthew was not quite 7.

While it is tempting to claim that some children learn to read by mere exposure, most children do not. Moreover, there is a danger that, in making such a claim, we trivialize the accomplishments of Janet, of my son Michael, and other children who do learn to read without instruction. We may also fail to give appropriate consideration to those factors that contribute to their success. Recent research indicates that oral activities, particularly rhyming, may contribute significantly to later success in reading. In particular, children who are able to produce rhyming segments and to identify non-rhymes at age 4 and 5 are, in general, better readers 2 years later than children who lack such ability. Peter Bryant and colleagues at Oxford University have found that rhyming and alliterative abilities are distinct from general language ability and from sociolinguistic background. In other words, it seems to be the case that children's ability to recognize and produce rhymes and alliterative forms is independent of factors such as being read to in the home. This is not to say, however, that what happens in the home is of no consequence. It is highly likely, for instance, that rhyming and alliterative abilities can be encouraged and practiced in very young children. Many of the popular Dr. Seuss books (such as *The Cat in the Hat*) provide excellent exposure to rhyme and alliteration. The fact that they are nearly universally loved by children points to the fact that children find rhyming activities natural and fun.

Educationally, the fact that preschool children are good at rhyming is significant for two reasons. As Bryant, MacLean, and Bradley (1990) point out, the fact that children have this ability indicates that they are able to analyze the constituent structure of words. Both rhyming and alliteration require the child to isolate the initial segment, the onset, from the vocalic nucleus, the rime, and thus shows that they are able to recognize sound units smaller than the word. The ability is also significant because research demonstrates that "there is a powerful connection between these abilities and the progress that children make later on when they learn to read and write" (p. 239).

Research linking rhyming and alliteration to reading is important because it suggests that early factors other than level of home literacy help determine later success in reading. It is an exciting finding for educators because it points the way toward an intervention that might have a positive effect. More precisely, it causes us to rethink our position on phonics, whether pro or con, and to reconsider the kind of phonics instruction that might be effective.

All of this is not to say that home literacy is unimportant, for it remains a highly significant factor. It is only to say that other kinds of oral language appear to be important as well. It may be the case that Janet learned to read on her own simply by being exposed to print. Or it may be the case that the early exposure to children's books, together with a rich oral culture in the home, ignited the spark that already existed.

In order to learn to read, the majority of children need some teaching. This teaching is easier, of course, if the children know the purposes of reading and have been exposed to a great deal of print. Torrey (1973), Ferreiro and Teberosky (1982), and Bissex (1984) all report studies of children who apparently learned to read without instruction. Some had the advantage of *Sesame Street* and *The Electric Company*, as did Janet, but others did not. What they all did have in common was the view that learning to read presented a challenge they wanted to meet and they were questioners. As Pflaum reports, it seems to be a characteristic of early readers that they "*ask very specific questions* and ... receive specific answers to those questions" (1986, p. 65).

We come then to the importance of social interaction. Clearly an important factor in children's learning to speak, social interaction might be thought of as less important for learning literacy. After all, reading and writing, unlike speaking, are activities that can be carried out in isolation from others. But apparently, *learning* to read and write are both facilitated by social interaction.

GRACE: THE LANGUAGE LEARNER

Grace was born in an extremely isolated region of the Ozark hills of Missouri 2 years before the Great Depression hit the United States. She was the middle of three (surviving) children of deaf parents. Her older brother, George, was born 2½-years before she was, and her younger sister, Bette, was born 8 years later. In her own words (personal correspondence), written in 2001:

The only neighbor was about 1/4 mile from where we lived. I guess you could say daddy was a hired hand for the man that owned the little house we lived in with a very small salary and rent free. There was no electricity, we heated the house with wood and also cooked with wood on a range. Water was carried from the spring which was about probably 2 blocks from the house. I started to school at age 5 and since there wasn't kindergartens then, it was the 1st grade. I remember some things that happened, even the doll that Grandma Stone sent me on my 2nd birthday. The doll was nearly as big as I, and I remember dragging it around by one of the doll's arms. When it finally came off then George and I buried it. The next day I wanted my doll but we didn't do a very good job marking the grave and could never find it. Also before I started to school I remember Mother would let us walk over to the main road and check the mail box, but I don't remember that we got much mail. But to get to the mail box we had to walk on the swinging bridge. George would make it rock side to side and scare me so that I would cry. I don't remember my first day of school except that I had to walk a long way with George to get there. Years later I went back to where we lived and drove from there to where the school had stood (no longer there) and it was 3 miles. No wonder I cried when it was cold as the bucket that carried our lunch was a syrup bucket and it got very cold without any gloves.

What I know of Grace's language learning, I know from her recollections as an adult and from my own acquaintance with her parents before they died in the 70s. Research, however, can fill in some of the gaps in our understanding of what her experience was probably like. There are, in fact, a number of studies that shed light on the process of language learning in hearing children of deaf parents. Most are case studies, and many of these show strong similarities between children acquiring English only and those acquiring English and **American Sign Language** (ASL) simultaneously. In contrast, one early study of 52 hearing children of deaf parents suggested that as many as 44% had "problems of speech, language, or both." Interestingly, however, "the amount of time spent with hearing adults or children did not seem to be related to speech and language difficulty" (Schiff & Ventry, 1976, p. 356). The researchers concluded, and Grace's experience living in a relatively remote community would support, that it is likely "the quality of interaction with a child [that] is more important than mere exposure to normal language" (p. 356). The number of children with speech or language problems in this study was, of course, much higher than would be expected in the hearing population. The researchers noted that one of the saddest things about working with their subjects was the children's parents' refusal to acknowledge that their children had problems. Thus, the children likely did not appear in speech clinics or come to the attention of language professionals. Nor did their problems solve themselves when the children began school, evidence once more that the early years are critical to language development.

Most hearing children of deaf parents acquire ASL and English simultaneously, the more common pattern being to learn ASL through interactions at home with parents and spoken English in interactions outside the home. This was true with Becos, an only child with normal hearing and growing up with parents whose primary language was ASL (Johnson, Watkins, & Rice, 1992). Becos was allowed to watch television; his parents believed that it would help with his English-language development, and he also had limited interaction with hearing relatives. They tested four specific hypotheses regarding the influence ASL would have on spoken English and found, in brief, that "Becos's pattern of spoken English development can be described by both expected developmental sequences for English and predictable patterns of influence from ASL" (p. 48). In other words, his English language development followed the same predictable sequence as monolingual English children but also included some identifiable influences of his other language, ASL. For instance, when he was just over 3, Becos's word order sometimes followed ASL word-order rules rather than standard English rules. The investigators point out, however, that the incidence of these forms was low (p. 49). This finding is entirely consistent with other research showing that hearing children of non-hearing parents manifest normal English developmental patterns with some influence of ASL. Prinz and Prinz (1979), for example, describe the sequence of semantic relations in their subject, Anya, the daughter of a deaf mother and a hearing father, as approximating "that both of children learning English and of deaf parents acquiring ASL" (p. 289).

In general, children such as Becos, Anya, and Grace will produce their first sign before the first spoken word and several months before hearing children are expected to produce a first word. It is also common that these early signs are semantically related to the first words—*mama* is common—and that early signs may be imperfectly formed just as first words are imperfectly formed. Prinz and Prinz report, for example that Anya's early signing of *mama* was produced with the little finger as opposed to the thumb touching the chin and that she demonstrated other variations before finally settling on the adult version.

Grace recalls:

> *I can't ever remember not being able to sign and George did too. I am sure the signing was limited until I got out among more people and found out there was more going on than what I knew. And Mother did talk to us but that too was limited and George and I pronounced words the same way that she did. As we got older and were around people more, then we realized that our way of saying things was not correct and we started to copy other people's pronunciations. We also had to learn a lot of words for things that we hadn't learned at home. I remember in first grade that the teacher told us what we were supposed to do if we needed to use the restroom, but whatever word she used was not one that I knew, and so I didn't understand. It made for a very uncomfortable time until one of the older girls felt sorry for me and explained in words that I understood.*

Grace and children like her are very interesting because they help to inform our understanding of both monolingual and bilingual language acquisition. Becos's experience is similar in many respects to the experience of children we meet in Chapter 5. It is interesting to note, though, that people who acquire both ASL and standard English rarely think of themselves as having two languages. Grace, for example, even though she still signs and speaks and writes standard English, considers herself monolingual. She would say, moreover, that she is "hopeless" at languages and could never learn another one. Since her education was interrupted by her entering the workforce during WWII, she never had the opportunity to find out, but I suspect she is wrong. Indeed, the evidence is that she already is bilingual and that standard English was her second language. In fact, the more I learn about Grace's experience, the more parallels I see between her and the children we typically think of as bilingual.

When bilingual children arrive in school, the differences are cultural as well as linguistic, as Grace's memories show us. I will end the chapter with another recollection that Grace has about her early school years. This one underscores the experiential differences faced by children growing up in relative isolation and with a means of communicating that is not shared by the majority around them:

> *At Christmas time during my second grade, all the kids were talking about Santa Claus coming and they were going to hang their stockings, to get goodies. I asked where they hung them and was told on the fireplace. I was excited about that although I didn't know who Santa was. Well we had an open fire in our fireplace, (this is when we lived in a log cabin) so I thought I*

would hang my stocking. I found a really good place on one of the rocks and so when I got ready for bed I took one of my stockings and managed to get it hung. I had asked when Santa would come and one of the kids at school said after I went to sleep. That was okay but imagine my surprise when I checked the next morning and my stocking had fallen partly in the fireplace and was really scorched. My thought on that was that since it wasn't still hanging, this Santa (whoever he was) just didn't see it. Oh well I would tell the kids I got lots of goodies in mine anyhow. They wouldn't know the difference.

When I asked Grace if the other children had, in fact, known the difference, she laughingly responded that they *wouldn't* have if she hadn't got carried away with her tale and added to the very believable *orange, a few walnuts, and a piece of candy* (the contents of most children's stockings in those days) her own ideas: a new doll, a dime (a penny *might* have been possible, but a dime was serious money for that time), and a new pair of socks. "I probably threw in a wagon and a dollhouse as well," she recalls. "My credibility was shot and by the time I figured out this Santa and Christmas business, I was much too old to believe it." As this unedited piece of writing shows, Grace grew up fully in command of the English language, and she still serves as an interpreter at the local hospital when the need arises, so she has not lost her facility with ASL either.

CONCLUSION

We have seen in this chapter a sketch of Janet's language development from the time she was born until she reached her teenage years. While a full description of her language growth at each stage would warrant an entire book, even the brief examples provided in this chapter have served to mark significant milestones in her acquisition of pragmatics, syntax, morphology, and phonology of her native language. We saw Janet grow from an infant whose precursory behavior was essential to the development of real language to a school-aged child already established as a lifetime member of her language community.

We also met Grace and learned about the extraordinary feat of learning oral English while living in an isolated community with non-hearing parents. We know less of her story, but what we did learn confirms that language learning is a very strong drive in children, that language and communication are, indeed, irrepressible. In the next chapter, we will learn more about what children accomplish and how they do it when they learn more than one language.

For Further Study

1. On page 97, the author identifies four types of syntactic/semantic structures Janet has used. Find an example of each in the data provided. Are there alternative descriptions possible for any of the sentences?

2. What is a cleft sentence, and why might it be used instead of another form?

3. Collect a short speech sample from a child in kindergarten. Analyze the adverbs used to see if they follow the pattern described by the author.

4. The author makes the following statement:

   Interestingly, children at this stage are better at producing the correct possessive form of boss than they are at producing the plural, although they sound exactly the same.

   Why might this be true? Have you heard other instances of this apparent anomaly?

5. The author states that learning to read and write are facilitated by social interaction. What evidence from your own experience suggests that this is true?

6. The author writes that research on children's knowledge or alliteration and rhyme is promising "because it points the way toward an intervention that might have a positive effect." What kind of intervention would be appropriate?

7. The author refers to language as a "conventional mapping relation." Explain what this means and how it pertains to language.

8. What research methods might be employed to determine that very young infants are able to discriminate between similar speech sounds such as /p/ and /b/?

9. Why might it be the case that hearing children of deaf parents produce their first sign before their first word and sometimes several months before hearing children might be expected to produce their first word?

For Further Reading

Chamberlain, C., Morford, J., & Mayberry, R. (Eds.) (1999). *Language acquisition by eye.* Mahwah, NJ: Lawrence Erlbaum.

Dale, D. M. C. (1975). *Language development in deaf and partially hearing children.* Springfield, IL: Charles C. Thomas Publisher.

CHAPTER FIVE

Learning Two or More Languages

North American educators have a tendency to consider monolingualism as the normal outcome of schooling. This view is common in certain parts of society despite the fact that Canada, among other nations of the world, is an officially bilingual country that functions well in both English and French without insisting that all its citizens be bilingual. Educators and governments, especially in English-speaking countries, give the impression that multilingualism is unusual. The growing popularity of "English only" legislation in the United States reflects this view very clearly. While there are very likely some very legitimate safety and bureaucratic grounds for such laws, there is also a darker intolerance and ethnocentricity among some who support establishing these laws. There is also a great deal of misunderstanding about the nature of and importance of **bilingualism**. One of the aims of this chapter is to examine the facts about children who acquire more than one language, either simultaneously or successively. Throughout this chapter, I use the terms *acquisition* and *learning* interchangeably, although I am well aware that some theorists, particularly Stephen Krashen, mark a distinction between the two.

People learn their languages for a variety of reasons and under a variety of conditions, but the fact that they do so suggests there cannot be anything especially difficult about learning an additional language. Yet, in North America, we seem to find foreign language teaching, and even English as a second language, particularly challenging. It isn't, of course, that Americans are afraid of or resistant to foreign language learning. It is simply a fact of their geography—unless they happen to live along the Mexican or Canadian border, they have little exposure to other languages. Moreover, few people have the opportunity to travel extensively abroad, so exposure and *need* to acquire another language are restricted. Nevertheless, because of liberal U.S. immigration policies, the country is a land of immigrants, and thus bilinguals are hardly rare. It is precisely because of this cultural "melting pot" that English dominates—a common language unites the nation. As a result, anyone who is bilingual is considered slightly exotic. And yet, the fact is that most of the world's population learns and functions in two, three, or more languages (Crystal, 1987, p. 360).

THE TASK OF LEARNING AN ADDITIONAL LANGUAGE

There is, however, no clear agreement on what it means to be bilingual. Some authors use the term bilingual to refer to people with *any* proficiency, even if it is only a few words, in a second language. Others insist that native-like control of both languages is necessary. But, in fact, McLaughlin is correct when he says, "Bilingualism is best described in terms of degree" (1984, p. 9). For our purposes, we will adopt Haugen's useful definition, also used by McLaughlin: "the ability to produce complete and meaningful utterances in the other language" (Haugen, 1956, cited in McLaughlin, 1984, p. 8). This definition does not assume balance. Moreover, the definition does not readily apply to all age groups. It would take some modification, for example, for it to be meaningful for very young children, because what is a complete and meaningful utterance for them? If we consider the intent of the definition—the ability to communicate in two languages—then we have a continuum along which we can place even the youngest learner. It is not uncommon even for young children to be more fluent in one language or to reserve one language for use in certain situations. It only assumes that children are able to communicate in either language at a level appropriate to their age.

There are many routes to bilingualism. Many children acquire two or more languages before they reach school. I have known a number of Canadian families in which a Francophone mother and an Anglophone father (or vice versa) bring up a bilingual child who speaks the appropriate language with each parent. Which language eventually dominates—and usually, one will—depends on what language is spoken in the surrounding community. Another young couple I know emigrated from China and speak only Chinese in the home. Yet their child, when she reaches school age, will be bilingual, having acquired English from her playmates, from television, and the sheer preponderance of English around her. Still another set of parents in a small community in Labrador speaks both English and Inuit with their children. With only limited exposure to English-language television and no native English speakers in the small community, the parents believe that their children's eventual success in school and, indeed, in the predominantly English society, will be jeopardized if they begin school without some prior knowledge of English. In Europe, some children are brought up in bilingual homes and then educated in a third language. Actually, this pattern is becoming more common in Canada where, for example, immigrant parents use both English and Japanese in the home and then send their children to French immersion or even (in Quebec) French-language schools.

Parents thus assume the responsibility for their children's second language learning. In all these examples, children are learning multiple languages simultaneously.

What about children who acquire a dialect of English at home that differs substantially from the standard English used in schools? While they are not, strictly speaking, bilingual, the experience in many ways resembles the acquisition of two languages. Remember the story of Lanny from Chapter 1, the girl who considered her Portuguese and her English as belonging to a single language—hers! Grace, from Chapter 4, acquired American Sign Language and English simultaneously, and her experience, too, was similar to that of children acquiring another natural language. In fact, it has become common to find accounts of children simultaneously acquiring ASL and English (or other natural language) in the literature on bilingualism; 20 years ago, this was rarely the case. (see Drasgow, 1993; Grosjean, 1992).

The distinction between *simultaneous* and *successive* or *sequential* bilingualism is generally made in the literature on second language acquisition, in part, to differentiate children who come to school able to function in two languages from those who cannot. Originally, however, the distinction was marked because researchers believed that there were fundamental differences in the process of acquisition in the two circumstances. It is a useful distinction to maintain although it is probably accurate to say that educators tend to pay more attention to sequential acquisition. The reason is obvious: Educators believe they need not be particularly concerned about teaching a second language if the child has already acquired it before coming to school. In fact, this thinking is somewhat misguided. Teachers should be acquainted with both kinds of bilingualism for the same reason they should have some understanding of first language acquisition. It is important to know as much as possible about children's cognitive development, and bilingualism has a significant impact on cognition. Also, by understanding the conditions in which children acquire their first and second languages simultaneously, they might gain insights to guide them in creating successful language learning environments in school.

A second reason that educators need to think about both kinds of bilingualism is the growing trend toward preschool education for bilingual children—in English, for instance, for immigrant children in the United States. While this would technically be considered sequential bilingualism, because the learners are much younger and the environment of the preschool is less formal and more homelike, the boundaries between sequential and simultaneous bilingualism are perhaps less clear. Certainly, preschool educators need to understand a great deal about language acquisition in the home setting.

In this chapter, we examine childhood bilingualism and the issues surrounding it. The first two sections correspond with the distinction noted previously. Next, we examine the issues that an adequate theory of second language acquisition must address. Because the focus of this book is children's language learning, we concentrate on the conditions affecting their second language learning, although in the description of the issues affecting theory there will be some discussion of adult learning.

A critical factor in assessing these conditions is the age at which the child begins acquiring a second language, for most other conditions will be influenced by that one. The distinction already noted between acquiring languages simultaneously and sequentially is not always a clear-cut one. It is not easy to assign an arbitrary age at which the acquisition of two languages ceases to be simultaneous and becomes sequential. Are children who begin to learn another language at age 2 or even age 3 *adding* a language to an established first language? Or are they acquiring two languages at the same time? We *could* adopt McLaughlin's arbitrary age 3 as the point after which children are assumed to be adding a second language. Certainly the child has a good head-start in the first language by that time.

We saw in the last chapter, however, that a significant amount of first language growth occurs between age 3 and the end of the preschool years. More importantly, there is a major difference between the conditions or environment for second language acquisition that occurs in the home and in the school. The former has been termed *natural language learning* and the latter *formal language learning*. While recognizing that these distinctions are sometimes useful, I have chosen instead to mark the distinction between home bilingualism and school bilingualism. The first refers to children who acquire two languages simultaneously from infancy or any time before they begin formal schooling, even in daycare or preschool. The latter refers to those children who begin to learn a second language at any time during the school years.

HOME BILINGUALISM

Children of bilingual parents, who speak both languages with the child from birth, are effectively learning two first languages. What may be more common, though, is the child whose parents speak the same language but who learns another language from a grandparent, nanny, or babysitter, if not from birth, from a very young age.

Studies of preschool children acquiring two languages (Leopold, 1939, 1947, 1949a,b; Ronjat, 1913; Tabors, 1997; Totten, 1960) strongly indicate that they are able to do so in much the same way as they learn different registers of the same language. Ronjat's detailed study of his son, Louis, learning his mother's language, German, and his father's language, French, indicates that the child learned German and French vocabulary, phonology, and syntax simultaneously and without confusion. According to Ronjat's observations, the child could produce the phonemes of both languages correctly by 3;5 (McLaughlin, 1984, p. 75). As we saw in the previous chapter, this is well within the normal range for a monolingual child, and Ronjat's son was bilingual.

Ronjat reported following his friend, Maurice Grammont's, advice to keep the languages strictly separated: "each language must be embodied in a different person" (cited in McLaughlin, 1984, p. 75). With his daughter Hildegard, Werner Leopold followed the same advice, speaking to her only in German and her mother speaking to her only in English. Although her learning in both languages was impressive, Hildegard never achieved the balance achieved by Louis Ronjat. This was likely because the family lived in an English-speaking environment and visited Germany only twice in her first 5 years. Therefore, while German was the language in which she communicated with her father, it apparently had little utility outside the home.

There was some mixing of Hildegard's two languages, most obviously in her early vocabulary development where she seemed for a time to adopt

> the strategy of giving things one name only. However, once she realized that there were two languages in her environment, this competition ceased and she managed to use the appropriate words in both languages (although the increasing predominance of English complicated this task). (McLaughlin, 1984, p. 80)

In general, however, Leopold found no evidence that bilingualism in any way influenced the development of either language. Each developed as they would in a monolingual.

Another study from early in last century is useful for comparison with Ronjat's and Leopold's. Madorah Smith reported in 1935 on the learning of English and Chinese by eight children from the same family. The parents were American missionaries, and all their children were born in China. The parents spoke both Chinese and English to the children, who apparently confused the two languages until about age 3. Their preference was for their parents' native English, but they sometimes used Chinese even when playing alone together. Unlike the Ronjats and the Leopolds, the parents of the children in Smith's study mixed the languages, each parent speaking Chinese at times and English at others.

Tabouret-Keller (1962) reported a more recent study of early bilingualism in a family where the parents mixed the two languages. The little girl's mother was raised in a poor rural area and spoke both her native German and the French she had learned in school. The child's father was a mine worker who had learned both German and French as a child. According to Tabouret-Keller's account, both parents mixed the two languages in speaking with the child, using French about twice as often as German. Not surprisingly, the child had a larger French than German vocabulary by the time she was 2 years old by a margin of about three to one. She also mixed German and French words in about 60% of her sentences. While mixing would be expected under the circumstances described, the amount of language mixing done by this child exceeded what would be predicted given the proportion of French she heard. But then, of course, the parents were not the only influence on their child's language growth. The family lived in an area where German was spoken and this was the language of the child's playmates.

Numerous other studies report the mixing of the child's two languages (Engel, 1965; Ruke-Dravina, 1965, 1967; Totten, 1960; Zareba, 1953) or three languages in the case of a trilingual environment (Murrell, 1966). One of these studies was particularly interesting for the conclusions it reached about the nature of language structure. Engel's son, who was learning both English and Italian, produced a number of hybrid words, usually English words with Italian endings, and experienced some semantic confusion between the two languages. The sound systems, however, were entirely distinct, leading Engel to conclude that the phonological system is somehow separate from the semantic and morphological systems.

Oksaar (1970) supported this conclusion in his study of a bilingual child. The child spoke Estonian with his parents and Swedish with his playmates. The sound systems of the two languages are similar, and it is usually the case that children have more difficulty keeping similar systems distinct. Even though the child was in constant contact with a Swedish-speaking playmate, Oksaar found no evidence that Swedish influenced her son's Estonian pronunciation. There was, however, evidence of mixing in his morphology and syntax. Like Engel's child, this one tended to add endings from one language to words of the other. In contrast, Itoh and Hatch, studying the language development of a Japanese-speaking child learning English from 2;6, found an early confusion especially in the sound system. Specifically, they found that the Japanese sound system influenced his English pronunciation (1978, pp. 80–83).

It seems that learning the sound system may be a different sort of task from learning other language systems. Johnson and Lancaster (1998) studied a child learning English and Norwegian, focusing on the speech sounds from 1;2 to 1;9. They found that the child did not treat the two languages as a unified system but appeared to maintain a separate system for each. Analyzing the language development of a 3-year-old Spanish-speaking child acquiring English, Hernandez "found that the influence of the new sound system was initially preeminent, suggesting that acquisition of the sound system is especially important for a child of this age learning a second language" (McLaughlin, 1978, p. 104). Hernandez also reported the more general observation that Spanish-speaking children attempting to speak English often resorted to using Spanish words and grammar with English pronunciation.

If children tend to keep the sound systems of their two languages separate, what about the other systems? While some children appear not to confuse or mix their two languages, early mixing seems to be much more typical. Crystal identifies three stages of development in early childhood bilingualism:

1. Children build a vocabulary of words from both languages, which only rarely are translation equivalents of each other.
2. When they begin to combine words in two- and three-word sentences, words from both languages are used within the same sentence. But the amount of mixing declines rapidly.
3. As the vocabulary grows larger in each language, children begin to learn translation equivalents (e.g., chat and cat or friend and amigo). (adapted from Crystal, 1987, p. 363)

For Crystal, these stages constitute evidence that acquiring a single language and acquiring two languages are different processes. On the face of it, this appears to be true but if we think about the processes from a broader perspective, they don't seem quite so disparate. Both bilingual and monolingual children initially acquire a single label for common objects or actions and only rarely have synonyms in their early vocabularies. When they begin to combine words into sentences, bilingual children use the words they have. Assuming that they attempt to express the same semantic relations as monolingual children, and there is no evidence to the contrary, then they must necessarily mix their two languages. Otherwise, given the nature of their vocabularies, they would be limited in what they could express. As their vocabularies expand, monolingual children *and* bilingual children add synonyms. So while a case can be made for different *behavior* in bilingual and monolingual children, the different behavior may not signal different acquisition processes.

In addition to the ones cited here, there have been a number of other studies of early bilingualism, most of them case studies and thus inconsistent in their objectives, observations, and purpose. Even with such inconsistency, however, it seems that certain conditions facilitate the acquisition of two languages. In general, it seems to be the case that Grammont's advice to his friend Ronjat was sound. Young children experience less confusion between their two languages if those two languages are kept distinct. They seem to have little trouble learning the separate languages of their two parents, or the language of their parents and the language of their peers or other caretaker. The distinction, however, need not be embodied in people. Ruke-Dravina (1967) observed situational specificity in which children playing with the same playmates used their parents' language, Swedish, when playing in the home and Latvian, the playmates' language, when playing outside. The studies also agree that balanced bilingualism is rare and sooner or later one language dominates. It also seems to be true that once a particular language becomes predominant, it is difficult for the child to switch back to the other language. There may even be a period during which the child refuses to use either language, a silent period until some degree of balance is attained (Engel, 1966; Leopold, 1949b).

What is abundantly clear is that children who grow up bilingual or multilingual are neither linguistically nor educationally at risk. There is no evidence whatsoever that acquiring more than one language is detrimental. On the contrary, "By the time these children arrive in school, the vast majority have reached the same stage of linguistic development as have their monolingual peers" (Crystal, 1987, p. 363). In addition, they have another language. Bilingualism is clearly an advantage.

SCHOOL BILINGUALISM

The most obvious differences between home and school bilingualism are the age of the child learner and the setting in which the languages are acquired. These are, indeed, compelling differences, but common sense tells us that there are more. As every parent knows, children appear to perform amazing feats of learning—linguistic and otherwise—during the first few years of life. But as every primary teacher knows, the learning feats of young school children are no less impressive. Moreover, for all the emphasis we place on the home environment for language acquisition, we know that there is a great deal of variability in children's homes—in the amount and variety of talk and reading, for example. And yet, children from all homes learn one, two, or more languages with apparent ease. All this argues that influences other than age and setting account for differences between home and school bilingualism. Another major difference between home and school bilingualism appears to be the kind of language that occurs in school. A number of researchers and educators have observed that the language used in schools is significantly different from the language used outside classrooms. Margaret Donaldson (1978) characterizes the difference in terms of children's thinking. They are quite capable thinkers before they begin school, but their thinking tends to be "directed outwards on to the real, meaningful, shifting, distracting world." Success in school, however, requires them to learn "to turn language and thought in upon themselves," to direct their own thought processes in a thoughtful manner. Linguistically, this means that children must be able not only to talk but to choose what they will say, "not just to interpret but to weigh possible interpretations." In short, they "must become capable of manipulating symbols" (pp. 87–88). Children must learn these new thinking and language skills in contact with the language of the school—the formal, abstract language that is largely decontextualized, logical, and expository. The informal language of the home is, in contrast, context-bound, sequential, and intuitive.

Learning language in school is made easier when children have been previously exposed to the literary functions of language by being around people who read and by having books read to them. Still, a great many children find the language demands of the school very difficult to meet. When the language of the school is also a second language for the child, the problem is compounded. Children learning a second language benefit, as do monolingual children, from literate homes. Monolingual or bilingual, children who know about books and the language of books have a better chance of success. Unless, of course, the language of the school can be better suited to match the experience of the children. As we shall see, in school second language programs, this seldom happens.

The majority of children in North America achieve whatever degree of bilingualism they possess in school. Whether they are adding the dominant language (usually English) to their home language or adding a minority or foreign language, children may encounter any one of a number of different formal language programs. These include immersion, two-way immersion, bilingual, FLES (foreign languages in the elementary school), and a hands-off approach, sometimes called submersion.

Immersion

One of the most promising of the second language programs in elementary schools is immersion. The most comprehensive research literature comes from the Canadian experiment in bilingualism, French immersion. Swain (1976) listed 114 such research reports, and dozens more have appeared each year for the past two decades. Throughout Quebec in the 1960s, the protection of the French language became a sensitive political issue. It became apparent to Anglophone parents that their children's future in Quebec would be brighter if they spoke both their native English and the language of the majority of the population of Quebec, French. Thus began what has since become a national movement in bilingual education, government-supported French immersion programs. The identifying characteristic of immersion is the exclusive use of the second language in school. Teachers must be bilingual because the children will initially speak only in English. Teachers, however, will respond in French, and gradually children start to use French themselves. For the first few years, all instruction in all subjects is in French. For children who begin immersion in kindergarten, English is usually introduced in third grade (or in fourth grade in some programs), and the amount of English gradually is increased until the proportion is approximately 60% English and 40% French.

The children in the first immersion classes are in or have completed university as of this writing. As might be expected, they have been studied rather extensively. The results are, on the whole, positive. Not only do children acquire a better level of competence in French than those in more traditional language classes, they also tend to have more favorable attitudes toward French-Canadians. The research does not indicate, however, that immersion is a panacea. Although their language proficiency is impressive, children from immersion classes are a long way from native proficiency, partly because they have extensive academic or "school" competence but less social language proficiency in French. One very important finding on which nearly all studies agree, however, is that the children's proficiency in English is not at all adversely affected by their acquisition of French in immersion programs. Although they may lag slightly behind their peers in second or third grade, by fifth or sixth grade, they catch up.

Since the original immersion programs began, there have been other experiments with variations—early partial, delayed, late, and double immersion among them. *Early partial immersion* begins either in kindergarten or first grade with the day divided between the child's first and second language. Initial evaluations of English-speaking children in French partial immersion have shown that their English language skills are no better than peers in total immersion and that their French skills are worse (although better than children in FLES programs) (Barik & Swain, 1974; 1975; Genesee, 1983; Swain & Lapkin, 1982). Even though early immersion has been largely successful, the program has suffered very heavy attrition rates across Canada. The attrition rate suggests that immersion is not the right program for every child. Moreover:

> Clinical studies indicate that there may be a subgroup of children for whom early programs are not suitable. These children could be termed developmentally immature in the sense that their cognitive and linguistic skills are not developed adequately to meet the demands of a bilingual academic environment. (Wiss, 1989, p. 518)

Rather than have their children face the possible stigma of withdrawing from immersion, and worrying that their children's education may suffer if they begin French immersion too young, some parents prefer to delay French until later. *Delayed immersion* is essentially the same as early total immersion except that it begins in third or fourth grade. *Late immersion* is yet another alternative for some children. It begins in sixth grade or later and lasts for 1 or 2 years. Results of evaluation studies of late immersion indicate that the students suffer no harmful effects to their native language, do very well in French, and develop positive attitudes toward French-speaking people. They do not, however, do as well in French as children of the same age who have had either early or delayed immersion (Barik, Swain, & Guadins, 1976; Connors, Menard, & Singh, 1978; Swain, 1974).

Success in immersion led some educators to experiment with *double immersion*. Taking the view that if immersion in one language works, some schools are trying immersion in two languages. A study conducted in Montreal of English-speaking children immersed in both French and Hebrew showed promising results in both languages without detriment to English (Genesee & Lambert, 1983; Genesee, Tucker, & Lambert, 1976, cited in Reich, 1986, p. 222).

FOREIGN LANGUAGES IN ELEMENTARY SCHOOL (FLES)

Although immersion is a fairly common educational program in Canada, it is not widespread on the continent. More familiar, perhaps, is the taking of at least one foreign language in school. These courses, unlike immersion and bilingual programs, do not attempt to teach other curricular subjects *in* the foreign language. Rather, language is treated as a subject in its own right. Typically, both the amount and the kind of exposure to the new language is limited in comparison to immersion. The time devoted to the foreign language might be as little as 20 minutes three times per week or as much as 50 minutes per day. During that time, teaching is likely to focus more on the language itself than on content or meaning.

McLaughlin (1985) reported that early FLES programs were not dramatically successful. Although there was greater acceptance of foreign language classes beginning in the elementary school, children did not learn the languages quickly and easily when taught for only one hour per day. One study did report that students who began learning a second language in elementary school generally performed better than children who began in high school (Vocolo, 1967), but most evaluations reported that children lost interest by fifth or sixth grades and motivation became a major problem (Page, 1966). These studies are strongly at odds with the immersion studies, and the reason likely lies in the teaching method. Until recently, and even now in some schools, most FLES teachers used a behaviorist approach. As they grew older, the children tired of pattern drills and structure manipulation. Since these constituted the children's only exposure to the language, their learning declined. Such methods were never used in immersion where the focus was on the subject matter being taught rather than the structure of the language.

More recent FLES programs have employed different methods with more positive results, but the language proficiency level achieved is still far less than that in immersion programs. Recent FLES programs have also been less ambitious in their goals, emphasizing oral skills and cultural awareness. Full communicative competence in the target language is not expected, and both parents and students are told so from the beginning. The most common languages taught in current FLES programs are Spanish, French, and German, although Japanese, Cantonese, and Mandarin are gaining in popularity.

Immersion and FLES programs are intended for children who speak the dominant language to learn a second language. Educationally, they are important, but they are not critical to the life of the child in the way that language programs for minority speakers are. There are hundreds of thousands of children in both the United States and Canada who speak a minority language at home and then face schooling in English. The next two types of programs attempt to meet their needs.

Two-Way Immersion

An increasing number of school districts in the United States are experimenting with programs designed to develop language proficiency in two languages while promoting academic achievement. Such programs are popular because they are seen as an effective way of educating both majority and minority children. Borrowing from the principles of immersion, these programs integrate majority and minority children in classes that provide content as well as language development in both languages. This approach permits minority children to maintain and develop their language and majority children to acquire a second language. It also permits minority children to learn English. These programs are seen as empowering minority children because they officially sanction their first language. Christian (1996), in her review of two-way immersion programs, points out that "the social interactional features of two-way immersion programs support better opportunities for language development. Both L1 and L2 acquisition are facilitated by interaction between the "novice" (the learner of the language) and "experts" (fluent speakers of the language)" (p. 67). In other words, children are able to learn from one another in an environment that gives equal value to both languages. They benefit from having native speaker models of their own age and interests.

These programs are relatively new and rare. Christian reports only 169 such schools in 92 school districts in the United States. Most of the schools with these programs offer them in Spanish and English in the elementary school level, and so it is still early to measure their effect. Emerging research, however, "point to their effectiveness in promoting academic achievement for minority and majority students, along with high levels of bilingual proficiency for both groups" (Christian, 1996, p. 72). There is also growing evidence that children in these programs develop friendships that are defined by neither race nor ethnicity. This is, in itself, an argument for these kinds of programs. As you will see in the following paragraphs, two-way immersion programs resemble certain bilingual programs. The difference is in the goals, particularly as they relate to the inclusion of majority English speakers in the model.

Bilingual Programs

Language programs intended to maintain the child's native language within an English-speaking environment or to ease the transition between the language of the home and the language of the school are commonly called bilingual programs. The introduction of English in school and the widespread use of English in the community may cause children to lose much of their native language proficiency, unless there is a concerted effort to maintain it. *Maintenance bilingualism* is intended to protect the native language while introducing English as the language of the school. Such programs are not popular in the United States, although a few exist in areas with concentrated non-English populations. There are also a few programs for Native American children, designed to maintain their native language and culture. A number of researchers report studies of children taking part in small experimental programs for Choctaw (Doebler & Mardis, 1980), Navajo (Rosier & Farella, 1976), and Hopi language programs (Haussler, Tompkins, & Jeanne, 1987). Some of these are maintenance programs while others might more appropriately be considered *transitional* (described in the next paragraph). In general, the researchers conclude that children benefit from such programs. Nevertheless, because of the small number of children and the limited print material available for educational purposes, the programs are not widespread. This is particularly unfortunate in the case of aboriginal languages, some of which have only a few hundred speakers left, many of them elderly. In Canada, on the other hand, with its official policy of bilingualism and multiculturalism, there are a number of bilingual maintenance programs operating in languages including German, Ukrainian, Hebrew, French, Spanish, Italian, Cree, and Inuktitut.

A second type of bilingual program is termed *transitional*. In this type of program, the child's home language is used in the early years of schooling and the dominant language introduced later. Transitional programs are widely used. In India, for example, where more than 200 languages are spoken, at least 80 are used in schools, mostly in the first 4 years, after which students are switched to one of the major languages (Khubchandani, 1978, cited in Reich, 1986, p. 224). Canada also has a number of transitional programs in place for Chinese, Ukrainian, German, Hebrew, Italian, and some aboriginal languages. The U.S. government as well as some state governments sponsor programs for as many as 58 different languages (Tucker & Gray, 1980), including aboriginal languages.

Surprisingly, very few evaluations of transitional bilingual programs have been published. The ones that have been, including one done in Mexico and one in the Philippines, addressed program effectiveness from the perspective of proficiency in the second language only. Not surprisingly, they revealed that the longer the children spent being educated in English (the second language in both countries), the better their English. Neither the children's native language proficiency nor their attitude toward schooling was considered, and many educators would consider these to be important factors in the overall development and education of the child. Similarly, a study on the effects of bilingual programming on Choctaw children measured only the children's performance in English. Even so, researchers Doebler and Mardis found that the bilingual program resulted in superior performance on two of five measures (social studies and science) and no significant difference on other measures. It should be pointed out, however, that in studies of bilingual programs, "no significance" is not negative. *No significance* means that there is no statistically significant difference between the scores of children in bilingual programs and children in monolingual programs. But as Zappert and Cruz (1977) pointed out, this in itself is significant since the bilingual children have the advantage of another language.

Although relatively few global studies have measured the effects of bilingual programs, there is an emerging body of research on the acquisition of literacy in such programs. Although most researchers and educators seem to agree that, in theory, a child learns to read a familiar language more easily than an unfamiliar one, the decision whether to introduce reading in the child's native language or English is not so easily answered. Haussler et al. (1987) argue very persuasively that the decision must be made on a case by case basis after considering a number of factors. A major one is whether children are "active participants in a biliterate environment" (p. 84). In other words, children need the support of an environment in which people practice literacy in both languages. If this condition is not met, success is less likely.

Submersion

The success of immersion in Canada and in some U.S. communities has led some educators to the erroneous conclusion that the best language teaching program is none at all. In other words, if immersion children can learn the new language in an environment where they are taught all the school subjects in that language, can't minority children do the same with English? In *submersion*, children are placed in classes where all their subjects are taught in the language of the school even though they may not know the language at all. According to Reich, this is the predominant teaching method for minority speakers in Sweden, New Zealand, China, Belgium, Australia, and many other countries (1986, p. 223). It is also the method by which many older immigrants learned English in the United States and Canada.

But is it effective? It is a great credit to the learning powers of children that it does work for some. But on the whole, it is neither an effective nor an humane way to learn a language. The U.S. Supreme Court recognized the inadequacy of submersion in the landmark *Lau vs. Nichols* case, proclaiming that submersion does not provide equal educational opportunity for children who do not speak English.

Although it may not be immediately obvious, there are several important differences between submersion and immersion. In fact, they have more differences than similarities. In Table 5.1, summarizing the differences, we see that the only real similarity between immersion and submersion is that children are not initially proficient in the language of instruction. A major difference is that children in immersion classes are all at the same level of proficiency in the unfamiliar language while children being submersed in English will likely have had varying amounts of exposure to the language. Immersion children come from the dominant culture where their language is protected and respected, and when they begin school, they are permitted to speak in their native language for the first few months. Their bilingual teacher understands their first language and encourages them in their second. In contrast, children submerged in English come from minority cultures, and there is little if any protection or respect for their languages. When they begin school, they must use English from the first day, and if they do not, their teachers will probably not understand them.

Table 5.1 Comparison of Immersion and Submersion

		Immersion	*Submersion*
Children	Same level of L1	Yes	No
	L1 "protected"	Yes	No
	Allowed to use L1 initially	Yes	No
	Members of dominant culture	Usually	No
	All speak same L1	Usually	Rarely
Teachers	Understand L1 and L2	Yes	Rarely
	Specially educated in L2 methods	Yes	Occasionally
	Understand children's culture	Yes	Rarely
Program	Optional	Yes	No
	Specially funded	Usually	Rarely
	Available to every child	Rarely	Yes
	Taught entirely in L2	No	Yes

In the immersion classroom, the teacher knows both the children's native language and the language being taught. The submersion teacher will know English and possibly one other language, but the children in the class will rarely all come from the same language background. The immersion teacher has been educated in language acquisition and in methods for teaching children who do not know the language in which she is teaching. Some teachers in the submersion situation may have had Teaching English as a Second Language (TESL) training, but many must rely on their usual teaching practices. Finally, immersion is optional and prestigious. If children or their parents are unhappy with the program or the children's progress, good educational alternatives exist. Immersion is also specially funded by a government anxious to promote bilingualism and enjoys an elitist reputation in the community. No one can make such claims for submersion.

We have seen that children acquire a second language under a number of different circumstances and that they do so with varying degrees of success. A number of questions are thus raised both for theory and practice. The practical issues will be addressed in Chapter 9 and 10 after we have looked at the particular circumstances in which two children acquired their second language very successfully. In the remainder of this chapter, we will see how situation, proficiency, and a number of other factors are addressed in theories of second language acquisition.

ISSUES IN SECOND LANGUAGE ACQUISITION THEORY

Complicated as it is, the task of formulating an adequate theory of first language acquisition is simple in comparison with the task of formulating an adequate theory of second language acquisition. This is true because the number of factors that may vary in second language acquisition is far greater than those in first language acquisition. Spolsky (1985) framed the problem by breaking down into its component parts the central question about second language learning: *Who learns how much of what language under what conditions?*

Who can be anyone of any age, ability, and intelligence and with any attitude or personality. *Learns* refers to the process itself and raises questions about the different kinds of learning there are, about innateness, about transfer between languages, and about conscious and unconscious learning, etc. *How much of* refers to the amount of language learning that takes place and what aspect of the language is learned (e.g., syntax, phonology, semantics, and culture). *What language* refers to the target language being learned, and *under what conditions* addresses the kind and amount of exposure to the second language, which leads to learning (pp. 269–270).

Because first and second language acquisition have two essential elements in common, namely learners and language, it is not surprising that the theories devised to account for them would have at least basic similarities. In general, they do, and some theories of first language acquisition fit the data of second language acquisition with little or no modification. For example, a behavioristic model has only the additional requirement that the habit of the first language be eradicated in the learning of the second. Second language acquisition theories, thus, are partly derived from first language acquisition theories, but because of the variability in the factors identified by Spolsky, they are necessarily more complex. In fact, no one theory has yet been put forward that is comprehensive enough to account for all these factors and the interactions among them. Nevertheless, there has been no reluctance to theorize about second language learning. The details of the many theories that have been advanced in recent years are well beyond the scope of this chapter. Table 5.2, however, identifies nine such theories together with the researchers usually credited with proposing them, sources for recent discussion or evaluation, and some indication of their scope.

Under the heading *scope* in the table are the designations *learner, process, proficiency, language,* and *condition.* These correspond to different aspects of Spolsky's question. Learner variables (*who*) are those attributes of learners that influence their success in language acquisition. These include, among others, age of the learner, cognitive style, and socio-psychological attitudes toward speakers of the target language. *Process (learns)* refers to the internal systems devised by the learner or the strategies used in learning, understanding, and producing the new language. *Proficiency (how much of)* refers to those things that affect the amount of learning that takes place and the level of mastery a learner attains. *Language* takes a slightly broader view than Spolsky's and includes features of the target language as well as the nature of the input to the learner. Finally, *conditions* addresses the situational factors, (e.g., classroom or naturalistic environments) that influence second language learning. In the discussion that follows, I examine the variables in turn, noting the strengths of particular theories for dealing with each one.

Table 5.2 Nine Theories of Second Language Acquisition

Theory/scope	Origin	Evaluation/discussion
Acculturation		
Learner Proficiency Conditions	Schumann (1978a, 1978b, 1981a, 1981b, 1982)	McLaughlin (1987) Ellis (1985) Larsen-Freeman (1983) Larsen-Freeman & Long (1991)
Accommodation		
Learner Conditions Proficiency	Giles et al. (1977) Giles & Byrne (1982)	Ellis (1985)
Behaviorism		
Conditions Language	Skinner (1957)	McLaughlin (1978, 1984, 1987)
Cognitive		
Learner Process	McLaughlin et al. (1983); McLeod & McLaughlin (1986); Segalowitz (1986)	McLaughlin (1987)
Discourse		
Learner Conditions Process	Hatch (1978c, 1978d)	Ellis (1985) Larsen-Freeman (1983)
Interlanguage		
Process Language Proficiency	Selinker (1972)	McLaughlin (1987) Ellis (1985)
Monitor Model		
Learner Process Conditions Language	Krashen (1977a, 1977b, 1978, 1981, 1982, 1985)	McLaughlin (1987) Spolsky (1985) Ellis (1985) Larsen-Freeman (1983); Gregg (1984)
Neurofunctional		
Process Language	Lamendella (1977, 1979)	Larsen-Freeman (1983); Ellis (1985)
Universal		
Process Grammar Language	Chomsky (1980) Greenberg (1966, 1974); Wode (1981)	McLaughlin (1987) Gass (1984) Ellis (1985)

Learner Variables

It is fairly obvious that there is more variation among second language learners than among first language learners. Because second language learners are older than first language learners, they will have had a variety of linguistic, learning, and life experiences that infants learning their first language will not. While any number of learner factors may influence the course of language development, researchers have identified a number of general factors believed to contribute to individual learner differences. Among these are age, aptitude, cognitive variation, and personality traits.

There is a vast body of research literature that attempts to describe and explain differences that are attributable to the *age of the learner*. The results are mixed, as might be expected, but what has emerged with some clarity are the findings that:

> a) in general, the ability to learn languages does not diminish with age; b) more specifically, young children's superiority as language learners is restricted to their learning of the sound system. (see McLaughlin, 1981, pp. 23–32)

Some researchers believe that *aptitude*, or some kind of specialized language learning ability, plays a central role in language acquisition. The research findings are dubious, however, in part because it is impossible to know with any certainty just what cognitive abilities aptitude comprises. If there is an aptitude factor in second language acquisition, it is likely that it is a rather specialized aptitude that governs only the ability to learn in formal settings, and probably not all of these. Otherwise, there would not be so many successfully bilingual people in the world—in Asia and Europe, for example—who have learned their languages either at home or in school. For most educators, however, the question of aptitude is, *in practice*, not very important. Children need to and have the right to learn the language of the school whether or not some test judges them capable or not. The educator's major concern is not with measuring aptitude, if indeed such a thing could be done, but with planning a language learning environment that enhances every child's learning opportunities.

Cognitive style refers to the ways in which individuals process information or approach particular tasks. Although much of the literature on cognitive styles seems to suggest that they are dichotomous (i.e., that people tend to possess one trait or its opposite), it is more likely the case that people "show a tendency towards one pole or the other, with their scores on cognitive style tests arranged along a continuum between the poles" (Larsen-Freeman & Long, 1991, p. 192). A number of dimensions are included under the heading *cognitive style*, including:

1. types of learning inherent in cognitive tasks,
2. variation in *strategies* individuals employ, and
3. variation in personal *cognitive styles* of learning. (Brown, 1980, p. 80)

Types of Learning.   According to Robert Gagne (1965), people employ eight different types of learning for different tasks ranging from signal learning, involving a classically conditioned response, to problem solving, requiring "the internal events usually referred to as 'thinking'" (pp. 58–59, quoted in Brown, 1980, p. 81). Brown claims that learners use all eight types of learning depending upon a number of factors including the aspect of language being learned and the learner's previous experience of language learning. Because language learning is highly complex, it is unlikely that the different levels of learning will proceed independently.

Variation in Strategy.   An important part of language learning is problem solving. People vary greatly in how they reach solutions. In general, we distinguish between two broad types of strategies—learning strategies and communication strategies. The former refers to the ways in which learners attempt to work out meanings and structures in language and store them for later recall. The latter refers to how learners manage to encode and express meaning in order to communicate in a language. Learning strategies include such things as memorization, overgeneralization, and inference, and learners make use of different strategies and different combinations of strategies for different purposes. Moreover, it is likely that older children and adults have better developed processing capabilities and thus more to build on as they approach the learning of a new language (see McLaughlin, 1981, p. 30).

To communicate in a second language, learners generally rely on essentially the same strategies as they do in learning it. Brown (1980) claims, in fact, that learning and communication represent the input and output of the same process. Some strategies work equally well for both. For example, the strategy, *join a group and act like you know what's going on* (Tabors, 1997, p. 76) can work for both learning and communicating, though possibly better for learning than for communicating. Nevertheless, there are differences. It is very common for second language learners to avoid structures or words about which they are uncertain or which they find difficult. This strategy obviously has no parallel in learning. On the other hand, generalization (e.g., from a known form to an unknown form) is a productive learning strategy that also occurs in communication, although it is difficult to detect because its use results in a correct form. Overgeneralization, in contrast, is not a successful learning strategy, but is all too apparent in communication since it results in an incorrect form.

Variation in Personal Cognitive Styles.   The third dimension of cognitive style refers to the particular way in which a learner approaches a learning situation. In learning language, people may vary in the amount of explanation they want or need or in their preference for oral or written presentation. Other dimensions of cognitive style include field dependence vs. independence, reflectivity vs. impulsivity, tolerance vs. intolerance of ambiguity, and the tendency to skeletonize or to embroider in the recall of cognitive material (Brown, 1980, pp. 90–97; Hatch, 1983).

Personality traits are those attitudes, feelings, and emotions that may influence an individual's learning. They are sometimes called the affective variables and include the learner's attitude toward the language being learned and its native speakers, motivation for learning the language, and ego factors such as self-esteem, degree of inhibition, and capacity for empathy, among others.

Obviously, a complete theory of second language acquisition must account for learner differences attributable to personality and cognitive factors. For educators, however, the concern is a more practical one. They need to understand how such factors influence second language acquisition in order to have some idea how to plan instruction for the introverted as well as the extroverted child and the analytic as well as the synthetic thinker.

Situation

Situational Variables are those things in the language learner's environment that influence the learning and the use of the new language. In short, they encompass everything the learner sees and hears in the new language, and they are highly significant:

> The quality of the environment is of paramount importance to success in learning a new language. If students are exposed to a list of words and their translations, together with a few simple readings in the new language, they will perhaps be able to attain some degree of reading skill in language, but listening and speaking skills will remain fallow. (Dulay, Burt, & Krashen, 1982, p. 13)

ESL teachers have long lamented the fact that language forms that students apparently master in class sometimes give them all kinds of trouble outside. Several years ago, I had a similar experience with a Chinese graduate student who was taking an oral examination for his master's degree. Throughout the examining period, he answered the questions well but continually confused the personal pronouns, producing sentences such as "English is a difficult language because she is very different from Chinese," and "My mother could speak only one language and he was happy when I learned more languages." I had never heard him make these errors in the 2 years I had known him. The question of why a tense situation causes errors has potential impact on our understanding of the very processes of language learning and production, for clearly there is an interaction between situation of use and the learner's ability to recall correctly a previously learned form.

It would be impossible to identify all the environmental factors that potentially influence language learning, but researchers have identified four broad categories of factors that are believed to have a significant impact. These include:

1. the naturalness of the environment,
2. the learner's role in communication,
3. the availability of concrete referents, and
4. target language models. (Dulay, Burt, & Krashen, 1982, pp. 13–43)

Naturalness of the Environment.   Evidence suggests that learners perform better when they "are exposed to natural language, where the focus is on communication" rather than in "a formal environment, where focus is on the conscious acquisition of linguistic rules or the manipulation of linguistic forms" (Dulay, Burt, & Krashen, 1982, p. 42). Certainly, this conclusion is consistent with many of the studies reviewed earlier in this chapter and with the experiences of the children reported in Chapter 6. It also seems to be the case, however, that some exposure to the formal properties of language may be helpful for adult learners.

The Learner's Role in Communication.   The quality of language learning is also affected by the types of communication in which the learner is most frequently engaged. Communication exchanges may be classified as one-way, restricted two-way, or full two-way. One-way exchanges occur when the learner listens to or reads the target language but does not respond. Restricted two-way exchanges occur when the learner listens and responds either non-verbally (e.g., by nodding) or in a language other than the target language. In full two-way exchanges, the learner responds in the target language.

There is some evidence that in the earliest stages of language learning, one-way and restricted two-way exchanges, may actually facilitate language acquisition for some learners. A silent period lasting until the learner is ready to speak seems to be beneficial in some classroom situations. Gary (1975), studying 50 English-speaking children learning Spanish, found that the children who did not engage in any oral response during the first 14 weeks of the course performed better in listening comprehension than did children in classes where oral responses were required. What was more surprising, perhaps, was her finding that the children who had kept silent did as well in speaking as their peers who had been speaking for 14 weeks (cited in Dulay, Burt, & Krashen, 1982, pp. 24–26).

An important aspect of the language learning environment seems to be the availability of visible referents. It is much easier to understand a language in which one has limited proficiency if there is adequate context. I once witnessed Stephen Krashen illustrate this point in a simple counting task. He first stood before us and counted to 10 in a language I didn't understand. He could have been giving directions for making a moon landing for all I knew. He then repeated the exercise holding up one finger, then two, etc. as he said the corresponding number. The second time he did so, I was able to remember 6 of the 10 numbers. As a counter example, most of us could sit and listen to Radio Moscow for hours, days, or even weeks without ever learning six words of Russian. Talking about what is present and observable helps the learner understand and is thus crucial to acquiring language.

Another type of situational variable has to do with the source, or models, of language the learner encounters. The different people learners come into contact with influence the language they learn. It seems to be the case that learners neither learn nor even attend to all the language to which they are exposed. Research on speaker models indicates that learners apparently prefer some sources over others. Milon (1975) reported, for example, that when a 7-year-old Japanese-speaking child moved to Hawaii, he learned the Hawaiian Creole English of the children around him rather than the standard English of his teacher. Immersion studies in the United States and Canada have reported similar findings and also speculated that a child's language development is actually hampered when the only models are adults. Children who entered immersion in kindergarten were found to have some grammatical deficiencies in French even after 7 years in the program (Bruck, Lambert, & Tucker, 1975). Remember that there are no native-speaking peers in immersion classes. Children seem to prefer peers as language models over both teachers and parents. There is evidence, too, that they make more use of models who are members of their own social or ethnic group than those who are not (Benton, 1964). This is consistent with the immersion findings: Having no native-speaking peer group, the children served as models for one another and their language reflected the fact that they were non-native speakers. Language itself is, then, an important variable in the acquisition of a second language.

Language.   Learners are not solely responsible for their language learning. We saw in our discussion of social interaction theory in Chapter 3 that the attempts caretakers make to focus the child's attention or to focus their own language on what is occupying the child's attention contribute to the child's language learning. In second language acquisition, a great deal of research has gone into understanding the characteristics of the language input that promotes learning (foreigner talk) and into the feedback the learner provides and its effect on subsequent input (discourse studies).

Studies on language input focus on describing *foreigner talk*, or the modifications native speakers make when talking with someone they perceive to have less than native proficiency in their language. A number of common modifications have been identified. For example, native speakers typically choose topics concerned with the present, they check more often to see whether they are being understood, they repeat or paraphrase both their own utterances and the other speaker's, and they give shorter responses. Hatch (1983) has pointed out that ESL teachers commonly speak more slowly and use intonation patterns that help the learner to identify syntactic groupings and boundaries. The conversation between Wuxing, a Chinese graduate student, and his teacher in Table 5.3 shows the teacher making several adjustments to her speech to accommodate Wuxing's level of English proficiency, as she perceived it.

Understanding the adjustments native speakers make in talking with non-native speakers contributes significantly to our understanding of input, but it is only one side of the coin. Native speakers do not determine input nor the course of conversation all by themselves. Learners provide feedback and this feedback influences the subsequent input they receive. It makes sense, then, to study the interaction that occurs in conversations between native and non-native speakers. *Discourse studies* examine conversational turn-taking, how topics of conversation are nominated and developed, and how meaning is negotiated. They also examine the differences between interactions that occur between adult speakers and those that occur between an adult and a child.

Hatch (1978b) has identified certain characteristics of adult-child interactions. As she describes them, a typical interaction begins when the child requests the adult's attention. "Mummy, look!" would be a common way of opening the communication channel. The adult normally responds by naming the object that has

Table 5.3 Foreigner Talk Modifications

Example	Modification
Wuxing: I need, uh, the book. Terry Piper: The book? Which book?	*Repetition.* She repeats part of his utterance even though she has understood him.
W: From class. Yellow, I think. T: The yellow book from class. Let me see. The book about reading in a second language? W: No. Uh. Not about that.	*Repetition* and *expansion.* She expands his fragment into a well-formed sentence.
T: Not about reading in a second language. Was it today or last week? W: Last week.	*Self-repetition.* She repeats her own previous utterance.
T: Last week. (Removing a book from her shelf.) This one? W: No, about universals.	*Repetition* and *"here and now."* She repeats her own previous utterance and then offers visual aids.
T: Oh, language universals? Was it by Hatch? Who wrote it? W: I don't know.	*Repetition* and *confirmation check.* She paraphrases to confirm that he has understood her question.
T: Was it this one? W: No.	*"Here and now."*
T: Well, have a look. Books about universals are there. W: Yellow.	*Short response.* *Repetition.*
T: Yes. But I don't classify them by color. Do you understand "classify"? W: Yes. But maybe I, uh, blind to color.	*Comprehension check.* She asks overtly whether he understands.
T: You're colorblind? W: Yes, maybe. (Laughing)	*Expansion* and *confirmation check.*

attracted the child's attention: "Oh yes, a bluebird." At this point, depending upon the age of the child and the particular situation, this conversation might be abandoned and another nominating sequence begun, or it might be developed. Development usually proceeds with the adult requesting some comment on the established topic. "It's a pretty one, isn't it?" or "Why do you think it's sitting in the apple tree?" would invite the child to elaborate.

These conversational routines seem to help children to learn language, although it must be recalled that children in some other cultures appear to learn language without much overt assistance from adults. If children and non-native speakers learn language with these modifications to input and accommodation in discourse, and if they also learn language without them, there must be a variety of processing strategies that are sensitive to variations in input and feedback.

Process.   Essentially, there are two kinds of processes with which second language acquisition theory is concerned. *Cognitive processes* consist of the types of learner strategies discussed earlier. *Linguistic processes*, according to one view, "involve universal principles of grammar with which the learner is innately endowed. They provide the learner with a starting point. The task is then to scan the input to discover which rules of the target language are universal and which are specific" (Ellis, 1985, p. 17). This is, in essence, a *nativist*, or *universal-grammar*, perspective on the nature of linguistic processes.

Interlanguage theory (Selinker, 1972) takes the notion of process beyond the "starting point," referring to the learner's system at any one point in time and also to the system as it changes over time. This system is believed to be separate from the native language system and to be the product of five cognitive processes:

1. transfer of some features from the first language
2. transfer from the teaching process
3. learning strategies
4. communication strategies
5. overgeneralization of linguistic material from the target language.

The interlanguage hypothesis applies to adults and children who acquire their second language after the first is clearly established. Although it speculates about different influences on the system, the hypothesis makes little attempt to explain the learning process. Rather, it provides a useful framework in which to describe certain second language phenomena, but that is not the case with Krashen's Monitor Model.

Krashen's model rests on five hypotheses, all of which relate to second language processing. The first and, in Krashen's view, the foundational hypothesis is called the acquisition-learning hypothesis. It makes the claim that there is a distinction between acquiring language in an informal setting where attention is directed entirely at meaning, much as the first language is acquired, and learning language in a formal setting such as the classroom where attention is directed to form. Furthermore, this distinction is believed to be independent of the age of the learner or other learner variables. It is important to note that Krashen is not merely stating the obvious (i.e., the fact of environmental differences). He claims that the learner actually processes and stores language differently under the two conditions. Acquisition leads to subconscious internalization of language structures and rules while learning leads to conscious learning.

Although this distinction holds a certain intuitive appeal, there is little evidence to support it. The further claim that language, which is learned (as opposed to acquired), cannot eventually become subconscious knowledge is not only unsupported but "flies in the face of the evidence" (Spolsky, 1985, p. 271). An even more serious shortcoming of the hypothesis is that while it specifies two distinct sources of input, it fails to elucidate how the processes responsible for acquisition and learning differ from one another.

Perhaps the most important and the most controversial claim made by this hypothesis is the one that relates it to the Monitor Hypothesis. Krashen claims that the role of acquired language is to initiate utterances and control fluency while learned language is available only as an editor or monitor to correct the language output before it is uttered. What this implies is that there is no place for learned language in comprehension, and this too flies in the face of experience. Attempts to confirm the existence and use of a monitor in experimental situations have failed, and the hypothesis is further weakened by the doubt cast on the acquisition-learning hypothesis that supports it. Quite simply, if the monitor does not exist, there is no purpose for the acquisition-learning distinction and, conversely, if that distinction is false, then there can be no monitor.

The other three hypotheses, the natural order hypothesis, the input hypothesis, and the affective filter hypothesis falter in similar ways. The natural order hypothesis makes the claim that learners acquire the rules of language in a predictable order. The evidence for the claim comes mostly from studies on the order in which certain grammatical morphemes are learned by non-native speakers (e.g., Dulay & Burt, 1974; Porter, 1977). Once again, the evidence cited in support of the hypothesis is dubious. First, there are serious methodological problems with the morpheme acquisition order studies, not the least of which is that some measured accuracy of use rather than order. Second, other research has demonstrated that structures in the learners' first language influence the order and the accuracy with which they acquire the grammatical morphemes of English (McLaughlin, 1984, 1987).

The natural order hypothesis is dependent upon the fourth hypothesis, the input hypothesis. Assuming, "as Krashen does, that learners progress through 'natural' developmental sequences, we need some mechanism to account for how they go from one point to another" (McLaughlin, 1987, p. 36). Krashen claims that learners proceed from their current level of proficiency (i) to the next level (i+1) by understanding language that is just beyond their current level of proficiency. This is called comprehensible input and has the following characteristics: a) it is focused on meaning, b) it is roughly tuned to the learner's level of competence rather than finely tuned, and c) it is based in the here and now.

Among other "evidence" that Krashen states for the input hypothesis are the existence of simplified speech, the existence of a silent period, and the fact that older learners seem to make faster progress in language learning than do children. None of these is really arguable: It does seem to be the case, as we saw earlier, that a period during which speech is not required facilitates learning for some children, simplified codes play an important role when they are available, and older children and adults learn at a faster rate than younger children. Even if all of this is true however, does it constitute evidence for any particular internal process? McLaughlin, Spolsky, and Ellis think not, pointing out the absence of any explanation about how the mapping from meaning to structure occurs.

The final hypothesis comprising the Monitor Model is the affective filter hypothesis, and that it is widely questioned will come as no surprise to the reader. The affective filter is identified as "that part of the internal processing system that subconsciously screens incoming language based on what psychologists call 'affect': the learner's motives, needs, attitudes, and emotional states" (Dulay, Burt, & Krashen, 1982, p. 46). The affective filter supposedly reduces the amount of input available for natural learning by limiting what the learner pays attention to, what will be learned, and the speed at which it is learned. In other words, if a learner is extremely nervous or tense, as was the case with the Chinese graduate student described earlier, the filter purportedly keeps the learner from paying attention to certain kinds of language data. Or, if the learner harbors resentment toward speakers of the target language, the filter may limit the amount of learning that actually takes place. The learner may cling to a heavy accent, for example. But these are hypothetical instances and, as with the earlier hypotheses, the hard evidence for this one does not exist.

Unfortunately, the task of evaluating the affective filter hypothesis is further complicated by vagueness. Krashen and his colleagues have never explained just how the filter screens language intake. It would seem that unless the filter screens randomly, it would need to have available some grammar or grammatical template in order to separate those language items to ignore from those to attend to and admit. That being the case, several questions arise, including two obvious ones: What grammar is available to the beginning learner? How does the affective filter get constructed?

Fortunately, there are other theoretical approaches to processing issues. Cognitive theory takes a broader perspective than universal grammar, the monitor model, or even interlanguage, deriving its principles not from linguistic theory but from contemporary research in cognitive psychology. As we have seen, cognitive theories of language acquisition do not accord language a special status. Rather, learning a second language is viewed as learning a complex cognitive skill "because various aspects of the task must be practised and integrated into fluent performance. This requires the automatization of component sub-skills" (McLaughlin, 1987, p. 133). Automatization is one of two central concepts in cognitive theory; the other is restructuring.

In order to produce a meaningful utterance, a speaker must coordinate information of many kinds from a number of sources while making a simultaneous plan for the structure of the utterance and for its articulation. In order for all this to be accomplished in the very short time before the listener loses interest, the speaker must have automatized most of the component tasks. McLaughlin (based on Levelt, 1978) conceives of speaking as an hierarchical task structure in which the first order goal is to express a particular intention, the second is to decide on a task, and the third to formulate a series of phrases. Finally, the speaker must attend to lower-order goals, which include retrieving from memory the necessary words, activating articulatory patterns, utilizing appropriate syntactic rules, and meeting pragmatic conventions. When we consider, further, that *each* of these goals entails a number of sub-tasks, then we begin to understand the importance of automatization. Automatization occurs as a result of practice, of the repeated "mapping of the same input to the same pattern of activation over many trials" (McLaughlin, 1987, p. 134).

Restructuring refers to the constant reorganization of the internal system to accommodate new material. In second language acquisition, the internal system would be the grammar and lexicon of the target language. A beginning learner of English might, on the basis of limited exposure to English, construct the rule that all past tenses are formed by adding /d/. For *gaze, rhyme, fail,* and many verbs in English, this rule works, but then the learner encounters the past tense of *ring* and *sing*. The internal system must be restructured to accommodate this new information and the new rule might be that there are two past tense forms, with verbs rhyming with *ring* requiring a vowel change but no ending and all other verbs requiring /d/. The learner then encounters *bring* and *rust* and has to restructure the system yet again. And so on, and so on.

This particular cognitive theory is essentially human information processing. Although it is not the only cognitive approach to understanding language acquisition, it rests on the central assumption that language is acquired in the same manner as other complex cognitive skills. But this reluctance to accord a special status to language, to treat it as just another cognitive skill, is a position about which some researchers and theorists are highly skeptical.

Hatch (1983), for example, questions the closeness of the bond between cognitive development and language acquisition. She argues that the relationship cannot be causal (i.e., language acquisition cannot be dependent on cognitive development) and cites various kinds of evidence. The first is a study by Yamada (1981) showing that a child with low cognitive development (she was unable to count, although she could recite numbers, unable to give her correct birth date or age consistently, and could not name the days of the week) demonstrated complex syntactic ability (Yamada, 1981, cited in Hatch, 1983, pp. 220–221). Hatch also points out that there is no evidence that the operating principles Slobin (1973) identified for figuring out language (such as "Pay attention to the ends of words" and "Avoid exceptions") are truly cognitive strategies. They might well be unique to language. She cites as additional evidence cases of Turner's syndrome children (mentioned in Chapter 3) in which children with severe cognitive problems in visual-spatial tasks have superior language ability and cases of hydrocephalics who have linguistic abilities far in excess of their cognitive abilities. Yet, to be fair, cognitively based accounts of language acquisition and processing are very young and Hatch's criticism is not addressed specifically to information processing (although, clearly, information processing would have to be accountable to the same evidence). There has not yet been sufficient research done to evaluate the theory's worth as an account of second language acquisition.

Proficiency.   We come finally to the question of proficiency, or Spolsky's *how much*. Not all second language learners become fully proficient in the new language, and second language acquisition theory will ultimately have to account for the variability in levels of attainment. It is obvious that all of the variables we have discussed so far affect proficiency, and thus it may not seem necessary to address it separately, but two theories pay particular attention to the reasons that learners seem to stop learning. Acculturation and accommodation theories account for different levels of success in terms of social and psychological distance.

The acculturation model (Schumann, 1978a,b,c) is based on the belief that language learning is a central part of adapting to a new culture. Schumann argues that learners' success in acquiring a second language is controlled by their success at acculturating to the target language group. Further, both acculturation and second language acquisition are determined by the social and psychological distance that exist between the learner and the target language culture. Social distance depends on differences between groups in size, ethnic origin, political status, and social status. Psychological distance depends on such individual factors as culture shock, motivation, and language shock. Acculturation theory holds that:

> social and psychological distance influence second language acquisition by determining the amount of contact with the target language that the learner experiences, and also the degree to which the learner is open to that input which is available. (Ellis, 1985, p. 252)

Thus, when social and psychological distances are great, the learning situation is poor and the learner makes little progress. Schumann terms the failure to progress beyond beginning stages the pidginization hypothesis, referring to the simplified form of language that develops under certain conditions when two language groups come into contact. He maintains that when there is a social chasm between learners and the target language group, and thus a reduced motivation to learn the language, language learning may fossilize.

In his accommodation theory, Giles takes a similar view, that the causes for fossilization are rooted in socio-psychological factors. The major difference between accommodation theory and acculturation theory is that the former is concerned with perceived social distance and the latter with actual distance. Both view motivation as central to determining success in second language acquisition, but they see it as having different roots. Schumann apparently treats the distance phenomena as absolute while Giles believes the important factor is the perception of social distance. Specifically, Giles claims that what is important is how the learner's social group defines itself in relationship to the target language community (Ellis, 1985, p. 256). Giles claims that language proficiency is governed by a number of key variables:

1. how learners perceive their status in their own ethnic group;
2. whether learners make favorable or unfavorable comparisons between their ethnic group and the target language group;
3. how learners perceive the status of the ethnic group within the larger community;
4. whether learners view the ethnic group as culturally or linguistically distinct from the target language group or as linguistically related; and
5. the degree to which learners identify and perceive themselves as having status with other social categories, such as occupational, religious, or sex. (Adapted from Ellis, 1985, p. 256)

Both acculturation and accommodation theory are useful in helping to identify some of the possible reasons for the apparent limitations on second language learning that some people experience. Both are concerned to some degree with learner factors and with situational factors, but neither addresses the learning process itself and does not, therefore, constitute a complete theory of second language acquisition. As Table 5.2 shows, no one theory is complete, although several of them taken together represent a fair account of how it all *might* work. It might even be reasonable to say of them individually, as Ellis does about neuro-functional theory, that "they are perhaps best treated as affording additional understanding about SLA [second language acquisition], rather than an explanation of it" (1985, p. 275).

How the Variables Fit Together

It should be obvious by now that the major factors that influence second language acquisition are neither simple nor are they independent. We have seen that they overlap and that they interact in complex and largely unknown ways. The task of theory is ultimately to weave them together into some coherent explanation of how second language learning takes place. Theory is not yet at that point, but Ellis (1985) has provided a clear framework in which to think about the relationship among the different variables. He sees situational, input, and learner factors as influencing learning processes, which, in turn, influence the language produced (p. 276).

In the next chapter, we meet two children who have become bilingual under two different sets of circumstances. In witnessing the success of Quy and Lucy, perhaps we can more clearly understand what factors exert the greatest influence on second language acquisition in children and just what must be accounted for by theory.

Language Reacquisition

Before concluding this chapter, I would like to look at a relatively rare (at least in the research literature) but very interesting phenomenon known as *native language reacquisition*. Families who have spent any appreciable length of time abroad with a small child will have learned a great deal about second language acquisition. Most parents will notice that, in comparison with their own faltering attempts at learning the local language, their young children seem to soak it up like a sponge. Occasionally, parents who are able to communicate in the second language themselves will find that their children appear to lose their native language. Two studies of the phenomenon (Berman, 1979; Slobin Dasinger, Aylin, & Toupin, 1993) offer some insights into the language learning of preschool children. (Both children were under the age of 3 when they were initially exposed to the second language.)

The first language of the child reported in the Berman study was Hebrew, and during the period in which she was exposed to English, she appeared to lose her ability to understand Hebrew. When she returned to Israel after 1 year (at age 3;11), she had to regain both her comprehension and production abilities. The child reported in the Slobin study spoke English and was taken to Turkey where he maintained his comprehension of English. When he returned to an English environment at 3;0, after 6 months of speaking only Turkish, he nevertheless had difficulty with production. The Berman child, upon returning to Israel, had to function in both Hebrew and English while the Slobin child had only to function in English. Without going into detail here, the most interesting finding was the accelerated development of the Slobin child's first language. Any loss was quickly regained at a rate much faster than monolingual children experience. His speed of acquisition was also greater than the bilingual Berman child's, but this is perhaps to be expected given that the Berman child was effectively acquiring two first languages. Emphasizing the fact that, when returned to an English-speaking environment, the Slobin child was unable to take advantage of his ability to comprehend English in order to produce English utterances:

> This suggests that whatever the internal processes that may have been involved, they did not flow immediately into procedures for programming utterances for production. We would suggest, then, that serious attention be paid to the possibility that comprehension and production might play quite different roles in the processes of acquisition." (1993, p. 195)

The studies also demonstrate, once more, the amazing capacity that children have to learn language in the early years of their lives. Moreover, they serve to remind us that bilingualism is an asset, not a liability. The more we understand about how young children become bilingual, the better able we are to construct school curricula and activities that will build upon and foster language growth, in one language or in two.

For Further Study

1. Educators often encounter arguments such as "My grandfather came to this country without a word of English and he learned it all right. There were no high-priced ESL programs for him." Assuming that your school has or is planning to put into place an ESL or a bilingual program, how do you refute this argument?

2. It is often observed that in Canada, most fluent bilinguals were born into French-speaking families rather than English-speaking families. Why do you suppose this is true? Is there a comparable comment that can be made about U.S. bilinguals?

3. The author writes "Learners are not solely responsible for their language learning." In explaining why this might be true, discuss the relevance of age of the learner as a factor.

4. The author has categorized bilingualism according to whether it is attained at home or school and mentions that it can be classified according to whether a learner acquires two languages successively or simultaneously. Are there other ways of classifying bilinguals?

For Further Reading

For an easy-to-read account of second language learning in preschool children, see:

Tabors, P. *One child, two languages: A guide for preschool educators of children learning English as a second language.* Baltimore, MD: Paul H. Brookes.

CHAPTER SIX

Stories of Second Language Learners

In this chapter, I tell the stories of three children learning their second language under different circumstances. It would be a more symmetrical story if I had met them all at the same time in the same class. That way, with their shared classroom experience, I could have drawn some firmer conclusions about the influence of variables external to school on their language learning. I could have made some reasonable assumptions about the role played by family, age of first exposure to English, and other societal factors, but unfortunately, only two of the three were in the same class. The third lived 4,000 miles away and was born a decade later.

Two of the children, Quy and Lucy, I knew personally for a brief time. The third child, Jani, I never met. For her story, I rely, against my preferences as a scholar, on second-hand sources, principally the recordings and accounts of her parents and on the interviews that my own research assistants carried out with her parents and teachers. I'm sorry I never met Jani. Knowing Quy and Lucy, for even a brief time, provided a personal connection that made their stories easier to tell. There are also differences in the data I had available to work with, a fact that is especially important as time passes. I had more data on Lucy, much more first-hand data, than on either Quy or Jani, and more on Quy than Jani. Nevertheless, I will make every effort to describe the language learning experiences of all three children in as much relevant detail as possible. For 1 year during the early 1980s, I spent 2 or 3 days a week doing research in a kindergarten class in a school on the northern coast of British Columbia. It was there that I met both Quy (pronounced *Kee*) and Lucy. After only a few weeks, I was so struck by the progress they were making in English that I decided to study the two children more closely. What intrigued me then was the fact this Vietnamese boy and Portuguese girl, with such widely different experiences of both life and language, were coping so well with the demands of an English-speaking kindergarten. Their being in the same class as Michael, whom we will meet in Chapter 7, and whose second language learning was anything but smooth, made them all the more compelling as subjects of study. I decided to gather as much information as possible on their backgrounds, hoping that by so doing, I could come to understand more about the process of second language acquisition in children.

The account of both Quy's and Lucy's language learning from the time they began kindergarten is based on tape recordings made in their kindergarten class weekly for the first 3 months of the school year and once every 2 weeks thereafter. In most sessions, the children wore lavallier microphones during their regular classroom activities and also spent 15 to 20 minutes in private conversation with their teacher or with the researcher. These recordings are supplemented by the teacher's notes and formal evaluation reports, the latter written four times during the year, and by the observation notes taken by the researcher.

Quy's early language acquisition is based on his mother's recollections, recorded in interviews taken over a 2-month period in November and December of their kindergarten year. Her recollections were assisted by the diary she had begun to keep, at the suggestion of one of her new friends from the church, when she arrived in Canada. I was also able to interview two women who worked in the preschool that Quy attended from age 4;0 to 4;9. The account of Lucy's early language learning is also based on interviews conducted with the help of a Portuguese interpreter. These were conducted less frequently but over the 4-month period between mid-September and mid-December.

QUY'S LANGUAGE LEARNING

Quy from Birth to 22 Months

Quy was born in a refugee camp in Malaysia. During the 70s and 80s, there was a massive exodus of people from Vietnam, and Quy's parents were among the earliest to leave, under conditions so horrific that Quy's mother would not talk about them almost 10 years after the fact. Quy's father did not survive the journey, and it is something of a miracle that his mother, nearing her 8th month of pregnancy, did. Quy was born a few weeks after his mother reached the camp. Quy and his mother lived in the camp for just over a year before being accepted as refugees to Canada. During that year, his mother took English classes offered in the camp, but she was not a beginner, having learned some English in the job she had held in Vietnam during the war.

During their time in the camp, Quy's mother spoke only Vietnamese. That was the language used all around them, and essentially the only language that Quy heard. A month after Quy's first birthday, the young widow and her child boarded a plane for Vancouver, B.C., to begin their new life in Canada.

They arrived in the pouring rain, and the 10 °C (about 50 °F) temperature must have seemed very cold to the young mother and her child, but the Vancouver weather was almost balmy in comparison to the climate to which they were going. A church group in Prince Rupert, a small coastal community in northern B.C., had agreed to sponsor Quy and his mother. They met the new arrivals, and after one night in Vancouver, the two representatives from the church, Quy, and his mother boarded a plane for the hour-long journey north.

Quy's mother reported that she was in shock for several months. She was frightened about what the future held for her and her son, and she found the weather very inhospitable but not the people. She said that she seldom felt lonely and was grateful for the English she had learned because it helped her communicate with "the very kind people who wanted to help Quy and me." Her English improved rapidly, but she still spoke only Vietnamese with Quy. They did not have television, but Quy heard English spoken when members of the church group visited their home and when his mother took him to church.

When Quy was 16 months old, about 3 months after they arrived in Canada, his mother found a job. She was determined not to rely on the charity of her new friends but to support her son on her own. At first, Quy was cared for by another Vietnamese woman, a mother of four who also lived in Prince Rupert. The woman's husband was a fisherman whose income was sporadic, and she welcomed the few dollars that Quy's mother paid her. After about 6 months, however, a severe downturn in the fishing economy of the area meant the "fisherman's wife" had to find a job that paid more. Quy's mother then placed Quy in daycare, and his English language learning began in earnest.

Quy from 1;10 to 3;0

Although Quy had been exposed to some English before he went to daycare, according to his mother, he spoke only Vietnamese. Before he entered the daycare center, he had been very talkative, chattering away in Vietnamese. When playmates asked him questions in English, he would respond not by speaking but by nodding or shaking his head. She was unsure, though, just how much English Quy really understood. She was naturally worried about how he would adjust to an English environment. Unfortunately, his behavior during the first few weeks did little to ameliorate her feelings of anxiety. For the first few days, Quy didn't want to go to the daycare center. While he was there, he tended to play quietly by himself. After a few weeks, he stopped complaining and seemed to be happy about going. Sometimes, he even seemed reluctant to get out of the church van that delivered him to his home.

Quy celebrated his second birthday at the daycare center, and his mother was able to attend the lunchtime party in his honor. She reported that Quy seemed to be pleased with the party, and especially with the cake and ice cream, but he said nothing during the entire hour she was there, except a few words of greeting in Vietnamese when she arrived. When she asked the attendants at the center, they told her that Quy never talked. He didn't even speak Vietnamese with the other Vietnamese child, a 3-year-old girl.

Initially, Quy's mother wasn't worried about his silence, but then she started to notice that he was talking less and less at home. By the time he was 2;3, Quy spoke only when his mother insisted and then only in English even though she spoke only Vietnamese. He refused to speak Vietnamese and would sometimes respond to his mother's Vietnamese by saying "I don't know," which she took to mean that he didn't understand. Even though she knew that he did understand her Vietnamese, she reluctantly switched to English, which he would speak.

When Quy was about 2;4, his mother once again visited the daycare center. There she found Quy, not exactly talkative, but responding to his playmates in English. He greeted her in English when she arrived, and the attendants reported that he consistently greeted and responded to them in English although he was still reluctant to initiate conversation. At home, he was still mostly silent and still refused to speak Vietnamese.

It was natural enough for Quy's mother to worry that his refusal to speak Vietnamese would eventually lead to his losing the ability. Even though she knew that Quy would have to learn English to survive in Canada, she was anxious that he not lose this important link with their culture and history. She felt trapped. On the one hand, she desperately wanted to preserve his Vietnamese, but on the other, he refused to talk to her in Vietnamese, and she was worried about the effect of continued silence on her relationship with him.

Gradually, she relented and began to speak English with him. She would occasionally try to slip in a few words of Vietnamese, but he seemed to be intent on not understanding that language. Then, an event transpired that Quy's mother marked as highly significant in Quy's emergent bilingualism (and that speaks to the importance of motivation!).

Just before his third birthday, Quy was excited by the prospect of getting the tricycle he badly wanted. He was in town with his mother on a Saturday afternoon, and they walked past a hardware store that displayed a bright blue tricycle in the window. Quy pointed to it excitedly, saying, "There, that. Mama, I want that, please." Quy's mother did not respond, so he repeated his request, again in English.

His mother thought for a moment and then responded in Vietnamese that she was sorry but she could not understand him. He looked puzzled and repeated his request in English. She repeated that she did not understand. Quy merely pointed to the tricycle and said "Please." Quy's mother then told him in Vietnamese that she assumed he wanted a tricycle, but that since it was winter, he wouldn't be able to ride it anyway. It was Quy's turn to think. Finally, Quy laughed as though they were sharing a great joke and repeated his request for the tricycle. He went on to explain that he could ride it in the basement. All this transpired in Vietnamese. In perfect Vietnamese, his mother reported. He had not lost his first language, and it had not apparently deteriorated. From then on, Quy spoke whichever language was addressed to him.

Quy seldom confused his two languages, except in one sense. Sometimes, when talking to his mother about something that had happened in daycare, he would insert an English word into a Vietnamese sentence. She surmised that he had learned the names of certain objects and actions in daycare and simply did not know the Vietnamese equivalent. She would occasionally interrupt and tell him the Vietnamese word, which he would repeat and usually remember. It was her opinion that his Vietnamese pronunciation was fine, but she felt unable to judge the quality of his English pronunciation. We do not know, thus, whether Quy's Vietnamese influenced his English pronunciation.

Quy from 3;0 to 4;0

Quy stayed in full-time daycare until he was 4;0. During the year between his third and fourth birthdays, he made a great deal of progress in both his languages. At home, he increasingly spoke Vietnamese with his mother. Sometimes, she reported, when he began to tell her something in English, she would forget and respond in English. At the daycare center, he mostly spoke English. Just before his third birthday, however, two other Vietnamese children joined the daycare group. One, a girl of about the same age as Quy, spoke no English and was very shy. Quy began to speak to her in Vietnamese to which she eventually responded, and the daycare attendants credited Quy with easing her adaptation to the daycare environment. The two children spoke Vietnamese at first, but gradually she began to use English words partly as a result of Quy's teaching. She was observed to ask him in Vietnamese what the English label was for various objects. He would respond in English and at other times take the initiative in teaching her English words.

Quy from 4;0 to 4;9

When Quy was 4;0, he began attending preschool each morning. His mother had changed jobs and was working only part time outside the home. She was thus able to be at home with him in the afternoons where she worked doing tailoring and alterations. They also acquired a television set. According to Quy's mother, the television set had a significant influence on Quy's language growth. Initially, she put no limits on television, but after a few months she became concerned that he was engaging in fewer activities. After that, she limited his viewing to *Sesame Street* and *The Electric Company* in the daytime and one 30-minute program that he watched each evening with her. Nevertheless, she noticed a dramatic increase in his vocabulary, particularly in the use of idiomatic expressions of the type that she, as a non-native speaker, did not commonly use.

When Quy was about 4;7, during their bedtime routine, Quy's mother asked him, in Vietnamese, whether he needed to go to the bathroom before she read him a story. He replied, in English, "No way José!" She asked him, still in Vietnamese, "Who is José?" This time he replied in Vietnamese, "I don't know. Maybe he's a man on television."

From about this time on, his mother had difficulty in tracking his language development in either language, so great was his speed. She had worried, earlier, that his Vietnamese would suffer if she were his only contact with the language, but the church group sponsored other Vietnamese immigrants and there was soon a small community with whom Quy could communicate. His mother judged that Quy's two languages were pretty well balanced when he entered kindergarten at 4;9. She knew, however, that once he started school, English would win out. Not that it worried her. "In Canada," she observed, "that is necessary."

By the time he was 5 years old, then, Quy had acquired basic interpersonal communication skills in two languages. Strictly speaking, perhaps, Quy's accomplishment was different from the home bilingualism described in Chapter 5. He had, after all, learned his English not so much at home as in the daycare center and the preschool. On the other hand, his mother was bilingual, and although she was reluctant to do so, responded to his English as well as his Vietnamese. What Quy did have in common with Ronjat's Louis, Leopold's Hildegard, and other children who have learned two languages from an early age, was the embodiment of the two languages in separate people or situations. From the time he was 1;4, Quy used his two languages in two distinct environments, home and daycare, and with the exceptions already noted, mostly kept them separate. More importantly, however, was the fact that Quy, like Louis Ronjat and Hildegard Leopold, acquired basic interpersonal skills in English. He was different from Lucy, Michael, and many other children in the sense that by the time he faced the task of acquiring the cognitive academic language proficiency demanded in school, he already had the more basic language skills to build upon.

Quy in Kindergarten

To this point, Quy's story is the one told mostly by his mother as she recalled it a few years later. From the day he entered kindergarten, however, I was a frequent witness to his language learning. I met Quy on his first day in kindergarten. Anticipating a number of children who did not speak English, the kindergarten teacher, Colleen MacKenna, had asked me to assist her in determining the language proficiency levels of the 16 children in her class. In evaluating the language of a second language learner, teachers normally look at a variety of factors. They consider comprehension of the spoken language, the accuracy of forms in comparison to native-speakers of the same age, and fluency. The easiest way to evaluate all three is to talk to the child.

It is relatively easy to get a general indication of how much English a child understands by asking questions, as long as the teacher asks questions to which the child is likely to know the answers. Otherwise, it is not a test of language comprehension. Asking the child's name or the names of common objects is fairly safe. Some children, however, demonstrate culturally determined behaviors that may be misinterpreted. Some Asian children as well as some aboriginal American and Canadian children may respond to questions inaudibly if at all. This behavior is sometimes interpreted as meaning that the child hasn't understood when, in fact, the child is only behaving politely within the tradition of his or her culture. Quy had been in Canada long enough to have adopted Canadian behaviors in school, so there was no difficulty in getting him to talk. We determined very quickly that his comprehension was excellent.

Accuracy of form is a little harder to evaluate in children of Quy's age. The difficulty is that, unless they happen to be quite talkative, children may not produce the particular structures the teacher wants to evaluate. They have to be manipulated into producing the structures of interest. Means exist for doing so, as in the *Bilingual Syntax Measure* (BSM) (Burt, Dulay, & Hernandez-Chavez, 1975). Unfortunately, this measure and others of the same type provide only a few opportunities for a limited number of structures to emerge. Therefore, while they may be useful for charting development of a limited set of morphemes over a period of time, they tell us very little about how well the child knows the structures of English. The BSM probably tells us more about comprehension since the child has to answer a series of questions designed to elicit certain structures. In talking with Quy, we learned that most of the inflectional morphemes seemed to be in place, although he did show a tendency to overgeneralize certain morphological patterns as shown in Figure 6.1. When we compare the similar forms that Janet produced at 4;4 (Figure 4.4), we can see that Quy behaved just as a native speaker of English might. In fact, his behavior was so natural that I hadn't noticed it until I read the transcripts.

Fluency refers to the ease with which a speaker produces oral language, and it seldom requires a formal test to determine a second language learners' fluency. Certainly, it was clear enough that Quy had little difficulty expressing himself in English. A recording made of Quy retelling a story to his teacher during the third week in September shows why:

Terry Piper: *Have you read this book, Quy? Do you know the story?*

Quy: *Yes. I know.*

T: *Will you tell me?*

Q: *Yep. There was a woman and she was — she didn't have much money. So she lived in a shoe. Great big shoe. She had lots and lots of uh, boys and girls . . .*

T: *Children?*

Q: *Yep. Children. She had lots and lots of them and they all gots hungry. Real hungry. (He hesitates.)*

T: *Yes? And so what did she do?*

Q: *I don't know.*

T: *You don't remember? Why don't you tell me what you THINK happened?*

Q: *(After thinking for a moment) She wented to the Co-op and boughted some turkey!*

Tran nots here.
Lucy doesn't gots the glue.
My Mom, she boughted it at the co-op.
Mrs. 'Kenna didn't wanted it.

Figure 6.1 Quy's Overgeneralizations at 4;10

Fluency also entails a good, but not necessarily perfect, command of the grammar, vocabulary, and pronunciation of a language. Without administering any special tests, Quy's teacher and I could tell that Quy had near-native proficiency in all these areas. His pronunciation was native-like, although he had a slight tendency to devoice word-final consonants. This was apparent mainly in the plural ending on words such as *dogs* and *beds*. Since even native speakers have a tendency to slightly devoice word-final consonants, Quy's doing so was not a cause for concern.

The only other thing that revealed that English was not his first language was his hesitancy in providing the appropriate labels in English for certain body parts and items of clothing. Sometimes children who have learned these common lexical items at home in their native language will have trouble remembering the English equivalent. This is understandable since these are common vocabulary items that the child may not have been exposed to outside the home, or at least with any great frequency. This is likely the case with Quy. He had first learned the Vietnamese words for body parts and common articles of clothing. More familiar with the Vietnamese words, he had to search a moment longer for the corresponding English words. But he did know them, as we discovered when we administered the Peabody Picture Vocabulary Test (PPVT) (Dunn & Dunn, 1981). The PPVT was administered to all children who entered kindergarten with the exception of those who quite obviously did not know enough English to complete it. Quy's score on the test was 4;6, within normal bounds for his actual age of 4;9.

There were two other Vietnamese children in the class, a girl named Thuy (pronounced *twee*) and a boy named Tran. Thuy's family had insisted that she have an English name for school, and she had decided on "Doreen," although by Christmas she had changed it four times, to Dolly, Linda, Shelly, and Suzie. Just after she had decided to call herself Dolly, I recorded the following conversation between her and Quy:

> **Quy:** *Thuy, give me the white glue.*
> **Thuy:** *Not Thuy. Dolly.*
> **Q:** *Why "Dolly"?*
> **T:** *(Speaking in Vietnamese) Because I like it.*
> **Q:** *(Speaking in Vietnamese) Well, I don't. (Switching to English) I'm going to call you Thuy!*

It is interesting to note that Quy switched to English even when he was talking about the girl's Vietnamese name. During the many hours of tape recordings of Quy, he only rarely spoke in Vietnamese, although he often played with the other Vietnamese children. He seemed to be reluctant to repeat the role of language teacher that he had played earlier at the daycare center. He was, however, willing to help out in other ways. An old hand at "school," having spent 6 months in preschool, Quy sometimes provided rapid Vietnamese explanations of school routines. On one occasion, for example, he explained to Tran that he should wipe the finger paint off his hands with the paper towels kept at the teacher's desk. Although Tran's English was good enough for him to have understood, Quy chose to speak in Vietnamese, as he only rarely did. I wondered as I read the translation whether he had helped Tran to save face by not exposing his ignorance in front of the other children.

When I asked his mother which language he spoke when he was playing with these same children outside school, she replied that they switched back and forth, depending on what they were playing. In playing a traditional Vietnamese game they enjoyed, for example, they used Vietnamese. When playing with G.I. Joe, with a soccer ball, or any of the games they had learned at school, they used English, even though the other two children were far less fluent than Quy.

Quy seemed to be, in all respects, comfortably bilingual. His English language development throughout kindergarten ran a parallel course to that of his monolingual peers. At home, he continued to speak Vietnamese with his mother and usually with the Vietnamese friends who visited them. With his Vietnamese playmates, he switched back and forth between languages as noted earlier. Quy was so obviously untroubled by his two languages that I had to wonder the degree to which he was aware of having them.

Other than the few instances of language switching cited earlier, only one other incident suggested that Quy was aware of his two languages. Once, early in the year, the children were counting aloud. Quy, wearing his microphone, was counting along with the other children. They all reached 10, counting in English, and stopped. Quy paused, laughed, and continued in Vietnamese very softly, as if to himself. When I had the tape translated, I learned that he had continued counting to 20 in Vietnamese.

I wasn't about to repeat the mistake I had made with Lucy by asking Quy to think *about* language. I had learned that if I wanted to know if Quy felt his two languages to be distinct, I would have to find an indirect way. I devised a number of schemes. Once, when we were sitting together looking at a Big Book, I began to point to various things in the pictures, asking Quy if he knew another word for them. I hoped thereby to get him to tell me a Vietnamese word. But Quy wasn't playing:

> **Terry Piper:** *(Pointing to a bird) Do you know what that's called?*
> **Quy:** *A bird.*
> **T:** *Do you know another word for "bird"?*
> **Q:** *Robin?*
> **T:** *No, I don't think that's a robin. Can you think of ANY other word?*
> **Q:** *Mmm. Sea gull?*
> **T:** *Well, that IS another bird. Do you have a word for "bird" in Vietnamese?*
> **Q:** *(Looking puzzled). Bird. That's a bird.*

At that point, Quy turned the page, fed up with my silly game. On another occasion, I enlisted the aid of his mother. I asked her to show him pictures and ask him to name them in Vietnamese and then to ask him for the English equivalents. She tried, but had little more success than I did. In desperation, I tried a trick. I explained to Quy the directions for making a Halloween pumpkin from construction paper. Knowing that Tran was far less able in English than Quy, I asked Quy to explain the directions to him. Translation is a highly complex cognitive skill requiring that the child keep in mind the entire message while simultaneously constructing a completely equivalent utterance in the other language. In order to translate, Quy would have to be aware that the two languages were separate. But instead of translating, he turned to

Tran and in greatly simplified and somewhat pidginized English explained exactly what he was to do. I gave up.

Once I abandoned my tricks and turned to the transcripts, I found that even though there was no direct evidence of his being aware of having two languages, Quy did have some language awareness. Just before Christmas, when the children were making Christmas decorations, Quy and Thuy were working together at a table. Quy began to sing a song that the class had been rehearsing for the school's Christmas pageant. Thuy joined in, singing "Shingle bell, shingle bell, shingle all the way...." Quy interrupted her, "No, Thuy. It's not 'shingle.' It's jingle. It starts with j- not sh-." It is interesting to note that Quy did not tell Thuy that "bell" should be plural. The reasons are pure speculation, of course, but it is possible that the phonemic distinction was more salient to him than was the singular/plural distinction. Some support for this reasoning comes from evidence that awareness of the phonetic properties of language is one of children's earliest types of awareness, appearing in some children by the age of three (Dickinson, Wolf, & Stotsky, 1989, p. 229).

Quy also joined eagerly in rhyming games, again showing awareness of the sound of language as it exists apart from meaning. Otherwise, I had only the indirect evidence supplied by his mother of his behavior when he was younger from which to make any judgments about his awareness of his bilingualism. It seemed reasonable to conclude that Quy treated his two languages as two registers of the same language, to be used for distinct purposes. As we shall see, this seemed to be Lucy's view of her two languages, one of which she began to learn much later than Quy.

LUCY'S LANGUAGE LEARNING

A great many children who enter school with little or no English are not immigrants. Lucy was such a child, having been born in Vancouver, B.C. When she was a few months old, the family moved to the north coastal community where her father owned a large boat and employed a number of fishermen. Lucy's family, her mother, father, a sister 17 months younger, and a baby brother born during her kindergarten year, spoke Portuguese. Neither of her parents knew more than a few words of English, and since they lived and worked within the small Portuguese community, they had little reason to learn it.

Lucy's first extended exposure to English came when she attended a playschool for a few months during the year before kindergarten. Her mother reported using the playschool more as a babysitting service and that Lucy attended only occasionally, no more than once a week. The playschool teachers spoke only English as did roughly half the children. The others spoke a number of different languages, including Portuguese, Vietnamese, Chinese, and Italian.

When I first met Lucy in kindergarten, it was obvious that she understood some of what was said to her, but she was essentially a beginner in English. She did not have a sufficient vocabulary in English to reach even the minimum age-equivalent score of 2;6 on the PPVT. The school's ESL consultant (with an interpreter) visited Lucy's family at home and reported that Lucy was a very talkative child who was not at all shy and had a tendency to be a bit bossy toward her younger sister. She also reported that Lucy's family appeared to be well educated. There were many shelves of books in their home, and they subscribed to several Portuguese-language newspapers and magazines. While the ESL consultant and interpreter were visiting, Lucy brought out one of her books and started to read aloud. The interpreter was astonished to find that Lucy either had an excellent memory for a book that had been read to her many times or she really could read.

Given this kind of evidence about her use of Portuguese, I should not have been surprised by Lucy's progress in English, but I was. When she began, she could give her name when asked and could point correctly to most body parts and pieces of clothing. At this point there was no accuracy or fluency to measure since she spoke very little English.

Just 5 weeks later, all that had changed. The teacher gave her the PPVT, and this time her score indicated that she had the English vocabulary of an monolingual child of 3;6. At this point, it occurred to me that Lucy's previous exposure to English must have had a greater effect than I had initially thought. Either that or Lucy was a phenomenal language learner. By the end of October, I was convinced that both explanations must be true. This time, the last time Lucy was given the PPVT, her score was 4;0. She was also given the BSM, and some of her responses to those questions, reproduced in Figure 6.2, demonstrate that her comprehension and accuracy were both excellent.

With one possible exception, Lucy correctly understood all the questions asked. She responded incorrectly to the question "What would have happened to the food if the dog hadn't eaten it?" Her answer showed her to be focusing on the dog in the sentence and not the food. Indeed, the dog figured as the subject of all her responses in this section of the BSM. Besides, the question *is* very difficult, calling for the understanding of two conditionals and focus on the semantic object (the food) rather than the agent (the dog). Lucy's response would not be unusual in a native English speaker of the same age.

For the most part, Lucy's responses indicated a high level of both accuracy and fluency. Notice that her syntax was, for the most part, excellent. She had a good command of basic sentence structure and deviated significantly from adult forms only by omitting frills—modals and the copula, for example. Her developmental "errors" tended to be morphological—using *them* for *they* and using the uninflected form of the verb in *eat* and *drop*. At first glance, it might seem odd that Lucy had such good control of English syntax at a time when she was still making a great many such errors in morphology. However, when we look at what morphology Lucy *does* have, then we begin to understand the principle that guides her learning. She has the plural form; one bird differs from two and one cookie from a dozen. It is a meaningful distinction for her to mark. She has *that* in *'Cause that house fat. That* is a demonstrative; it is used to indicate which object the speaker is talking about. In contrast, the morphology she does not yet have tends to carry less meaning. The modal *would*, for example, does not convey much meaning in the presence of *then* (*Then dog die*), and the copula is almost totally redundant semantically.

It might be argued that the overarching principle governing Lucy's second language learning is to pay attention first to those elements that are the most useful for expressing meaning. This makes sense as a comprehension strategy. When one does

Terry Piper: What are these?
Lucy: Birds. /bɔds/
T: What is the mommy bird going to do with the worm?
L: Give it to the birds.
T: Why?
L: 'Cause them hungry and crying.
T: Why's he so fat?
L: He eat too much.
T: And why's he so skinny?
L: He eat nothing.
T: What are these things?
L: Houses /hausɔs/.
T: And these?
L: Noses. /nozɔz/
T: Why do you think this man lives in this house?
L: 'Cause that house fat.
T: What's he doing to the floor?
L: Wipin' it 'cause it all wet.
T: What did he do with his shoes?
L: Man wet them. (meaning 'He got them wet.')
T: Why is the dog looking at the king?
L: 'Cause dog hungry.
T: What happened to the king's food?
L: Dog eat it.
T: What would have happened to the food if the dog hadn't eaten it?
L: Then dog die.
T: What happened to the apple?
L: Dog drop it.

Figure 6.2 Lucy's Responses to Selected Questions from the BSM

not have sufficient control of a language to attend to every lexical and grammatical feature, then one must focus on those that are most significant for understanding the message. These would, then, be the earliest items to appear in speech, given that the intent of children's speech is to convey meaning.

The answers she gave to the questions in Figure 6.2 give some indication of Lucy's fluency at this point. Her retelling of a story she had heard a number of times before is an even better indicator. Figure 6.3 reproduces part of a transcript of Lucy telling *The Three Little Pigs* during the first week in November.

One of the more revealing statistics of Lucy's story is the fact that she used only 40 different words in telling her story of 122 total words. She told it without major hesitations and entirely without false starts, both indicative of a fluent speaker. She was not yet a native speaker, however, and it might be useful to compare her story with one told by Quy at approximately the same time. His narrative, reproduced in Figure 6.4, differed from Lucy's in significant ways.

Well. Three pigs. One pig say he make house with straw. Hims brother pig say "No good. I make house with mud." Hims brother pig say "No good. I make house with brick. Very strong." Then the wolf came. He say "I huff and I puff and I blow house down." And he blow down straw house. Little pig cry and run away. He say "I huff and I puff and I blow house down." Then he blow down mud house. Other little pig cry and run away. Then wolf say "I huff and puff and I blow house down." He blow and blow and hims face look funny. But house toooo strong. So pig laugh and wolf cry and run away.

Figure 6.3   Lucy's Telling of *The Three Little Pigs*

Once upon a time there was a boy and a girl. Hansel and Gretel were their names. One day they went for a walk to the woods. Their mother told them not to go to the woods 'cause bad people live there, but they were very bad children and so they went anyway. Then they went way, way back in the woods where it was very dark and scary and they were scared and Gretel says "I'm hungry," and Hansel says, "Me too." And then they see the witch's house and she came out and she had a big sore on her nose. She said "Please come into my house." And they did and so she gave them lots of things to eat—bread and meat and cookies and apples. Then they got sleepy and she put them into her oven to cook them. Then a man heard them crying and he came and he killed the witch and they went home. The end.

Figure 6.4   Quy's Telling of *Hansel and Gretel*

Quy's story had many features that Lucy's did not. First, he used more than twice as many different words (89) in his 164-word story. Since he had had far more exposure to English, a larger vocabulary would be expected. Quy's sentences were longer than Lucy's, mostly because of his use of the conjunctives *and* and *then*. He also used the conventional ways of beginning and ending fairy tales. Lucy, at this point, did not. We know that Lucy had been read to and that she was an emergent reader in Portuguese. The fact that she did not use the standard frame for her story in English likely reflects her relative lack of experience with English stories. What is more important, though, is the strong sense of story conveyed by both children. It is obvious that neither child had memorized the story being told, although there is some evidence of semantic memory operating in repeated expressions such as "no good," "cry and run away," and "I huff and I puff and I blow house down" in Lucy's narrative. It seems likely that both children remembered the stories in episodes— that they had personalized the events in what is called episodic memory (Glucksberg & Danks, 1975).

COMPARING LUCY WITH QUY

There is no doubt that Quy was a more fluent speaker than Lucy at this time, but Quy was a more experienced second language learner. That Lucy was becoming rapidly fluent was obvious to her teacher. In class, Lucy was a real chatterbox. From the beginning, she made very full use of all the English-language resources she had. She was never heard to use Portuguese, even with her two Portuguese friends in the same class. Jenny, Hilda, and Lucy played together both in and out of school, and most of the time, when they were playing in one of their homes, they spoke in Portuguese. At school, however, Lucy always spoke English, at least until mid-January.

Many teachers have observed that ESL children who share a native language will often use that language when they are together and use whatever English they possess when they are talking with teachers or playing with English-speaking playmates. Such children may be following the principle *une personne, une langue* recommended by Grammont (Chapter 5). There are also children, however, who behave as Lucy did, coming to school with little or no English but learning it very quickly and using it exclusively in the school setting. They are also following a principle. They decide which language to use not on the basis of the native language of their playmates but on the situation or setting. That is, if they have a choice. Choice implies awareness, and there is little direct evidence that Lucy was aware of having two languages. There is, in fact, at least one suggestion to the contrary.

I was visiting Lucy's classroom a few weeks before Christmas and was sitting at a table with Lucy. She had been identifying some pictures for me as part of an informal vocabulary test, but as usual, she was impatient with the task and eager to talk about something else. On that day, the topic was her baby brother who had been born a few weeks earlier. She told me how tiny he was, that he always seemed to be hungry, and that he woke her up before she was ready to get up — "before wake-up time" as Lucy put it. She also said that he couldn't talk at all. When I asked if she knew why, she replied that she didn't. I asked then how she knew that he was hungry, to which she replied, "'Cause he cry." I explained that his cries were his way of talking and promised her that eventually he would be able to talk just as she did.

On an impulse, I asked her "Which language do you think he'll speak?" She didn't appear to understand the question, so I tried again. "How many languages do you speak, Lucy?" Her response this time was prompt and very definite. "One."

"Which one?" I asked, although I really should have known better.

"Mine!" Lucy replied and let me know with her tone that she was not likely to put up with much more of this silliness!

This exchange provided a clue about how Lucy viewed her two languages. She seemed to treat her second language as a second register of *her* language. In other words, for Lucy, English and Portuguese may have been a single language with two registers, one for home and one for school. Many native English-speaking children do, after all, learn quite a different variety of English for use at school. It just happened that in her case one of the registers was Portuguese and the other English.

Under this interpretation, it would not be unusual to find some mixing of the two languages, yet her teacher could not recall ever hearing her speak Portuguese. Nor did the transcripts reveal any use of Portuguese until late January of the kindergarten year. When Lucy did begin to use her first language at school, however, it was for quite a specific purpose. It was also clearly apparent that Lucy had begun to mark a distinction between the two languages. After Christmas, a new child began kindergarten, another Portuguese speaker named Maria. Maria knew a little English, but it was clear that she did not always understand what was going on around her—clear to Lucy, anyway, who took it upon herself to teach her. Frequently, when the teacher gave a direction, Lucy would turn to Maria and provide her the instructions in Portuguese. As noted earlier, translation is a highly complex cognitive skill, and it is unlikely that Lucy could have undertaken it without being conscious of the fact that her two languages were distinct. So whether or not she was aware of the distinction between her two languages earlier, by the end of January she was clearly treating them as separate.

From this point on, it would not have been uncommon to find some mixing of the two languages, but if there was any, neither her teacher nor I heard it. Nor was there any evidence that Lucy's English language learning was in any way inhibited by her work as an unofficial translator. Lucy continued to make impressive progress with English, evident in the story she told me in early March. She was looking at a picture-only version of *The Three Bears* and, with very little prompting, told the story transcribed in Figure 6.5.

Here, we can almost hear the language spilling forth from Lucy. So eager was she to tell her story that she took grammatical "short cuts" that eliminated some of the structural niceties of the language without damaging the meaning. Sometimes she spoke in short, telegraphic sentences, neglected a past-tense ending, or left out entire phrases (*Baby bear, his tiny voice*). However, because she demonstrated in the telling of the story that she had full command over highly complex morphological and syntactic structures

---

Terry Piper: What do you see in this picture?

Lucy: There's Goldilocks playing with her toys. There's a big bed for papa bear, a middle size bed for mommy bear, and a weeny, weeny, tiny bed for baby bear.

T: Right. And what is Goldilocks doing?

L: Get in baby's bed. Trying them. Sleep. Now they're trying their porridge. Papa say in his loud voice "Somebody's eatin' my porridge." Mom's on the other side going "Somebody was eatin' my porridge." Pretty soon there's a tiny voice crying "Somebody's eaten my porridge and it's all gone." So Papa say in big voice "Somebody sleep in my bed." Mommy say in middle size voice "Somebody sleep in my bed." Baby bear, his tiny voice, "Somebody's sleep in my bed and here she is." She open her eyes and shouted "Who?" Then she ran home. The end. Do you want me sing a song?

Figure 6.5 Lucy's Telling of *The Three Bears*

(*Mom's on the other side going "Somebody was eatin' my porridge"*), it is likely that her short cuts were just that. To put it in Chomskyan terms, her performance did not accurately reflect her competence.

The likelihood that Lucy initially considered her two languages as a single code and the fact that she kept them separate according to situation of use constitute an argument that Lucy learned her two languages in much the same way as younger children such as Quy and other simultaneously bilingual children (i.e., as two first languages). The best counter-argument is Lucy's age. At 4;9, she clearly had a well-established first language, so her subsequent language learning had to be successive rather than simultaneous. Yet the speed with which she learned the language and the apparent absence of interference from Portuguese suggest that she approached the learning of English in much the same way as she did Portuguese.

Fortunately, for educators, it doesn't matter how we designate either child's language learning. What is important is that we understand what motivated their learning and the circumstances under which they achieved their bilingualism. The story that follows is clearly one of school bilingualism. Unfortunately, there are fewer details available about Jani than Lucy and Quy. There is, nevertheless, much to be learned from Jani, whose language learning experience has only just begun.

JANI FROM LABRADOR

When Jani began kindergarten in her Labrador community, Carla Doyle, the English-speaking teacher, became concerned after only a few days about her language abilities. Carla knew that Jani had only limited English, but she had observed her in the Inuktitut portion of the bilingual class and noted that she had little to say in that language either. Carla took up the matter with Mag, her Inuit co-teacher, who taught the Inuktitut part of the class. The Inuit teacher was surprised by the assessment. Jani, she assured her, had very good language skills in Inuktutit. "How do you know?" Carla asked, having herself observed Jani to say very little.

"She does what I tell her," Mag responded.

Indeed, Carla thought, that seemed to be true. Yet she was surprised by how little evidence Mag seemed to require to ascertain that the child was proficient in her native language. So she persisted, "Does she ever say anything? I mean, how do you know that she has acquired Inuktutit?"

Mag looked puzzled but answered. "Well, this morning, when I told her to get the Big Book and put it on the stand so the other children could see it, she did. She also sat down when I told her to."

The misunderstanding between Carla and Mag is a cultural one. In Carla's culture, a child's language is usually assessed in terms of production. Parents busy themselves trying to figure out the "meaning" of the child's early utterances and tend to take their comprehension for granted. Inuit parents, on the other hand, judge their children's language acquisition by their ability to understand what they hear and to do what is asked of them.

Jani's success in school will depend, in part, on the ability of her teachers to match their teaching to her and her classmates' experience and background. For the first few years, she will have the benefit of a bilingual classroom, taught in this community where fully bilingual teachers are rare, by two teachers, one from the English language and one from the Inuit culture. Later, in fourth or fifth grade, the language of instruction will be entirely English. Finding, or rather *creating* the match between home and school experience requires that Carla and the other English-language teachers whom Jani will encounter later come to understand more about Jani's world.

Like all the Inuit of Labrador (as well as those of Arctic Quebec), Jani speaks Inuktitut. Some linguists and anthropologists predict that this is "one of the few languages of native North Americans with a possibility of long term survival" (Foster, 1982; Priest, 1985, quoted in Crago, 1990). The Labrador community, where Jani lives, is harsh of climate and geography. The village where she lives is in a tundra-like land that is snow-covered from October until June. The people in the village of 200 live a very traditional existence, although it is obvious that their culture has been influenced by their Canadian and U.S. neighbors to the south.

Jani lives with her adoptive parents in an extended family of aunts, uncles, cousins, and grandparents, 14 in all. As Crago (1990) points out, such an arrangement is not unusual because in "the majority of cases, Inuit children are raised in extended families with several members of the family involved in the caregiving and handling of the baby or toddler" (p. 74). Children are full members of the family, going everywhere the rest of the family goes from a very young age. They go to the store, to visit friends, to community meetings, to church, to fish, and to pick berries. "An Inuk child is part of a richly woven fabric of kinship relations made up of blood relatives, adoptive relatives and fictive kin" (p. 74).

Jani's parents adopted her at birth; she is, in fact, the daughter of her mother's younger sister who has since left Labrador and moved to Montreal. Again, we see a difference between the values of the Inuit and those of their Canadian neighbors to the south. Crago (1990), in fact, noted that in the two communities she studied in Arctic Quebec, 40% of the children had been adopted into their families. "Inuit adoption, both traditionally and today, is a widely prevalent and socially valued practice which does not have the same value structure as adoption in southern Canada" (p. 74). Keeping with Inuit tradition, Jani' parents gave her the name of a recently deceased member of the community. The Inuit believe that when a child assumes another person's name, he or she also assumes certain attributes of the dead person's character. Moreover, people who share the same name share the same place in the familial structure. Thus, Jani, who was named after her grandmother, is addressed by her own mother as "Grandmother." The naming ritual helps children to learn the rather complicated kinship terminology of their language, a behavior that is highly valued in their society.

In school, Jani is perhaps more fortunate than many aboriginal children. Her language is protected and valued in her school, a school that is officially and actually bilingual. Throughout the years of schooling, Jani will find that teachers implement the bilingual policy differently. In most cases, English is clearly the dominant language of instruction for most of the day, and the Inuit-speaking teacher provides support by way of instruction or explanation in the native language. In addition, there are formal lessons in Inuit language and culture designed to preserve native values in the younger generation. In most cases, English-speaking and Inuit-speaking co-teachers work together to ensure that children become literate in both languages and become knowledgeable about both cultures. More important than "knowledge" for the children is the valuing of their culture that occurs in classrooms such as Jani's.

Unfortunately, there is only limited data from which to reach conclusions about Jani's language learning. At the time of the second edition when this story was originally told, Jani was still in kindergarten, and her teacher reported that Jani's oral language grew impressively in the first few months. She was attentive, seemed to enjoy school, and especially liked the books the teachers read to her. Carla reported that she had a slight accent when speaking English, but that may have been misleading. Jani may simply have adopted the dialect of her own community, a dialect that differs markedly in pronunciation from Carla's more standard dialect. She could write her name and read a few words in both languages, more in Inuktukit than in English.

I reported, then, that both Mag and Carla were optimistic about Jani's success in school since the indicators were mostly positive. The school that Jani attended typically achieved higher results (on the Canadian Test of Basic Skills) than other schools in the Canadian north. Unfortunately, this is still below the Canadian average. Nevertheless, Jani was well on her way to becoming bilingual and to acquiring the education she would need to function in either or both cultures. Jani went on to complete fourth grade in the same school with, I am told, similar results. During the following summer, however, Jani's adoptive mother was killed in an accident and Jani was removed from the community and taken to live outside Montreal with her biological mother, making it impossible to track her progress further.

THE CONDITIONS FOR SUCCESSFUL SECOND LANGUAGE ACQUISITION

At the very least, Quy, Lucy, and Jani teach us that children can become bilingual in either the home or the school setting. This is good news, particularly since much of the research reported in Chapter 5 suggested that the home provided the best situation for acquiring two languages. Lucy, in particular, teaches us that the school can be a good environment for second language learning *if* the language of the school is meaningful and purposeful and if it is spoken by other children and not just teachers. In daycare and preschool, Quy was not taught English but learned it in order to become a member of his peer group. In the kindergarten class, Lucy and Jani were not taught English either; it was simply there for the learning.

In taking a naturalistic approach in their classes, Colleen and Carla did not ignore the needs of their pupils. Both used non-intrusive methods of "teaching the language." They used more repetition than they normally would, repetition of whole-language events such as rereading and retelling certain stories as well as rep-

Mrs. Mac: What have you got there, Tung?

Tung: (He holds up a painted wooden cup but doesn't speak.)

Mrs. M: What a pretty cup! Cup. Can all of you see Tung's cup? Isn't it a pretty one? (As the other children look at the cup and comment upon it, Mrs. MacKenna turns to Tung and speaks softly.) Can you say "cup" Tung?

T: Kuh.

Mrs. M: Right! Where did you get your cup. Tung? Is it your Mummy's cup?

T: Mom kuh.

Mrs. M: (To everyone) This cup belongs to Tung's mother. What do you think she does with it?

Children: She drinks tea. Maybe put flowers in it. My mommy drink coffee.

Mrs. M: Those are good ideas. Tung, what does your mommy do with the cup? Drink tea? (She pantomimes drinking.)

T: (Shaking his head.) No.

Mrs. M: She doesn't drink from the cup?

T: No drink. Old.

Mrs. M: Oh, the cup is old? (Tung nods.) So she keeps it in a safe place to look at. (Tung nods again.)

Figure 6.6   Tung and Mrs. MacKenna Telling a Story

etition of language units — structures, for example, and the words for common classroom objects and activities. Colleen paired native speakers (or very fluent non-native speakers such as Quy) with non-native speakers for many activities in the kindergarten. There were no native English speakers in Carla's class, but she paired stronger pupils with weaker ones and encouraged cooperative activities, a way of working very common in their culture. Carla and Colleen talked to the children about nearly everything that touched their lives — about the toys and other objects they brought to show Carla, about books, about family and community events, and about fishing. Carla made the classroom such an exciting place to be that children were eager to share their observations and experiences. The children were highly motivated to learn enough English to participate, but even before they had much English to use, they had able teachers to help them out. Colleen was able to negotiate meaning even with beginners, as we see in Figure 6.6. The child, Tung, was a beginner in English who had been in Colleen MacKenna's class for 2 weeks when he stood up to tell this story in class.

Although he used only seven words in the entire exchange, Tung managed to convey his message: His family owns an old, wooden cup that is not used for drinking but is decorative and kept in a safe place. Tung's rendering of his story is very revealing of the kind of language learning environment that the children in this kindergarten enjoyed. It is a small wonder that they learned so much English so rapidly given the amount of help and encouragement from their teacher!

There is another similarity in the three children's language learning that may not be immediately obvious but that is, I believe, essential to their success. I pointed out earlier that when Quy began kindergarten, he already had basic interpersonal communication skills in English. Lucy and Jani did not, but they did have them in their first languages. All three children might, then, have been able to build the more abstract kind of language of the school, cognitive academic language proficiency, on that base, but they did not have to. Colleen MacKenna and Carla Doyle encouraged the children to develop basic interpersonal skills in English first. By not "teaching" English and concentrating instead on communicating with the children, these teachers helped them to "grow" the foundational language on which they would later be able to build the more abstract language of the school.

This approach was especially helpful for beginning ESL learners such as Lucy and Jani. There are likely two reasons why it was so important. The first is that however easy children might make it seem, second language acquisition might not be as easy as adults think. In reporting their study of a 2½-year-old Japanese child learning English, Itoh and Hatch (1978) pointed out that the affectionate interaction with an adult produced the change in attitude toward learning a second language that contributed to his ultimate success (p. 77).

The second reason is that a child's success in acquiring a second language in the school setting seems to be directly related to the *language interdependence hypothesis* (Cummins, 1980). The hypothesis holds that the

> cognitive-academic aspects of a first and second language are thought to be interdependent, and proficiency in a second language in a school setting is predicted to depend largely on previous learning of literacy-related functions of language. (McLaughlin, 1981, p. 28)

As noted earlier, there is a basic difference between the cognitive academic language required in most school situations and the more informal, natural interpersonal language that children learn outside. In second language learning, this means that the language children learn on their own outside school is usually very different from what is involved in most classroom learning. Colleen MacKenna's classroom was not "most classrooms." Instead of beginning with the more abstract "literacy-related" functions, she first helped the children to develop their informal language within the classroom. At the same time, she prepared them for "school language" by reading them a minimum of two stories each day, telling stories, and talking about stories.

From the studies reviewed in Chapter 5 and from the experiences of Quy and Lucy in Colleen MacKenna's class and Jani in Carla Doyle's, we have begun to uncover some of the prerequisites for success in second language acquisition. We know, in short, that the conditions for success strongly resemble those for success in first language acquisition. The implications for the classroom are obvious and fairly easy to implement. They are based on five simple maxims (Figure 6.7). Put into practice, these rules mandate a classroom that is friendly and accepting of learners' language, in large part, because they are based as much on common sense as they are on research and theory.

1. Focus on meaning rather than language.
2. Don't worry about "interference" from the first language.
3. Provide a positive and accepting environment.
4. Make sure ESL children have ample opportunity to interact with other children.
5. Establish routines that help children make connections between language and activity or events.

Figure 6.7   Five Maxims for Helping ESL Children

1. *Focus on meaning rather than language.*   All too often it is the case that the first lesson minority children learn is that what they say is less important than how they say it. This lesson does little to facilitate their learning. We will do well to recall the observation made earlier that adults facilitate children's language learning when they focus their attention and talk on whatever is occupying the child's attention. Quite simply, the best motivation for a child to learn a new language is the strong desire to talk about something or to someone in that language.

2. *Don't worry about initial language mixing or "interference" from the child's first language.*   Such mixing is probably more likely to occur when the focus is on communication for the simple reason that in trying to make themselves understood children may call upon whatever linguistic resources they have. Children are less likely to do so when attending to the form of what they say. Nevertheless, there seems to be a great deal of variation among children in the amount of mixing and the conditions under which it occurs. Both Colleen MacKenna and Carla Doyle report that among the children in their classes, even those of comparable backgrounds had very different patterns of language interference. Language mixing, therefore, should not be seen as evidence that there is anything amiss in the child's second language learning.

3. *Provide a positive and accepting environment.*   We saw in all three stories the importance of language environment. No teacher of young children needs to be reminded of the importance of the learning environment. For ESL learners, special care should be taken. Praise and encouragement are more effective than correction. Since young children make little use of correction anyway, it makes sense to replace it with support and reassurance. No doubt, some kinds of support are more effective than others. For instance, the teacher who makes a genuine attempt to negotiate meaning with children is offering better support than one who idly praises correct pronunciation.

A bilingual class provides a special and very nurturing kind of support for young children. There are a growing number of schools that provide such an environment, as we will see in Chapters 10 and 12. Such programs are relatively expensive, and where language groups are small or mixed, impractical. Teachers and parents should not worry, however, if their school is unable to provide a bilingual experience. A language-rich environment that provides incentives for children to learn and that values the culture they bring to the classroom will go a long way toward compensating for a monolingual environment.

4. *Make sure that children have ample opportunity to interact with other children.* Playing with children their own age provides second language learners with models of language appropriate to their needs and interests. Other children are better models of age- and situation-appropriate language than are adults. Besides, they provide the incentive for the second language learner to learn their language.

5. *Establish routines that help children to make the connection between language and activity or events.* Most children are creatures of habit and appreciate the predictability of routines. For non–English speakers, however, routines provide not only the comfort of predictability, they also provide an opportunity for real repeated practice. Rest time, snack time, and story time all provide children with an opportunity to learn the language associated with these activities—a different set of 3 R's if you will: regular, repeated, and *real* practice.

In the stories of the three children we met in this chapter, we saw that the conditions for success are varied but had certain commonalities. These five rules represent an attempt to define those commonalities. Following them will not guarantee that every ESL child becomes fully fluent in a short time, but it will help to make the task of learning a new language easier and more natural.

For Further Study

1. Can you think of additional ways of helping ESL children to gain Basic Interpersonal Communication Skills?

2. Often, older children arrive in an English-speaking country with knowledge of only written English and few if any oral skills. They may be placed into junior or senior high school classes where the language demands are more academic than they are in the lower grades. Would a teacher be justified in assuming that the pupils have Basic Interpersonal Communication Skills in the first language and moving directly into cognitive academic English?

3. Interview a bilingual adult and try to ascertain the key conditions that contributed to his or her bilingualism. Be sure to find out the age at which the second language was introduced and the environment (home or school) and any other factors that might have been relevant.

For Further Reading

Patton O. Tabors has an excellent portrait of a 4-year-old Korean boy learning a second language in *One child, Two Languages: A Guide for Preschool Educators of Children Learning English as a Second Language*, published by Paul H. Brooks, Baltimore, 1997.

See also:

De Houwer, A. (1990). *The acquisition of two languages from birth: A case study.* Cambridge: Cambridge University Press.

Lanza, E. (1997). *Language mixing in infant bilingualism: A sociolinguistic perspective.* Oxford: Clarendon Press.

CHAPTER SEVEN

The Miracle Makers:
Michael and Kenny

LANGUAGE DISORDERS IN MONOLINGUAL
AND BILINGUAL CHILDREN

The children we met in Chapter 6 as well as Grace, in Chapter 4, are in a real sense linguistically blessed. By the time they were a few years into their schooling, they had two languages and, as we have seen, there is no reason why their bilingualism should be anything but an asset in the educational process. Of course, the educational system does not always function ideally for every child, but it is nevertheless true that bilingualism can be considered an asset that *should* facilitate a child's education. Unfortunately, not all children are blessed in this way. Some are born with or acquire disorders that inhibit their ability to learn or function in language. Some children have physical handicaps that impair their language ability in varying degrees, and others have emotional or learning disorders that make language learning especially challenging. A complete description of the disabilities and disorders that may have an impact on language and learning is beyond the scope of this book. Besides, there are excellent books devoted entirely to the topic. Some familiarity with the nature of language disorders is, however, necessary for teachers and anyone else interested in children's language and learning. This chapter offers a broad description of some of the more common language disorders that teachers might encounter. The stories of two boys, Michael and Kenny, are also told to demonstrate the wide range of language problems a teacher might encounter.

We begin with an overview of four broad categories of language disorders and conclude the chapter with the stories of two children with two very different and somewhat unusual language disorders. Both children are monolingual, though Michael, in an ideal world, would have been bilingual. The first child, Kenny, is a monolingual child with a mild form of Asperger syndrome, a particular kind of autism that can be difficult to diagnose because often the children have extraordinary language abilities early in their lives. Michael has what might be called "induced language delay." His is a type of disorder that affects a small number of bilingual children whose parents are not part of the dominant language and culture. In attempting to understand Michael's language development, we come to an even greater appreciation of the importance of environment. The final section of the chapter will consist of a brief discussion of the problems associated with diagnosing language disorders, particularly in bilingual children.

A discussion of language disorder or handicap can be organized in a number of different ways. The two most common classifications are according to apparent cause and according to effect on the language output of the child. The first entails an examination of the language problems encountered by children with particular disorders—hearing impairment, for example, or cognitive disabilities. The second entails an examination of aspects of the language produced—voice quality, for example, or problems with the rate or rhythm of speech. However we structure our discussion, we are really talking about a continuum of dysfunction, from severe disorders resulting in total non-communication to relatively mild disorders such as hoarseness of voice or an inability to produce sibilants.

Few disorders are linked to a single cause. Although certain disabilities tend to result in certain language dysfunctions, the same problem, or symptom, occurring in two children may have entirely different and unrelated causes. For these reasons, I have chosen to organize the discussion around descriptions of particular language disorders. Before doing so, however, it is important to mark an important distinction between communicative disorders and communicative differences.

Disorder or Difference?

Communicative disorders result in speech that is so defective that it interferes with one's ability to convey messages clearly and effectively during interactions with community members who speak the same language and dialect (Mattes & Omark, 1984, p. 2). Children with communicative disorders should receive remedial assistance, but children with communicative differences do not require, and could be adversely affected by, attempts at remediation. Communicative differences are variations from the language "norm" of the community that arise out of dialect or language differences. Obviously, where the "norm" of the community is a particular dialect or a particular language, communicative differences are likely to appear in bilingual, bicultural children. We have already seen that the phonology of children's first language may temporarily influence their pronunciation of the second. Indeed, certain pronunciations are expected and almost legendary, such as the *l/r* confusion experienced by many Asian learners of English. But we also find language differences among speakers of the same language. There is, or should be, a wide range of acceptability that permits certain of these differences—such as both the British and the American pronunciation of erudite. We must not label as "disorder" those things that are only "different," for the latter:

1. may be developmental and will change as the child becomes more proficient in the language, or
2. may not need to be changed.

Certainly, dialect should not be confused with disorder. If children demonstrate any speech behavior or language use that others in their peer group or ethnic community also demonstrate, then it is obvious that their language is not disordered but different. Theirs is a legitimate means of expression and not in need of remediation. The child, Bob, whom we encounter in Chapter 10, is a good example of a child whose English, though not standard, is the English of his community. He is confused by attempts at correction. "Different" language should, in other words, be left alone.

The distinction between disorder and difference may seem obvious, but it is not one that is always made. Bilingual children with imperfect command of English (i.e., the language of the school) are too often counted as functionally handicapped because their communicative ability is "impaired." That this impairment is really only a developmental stage escapes the notice of some educators who send these children to speech or language pathologists for remediation. Of course, bilingual children may have language disorders, but they are no more prevalent in the bilingual than in the monolingual population (although non-mainstream children are more often referred for intervention), and special care must be taken in diagnosing language dysfunction in bilingual children.

Four Types of Communicative Disorder

The most common communicative disorders that a teacher is likely to encounter are related to:

1. voice,
2. fluency,
3. articulation of particular sounds, and
4. language processing.

Each type may occur with varying degrees of severity and in both monolingual and bilingual children. We will consider each in turn.

Voice Disorders

Any non-temporary affliction that affects the quality of the voice is considered a **voice disorder.** Conditions, such as chronic hoarseness not caused by colds or laryngitis, extreme breathiness, or hypernasality *may* be classified as voice disorders. In severe cases, the pitch, volume, and timbre of the voice may be so distorted that the speaker is unintelligible. In milder cases, the vocal quality may simply be inappropriate to the speaker's age or sex or to the situation but impede intelligibility only slightly. Essentially, there are two types of vocal disorder; those associated with phonation, or abnormalities in the vibration of the vocal folds, and those associated with resonance, or abnormalities in the modification of the sound as it passes through the vocal tract. Excessive breathiness and hoarseness would be examples of phonation problems while excessive nasality would be a resonance disorder. Vocal disorders have a number of causes, but only about one third of them are anatomical or neuro-physiological. Most have other causes such as emotional stress or abuse of the vocal apparatus caused by excessive use of the voice in singing, speaking, or shouting. Such abuse may result in a temporary physical disorder such as nodules or ulcers on the vocal folds, but treatment other than rest is not usually required.

Unless they happen to be working alone in a one-room school in an isolated community, teachers need not worry about the accurate diagnosis of a vocal disorder because competent professionals are available to do that. Their main concern is in detecting that a vocal disorder might exist, a task that might not be as straightforward as it sounds. As Mattes and Omark (1984) caution, even vocal disorders come with cultural values and biases attached. Cultures vary, for instance, in the degree of breathiness or nasality they consider normal or acceptable in speech. For this reason, educators should exercise some caution in deciding which conditions should be remediated. A sensible guideline is to refer those conditions that result in reduced intelligibility or are esthetically displeasing to the others in the child's own culture (p. 2). It would not be possible, then, for a teacher who is a member of the dominant culture to determine the effect on members of the child's culture. Whenever possible, bilingual children should be tested for vocal disorders in their first language. Otherwise, it may not be possible to distinguish certain normal vocal behaviors of the first language from those that are indicative of a disorder. In general, classroom teachers need not worry about making an accurate diagnosis of vocal disorder. If something unusual about a child's vocal quality persists and is not apparent in others of the child's peer group, then the child should be referred to a speech or language pathologist or the family physician. A true voice disorder should affect both languages, but since the teacher cannot be sure whether the child is transferring first language vocal habits to English, she or he should make every effort to have an assessment done in the child's native language.

Fluency Disorders

Children with **fluency disorders** have difficulty in speaking rapidly and continuously. They usually speak with an abnormal rate, rhythm, or both. The best known of the fluency disorders is stuttering, but there are others that impede the comprehensibility of speech. One of these is cluttering, a less common disorder involving the excessively rapid production of speech. Children with this disorder are "unable to control their speech rate, and as a result introduce distortions of rhythm and articulation into their speech" (Crystal, 1987, p. 278). Unlike stutterers, they also seem largely unaware that their speech is either partly or totally unintelligible to the listener.

There are a great many theories, but at this time there is no consensus about the cause of fluency disorders. Physical origins have been suggested, as have psychological and neurological ones. Fortunately, treatment programs are in advance of theory; a great many programs and methods exist for the treatment of stuttering, in particular. For the classroom teacher, the most important issue is not the treatment of fluency disorders but referring children who require it.

Children learning their first language frequently experience a temporary fluency dysfunction. The most common symptom is lengthy hesitation and it occurs typically in children around the age of 3, although it can affect speakers of any age. Most people, when speaking under pressure, will find themselves pausing as they search for an elusive word or repeating themselves unnecessarily. Care must be taken to distinguish both developmental and temporary, stress-induced disfluency from the type that may be a true pathology.

Care must also be taken, as in the diagnosis of voice disorders, to assure that bilingual children are correctly diagnosed. Once again, there is the possibility that what appears to be a dysfunction may be only a difference caused by either the transfer of first language speech and cultural patterns to the new language or by limited proficiency in English. While neither severe stuttering nor cluttering are culturally induced, it is the case that not all cultures take the view of stuttering that we do. Mattes and Omark (1984) report that cultures differ in their views about what should be remediated. North American Cowichans sometimes view stuttering as supernatural, for example, and some other cultures are far more accepting of fluency differences (p. 4).

A more common diagnostic problem occurs with bilingual children. Children learning English as a second language, for instance, may speak with hesitations, false starts, and frequent repetitions that impede the easy flow of speech. These occur when the child has difficulty in thinking of the appropriate word in English, or perhaps doesn't know it, or when the child is in any way unsure of the language. It would be a mistake to classify these developmental differences as fluency disorders; they will in all likelihood disappear as the child learns more of the language.

Articulation Disorders

Articulation disorders comprise a wide range of problems. At one end of the spectrum are difficulties with the pronunciation of a particular sound that have little impact on intelligibility. Lisping is an example of one of these milder disorders. At the other end are phonological systems that are so severely impaired that speech is totally incomprehensible. Sometimes these disorders result from serious injury to the brain. Children with disorders of this magnitude are easily identified and referred for treatment. The more problematic case for classroom teachers is children whose misarticulations are minor and may not need remediation because they are developmental.

As we saw in Chapter 6, although the phonological system is largely in place by the time a child is school-aged, certain distinctions may be still need to be worked out. A few children may still produce /w/ for /l/, /r/, or both even after they have begun school. Usually, these three sounds are acquired by the age of 4, but occasionally the distinction is not worked out until a year or so later, even though speech is normal in all other ways. As Crystal (1987) has noted, "many of the pronunciation problems that cause parental concern are due to a general delay in the ability to control movements" (p. 277). Delay is not the same as deviance. If we find that a child's pronunciation is different from her peers', then there are two possibilities. If the school-aged child's phonological system appears to be essentially the same as that of a younger normal child, then it is not deviant but simply delayed. It is simply a matter of slower development than is usual. However, if there are "patterns of acquisition that never appear in young normal children," then "we can say the child has a deviant system" (Ingram, 1976, p. 98). In the case of phonological deviance, the child should be referred for remediation. The speech therapist or language pathologist will be able to distinguish delayed from deviant speech if the teacher is in doubt about the cause of a child's mispronunciation.

Bilingual children may present particular diagnostic problems. Because articulation disorders may result from regular but different phonological processes, a bilingual child may possibly experience interference between the sound systems of the first and the second languages. This is one reason that some children learning English as their second language pronounce words differently from monolingual English speakers. It has been observed, for example, that French children sometimes substitute /d/ or /t/ for the /th/ sounds in English. It is thought that this is because French has no /th/ sound. Spanish and many other Romance languages simply have fewer consonant and vowel sounds than English, and thus speakers of these languages who are now learning English must learn additional sounds. While they are doing so, they may substitute related sounds, either from English or from their own language, for a time. Another type of phonological difference can occur when two languages have the same sound or sounds but produce them slightly differently. Portuguese, for example, has the /p/ sound, but it is not aspirated as it is at the beginning of English words. When a Portuguese speaker produces a /p/ in the manner of Portuguese, it may sound more like a /b/ to an English speaker.

The distribution of sounds in words differs between languages and contributes to some of the articulation problems experienced by non-native speakers. In Mandarin, for example, the only consonants occurring in word-final position are nasals. Chinese children may, thus, leave off final consonants that are not nasal. The important point for the teacher to remember is that, in children, these articulation problems are developmental and will be overcome as the child becomes more proficient in the language. Although certain techniques that speech therapists use *may* be useful with ESL learners whose developmental errors persist, these children should not, as a rule, be referred for therapy. The question arises, then, of how the classroom teacher knows which pronunciation problems are indicative of an articulation disorder. We return to the criteria discussed previously. Bilingual children should be assessed in their native language and referred for therapy only if an articulation disorder is present in that language. If first-language assessment is not possible (e.g., one cannot find a Cowichan speaker in Boston), then the teacher should proceed under the assumption that there is no articulation disorder. If the child's pronunciation remains heavily distorted over an extended period (more than a year for a child in kindergarten, first, or second grade, or more than 2 years if the child is older), a speech therapist might be able to do a complete profile of the child's English phonology and make some reasonable guess about the causes of the pronunciation problems. Happily, young children tend to acquire native-like pronunciation fairly easily. Bilingual children may have difficulty with English pronunciation because they have had relatively less exposure and opportunity to practice it, but they are no more prone to articulation disorders than the monolingual population.

Language Disorders

Also known as language handicap, **language disorder** refers to "any systematic deviation in the way people speak, listen, read, write, or sign that interferes with their ability to communicate with their peers" (Crystal, 1987, p. 264). As with voice, fluency, and articulation disorders, language disability covers a wide spectrum of dysfunction and may affect the structure, content, or use of language. The causes are various, but in a large proportion of cases, there are clearly physical origins. Brain damage, causing mental or physical disability that may have a serious effect on language skills, and deafness are the two principal physical impairments underlying language disorders.

The disorders themselves vary in severity and in the level of language they affect. Language impairments that result from specific brain damage are collectively called aphasias. Aphasia refers to the loss of ability to use and understand language and excludes language disorders associated with other physical conditions such as deafness. Although there are a number of different kinds of aphasia, corresponding with the particular area of the brain that is damaged, they can be broadly classified into *receptive, expressive,* and *global aphasias.*

Receptive aphasia, also called sensory aphasia and *Wernicke's aphasia,* results from a lesion to a region in the upper back part of the temporal lobe of the brain called Wernicke's area. People suffering from this type of aphasia typically exhibit no articulation difficulty or disfluency. In fact, their language may be characterized by excessive fluency. What is affected is comprehension, and as a result, speech may be marked by repeated patterns or formulaic phrases, unintelligible sequences of words, or odd combinations of words or even phonemes. Sufferers of receptive aphasia may also experience problems in retrieving words from memory (Crystal, 1987, p. 271).

Expressive aphasia is also known as *motor aphasia* and as *Broca's aphasia,* after the French neurologist who found that damage to the lower back part of the frontal lobe interferes with speaking ability. Patients with expressive aphasia suffer severe impairment to their articulation and fluency. Speech is often very slow and labored, with many hesitations and disturbances in the individual sounds and in the prosodic features of the utterance. Sentences tend to be very short and telegraphic in structure (i.e., composed of few words with little attention to the requirements of grammar). In contrast to receptive aphasics, expressive aphasics have little difficulty with comprehension.

In patients with global aphasia, the symptoms of expressive and receptive aphasia are combined. They have minimal speech capability and their comprehension is also very limited. Because the prognosis for recovery, or even for significant improvement, is poor, this type of aphasia is sometimes known as "irreversible aphasia syndrome" (Crystal, 1987, p. 271).

The diagnosis and treatment of aphasic children rests beyond the expertise and responsibility of classroom teachers. Most school systems provide specialists to whom children can be referred in the unlikely case that they have not been identified before they reach school age. It would not be unlikely, on the other hand, for teachers to encounter children with some degree of hearing impairment, since an estimated 6 to 7% of the population suffers some degree of hearing loss. Again, specially trained speech and language pathologists are available in most districts to provide advice, but some knowledge of developmental trends in deaf children's language is useful for all teachers.

We saw in earlier chapters that the language environment is essential to language acquisition. Children need to hear language and have opportunities to use it. Hearing-impaired children have been deprived, in varying degrees depending on the severity of their hearing loss, of the sensory input of language. Without that input, they will not develop speech.

Children who are born with hearing impairment that limits their perception of sounds to those exceeding 60 decibels (db), or about the intensity level of a baby's cry, generally will not be able to develop spontaneous oral language that approximates that of normal children. Children born with losses exceeding 90 db are considered deaf and will not develop speech and language skills without educational and therapeutic intervention (Ratner, 1989, p. 370).

In general, the severity of the loss corresponds with the degree of language handicap. In other words, when children can hear only a limited range of the sounds produced in normal speech, they will likely develop speech that is difficult to understand. The greater the degree of deafness, the more distorted the pronunciation, for example. If the hearing loss is only minor, though, children will benefit from most of the language around them. They may not hear whispering or softly spoken language from a distance or outside their line of vision, but in most ways their language will develop more or less normally.

As Ratner points out, an articulatory disability is less influential on children's school success than are disabilities in syntax and semantics that directly influence their ability to develop proficiency in reading and writing. "Over the years, repeated surveys of the reading abilities of older deaf children and adults suggest that their reading ability may never surpass that of 4th- to 5th-grade hearing children (Hammermeister, 1972; Trybus & Karchmer, 1977)" (cited in Ratner, 1989, pp. 373–374). Other studies point to an incomplete grasp of syntax as the reason underlying the reading problem. Some of the syntactic problems that deaf children have are similar to those experienced by normally developing hearing children, but they also have particular problems with the verb phrase—in particular, modals and other auxiliary verbs as well as infinitives (e.g., To see is to believe) and gerunds (e.g., Seeing is believing). Other syntactic structures that cause problems in comprehension include negation, question formation, relativization, and complementation. Deaf children are more likely to produce sentences such as:

Sheila take the cat no. (negation)

Who the girl take the cat. (question formation)

I saw the girl that the girl took it. (relativization)

Mommy goes to shopping. (complementation)

Because language disorders of this severity are caused by a dysfunction in the process underlying the surface production of *any* language, children with more than one language will have all their languages affected. It is not possible for a systemic language disorder of this fourth type to affect only one of a bilingual's languages. It is, thus, important for teachers who suspect systemic disorders in bilingual children to have their language evaluated in both languages.

Asperger syndrome, or hyperlexia, is sometimes referred to as "high IQ autism." I have not discussed autism, per se, because it is not primarily a language disorder but rather a term used to describe individuals who exhibit a variety of physical and mental disorders including extreme self-absorption, severe social and communication problems, and behavior problems. One form of autism, however, called Asperger syndrome, at least in its milder forms, has particular relevance for language teachers. I have known two such children very well, one in my professional life and one in my personal. It is Kenny, whom I have known since he was born in 1970, whose story I tell in this chapter.

KENNY'S EXPERIENCE

All forms of autism exist in varying degrees. Kenny was not as severely autistic as many children, and this fact made it harder to diagnose his condition. In fact, Kenny's condition was not identified until he was in high school. Kenny was his mother's first child, born on his due date in April of 1970. His mother described him as an easy child, sleeping through the night when he was only a few days old. When she would go into his room at 5:30 or 6:00 a.m., she would often find him awake and staring at the colorful mobile above his crib. Later, she would hear him gurgling and go in to find him kicking his legs and trying to reach the mobile or staring intently at the crib bumper pad. There is a family photo of Kenny taken when he is only 2 or 3 months old, sitting in his father's lap while his father reads a newspaper. In the photograph, Kenny appears to be reading the newspaper or, at least, trying to focus on it. He isn't reading, of course, but the photograph is strangely prophetic.

The first 2 years of Kenny's life were unremarkable except that he continued to be an amazingly confident and uncomplicated child. Very early, he showed signs of remarkable intelligence; another family photo shows him at 2 years working on a wooden puzzle. The puzzle was one intended for children between 4 and 6, and yet

Kenny had not only the manual dexterity but the cognitive ability needed to complete it successfully. He had a large collection of such puzzles and entertained himself for hours at a time working and reworking them. Kenny did not have the problems with fine motor coordination that are common with Asperger syndrome, but as we shall see, he later demonstrated many of the other symptoms. He also loved books, especially the Dr. Seuss collection, and television. His parents restricted his viewing to PBS children's programs and the occasional cartoon, but they soon discovered that their son had a mind of his own. He would get up very early in the morning or very late at night, go downstairs, and turn on the television. It was only after they began to unplug the set and seal the electrical receptacle that he stopped this behavior.

Just before Kenny's second birthday, another child was born, a brother named Christopher. Kenny was not happy about the arrival of a baby brother, and while he did not appear to object to his mother's attention to the infant, she quickly learned not to leave them alone together because Kenny tended to be overly aggressive. This behavior, however, diminished over time. In retrospect, Kenny's mother sees this as a result of Kenny's beginning to turn inward.

In May of 1972, Kenny went with his mother to a well-baby check-up for Chris. While they were waiting for the doctor, she handed Kenny a book from the office collection that he had not seen before. It was a children's book intended for a child just beginning to learn to read. He looked at it and then began to read aloud, slowly and mispronouncing a word here and there, but there was no doubt that he was reading. She knew that he could identify words, that he had mastered the alphabet, but she had attributed his reading at home to extreme familiarity with his collection of books. Admittedly, he had many of them, but she and his father had also read them to him many times. It was now apparent, that at 2;1, Kenny could read.

Concerned that her son didn't have playmates his own age in their neighborhood and worried about his socialization, Kenny's mother arranged for him to have regular play dates with other children roughly his own age. She noticed that although he wasn't antisocial in his behavior, Kenny tended to play alongside other children rather than with them. She didn't know then, of course, but "the difficulty in developing fluent interpersonal skills is probably the most noticeable symptom of children with Asperger syndrome" (Cumine, Leach, & Stevenson, 1998, p. 39). Kenny was also typical of children with this syndrome who are characterized as less antisocial than asocial. Years later, after Kenny was diagnosed, his mother recalled that she had often referred to him as asocial. Sometimes he did appear to enjoy playing with older children, when they would allow him to, and with younger children whom he tended to "instruct," but he never formed lasting friendships until he was at a university.

When Kenny was 4 and Christopher was 2, their mother enrolled them in a Montessori school. Unlike his younger brother, Kenny had little interest in the social aspects of the school, preferring to work alone rather than on group tasks. He did find it an intellectually stimulating environment, though, and complained on weekends when he couldn't go. After he had been there for only a few months, one of the teachers asked to speak to his mother when she came to pick him up. The teacher asked whether either she or Kenny's father had noticed that their son had a gift for mathematics. They had suspected as much, but neither parent knew a great deal about what constituted normal intelligence in a young child and were, thus, not sure what constituted above average intelligence. Although they had reservations, on the advice of their pediatrician, they had Kenny's IQ tested at age 6 when they were preparing to enroll him in the public school system. He scored 163 on the Stanford-Binet test, putting him in the category of the extraordinarily gifted. They decided to leave him in the Montessori school for a while longer even though it was putting a financial strain on the family. To ease the burden, they put the younger child, Christopher into a public kindergarten when he was 5 (the year that Kenny began second grade at the Montessori school), a decision that was fine for Christopher but contributed to Kenny's social isolation in the school. Nevertheless, he flourished in the school that allowed him to progress at his own pace and spend more time with the subjects that particularly interested him.

At the beginning of third grade, Kenny's father had decided to change jobs, a decision that brought a decline in the family fortunes as well as a move to another community. They decided that since Kenny would have to change schools anyway, it was a good time to consider the public school system. After consulting with the school principal, who assured them that the school could cope with an extraordinarily gifted child, they enrolled Kenny in third grade in September. At first, Kenny seemed to adjust. He even tried to join in with other children in games at recess, but he often finished up hanging around his younger brother and his friends. He told his mother that he didn't understand what he was supposed to do with other kids since they didn't seem to "want to do anything." By that he meant that they did not share his interests. He had taken up chess, and it was true that there weren't a lot of third-graders who shared his passion for the game that he played with his father almost every night. During her first conference with the teacher, Kenny's mother became concerned when the teacher reported that he had trouble with reading. "How can that be?" his mother asked. He had been reading since he was 2, and at home, he read books on chess, science fiction written for adults, and pored over his father's university chemistry and physics texts. The teacher responded that he never completed the "reading activities," to which his mother replied that surely reading was its own activity. The teacher also said that he was "antisocial," not at all aggressive in his behavior, but not wanting to play or work with other children. Kenny's mother answered that it wasn't so much that he didn't want to but that he didn't know how. She also explained that he had spent several years in Montessori school where individuality was encouraged and where he was responsible for the pace of his learning. It was clear that the teacher was not impressed, but neither Kenny nor his mother were impressed with the teacher, either, so she arranged for a conference with the principal. The principal recommended advancing Kenny to a fourth-and-fifth-grade split class with a much more experienced teacher who had worked with gifted children in the past. As well, they would work out a schedule that allowed Kenny to take advanced courses in math with high school students. Although both mother and principal were concerned that they were not addressing the social aspects of Kenny's education very effectively, they believed that he would be no worse off than he was in the current situation. The solution worked for the year, but each year, parents, teachers, principal, and Kenny himself were faced with cobbling together some kind of educational program that attempted to meet the child's needs.

With each successive year, the solutions were harder to find and less successful. Kenny was almost 2 years younger than his classmates, but given the degree of his social isolation, this seemed not to matter much. At first, he did better socially with the high school students, but of course, they had little time for him outside class and so his social isolation increased. He and his brother fought, as siblings do, but Chris's friends became his only social outlet, and Kenny often misunderstood their social cues. Chris's friends considered him a "dork," and Kenny often misunderstood their laughter as approval and thought that he had friends when, at most, they tolerated his presence. Thus, Kenny spent a great deal of time with his parents, and I can recall his mother telling me when he was only 5 years old that Kenny was very good company with his intelligent conversations and probing questions but that he simply didn't understand small talk or jokes unless they were very pointed or very intellectual.

For 2 years, when he was in eighth and ninth grade, Kenny attended a private school with special programs for gifted children, but although he did well academically, he became depressed and his parents removed him. Kenny went back to the public school system, and his high school record is extremely uneven. He excelled in math and science and in languages, learning Spanish and French easily. He asked to take Japanese and his parents allowed him to enroll in an evening class at the local community college. At high school, though, he either refused to attend or paid little attention to classes such as history or English that didn't interest him, and he absolutely refused to take physical education. As a young child, he had taken gymnastics classes and, while he had mastered many of the routines easily, he lacked the natural grace needed to become a serious competitor.

At the end of his senior year, Kenny left high school but without a diploma. He had not completed all the mandatory classes. His SAT scores, however, were predictably outstanding, and he was admitted to a large state university in the Midwest on the basis of those scores. He spent 7 years as an undergraduate, taking a total of four majors before graduation: computer science, mathematics, philosophy, and Japanese. It was while at university that he was finally diagnosed as having Asperger syndrome, and he instantly became an expert on the subject, educating his parents and everyone else who would listen. He told me that it gave him a great sense of freedom; he no longer felt inadequate and felt that knowing what his problem was, he could deal with it. One of the reasons that Kenny stayed at the university so long was his fear of change. People with Asperger syndrome are often more comfortable with repetitive activities than new activities. Eventually, he did graduate and even enrolled in a graduate program, but he left that after 1 year, declaring himself finally tired of school

As of this writing, Kenny is 31. He works as a head waiter in a 4-star restaurant near Chicago, a job that he likes. Before getting this position, he lost many, many jobs as a waiter because the social conventions that are required in treating customers appropriately were so difficult. Finally, by his own account, he succeeded because he watched what other waiters did, memorized and analyzed what was said, and tried to work out the rules. For him, it eventually worked. He still has social problems, but knowing what they are and why has helped him to cope. He also found a support group of others from the University community who have the same condition. Would it have mattered if Kenny's hyperlexia had been identified earlier? No one

- General social "clumsiness" and problems with social interaction
- A tendency to "instruct" or teach; pedantic tone
- Poor motor coordination and/or atypical gait or posture
- Resistance to change and enjoyment of repetitive activities
- Excellent ability to memorize
- Restricted non-verbal communication skills

Figure 7.1   General Indicators of Asperger Syndrome

can answer that with certainty, but I suspect that it would not have. The schools had enough difficulty dealing with him as an extraordinarily gifted child. The label, in the absence of special programs or extremely cooperative educators, would have done little to improve his experience with education.

Why, then, is Kenny's case important to us here? On the surface, language seems to have been the least of his problems, but in fact, that is not true. Children who are asocial may have serious communication difficulties for the simple reason that they are unaware of the needs of the listener. Their talk tends not to have a social purpose and, therefore, may lack the social conventions of politeness and turn-taking that constitute effective communication. While Kenny had no difficulty with the *formal* properties of language and he learned to read early and well, communication is about more than that, and his failure to understand the social dimension of language use created educational and social problems for him throughout his life. Unlike children with other kinds of autism, children with Asperger syndrome are more likely to appear in regular classes and to escape diagnosis or be wrongly diagnosed as having behavioral problems such as being antisocial. More boys than girls are afflicted with Asperger syndrome, which affects approximately 3 in 1,000 children. Fortunately, there are excellent resources for teachers and for caregivers, both in print and on the web. One particularly useful book is *Asperger Syndrome* by Val Cumine, Julia Leach, and Gill Stevenson (1998). The diagnostic criteria in Figure 7.1 are not exhaustive, but they can be helpful in guiding teachers to refer children for more thorough assessment. One final caution about children with Asperger syndrome: Children with this disorder are more likely to be trusting and to take what is said to them at face value. This makes them especially vulnerable to bullying, and teachers may have to take special care to ensure that all children understand that bullying is unacceptable behavior.

Language Problems of Bilingual Children

When bilingual children were studied earlier in this century, researchers were mainly interested in how bilingualism facilitated or interfered with language development. Many of these studies concluded that monolinguals performed better than bilinguals on measures with one language only. Bilingual French/English children would, for example, perform worse on tests of either English or French than would monolingual children taking language-appropriate tests. Bilinguals were found to have smaller vocabularies (Barke & Parry-Williams, 1938; Grabo, 1931; Saer, 1922) and to make more grammatical errors (Carrow, 1957; Smith, 1933, 1935, all cited in Abudarham, 1980, p. 236). The flaw in these studies was that most of them considered only one of the bilingual's languages or each language separately. They did not consider the totality of the language system of the bilingual (i.e., the full communicative capacity provided by the two languages) (Abudarham, 1980, p. 236). Yet researchers all too often reached the conclusion that bilingualism was a disadvantage to the child. As MacNamara wrote, "there is some firmly grounded evidence indicating that the bilinguals have a weaker grasp of language than monoglots" (1966, cited in Abudarham, 1980, p. 236). More recent research has attempted to correct this flaw by testing bilinguals' proficiency in both their languages. These studies have been useful in affirming the linguistic "normality" of bilinguals, but they have not provided specific measures to be used to diagnose language disorders in bilingual children.

Any language disability that can affect monolingual children can also affect bilinguals. On the other hand, educators have identified certain language problems associated *only* with bilingual children. It has been noted, for example, that children being educated in a second language are usually successful when their native language is the dominant language of the community (Cummins, 1979a). This is the case, for example, with English-speaking children in French immersion programs. In contrast, children whose native language is a minority language fare less well in school. It has also been noted that some children "seem to enjoy cognitive advantages tied to their bilingualism while others do not" (Peal & Lambert, 1962, cited in Edelsky et al., 1983), and that older children being educated in a non-native setting are generally more successful than younger ones (Toukomaa & Skutnabb-Kangas, 1977, cited in Edelsky et al., 1983).

To explain these somewhat contradictory observations, Canadian researchers Jim Cummins and Merrill Swain proposed the distinction between cognitive academic language and language used for most interpersonal communication, suggesting that school success is more closely related to children's cognitive academic language proficiency (CALP) than to their proficiency with the language used for basic interpersonal communication skills (BICS). Cummins also developed two hypotheses, the threshold hypothesis and the developmental interdependence hypothesis which, along with BICS and CALP, were intended to account for the differences in school success among bilingual children. According to the threshold hypothesis, a second language learner must attain "a certain 'threshold' level of proficiency... in that language before the learner can benefit from the use of the language as a medium of instruction in school" (Richards, Platt, & Weber, 1985, p. 293). Cummins also asserts that the level of proficiency children attain in the second language "depends upon the level of proficiency the child learner has reached in the first language at the time when extensive exposure begins" (Richards, Platt, & Weber, 1985, p. 293). This is the interdependence hypothesis.

Minority children who come to school without having attained cognitive academic language proficiency in at least one of their languages are supposedly educationally at risk. Children who begin school with neither CALP nor BICS are sometimes labeled as **semilingual**. Although the term is no longer widely used in North America, semilingual is used in Europe, principally in Scandinavia, to refer to bilingual children who have not mastered either of their languages "well enough to handle 'abstract cognitive/language' tasks involving meanings for abstract concepts, synonyms, etc. as well as vocabulary" (Toukomaa & Skutnabb-Kangas, cited in Cummins 1979a, p. 231).

Researchers such as Carole Edelsky and her colleagues (1983) and Martin-Jones and Romaine (1986) have pointed out, however, that the BICS and CALP distinction, the threshold hypothesis, the interdependence hypothesis, and the assumption of semilingualism are dangerous and wrong. They are dangerous because they essentially constitute a "blame-the-victim" theory: Bilingual children have trouble in school because of something they did not bring, namely the degree of proficiency in English that the school deems necessary. This view fails to recognize and to take advantage of the totality of the language that these children *do* bring. The two hypotheses and the label semilingual are often wrong because they rely on data from tests and test settings that are inadequate to assess children's language competence.

In general, school personnel test those aspects of language they know how to test. These include pronunciation and vocabulary, frequently measured by worksheets and standardized tests. These fragments of language are quantified "without regard for their interrelationship with other levels of linguistic organization" (Martin-Jones & Romaine, 1986, p. 29), and in such a way that they tell us more about what children do not know than what they do know about language. Basing his claim on his own clinical experience in Britain, Abudarham (1980) asserts that standardized tests such as the Peabody Picture Vocabulary Test have "little, if any, diagnostic or prognostic value" with dual language children (pp. 231–232), in large part because they reveal deficits in the second language without tapping children's native language resources. The fact that such measures tell us little about what children know about language or what they can do with language does not deter well-intentioned educators from using them nor from reaching conclusions about bilingual children that may be faulty. As Martin-Jones and Romaine (1986) point out, most language tests given in schools "are only indirectly related to common sense notions of what it means to be a competent language user" (p. 29). This being the case, it is easy to see the potential for abuse. As the authors point out,

> When notions like "the ability to extract meaning" become operationalized as scores on, for example, reading tests, a child who fails is then labelled as one who is "unable to extract meaning." Similarly, when the "cognitive aspects" of language are tested in terms of, say, being able to produce synonyms, then the child who can't is branded as "lacking in the cognitive aspects of language development." (p. 29)

Once educators who make decisions on behalf of bilingual children get it into their heads that such things as mastering complex syntactic structures, providing synonyms on vocabulary lists, and even correct spelling are valid indicators of language proficiency, they cease to question the real nature of language ability and how it might or might not be revealed by such measures. In a real sense, then, the explanation attempted by the BICS and CALP distinction and by the threshold and the interdependence hypotheses constitute a deficit theory: Bilingual children's lack of success in the majority language and in school is attributed to that which they do *not* bring to school and not to any deficiency in the school's assessment of such children or in their curriculum for or teaching of bilingual children.

Nevertheless, from time to time, a bilingual child will enter school with a particular language disability that is related to decisions made in the home. Such a child has severe and obvious difficulty communicating in *either* language and, in the past, would have been labelled as semilingual. Today, however, the term has such negative connotations that it has largely been abandoned in North America. Michael is such a child, and the story of his language development is revealing for what it says about the importance of language environment.

MICHAEL'S LANGUAGE DEVELOPMENT

Michael was in the same kindergarten class as Lucy, the child we met in Chapter 6. I first met him when I visited the class in September, about 2 weeks after the beginning of the school year. He was sitting on the floor with the other children listening as the teacher read *The Three Bears*. He seemed to be engrossed in the activity and watched the teacher intently as he listened. He laughed when the other children laughed but otherwise remained silent. Many of the other children, in contrast, would respond to the teacher's occasional question by calling out answers— "Goldilocks!"—or would comment on the familiar story. During that visit to the classroom, I met with the children individually to try to determine their level of English language proficiency. I sat at a table in the back of the classroom and called the children to me one at a time. When I called Michael's name, he looked up but did not move, nor did he respond to my request to join me, although when I called his name a second time and motioned to him, he did come to the back of the room.

He sat quietly at the table, following my eyes with his as I talked to him. The only response he made to any of my questions was to give his name when I asked. I tried asking him the names of various objects—shoes, a book, his nose, his shirt, a picture of a bird—but he merely looked at me. I then tried to get him to repeat the names of these same objects. When he appeared not to understand the task, I demonstrated with another child. His repetitions were mostly highly nasalized monosyllables that all sounded something like "muh."

At the end of the day, I talked with the kindergarten teacher to try to learn something about Michael's background. Unfortunately, the ESL consultant who usually visited the homes of new pupils had not yet visited Michael's home and the kindergarten teacher knew very little about him. She thought it likely, given his last name, that his family spoke Italian at home, but she had not been able to verify this fact. His registration card was only partly complete, and she was able to ascertain only that he was 4;5, and that he had one older sibling who was not in school. She reported that Michael seemed to enjoy coming to school, caused no problems in class, but had not spoken except to say his name when asked. He seemed very attentive and often smiled or laughed at the actions of the other children. Neither the teacher nor I was particularly concerned about his silence; we assumed that he was a beginner in English, and we both knew that an extended silent period is quite normal in young second language learners.

Michael was absent during my next visit to the class, and it was nearly 3 weeks later when I saw him again. I could tell by the expression on his face that he remembered me and came immediately to my table when I called him. Once again he watched me closely and he seemed to understand more of what I said. He responded correctly when asked to name pictures of a house, a bear, and a bed from *The Three Bears.* He also responded "I don't know" when I asked him what a picture of a tree was and again when I showed him a picture of a bird and asked what it was. To the other questions he gave no response at all. In all his utterances, his pronunciation remained badly distorted. His teacher had learned nothing more about his background but told me that he was an even-tempered child who seemed to enjoy school, but as a watcher rather than a joiner. He seldom participated in his classmates' activities and waited patiently for crayons or toys to become available. He was still silent, speaking only when he was alone with his teacher and then only repeating the names of objects after her. She could recall no instance of his initiating speech.

Although I visited the class on a number of occasions during the next month, it was not until late November that I learned anything more about Michael. The ESL consultant had visited his home and had met both his father and mother whose native language was indeed Italian. The parents, she reported, spoke very limited English, but the father seemed to understand most of what she explained about the school's kindergarten and ESL programs. She also learned that Michael's grandmother lived with the family and that Michael had a teenaged sister who did not live at home. In short, she was able to learn very little more about Michael.

Michael's teacher, however, happened to meet his sister and had learned from her more about Michael's background. His sister had been born in Italy and had moved with her family to Canada when she was 9 years old, 6 years before Michael was born. She said that she had found it very difficult to learn English, although it was the impression of the teacher that she spoke fluently and with no foreign accent. She struggled through school, a fact that caused her parents a great deal of anxiety, but eventually completed high school. At that point, when Michael was approximately 2;6, she left home and had only infrequent contact—perhaps once a week—with her younger brother. Before she left and occasionally when she returned to visit the family, she would read aloud to Michael, although infrequently, and sometimes played children's records for him. When the teacher asked her which language she used in communicating with Michael, she gave an answer that was extremely revealing—English, she said, was the only language her parents permitted to be used with Michael.

Convinced that their daughter's problems in school were a result of her limited English proficiency, his parents had determined that Michael would learn *only* English. Unfortunately, they spoke very little English themselves and his contact with his sister and her English-speaking friends was minimal. According to his sister, Michael understood Italian and spoke a few words, but his parents discouraged conversation in that language and Michael seemed content to listen. They did not read to him in Italian and could not read to him in English, although they did provide a number of

English-language children's books and records for him. Michael's teacher found this last observation especially interesting because she had observed that he seemed to be familiar with some of the songs played or sung in class even though he never joined in singing them.

To complicate Michael's learning of English even further, both his parents worked outside the home and he was left in the care of his paternal grandmother who spoke no English at all. She had been instructed not to speak Italian to Michael because the parents were adamant that Michael not learn Italian. Very likely, she did speak some Italian to the child, for it is hard to imagine that she would love and care for him in total silence. But whatever communication occurred between grandmother and grandson was not sufficient for him to acquire a functional first language, at least so far as we were able to determine.

From this time in November until the end of the school year, I took special care to observe and to document Michael's language learning. During that time, there were many occasions on which I was disheartened, convinced that Michael was making no progress at all. He was always attentive in class and in conversation with me, but he rarely spoke except in private conversation with his teacher or with me. At various points in the year, when I compared his language development with that of the other ESL children in the class, I could see that Michael's vocabulary was extremely limited, his sentences short and filled with errors that the other children had either not made or had long since stopped making, and his pronunciation, though improved, still greatly distorted. At the end of the school year, his teacher, the ESL consultant, and I agreed that Michael was not ready to go into first grade in the coming term. His oral language development lagged so far behind that of his peers that it seemed highly unlikely that he would be ready to cope with the demands of literacy in 3 short months, particularly if he had little practice in English in the summer months. Unfortunately, the ESL consultant had made little headway in convincing Michael's parents to speak and read to him in Italian, so it seemed likely that Michael's exposure to *any* language would be curtailed during the school break.

When the school year ended, then, my assessment of Michael's language learning and my prognosis for future language development was not a positive one. As I began to listen to the tape recordings and read the transcripts from the previous 9 months, however, my assessment of his progress changed. At the end of May, Michael's language, when compared with other children in the class, seemed painfully underdeveloped. As I retraced his growth during the year by listening to the tapes and reading the transcripts, however, I realized that he had made a great deal of progress. His rate of development and the degree of fluency he had attained by June were well below those of any other child in the class, but when I considered his language on its own merits, I could see growth. His pronunciation, which in the fall had been almost unintelligible, retained some distortion but was intelligible and showed improvement every month. Even at the end of the school year, when he added a new word to his vocabulary, the pronunciation would initially be highly distorted but would soon improve. In other areas of language, Michael showed more impressive growth. His comprehension, accuracy (both in syntax and in choice of words), fluency, and communicative competence all improved dramatically over the school year.

Comprehension

For kindergarten-aged children, comprehension refers only to the understanding of oral language and not written language. It is usually gauged by assessing their verbal and non-verbal responses to the language they hear. Throughout the school year, Michael's teacher had administered the Bilingual Syntax Measure (BSM). The BSM is a test sometimes used to assess English language proficiency in children from about kindergarten through about third grade. It consists of a set of simple, brightly colored pictures and questions designed to elicit certain grammatical structures such as tense markers, plurals, and possessives as well as more complex forms such as the present perfect and conditionals. While this is not a test designed to measure comprehension, it was very clear in the early attempts to administer the test to Michael that he did not understand the questions. For example, in January, his response to the question, "What is the mommy bird going to do with the worm?" was "Eat it." But the picture makes it abundantly clear that she is going to give it to her baby birds. Thinking that he may have meant that the baby birds were going to eat the worm, I asked him "Who will eat the worm?" to which he replied by pointing to the mother bird. In March, however, and again in June, his responses, "She's give them food" and "Give it to babies," indicated that he had understood the question.

The same pattern appeared in his responses to the question "Why is the dog looking at the king?" the expected answer to which is "Because he's hungry" (the dog, that is). In November, Michael responded "Doggy looking that turkey." In January, he responded "Cause he eat, him eat," which may have indicated correct comprehension and problems with sentence formation. It was clear in March, however, that he could both understand the question and produce the appropriate response: "Because him hungry."

The evidence from the BSM would not be adequate for assessing Michael's level of comprehension. In Michael's case, however, his difficulty in comprehension was apparent for several months in much of the interaction between Michael and me and between Michael and his teacher, but the same improvement that appeared in his performance on the BSM was also evident in other situations of language use. While it is sometimes difficult to distinguish comprehension errors from production errors—in other words, to know whether a child hasn't understood what is said or does not know how to respond appropriately—it is certain that no language development would have taken place over the school year unless he had first experienced improved comprehension. Learners' ability to speak a second language nearly always lags behind their understanding of it.

Accuracy

One of the problems in evaluating how much a child's accuracy in using the language has improved is this confounding of accuracy with comprehension. With the BSM, however, this problem is minimized through the use of simple, unambiguous pictures and by the teacher's assuring before beginning the procedure that the child knows the names for the objects and the actions portrayed. In assessing Michael's

Table 7.1   Selected Answers and Responses to BSM

Question	Response
What is the mommy bird going to do with the worm?	She's give them food. (March)
Why's he so fat?	Because him eat too lots. (June)
And why's he so skinny?	Because he was eating. (March)
	Because he's not eating. (June)
Why are their eyes closed?	Because them go bed. (March)
Why do you think she's so happy?	Her like it outside. (June)
Why do you think this man lives in this house?	Because him house is fat. (March)

accuracy in answering the BSM questions, once it was clear that he understood them, it was obvious that he responded with semantic accuracy long before he had mastered syntactic accuracy. The excerpts in Table 7.1 illustrate this.

All of Michael's talk with adults and his infrequent spontaneous speech were marked by the same kinds of grammatical errors as his responses to the BSM. What is more interesting, however, is the fact that his grammatical system at any one time seemed to be mostly consistent. It would be surprising if a child acquiring a second language were to manifest a completely stable grammar, especially for an extended period of time. As language learners are exposed to more and more language, they figure out the rules more accurately and their grammar undergoes changes. This is the central claim of the interlanguage hypothesis we examined in Chapter 6, and it is certainly true for Michael. We can see an example of his grammar in transition in two of the answers in Table 7.1. He says at one point "Because him eats too lots" and a few minutes later, "Because he's not eating." The third person subject pronoun is an unstable form for Michael at this time, most likely because he was in the process of modifying his previous grammar, which used "him" and "her" in subject position. This is a process that began earlier and was well underway in June. The following September, I went back to the school to find out whether a number of the observations and predictions I had made about Michael's language growth had been accurate. I found out that when he returned to school in September, he had sorted out the distinction for both the masculine and feminine pronouns.

Fluency

In second language acquisition, fluency refers to the ability to produce language with relative ease and to communicate ideas effectively. Fluency has little to do with either grammatical accuracy or correct pronunciation unless severe deficiency in either impedes the flow of language. There are a number of ways of measuring fluency, including the number of times a child initiates speech. We have already seen why this might provide us with faulty information with certain minority groups. With Michael, this measure would indicate no fluency at all. In his case, a rough indication was obtained simply by counting and comparing the number of words produced in response to the same set of questions over time. In November, the 21 questions of the BSM elicited 28 words in response, or an average of 1.33 words per response. By January, the number of words jumped to 52, or an average of 2.48, and by the end of the school year, there was an increase to 69 for an average of 3.29. During the school year, then, there was an appreciable increase in fluency as indicated by the number of words produced in this highly controlled situation. With a great deal of prompting and the use of a picture book, Michael was able to tell me the story of *The Three Bears.*

Terry Piper: *Will you tell me a story Michael? What do you see?*
Michael: *The girl leaving in … [long pause]*
T: *What is the girl doing?*
M: *Leaving in bear bed.*
T: *What's she doing now?*
M: *Look in kitchen.*
T: *And what's she doing here?*
M: *Her [unintelligible] chair.*
T: *What did she do to the chair?*
M: *Wreck chair.*
T: *Right! And now what's she doing?*
M: *Sleepin' in bed now.*
T: *Yes?*
M: *That's the end.*
T: *No, not yet. What are these?*
M: *Those are bear.*
T: *What are they doing?*
M: *Them, them, this—the girl eat them.*
T: *What's this bear doing?*
M: *Him [unintelligible]*
T: *What?*
M: *That girl eat again.*
T: *What's happening here?*
M: *That bear—her sleeping on her bed.*
T: *And now what's the girl doing?*
M: *[unintelligible] out window.*
T: *Okay. And what are the bears doing?*
M: *Lookin' out. [long pause]*
T: *Is that the end?*
M: *Yeah.*

Michael's telling of the story took a great deal of effort both for him and for me, but eventually he more or less got it told. This is not by any means a fluent telling for a child at the end of the kindertgarten year, but when we recall that Michael did not speak at all in September, we have to count his hesitant retelling as significant progress. Lucy was far more fluent, and Kenny probably could have retold *2001, A Space Odyssey* with more fluency.

Other samples of Michael's speech showed the same pattern and rate of growth in fluency—steady but very, very slow. Improved fluency results from improved comprehension and productive ability as well as improved confidence. Confidence is part of that somewhat more amorphous aspect of language ability called communicative competence. We have seen that language acquisition has its roots in the child's wish to make meaning, to communicate. As a child's need and desire to communicate grows, language learning takes place. The most important index of language learning, then, is the overall growth in communicative competence.

Communicative Competence

The ability to communicate competently involves more than the ability to form grammatically correct utterances. It includes knowing the rules of speaking, how to use and respond to requests, apologies, invitations, thanks, etc., and how to use language appropriately. We have already seen that this was Kenny's major linguistic shortcoming. Communicative competence is difficult to measure or quantify, but it is not difficult for a teacher or other observer with extensive opportunity to observe a child to reach a fairly accurate and useful conclusion about the level of communicative competence a child has attained.

In Michael's case, there was little spontaneous speech from which to judge his communicative ability. Over the course of the school year, there was some growth. In March, the following dialogue was recorded:

> **Terry Piper:** *What are these children doing, Michael?*
> **Michael:** *I need big dog.*
> **T:** *Do you? Why?*
> **M:** *'Cause, mm, I leave my mom.*
> **T:** *You need a big dog when you leave your mom?*
> **M:** *Yeah. Dog, mm, dog go school.*
> **T:** *The dog would go to school with you?*
> **M:** *Yeah.*

As brief as it was, the exchange provided some evidence that Michael was increasing his repertoire of language functions. Michael declined to talk about the topic I introduced but used language instead to say something that *he* wanted to say. He was obviously trying to tell me something about his wish for a dog and what that dog would do. The fact that he rarely initiated speech is not in itself an indication of poor communicative ability. We have already seen that in many cultures such behavior is discouraged. It does suggest, however, that Michael was using only a limited number of the possible functions to which language can be put. The transcripts revealed a small number of spontaneous utterances, of Michael's using language to express his own meanings. As before, comparison with other second language learners in the class made Michael seem extremely reticent. Late in the year, however, an exchange took place with other children that suggested that he was beginning to use language for his own purposes. Michael was sitting with Rapinder and Jenny at a table during snack time. Jenny had brought a mandarin orange for her snack and Michael clearly craved it:

Michael: *What dat?*
Jenny: *It's a mandarin. My mommy gived it to me.*
Rapinder: *I got apple.*
M: *Me too. You want? [offering it to Jenny]*
J: *No, I want this.*
M: *Me too. You take. [offering the apple again]*
J: *No. I want mandarin. [she starts to peel it]*
R: *Michael want to trade.*
M: *Yeah, want trade.*
J: *No, I give you one piece. [she continues to peel the mandarin and hands Michael a piece]*
M: *Thank you.*

It would be presumptuous and likely wrong to label Michael as a semilingual if for no other reason than we had no accurate indication of his proficiency in Italian. Moreover, his English was growing—very slowly, but growing. Nevertheless, Michael was obviously a child at risk in the educational system. Bilingual children with similar but usually less severe language problems do appear in elementary schools from time to time. It may be frustrating for educators who have no appropriate label for them to plan for their education, but it is possible and does not require administering sophisticated tests. In Michael's case, no standardized tests were attempted, and the only test administered was the Bilingual Syntax Measure. Even with this simple test, the results were not used to label, place, or plan instruction for the child. Rather, the teacher relied on information gathered from the parents, on her own experience of other children of the same age, on her direct observation of and conversation with the child, and on her professional common sense in planning language experiences for Michael.

Michael and his family remained in the community during the years I was in contact with it. When I left for good 4 years later, I lost contact with Michael. I did learn, by asking around during a visit a few years later, that he was in high school and, though not in the top 10% of his class, his performance was acceptable. Michael is in his 20s now and is working in the fisheries in northern British Columbia. He did not complete high school. His parents returned to Italy after Michael left school.

PRINCIPLES AND GUIDELINES FOR ASSESSING BILINGUAL CHILDREN

What Crago and other researchers have learned from their ethnographic research, Michael's teacher learned in her own classroom. She adopted and applied a principle that is very basic in assessing the language of bilingual children. No decision about a language disorder can be made without first assessing the child's entire linguistic repertoire. In bilingual children, this includes both languages and, in some children, the merger of the two. In Michael's case, it would have been impossible to begin to understand his language problems in school without benefit of the additional information about his situation at home. We saw that Michael suffered from delayed development in his first language, and it was not, therefore, surprising that he had a problem learning English as a second language. We must also keep in mind however, the bilingual child who has normal first language development, which brings us to the second principle in assessing language disorders in bilingual children: If a child does not have a language disorder in the native language, then whatever communicative disorders that may *appear* to occur in the second language cannot be true language disorders.

Once again, we see that assessment in the child's native language is important, but is it possible? There have been efforts to create language proficiency tests that can be standardized in two languages. In the United States, for instance, the Test of Auditory Comprehension of Language is standardized in both English and Spanish. The problem with such a test, however, is that it measures the child's performance in each language independently and does not provide any indication of the child's overall language ability. As Abudarham (1980) points out, "If a child knows the correct response in the language not being currently tested, he is not credited with a positive score" (p. 239). Abudarham identifies another problem with most language tests used with bilingual learners. Because most language tests assume a developmental sequence, earlier test items are likely to use and test vocabulary appropriate to early childhood and later items will require vocabulary appropriate to older children, etc. For bilingual children who may have acquired their second language after early childhood, any early childhood words that appear on the test may be unfamiliar. They may well know other words, and they may also know words appropriate to their age at the time of testing, but their test results fail to reveal what they *do know*.

School personnel use tests because they are available, but also because they do not know of alternatives. Yet, if the tests are not providing reliable data, then they must be abandoned. But abandoned in favor of what? We have already seen how one teacher gathered information about the language background of one of the children in her class. Of course, not all teachers have access to such information. The following guidelines are intended to help educators in identifying language disorders in bilingual children:

1. Gather all possible information about the child's language background. Without intruding on the family's privacy, try to find out whether the child is a talker or is especially reticent, whether he or she has been read to and enjoys books, and the parents' attitude toward school. It is also useful to know whether the child has siblings and what languages are spoken by the child's playmates. Enlist a bilingual adult, ideally another teacher, or an older child if necessary.

2. Exercise care in using the information you gather. You must ensure the confidentiality of anything you do learn and take particular care to interpret the findings correctly. If you are not familiar with the cultural traditions of the child's family, find someone who is to advise you. This latter point is especially important. If you learn, for example, that the child says very little, do not jump to the conclusion that he or she does not have adequate knowledge of the language. It may be that such behavior is normal within the child's cultural group, which brings us to the next point.

3. Whatever language behavior you observe should be compared to that of other bilingual children with similar cultural and language background. If you find even one other child who manifests the same or a similar phenomenon, then you should be very doubtful that you have uncovered a true language disorder.

4. Expect second language learners to make grammatical errors. These may resemble errors made by first language learners at an earlier age, or they may be unique to second language learners. In acquiring the system of the second language, learners often make generalizations about that system that are only partly true, but these do not constitute evidence of a language disorder. As an example, many people from the Indian subcontinent produce the tag, *isn't it?* in sentences such as *It is a beautiful day, isn't it?* or *She looks very beautiful, isn't it?* They have obviously made an error in their hypothesis about how tag questions are formed in English, but it is a common error among non-native learners of English and is not evidence of a language disorder.

5. Under some circumstances, children may lose proficiency in their first language. It is not exposure to the second language per se that leads to this loss. Rather, children who lose opportunities to use their first language may lose ground in that language. If, for example, a young Cree-speaking child moves with her family to the city and loses the extended family and Cree community, her Cree language *may* suffer. Surrounded by English, she no longer has the opportunities to use her own language that she once had. There is also pressure from the school to learn English. If school personnel manage to test her in the Cree language, especially after she has been away from the Cree community for a year or more, they may find that her language seems to be underdeveloped, but the school will have failed, not only in their assumption of abnormal first language ability, but in not measuring the *totality* of the child's language.

6. Remember that it is normal for some children to use both languages to communicate. Mattes and Omark (1984) differentiate between linguistic borrowing and code switching. The former occurs when speakers incorporate elements of one language into another, particularly words. An example of borrowing would be the use of a single word from one language in the sentence of another, and it is especially common when the speaker does not know the word in the other language. The latter involves switching back and forth between languages but is not limited to individual words. A speaker may begin a sentence in one language and switch to another for a phrase and then back to the original. Both borrowing and code switching are normal phenomena in bilinguals. They represent a legitimate means of communication and should not be taken as evidence of any kind of disorder.

7. Look for possible cultural and language bias in any test or other instrument used to make decisions about bilingual children. In order to do this, it will be necessary to . . .

8. Learn as much as possible about the traditional and contemporary lifestyles of the cultures that you encounter in your community. Try to understand, for example, the different patterns of human development within different cultures as well as their value systems and beliefs and assumptions about education. Remember, however, that...

9. Each child is an individual whose own linguistic and cultural experiences will be to some degree unique. Do not assume that what you have learned about one child will always pertain to others from the same or similar background.

10. Finally, learn to trust your own judgment based on your experience with children of the same age. When there is doubt about the child's language, adopt a wait-and-see attitude. Many patterns of second language learning are normal, and it would be a mistake not to give a child adequate opportunity to learn with a friendly and facilitative classroom environment.

CONCLUSION

Often, we learn more about language learning from children like Michael and Kenny who experience difficulty with it than we do from children who proceed normally. These two boys had very different kinds of problems—almost at polar ends of a spectrum. Michael had very little language of any kind when he entered school while Kenny appeared to be years ahead of his peer group, but formal education was difficult for both of them. From Michael, we learned that although the preschool years are *very* important, it is possible for a child to overcome early deprivation, to catch up, for the most part, and to learn to function in the language of the school. From Kenny we learned that language fluency does not tell the entire story, that communication and social problems may reside alongside excellent reading and speaking skills. Both boys remind us that whatever generalizations we may be able to make about children's language and learning, it is ultimately subject to individual variation and we must look to the children themselves to guide us in the educational decisions we make on their behalf. Children's need and wish to communicate is so great that they are frequently able to overcome severe disabilities to acquire language. As teachers, our job is to be observant so that we will know when to refer, when to give the child time, and, for all children, how to provide the most encouraging environment possible for the learning of language.

For Further Study

1. The author writes that "as a rule" ESL children having pronunciation problems should not be referred for therapy. Why do you think this is true?

2. Go back and re-read Lucy's retelling of *The Three Bears* on p. 167. What strikes you as the most significant differences between her account and Michael's?

3. Why do you think it so prevalent for teachers to think of second language learners in terms of deficits, or what the students do *not* know about language? Is there any danger to a teacher holding that view?

4. Search the Internet for at least three websites on Asperger syndrome. Find three traits of Asperger syndrome not identified in this chapter.

5. What are the critical differences between Asperger syndrome and non-Asperger giftedness?

For Further Reading

The sources cited in this chapter all have excellent material on Asperger syndrome, but I would particularly recommend:

Cumine, V., Leach, J., & Stevenson, G. (1998). *Asperger syndrome, a practical guide for teachers.* London: David Fulton. (Also, there are excellent websites devoted to this subject as well as to semilingualism.)

Gutstein, S. (2001) *Autism/Asperger's syndrome: Solving the relationship puzzle.* Arlington, TX: Future Horizons.

Miller, S. (1993) *Reading too soon: How to understand and help the hyperlexic child.* Elmhurst, IL: Center for Speech and Language Disorders

CHAPTER EIGHT

Learning to Use Language

The research on children's language learning focuses heavily on how they acquire the sound system, words, morphological endings, and sentences. As a linguist, I spent many years studying how children learned these building blocks of language. And yet, anyone who has attempted to learn a foreign language knows that the learning of the structural components is necessary but not sufficient for learning a language. It is somewhat surprising that researchers have focused so heavily on these areas given that, particularly in young children, so little of language use is confined to the sentence. Children—and indeed adults engaged in everyday conversation—use language in chunks both larger and smaller than sentences. What is perhaps even more important is that they learn to match language use to social context, a significant feat that one never completely stops learning. Conversational skills take longer to master than the structural component parts. Some children, such as Kenny whom we met in Chapter 7, never do fully master them.

One way of thinking about how children learn the many uses of language is to conceive of a child's social circle as an ever-widening one, starting with the mother (or other principal caregiver) and moving outward to encompass first the immediate and extended family, then other relatives and playmates, neighbors, shopkeepers, friends of siblings, and eventually, teachers and all the other folk who populate schools. As the circle widens, so do the opportunities for and the demands on language. Children learn that what is appropriate with the inner circle may be less so with the outer circle and vice versa. As they learn language, children learn at the same time the social rules of language and how to manipulate or modify the use of these rules to fit the situation. In fact, it can be argued that outside literacy, the most dramatic language development of the school years is in pragmatics, or the appropriate use of language. Children begin school with some facility with a range of language functions, but it is during the school years that they develop their conversational ability. Through these years and beyond, one of the principal tasks of language learning is learning the art of effective communication for a large variety of purposes and in all the different situations one is likely to encounter.

In this chapter, we will examine some of the social aspects of language in children's lives, particularly in the school years. The framing notion of our discussion is how children learn to use language appropriately. Doing so requires, of course, learning the various functions of language, encountering and acquiring gender differences, acquiring conversational skills, and constructing narrative.

BUILDING CONVERSATIONAL SKILLS

Pan and Snow (1999) capture the essence of the task of acquiring conversational abilities by describing what one would have to program into a computer to enable it to engage in meaningful conversation. Acknowledging that it is *theoretically* possible to program a computer to recognize and produce "thousands of phonologically and grammatically correct sentences," they go on to state the obvious, that "writing software to enable a computer to engage in unstructured conversation with a native speaker is a much more challenging task" (p. 229). Children have advantages over computers, of course, and we do not have to program them, but it is important to understand what children need to know and do in order to acquire the conversational skills that they will need for their entire lives.

The elements of conversational competence include the following:

1. becoming sensitive to the listener's perspective
2. becoming adept at turn-taking
3. learning to make conversational repairs
4. becoming sensitive to relevance
5. learning to make (and to understand) indirect requests
6. acquiring gender-based distinctions

We shall consider each of these in turn beginning with the one that is fundamental to all the rest, understanding that the listener has a perspective that differs from the speaker's.

Becoming sensitive to the listener's perspective is a prerequisite to effective conversation. Unless a speaker is aware of the listener's attention and comprehension, he is unable to structure his narrative or information in a way that makes sense to the listener. One indicator that a child is aware of the listener's perspective is the use of definite and indefinite articles. In general, English speakers use indefinite articles to introduce into the conversation a topic that is new to the listener. We would normally say, *A woman came into the store where I was shopping* rather than *The woman came into the store where I was shopping* unless the speaker was referring to a specific woman who had been previously introduced into the conversation. There are exceptions, of course, such as *This woman got on the bus and sat down beside me.* Even though *this* is definite, and the woman has not previously been introduced, the speaker is using it colloquially as an indefinite pronoun. By the time they reach school age, most children are able to use definite and indefinite articles correctly. At that age, they are not, however, reliable in using the indefinite article to introduce a new topic into the conversation.

The kind of understanding that a child needs to have in order to use the indefinite article correctly is similar to what is needed to estimate accurately the background knowledge the listener needs to understand a story or a conversation. We have all known people who begin to speak about a subject without providing adequate background. A friend of mine routinely comes into my office and begins a conversation with me that he is obviously in the middle of in his own mind. "I just don't know why she can't figure it out," he will start, without my knowing who "she" is or what she is having so much trouble understanding. In this kind of situation, the listener will usually wait to see if further information is forthcoming or whether he can otherwise figure out the context, but it would be more useful if the speaker were to supply the context and not risk the listener's frustration. Understanding the listener's perspective also entails judging how much information a listener is likely to have and to need—in other words, providing sufficient information but not redundant or superfluous information.

As children become more able conversationalists, they learn to do *comprehension checks* to ensure that listeners are understanding the intended meaning. I was once traveling in China with a friend who did not have, as I had, experience teaching English as a second language. We got into a taxi outside our hotel one morning, and he gave directions to the taxi driver in English. The taxi driver obviously didn't understand, and we secured the assistance of the doorman. The driver, he said, had understood where we wanted to go; he just didn't know where it was. My companion responded that it was near and that he would direct. He proceeded to do so, rather offhandedly, in the manner of "Take a left at the second light." Some time later, he interrupted his conversation with me to observe that the driver should have turned at the previous light as he had been told. I couldn't resist pointing out that he had not done any comprehension checks to determine that the driver had understood his directions. The point for our discussion here is that effective communication depends upon being able to put oneself to some degree in the role of the listener. As children move out of the egocentric stage, their awareness of those around them increases, and this awareness leads to an increasing awareness of their needs as listeners.

Another aspect of effective conversation concerns what children know and the language they have available for talking about their knowledge. As Hulit and Howard (1993) point out, "It is difficult for any speaker to provide information to his listener if his own understanding is lacking" (p. 242). The school-age child knows more about the world than the preschool child and has more language to express it. Throughout the school years, children continue to add to their store of general knowledge about the world. This, combined with their improved cognitive abilities and language competence, makes them much more effective conversationalists.

Becoming adept at turn-taking is also foundational to building conversational skills given that conversation, by definition, involves more than one participant. Otherwise, talk would consist of a series of monologues. Children do not arrive at school completely devoid of experience in turn-taking, however. Even in infancy, they engage in rudimentary turn-taking with their mothers as they coo or babble and their mothers respond. Mothers respond to their babies' non-linguistic behaviors such as smiling, laughing, crying, and even burping with language, thus establishing the early patterns of conversational turn-taking. As children grow older, adults become more selective in what they respond to, responding only to language or language-like noises. Some researchers have claimed that when a turn is passed to children who do not know what to do with it, they will use fillers (*hmmm, well, uh,*) or simply repeat what the adult has said. It is likely that we all know people for whom these behaviors have persisted into adulthood. Pan and Snow (1999) have pointed out that normally mothers and their infants take turns quite smoothly, probably "because adults rarely compete with young children for the floor" (p. 231). This orderly exchange is less likely with peers, of course, because peers are more likely to compete for "air time." By about age 4, most children have become adept at holding the floor with a continuous stream of *ands* or *and thens*. The much more difficult job is to learn to yield the floor!

Learning to make conversational repairs is related to being sensitive to listeners. If the listener does not understand what the speaker has said and the speaker is aware of that, he will attempt to correct the conversational breakdown. Becoming competent with this facet of conversation entails the ability to request clarification, the ability to perceive when clarification is required, and the ability to provide clarification. These are skills that children must acquire during the school years to become effective communicators. Preschool children will attempt to repair a wayward or broken conversation if asked to do so, but they will not be terribly successful. They will only rarely perceive the need to repair the conversation without being asked directly, but they are more successful with requesting clarification, although their methods may differ from adults'. A conversation between two preschool children might go something like this:

Mary: *We went to Disneyland.*
Jo: *Me too.*
M: *When did you go?*
J: *Sunday or maybe Saturday.*
M: *We flew in an airplane.*
J: *Why?*
M: *Because it's a long way.*
J: *No, it's not!*
M: *Yes it is! You're stupid!*

This is not the recommended way for clearing up what was essentially a misunderstanding between Mary, who had been to the California theme park, and Jo who had seen *The Wonderful World of Disney* on television and who may not have even known about the existence of the park.

Sometimes, when the first attempt at repair fails, subsequent repairs are attempted. These are called stacked repairs. These can occur with nearly any topic and are most frequent when one conversationalist has more knowledge about the subject than another or when the primary context for certain lexical items differs for the speakers. Such a case occurred a few years ago between my friend Bernadette and me:

> **Terry Piper:** *You'll never guess what I did this weekend.*
> **Bernadette:** *I'm afraid to.*
> **T:** *I went shopping.*
> **B:** *Oh, oh. Sweetn's? (a local boutique)*
> **T:** *No. I bought a Suzuki.*
> **B:** *A what?*
> **T:** *A Suzuki X-90. Actually, I leased it.*
> **B:** *Why?*
> **T:** *Well, I thought it was about time. And I got a really good deal on it.*
> **B:** *(Looking thoroughly bewildered.) But, Terry, what are you going to do with it?*
> **T:** *(Finally catching on that we're talking about different things.) Bernadette, I'm not talking about a motorcycle!*
> **B:** *I didn't think you were. I thought you meant a violin.*

The repair was left so late in the conversation, not because I was unaware of her response, but because I attributed it to the wrong reasons. I assumed that she was surprised by the size of the financial commitment or that I'd actually bought a car after depending on public transport for so long. In fact, her main context for Suzuki was violin and not vehicle.

A memorable conversation that occurred between my British husband and me a few days before our first Christmas together is illustrative:

> **David:** *Rob and Cynthia are coming over tomorrow night. I promised them we'd have mince pies.*
> **Terry:** *Mince, hmm. Not my favorite. Are you sure?*
> **D:** *Of course! Can't have Christmas without mince pies.*
> **T:** *(doubtfully) Okay. I'll have to get some mincemeat.*
> **D:** *Do you have tins?*
> **T:** *Pie tins?*
> **D:** *Yes, for the pies.*
> **T:** *Well, I've got two or three.*
> **D:** *You have to make more than that!*
> **T:** *For four people? I don't like the stuff, and I doubt that Cynthia is that crazy about it either since she's also an American.*
> **D:** *Okay, but I'll eat at least four and so will Rob, so shouldn't you make a dozen to be safe?*
> **T:** *You want me to make a dozen pies for four people for tomorrow night?*
> **D:** *Yeah, although you might as well make two dozen and save the rest for Christmas.*

> **T:** *How many people did you invite for Christmas?*
> **D:** *None, just you and me.*

The source of the misunderstanding was lexical, and I didn't identify it until we went shopping for additional pie tins. I picked up a package of foil pie tins, 8 or 9 inches in diameter. David looked at them with disbelief. He had a muffin tin in his hand, but apparently what we were looking for were shallow tart tins. What I had grown up calling tarts were pies to David and his countrymen. I'm glad I discovered that before I bought gallons of mincemeat. In this case, the repair wasn't made during the actual conversation in which the misunderstanding occurred.

Becoming sensitive to relevance is a task a child must accomplish on two levels. The first is *topic relevance*. During the school years, the child becomes increasingly aware that adults and older children will be more interested in a conversation whose topic is timely, pertinent, or useful. They will engage for only so long if they perceive the topic to be of no interest to them. Topic relevance is a skill that some people never fully master, and the result is either a reticent conversationalist, reluctant to tackle topics that might not interest other people, or the opposite kind who talks about whatever topic pops into his head without regard for audience.

The second kind of relevance is *intraconversational relevance*. Part of successful conversation is contributing useful, relevant commentary, and this is something that the child must learn, as with most language, without actually being taught. A further lesson is that the child alone will not be the arbiter of what is relevant. Preschool children (and some adults!) sometimes engage in parallel monologues, primarily because they have not mastered the notion of relevance. The following is an example:

> **Janie:** *I don't want to play checkers.*
> **Doug:** *I don't want to play dolls.*
> **J:** *Checkers is boring.*
> **D:** *Dolls is more boring.*
> **J:** *Mom wouldn't let me go to the party with Candace.*
> **D:** *My dog had to go to the doctor.*
> **J:** *It's not fair.*
> **D:** *But he's sick.*
> **J:** *What? Who's sick?*

Learning to make and to understand indirect requests is a skill that makes one a more popular companion. Adults learn to say *It's dark in here* or *Don't you think it's a little dark in here?* as a way of getting the lights turned on rather than *Turn on the lights.* At age 4 or 5, children will understand *Don't you think it's a little dark in here?* not as a request to turn the lights on but as a question asking for an opinion, but during the school years they come to understand the intent. Adults understand the importance of indirect requests for preserving relationships. For example, when my husband asks *What are you having for breakfast?* he is not asking what I plan to ingest. The real meaning is *What might you make ME for breakfast?* Likewise, *Are you having lunch?* means that he is hungry and hoping to take advantage of whatever preparation I might be making.

Children have to learn a number of different rules in learning to deal with indirect requests. According to Ervin-Tripp and Gordon (1986), the child uses two simple rules: Be brief and be creative enough not to seem demanding. Learning the rules of politeness—whom to interrupt and when, the necessity of being more polite when trying to win favor, and the degree of politeness that must be evident to make a very large request as opposed to a small one—is an important aspect of learning to deal with indirect requests.

Acquiring gender-based distinctions is an important aspect of sociolinguistic competence. There is little doubt that these differences are a result of socialization, a process that begins at home and continues in school. Males and females differ both in the vocabulary they use and in their style of speech (and perhaps writing, although that may be more difficult to detect except in any but personal writing). It will be interesting to see in the next several decades whether closing the gender gap in education, employment, and politics will eventually narrow or close the gender gap in language as well. Some of the differences children will eventually manifest if this gap does not close include the following:

1. Men tend to talk more than women do. Their conversations are longer with other men than they are with women (Swacher, 1975).

2. Men talk louder than women do and use volume, as opposed to pitch change, for emphasis (Glass, 1992).

3. Men tend to use three tones while women typically use five. The effect is more monotonous (Glass, 1992).

4. Men interrupt more, and they are more likely to interrupt women than other men (Parlee, 1979).

5. Women are more likely to interrupt women than men (Willis & Williams, 1976, reported in Hulit & Howard, 1993).

6. Women more readily surrender the topic of conversation as well as their turns.

7. In conversations in which both men and women participate, only about one-third of the topics introduced by women into conversation are sustained, while nearly all topics introduced by men are sustained (adapted from Ehrenreich, 1981).

8. In conversation, women tend to disclose more personal information than do men (Glass, 1992).

9. Men tend to use more declarative sentences than women, who tend to be more tentative. Similarly, men ask fewer questions to stimulate conversation than do women.

By the time they reach school age, children in the dominant culture have begun to use gender-appropriate language. From the time they are about 4, their topics of talk are differentiated along the same lines as adult male/female talk. Moreover, according to research done by Carol Edelsky (1977), when they begin school, children are already able to distinguish between male and female speakers on the basis of vocabulary used in emotional expressions. Early socialization into these roles occurs, of course, in the home. Research has shown that caregivers talk differently to boys and girls. For example, while mothers are likely to use nicknames for either sons or daughters, the kinds of nicknames differ. Fathers are more likely to use nicknames for their daughters and typically choose terms of endearment or food terms (e.g., *Daddy's sweetheart, cupcake,* or *pumpkin*). When they do adopt nicknames for their sons, they choose names such as *ding-a-ling* (Berko-Gleason & Greif, 1983), *sport,* or *champ.*

Conversation, of course, is only one of the language skills that children master during the school years. Another one, perhaps even more important to school success than conversation, is the ability to tell a coherent tale, that is, to construct a narrative.

Learning to Construct Narrative

Certainly, conversation can entail narrative, but generally conversation is characterized more by turn-taking than by narrative monologue (although some people appear not to know the difference). The differences are obvious—a narrative involves one person telling a story to one or more other people. It is largely uninterrupted (when it is, it becomes a conversation), and the full burden falls on the speaker. Learning how narratives are constructed is important to reading comprehension, writing, and oral language development. What children have to learn about narrative includes the various components of the narrative as well as the structure of the narrative.

Pan and Snow identify three genres of narrative, the script, fiction or fantasy, and personal. *Scripts* are those generalized accounts of recurrent events such as an account of what happens when a plane lands or how to make pizza. *Personal* narratives recount events that the speaker has experienced, and *fantasy* or *fiction* is the genre that children engage in when they pretend.

With assistance, very young children can recount recurring events such as what happens when Daddy comes home, and over time, they will learn to use the more common features that define the genre, features such as "timeless present tense, the general pronoun *you,* and a timeline that follows real-event chronology" (Wolf, Moreton, & Camp, 1994, cited in Pan & Snow, 1999, p. 243).

Before they reach school age, children begin to create their own imaginative stories using devices they will encounter later in print. They will use what they have acquired in the early years as a basis for constructing more complex narratives in both speech and writing. One of the skills that is foundational to constructing narrative is the ability to take alternative stances. When children learn to pretend, they are taking alternate stances, and this helps later as they learn to construct narrative. Very young children engage in fantasy talk with older speakers, but at the beginning, they only respond to fantasy—they neither initiate it nor use the linguistic markers associated with pretense. But by the time they reach school age, however, "Children not only initiate fantasy autonomously, but also use a variety of means, both linguistic… and non-linguistic…to signal shifts between real-world and fantasy-world talk"

(Wolf, Moreton, & Camp, 1994, cited in Pan & Snow, 1999). They use, for instance, a changed (often falsetto) voice or a style of speaking that differs from the one they normally use.

By the time they begin school, most children have begun to create their own stories using devices that they will later encounter in print. A narrative consists of a setting that provides information about the location, the characters, and any relevant background information to the episode. The episode is the heart of the narrative and contains information about the event that caused the main character to act, the character's action, and success or lack of success in carrying out the action and the consequences of the plan. It might also include the character's own feelings about the action. When a hearer (or reader) complains about not being able to understand a narrative, it is usually because critical elements of the episode are missing.

Children acquire the ability to narrate in regular stages related to both age and culture. Primitive narrative structures begin to appear sometime after the age of 3. These first attempts lack setting and organization. Little information is provided, and the child depends on prosodic devices to convey much of the tale. Gradually, the child starts to organize the narrative temporally. These narratives will have a discernible beginning, middle, and end, but there will be little information provided about motivation, and the plot will be thin or non-existent. By the end of the first or second year of school, plots begin to emerge, and, partly as a result of increased exposure to printed stories, the devices for carrying the plot forward become more sophisticated. They will learn stylized beginnings and endings, for example, for fictitious narratives (i.e., *Once upon a time... they lived happily ever after*) as well as the use of the past tense and connectives (*and then...*) for personal narratives. This pattern of development applies to English speakers.

Dickinson, Wolf, and Stotsky (1993) point out that culture plays a major role in the development of narrative. "The narratives of African-American [girls especially] tend to have a structure distinct from that of middle-class white children. They use an approach referred to as topic-associating, which juxtaposes thematically related incidents to make a point implicitly" (p. 373). To those unfamiliar with this narrative structure, the resulting stories are difficult to follow because they lack the familiar explicit indicators of shifts in time, character, or setting. Japanese children's narratives also have a distinct character. They tend to be succinct and, consistent with the Japanese haiku, told in sets of three episodes (p. 373).

Whatever their previous cultural experience of narrative, when they get to school, children will face the task of linking oral and written language. Narrative is the principal link between the two. There are two kinds of evidence that this is an extremely important link. The first is that children with moderate to severe reading problems frequently have deficient narrative skills. The second is the evidence that, in kindergarten children, there is a significant and positive correlation between the ability to name letters and to write and the ability to understand stories (Dickinson & Snow, 1987; Dickinson et al., 1993).

LANGUAGE FUNCTIONS

A very concrete way of categorizing children's language development within a social interaction theoretical framework is to define the different functions that language serves in their lives. Thinking about language growth as a child's expanding the number of functions language plays and the quality of interaction within each function also helps us evaluate the quality of language in the classroom. It would be possible, of course, to theorize about language acquisition from the perspective of language function, as Halliday (1975, 1978) did. A purely functional analysis of language acquisition, however, is somewhat problematic.

Useful as it is, there are three problems with a purely functional analysis. The first has to do with intent. Using the example of a doctor lecturing a patient on the likely consequences of overeating and smoking, D. Piper (1992) points out that the doctor might not consciously conceive of her diatribe as a warning but might view it as a "dispassionate description of facts" (p. 244). Similarly, a mother, worried about her child being late getting home, might, upon the child's tardy arrival, demand "Just where do you think you've been?" She might believe that she is asking the child for an explanation (as she probably is) and not recognize the further function of the question—to express her fear and perhaps a warning to the child.

The second problem also relates to intent, and that it is often difficult for a researcher (or a teacher) to determine just what was intended. A full understanding of the situation, and perhaps a personal history of the speakers, would be required to get the correct meaning from a sentence such as those in the previous paragraph. A final problem exists even if we are able to solve the first two. This is the problem of polyphony in adult speech and, thus, to some degree in children's speech. In other words, utterances have many functions, intended or not, and some of these might actually change during the course of the utterance as a result of situational feedback.

These problems with functional analysis are significant not only to researchers but to teachers because they point to the difficulty of assessing a child's functional competence. The importance of understanding the multitude of functions language serves in children's lives, however, is not to assess them but to ensure that children's experience of language in school is as functionally rich as it was at home. Besides, one thing is clear. Language learning is indistinct from learning to use language in functional ways. Common sense tells us that this is true. How could we, after all, claim that we had mastered a language if we had mastered the grammar and phonology and knew thousands of words, yet could not use it in any social setting, to any practical use?

In the next pages, I will attempt to characterize the roles language plays in the lives of preschool children so that later we may compare this early experience with the typical school experience of language and learning. We will begin by looking at the uses to which children put language as they learn it.

THE FUNCTIONS OF LANGUAGE
IN CHILDREN'S LIVES

We saw in earlier chapters that linguists and others interested in language acquisition may study it from a number of vantage points. For teachers, whose interest is in working with children to provide language-rich environments in which their language can continue to flourish, a particularly useful way of thinking about language acquisition is in functional terms. A number of researchers have examined language acquisition and language use from that perspective. Because their purposes and methods differed, each researcher came up with a distinct set of functional categories. We will not consider here all the functional schemes proposed by researchers, but will concentrate on four, those of Halliday (1975, 1978), Shacter Kirshner, Klips, Friedrickes, and Sanders. (1974), Tough (1977, 1979), and Shafer, Staab, and Smith (1983).

Four Perspectives on Language Function

One of the first and most influential researchers to use a functional analysis was M. A. K. Halliday, a British linguist who employed the notion of function in describing his son Nigel's early language acquisition. He identified seven early functions that accounted for all the uses to which Nigel put the words he was learning. In order to classify Nigel's early words in this manner, Halliday had to make judgments about what meaning his son intended—what he was trying to accomplish with each utterance.

Ingram (1989) has pointed out that Halliday provides no operational procedures for researchers to follow in making such judgments, making it difficult for them to apply his method to the analysis of other children's speech in order to discover how universal the functions truly are. Ingram may be right, but he is writing as a linguist with particular goals in studying language acquisition and with rigorous standards for accomplishing them. Parents and teachers, in contrast, are accustomed to making precisely these kinds of judgments about children's intentions. Doubtless they are sometimes wrong, but even then there is opportunity for unraveling intent and recreating the fabric of meaningful discourse. Focused as they are on communicating with children, they find sense in a functional analysis (p. 171).

The functions Halliday identified included the instrumental, regulatory, personal, interactional, heuristic, imaginative, and informative functions. All these were present in the child's language before the age of 2. Later, he postulated, children make a transition to the more abstract uses of language that characterize adult speech. He therefore added four functional categories to account for the more mature uses to which children put language. These included the interpretive, the logical, the participatory, and the organizing functions (Halliday, 1978).

Schacter et al. (1974) proposed nine functional categories that were also based on the analysis of young children's speech. They recorded 6,000 utterances made by children playing in nursery schools and then classified them according to how the investigators perceived the intent of each utterance. The nine categories these researchers identified included: expressive, desire-implementing, possession-rights-implementing, ego-enhancing, self-referring-including, joining, collaborative, learning-implementing, and reporting. Notice that while most of these functions demonstrate the highly egocentric nature of preschool children, they also use language for social purposes (the joining and collaborative functions) and for learning (the learning-implementing and reporting functions).

Based on her own and on the work of previous work of Halliday, Vygotsky, Luria, Bruner, and others, Joan Tough established her own theory of language functions. According to her analysis of preschool children's language, Tough (1977, 1979) concluded that four functions account for their language use: directive, interpretive, projective, and relational. She went further to describe specific uses that children make of language within each function and also identified specific strategies they use to accomplish each use. Finally, Shafer et al. (1983) condensed Tough's categories to a set of five, which they used for their book on developing children's language functions in school. Table 8.1 shows the four different sets of functional categories proposed by the different researchers together with a description of each category.

The most comprehensive of the functional systems is Halliday's, which postulates seven early functional categories and four later ones. The least inclusive is Tough's with four, but she covers the same language use by developing an elaborate network of uses and strategies for implementing the uses for each function. Whichever system we might choose to follow, it is clear that children's capacity to function in language is rich and varied. Although I will refer occasionally to some of the early functions in Halliday's system, for the purpose of discussion henceforth I will use the functional scheme suggested by Shafer et al. (1983), not because it is more comprehensive than the others but because it was created with the stated purpose of helping "teachers to develop various language functions with children in order for them to succeed in school and throughout life" (p. 20).

Five Functions of Language

1. *Children use language to assert and maintain social needs.*   When very young children make a demand (*Want juice!*), they are asserting a need. When they lay claim to a favorite toy (*That mine!*), they are asserting their personal right to have the toy. This function has several subfunctions. Shafer, Staab, and Smith identify five. A 6-year-old who warns a playmate, *I'm gonna tell!* is using language to threaten. The same child who contends that *It's not fair,* or who argues that *It is not your truck!* is asserting herself in different but related ways, to give a negative opinion in the first instance and to argue in the second. When 5-year-old Janet complained (in Chapter 4) that Matthew's drawing was "like a baby's," she was using language to criticize.

Children are also using this function when they assert positive expressions (*That looks pretty, Mom*) or when they ask an opinion (*Do you like this one?*). Incidental expressions such as *Oh, No!* are considered to belong to the same function. All exemplify ways in which young children assert their rights and their identities as individuals. This

Table 8.1 Rough Equivalents of Four Functional Systems

Description	Halliday	Tough	Schacter et al.	Shafer, Staab, & Smith
Early Functions				
Satisfy needs; get things done	Instrumental	Directive	Desire-implementing	Social needs
Control behavior of others	Regulatory	Directive	Possession-rights-implementing	Controlling
Tell about self	Personal	Relational	Ego-enhancing	Social needs
Get along with others	Interactional		Joining; collaborative	Social need; projecting
Find out and learn	Heuristic		Learning-implementing	
Pretend, make believe	Imaginative	Projective		
Communicate information to others	Informative		Reporting	Informing
Later Functions				
Interpret whole of experience	Interpretive	Interpretive		Forecasting and reasoning; projecting
Express logical relations	Logical	Interpretive		Forecasting and reasoning
Express wishes, feelings, attitudes, judgments	Participatory	Relational	Possession-needs-implementing; self-referring-including	Social needs
Organize discourse	Organizing			Forecasting and reasoning; projecting

is an early function to appear in their language because young children are egocentric, and it continues to develop well into the school years. As they approach school age, children's ways of expressing their personal rights and needs will conform more to the socially accepted forms of the adult world. Also as they grow older, they hear and learn to ask others' opinions, which has the effect of clarifying their personal needs but may also serve to keep the conversation going. Incidental expressions such as *Oh yes?* or *That's right* serve a similar function of moving the discourse along. Children will become increasingly able to voice agreement with and compliments of others, which contributes significantly to their ability to use language to maintain social relationships. This function is comparable to Halliday's instrumental function and is one of the earliest to develop.

2. *Children use language to project into novel situations.*   Play is very important in children's lives, and language is an important part of much of that play. When children enter into make-believe worlds and roles, they use language to project themselves into the part. Most of us have heard a young child at play alone, playing two or more parts in an imaginary situation. The child will use a different pitch and manner of speaking for the various characters. "Projecting is the function of reaching out into other person's experiences or into novel circumstances that we have not actually encountered ourselves" (Shafer et al., 1983, p. 103). This may be real or imagined. Because they are egocentric, young children's use of projecting language for real situations may be somewhat limited until they approach school age. It is difficult for them to assume another person's perspective. Still, there are circumstances that demonstrate that even very young children have the capacity to project themselves into the identities or experiences of others.

When children engage in make-believe, they are reaching outside their identities into another experience. When they engage in dialogues such as the following, they are using projecting language.

> Amy and Martha, both 4, are playing house:
> **Martha:** *I'm the mommy, and you can be the neighbor.*
> **Amy:** *No, I want to be the mommy.*
> **M:** *I'll let you wear my Mommy's pretty scarf.*
> **A:** *Okay. But Sally (a doll) is my baby. She wants to be my baby. Jilly wants to be yours. See, she's nodding her head.*

This is clearly an example of projecting language being used in an imaginative way to project completely outside their own experience. In preschool children, the projecting function includes projecting into the feelings, reactions, and experiences of others, both real and imaginative.

3. *Children use language for controlling the self and others.*   This is the language of getting the job done. It is akin to Halliday's instrumental function and to his regulatory function. It is the use children make of language when they direct others' actions or their own in expressions such as *Give me that truck* or *Look at this*. It is also the language used for requesting directions in utterances such as *What do you want me to do with this cup?* or *Where should we stick the red star?* and for seeking others' attention in commands like *Watch me*! or *Look at this*! Sometimes this function is directed toward the child's own behavior. A child playing alone, or with other children, might be heard saying *This goes here, and now it's done.* The comment is not directed to another speaker but serves the purpose of monitoring the child's own activity, much as adults talk themselves through complex or multifaceted tasks.

Shafer et al. (1983) point out that controlling language may consist either of very explicit statements such as *Shut the window*, or of implicit statements, such as *I think the plant looks dry*, which, if spoken with the intent of getting someone to water the plant, is equally controlling in function (p. 65).

Not only is the controlling function of language used to get things done, a very important function in the lives of young children, it also plays an important role in learning. When it is used to instruct the self or direct others in ways that facilitate understanding, it is helping children make sense of the world around them and is thus related to Halliday's heuristic function, which is a valuable tool for their early learning.

4. *Children use language to inform.*   Children no doubt hear a great deal of this type of language both before and after they begin school. It is the language for commenting on events past and present (*That's a fat frog; I saw one like it in the park*), for labeling (*That's a bus*), for talking about sequences of events (*You should wait to do that after we put the paint on*), and for talking about details (*It's not brown exactly, more like a funny red*). Other subfunctions include the language of comparison (*This blue is better than that one*), the language for making generalizations on the basis of specific events or details (*See the way it's smashed? Someone must have hit it*), and for requesting information (*What do you call this? What color was it before?*).

In the very earliest stages of language acquisition, children begin by labeling the objects in their environment—*Mummy, Ginger cat, truck, boat, juice.* Very soon, they expand this function. Any parent of a toddler knows, for example, that requesting information is one of the first types of informing language that children acquire. Children ask questions to sort out the workings of the world, and when parents answer their questions, they are exposing their children to even more informing language. We can see that this function of language serves children in some of the same ways as Halliday's heuristic function. Because it is the language used to discover, to test whether things are as they appear to be, and to question the world, informative language is an extremely important function for children to develop if they are to succeed in school.

5. *Children use language to forecast and reason.*   As we have seen, children put both controlling and informing language to uses that enhance their learning. The principal language function they employ in the business of learning, however, is the language of forecasting and reasoning, the language Halliday identified as heuristic. It is the language that expresses their curiosity and allows them to find out about the world. It is used with extreme frequency by toddlers asking *Why can't I?* or *Why does the wheel go around?* Subfunctions other than the requesting of information include predicting an event and forecasting or reasoning about causal relationships. Shafer et al. (1983) point out that the predicting of an event may be based on obvious reasons, either stated or not, or it may have reasons that are neither stated nor immediately apparent. Their example is of a child who looks out the window at a threatening sky and observes, I think it's going to rain. In this case, it is clear that the reason for the statement is the darkness of the sky. Another child, however, might look into a sunny sky and make the same prediction. In this case, there is no obvious reason for the speculation (p. 93). In the first instance, parents will usually respond by agreeing that the child's prediction is likely. In the second, they will usually try to draw out a reason for the child's gloomy forecast. In questioning the child and offering possible reasons or alternative conclusions, they engage the child in reasoning about an event and provide representative language for doing so.

While all the language functions provide a window on children's cognitive development, the forecasting and reasoning function of language is especially revealing. By carefully observing children's use of language to forecast and reason, we gain valuable insights into the growth in their reasoning. The following two dialogues illustrate this point:

Amy, age 4, is in trouble with her 12-year-old sister Sara:
Sara: *I told you to stay out of my things. Look what you did!*

Amy: *No.*
S: *What do you mean, no? Don't tell me you weren't playing with my nail polish.*
   You got it all over the vanity. Mom's going to kill us both. And it's all your fault.
A: *I didn't.*
S: *Then who did?*
A: *(Thinking for a minute.) Sam was here. I guess he...*
S: *Oh right. So when did Sam start polishing his nails with bright pink paint?*
A: *I don't know.*
S: *Well, will you at least help me clean it up?*
A: *(Relieved) Okay. We won't get in trouble, right?*
S: *Well, not if we get it all off. Go in the kitchen and get me a whole lot of paper*
   towels.

Six-year-old Danny and his mother are having a discussion about his afternoon plans. Danny wants to go to a showing of a children's film at the local library, something he usually does once a week.

Danny: *Why can't I go? James gets to go.*
Mother: *I explained already. You can't go because I have to work tonight and I won't*
   be able to pick you up. And Daddy's car is in the shop.
D: *Why can't I ride with James?*
M: *Usually, you can, but today James's mother is dropping him off and then his*
   Dad's picking him up
D: *I can ride with his Dad.*
M: *Not today because they're not going home afterward. They're going to James's*
   grandmother's house.
D: *I can go there, too!*
M: *No, you can't. You weren't invited this time. But I'm sure James will invite you*
   another time.

We see in the first dialogue that Amy is able to understand her sister's reasoning, helped along by the somewhat perilous situation in which she finds herself, far better than she is able to reason herself. Nevertheless, we see evidence that she is capable of causal reasoning in her *We won't get in trouble, right?* This question implies her understanding of the contingency—if they clean up the mess, they will avoid trouble. We also see her reasoning that, because Sam was also in the house, the blame might be laid at his feet, a slightly different type of causal reasoning.

In Danny, we find a child with more developed reasoning skills. As he makes his case for going to the film, we see an implied justification in his pointing out that James is being allowed to go. We find, too, that he is able to understand his mother's rather complex explanation of the reasons why he cannot go with James. Even though he doesn't accept the argument, he clearly understands it. The 2 years' difference in the ages of Amy and Danny makes a world of difference in their verbal reasoning abilities.

Language Functions Across Cultures

The examples used in our discussion so far have been from English-speaking children learning their native language. While it is certainly possible to examine the language growth of non-native speakers in terms of language function, care must be taken not to make faulty assumptions. It would be easy to do so given that functionality is socially determined (i.e., defined for the most part in terms of interactions). These differ widely from culture to culture. We have already seen how difficult it is to be certain that we have identified the speaker's intent correctly. We know that language functions are related to situations. People in different cultures react to situations differently, and the language that is appropriate for situations differs as well. We learned earlier that in Inuit culture children are deemed to have acquired their native language when they demonstrate their understanding by doing as they are told. Inuit children might use different expressions from native-English speakers to serve the same function or might appear not to have acquired the function at all. But when we are dealing cross-culturally, we have to be especially careful not to assume too much from what a child does not say. In judging a child's language attainment, remember that understanding of the function is just as important as producing it. Remember, too, that some functions are extremely difficult to observe, but that failure to observe a function does not mean absence of the function in the child's repertoire.

CONCLUSION

The purpose of this chapter was to look more carefully at the social aspects of language in children's lives; what they have to acquire in order to function as conversationalists in the many situations they will encounter in school and out. We began by looking at what children need in order to develop conversational skills. We examined the three kinds of narratives that children learn to construct and the language features typical of each. The chapter concluded with a categorical analysis of language functions, or the uses to which children normally put language. The purpose was not only to shed greater light on the accomplishment of language learning, but to establish linkages between the home experience and the school experience of language learning. In the next chapter, we see more linkages as we explore the relationship between language and cognitive growth. In our discussion of language functions in early childhood, we have considered the relationship from the perspective of language. In the next chapter, we will turn the mirror around and view the relationship from the perspective of cognitive growth. The two are not, of course, independent, but we gain a greater understanding of the relationship by viewing it from both perspectives.

For Further Study

1. List 10 nicknames or terms of endearment for male and female children or young people you know. Do you see a difference between those used for females and those used for males? Is age a factor?

2. Consider the following pairs of utterances, and speculate about whether the speaker was a male or female. What are your reasons for your choice?

   a. Who left the ice cream out?
   b. Damn, you left the ice cream out!
   c. Stop over there!
   d. Would you mind stopping at the dry cleaner?
   e. We've been invited to my boss's party.
   f. We've got to go to the boss's party.

3. Both men and women develop the full range of language functions, but some writers have observed differences in the ways in which such functions are expressed. Consider each of the following questions and determine whether men and women might use them to express different functions.

   a. Do we have any tea?
   b. Where's the butter?
   c. Aren't you ready yet?
   d. Are you watching that program (on television)?

4. Try to think of as many possible functions as you can for each of the following utterances. Be sure to provide the context for each.

   a. So, what do you think of the Yankees' chances this year?
   b. Is it midnight already?

5. What has the child had to learn in order to understand that the first request might be permissible and the second not?

   a. If you've finished with that section of the paper, could I have a look at it?
   b. If you're not doing anything this weekend, would you mind driving me to New Jersey? (assuming the speaker lives in Virginia).

For Further Reading

Eckert, P. (1990) Cooperative competition in adolescent "girl talk." *Discourse Processes*, 13, 91-122.

Eckert, P. (1989) The whole woman: Sex and gender differences in variation. *Language Variation and Change*, 1, 245-67.

Tannen, D. (2001). *I only say this because I love you: How the way we talk can make or break family relationships throughout our lives.* New York: Random House.

CHAPTER NINE

Language and Cognitive Growth

From the time a child begins to speak, there is evidence of cognitive development. Uttering the single word *dog* demonstrates that the child has already developed symbolization, or the ability to allow one thing (in this case, a word) to represent another (a canine). It gets a lot more complicated, of course. Many mothers have observed that their children could not tie their shoelaces until they could talk their way through the process. The fundamental question addressed in this chapter is how the medium in which we listen and speak is related to the medium in which we think. Of course, there are many issues embedded in that larger one, among them the relationship between language and memory, the role language plays in conceptual development and vice versa, and how language impacts academic achievement. Perhaps we should begin, however, by being perfectly clear about what is meant by cognitive development. In brief, cognitive development refers to the way in which the organizing and thought processes develop in the brain. It is intimately tied to memory, to conceptualization, to reasoning, and to language. I have maintained throughout the book, and most forcefully in Chapter 1, that language is special in children's lives. I have also stressed that language development is based in social interaction. But stressing the importance of social interaction in no way implies that language development occurs independently of cognitive development. Our best evidence is still, as it was 30 years ago, that language and cognition develop in tandem:

> … there is a close connection between words and thought, and at all stages language development is crucial to thought activity. The two are not identical, but they are interdependent, and the context within which the child acquires language has a permanent influence over the way he learns to think. (Yardley, 1973, p. 13)

I would go on to argue that the way children learn to think is tied to their ability to succeed in school, and so it is now time to talk in greater detail about language and its special relationship to learning. A main purpose of this chapter is to attempt to characterize the role language plays in the learning of preschool children so that in Chapter 10 we may compare this early experience with the typical school experience of language and learning.

Although language and cognition are related processes, the relationship is not well understood. There are those, including Vygotsky, who hold strongly that cognitive development, if not impossible without language, is certainly facilitated by it. Others, including philosopher Bertrand Russell, hold that language just confuses the issue. It is still a matter of intense inquiry among psychologists and linguists, but it seems to be the case that neither depends wholly upon the other. As Ratner (1993) points out, "… it is not clear that language development is contingent upon mastery of any specific subset of cognitive abilities…. It is more likely that linguistic and cognitive development may progress in parallel" (p. 335). It does seem to be the case, however, that language does influence cognitive growth in a variety of ways. In the pages that follow, we will look at those cognitive processes that appear to be most intricately connected to language.

Cognition is not a monolithic process, and its development is not a single process of change. In fact, what we commonly call cognitive development actually involves changes in a number of different capacities including perception, the ability to associate and categorize, memory, conceptualization, and academic skills. We will not talk at length here about perception because, even though there is little doubt that language plays an important part in human perception, the most interesting aspects of perceptual development occur in the first 6 months of life, before the onset of language. Rather, we will concern ourselves with the relationship of language to memory and conceptualization and to the child's achievement in academic thinking.

THE ROLE OF LANGUAGE IN MEMORY DEVELOPMENT

Not all memory is language-based. A person who misses a step on a stairway, for example, will often say, "There's one more than I thought," when, in fact, the memory of the number of stairs had likely never been "thought" much less articulated in language. Nevertheless, memory and language are usually linked. A simple experiment reported by Carmichael, Hogan, and Walter (1932) demonstrated how inextricably linked they can be. In reproducing line drawings they had been asked to remember, subjects in the study routinely distorted them in a way consistent with additional *verbal* information they had received. Language provides not only a means of encoding experience but influences the recall of that experience. In other words, they allowed what they were told to override what they had seen.

The simple fact of memory development is that as children grow older, their memories improve. But why? What makes this growth possible? Siegler (1991) offers four possible explanations. One is that as children mature, their basic capacity increases. In other words, the physical and physiological mechanisms responsible for memories expand. Another possibility is that children's memory strategies improve; through practice they get better at the procedures involved in storage and retrieval. A third explanation is that as children grow older they learn more about memory and how it works, and they use this knowledge to manage their own memories. Finally, it could be the case that because older children have greater prior knowledge of the content they need to remember, they have a sounder basis on which to remember new material (pp. 173–175).

It is likely, in fact, that all four explanations have some basis in reality, that is, that increased capacity, greater sophistication in using strategies, metamemory, and other experience all contribute to memory development. For our purposes, however, the question is not the degree to which any one contributes to cognitive growth but how language is involved in each.

Basic Capacities

Basic capacities include those frequently used components of memory that form the foundations for cognitive activity. Such processes as recognition, association, storage, and retrieval are prerequisite to all thinking. How language is involved may not be immediately obvious, but if we consider just what constitutes development of some of these processes, the relationship becomes clearer.

Recognition is at the heart of memory; cognitive development could not proceed without it. With regard to language, however, recognition is not an especially interesting phenomenon because the ability is amazingly well developed even in newborns. What role language plays in auditory recognition is unclear. We saw in an earlier chapter that very young infants are capable not only of recognizing human speech sounds but also of recognizing subtle differences between speech sounds. One interesting piece of research does, however, shed light on the nature of the interaction between language and early recognitory behavior.

Infants as young as 1 month are able to discriminate between certain speech sounds such as voiced and voiceless consonants. They seem to be able to mark these and certain and other speech distinctions no matter what language is being spoken around them. This very early ability would suggest that some innate mechanism is operating, and it raises a question about the point at which the infant's recognitory ability becomes attuned to a particular language. Two studies, reported by Reich (1986, p. 25), shed some light on this question. Researchers in one study found that infants in the first 6 months were unable to recognize certain acoustic distinctions that their Spanish-speaking parents recognized (Lasky, Syrdal-Lasky, & Klein, 1975). A second study of children who were 7 months old showed that children of Spanish-speaking parents could recognize the Spanish distinction better than children of the same age exposed to the English language (Eilers, Gavin, & Wilson, 1979). It would seem, then, that around 7 months is the age at which children begin to recognize the distinctions appropriate to the language around them. This does not mean, of course, that their ability to recognize sound distinctions is limited to one language from this early age; on the contrary, if two languages are spoken in the home, they will be able to mark the salient distinctions in both, although more empirical research needs to be conducted to determine the specifics of that ability.

Another aspect of basic memory capacity that is present at birth but increases with age is association. It also changes in character. Infants are capable of associating certain stimuli with certain responses. In one experiment with 3-month-olds, researchers attached a string from their ankles to a mobile. The babies quickly learned that kicking their legs caused the mobile to move. Another study showed that they could remember what they had learned as long as 8 days later (Sullivan, Rovee-Collier, & Tynes, 1979, cited in Siegler, 1986). As children get older and acquire language, they are able to make an entirely new set of associations, verbal associations, and their memory and learning capacities thus increase.

Further evidence that language is important in the development of memory is found in the phenomenon of infant amnesia. Adults have very long memories. Most of us can recall events that occurred or recognize people that we knew decades ago. Even young children are very good at recognizing pictures they have seen even though a considerable time has passed. Yet few adults have any memories of infancy. Those who claim to recall an occurrence from early infancy are usually found to be remembering someone else's account of those events. The passage of time alone cannot account for our inability to recall the first months of life. What likely does account for it is a difference in the way infants encode events and the way older children and adults encode events. As Siegler (1991) points out:

> Whether people can remember depends critically on the fit between the way in which they earlier encoded the information and the way in which they later attempt to retrieve it. The better able the person is to reconstruct the perspective from which the material was encoded, the more likely that recall will be successful. (p. 178)

And this is where language comes in: Older children have language as part of the context of experience and thus available as a means of encoding while infants do not. It seems probable that the onset of language represents an important device for increasing basic memory capacity. It also provides the child with a valuable memory strategy. We have all had the experience of repeating over and over something that we wanted to remember later. This strategy of rehearsal is one of several that are central to the development of memory.

Memory Strategies

Those conscious activities we engage in with the hope of improving our chances of remembering are called memory strategies. They occur at some time between the event or experience to be recalled and the act of recalling. Rehearsal is one such strategy, and language is crucial to it. Research has established clearly that the strategy of rehearsal plays an important role in memory improvement. Children who verbally rehearse the names of pictures can recall more pictures than children who do not rehearse the names. Without language, of course, they would be unable to do so.

A second strategy involves organization. Children of 5 and 6 years old make less use of categories than do children of 9 or older. That language plays a central role in our ability to categorize is easily demonstrated by an experiment commonly done in psychology classes. Consider the following list of words:

desk	dog
computer	hamster
telephone	tomato
bookshelf	lettuce
cat	radish
bird	cabbage

If you try to remember the list as a list of unrelated words, you may remember as many as half the items. If, on the other hand, you mentally organize the list into three categories, office equipment, animals, and vegetables, you will do much better. If you go even further and subcategorize the latter two as household pets and salad ingredients, you will do better still. The ability to categorize is closely associated with language; it is impossible to do it effectively without the verbal labels for classification.

One additional strategy for improving memory deserves mention because it is closely related to linguistic development. Elaboration can be similar to organization in that it involves making connections between items or events, but it differs in that it can occur even when no categorical relations exist between them. Elaborations can be images, as when a girl trying to remember to buy an umbrella, a bottle of ink, and shampoo forms a mental picture of herself holding the umbrella to protect her clean hair and the bottle of ink she is carrying, or they can be verbal. *Mnemonics* are common verbal elaborations. Many of us can recall learning the names of the lines of the treble clef (e, g, b, d, f) by using the phrase *Every Good Boy Does Fine* and the spaces by spelling *FACE*. There is evidence that children 4 years of age can be taught to form verbal elaborations for remembering two terms and use them successfully in recall. Attempts to teach them to form visual images are less successful. Language is clearly involved, then, in the strategies children employ to store and to retrieve experience. It is also involved in the improvement of metamemory.

Metamemory

A component of metacognition, metamemory refers to the knowledge children have about how memory works. It is not hard to find examples of metamemory being called upon. Take the adult who is watching a television drama and reading the newspaper at the same time. She goes back and forth, sampling information from the television screen and the newspaper page in turn. The procedure goes smoothly enough until she discovers she has missed something, say in the television program, and what is happening no longer makes sense. What she will do in such a case is abandon the paper and pay close attention to the television, hoping to find clues to what she has missed. Usually in television, this strategy works, but it is the decision to employ the strategy that constitutes metamemory. As children grow older, they learn about the limitations and the fallibility of memory, and this knowledge directs them to develop a feeling for what is hard to remember as well as strategies for remembering those things.

At the very heart of metamemory is the act of monitoring, and an experiment conducted by Markman (1979) sheds light on the nature of monitoring growth in young children and on its relationship to language. Children between 8 and 11 years were read a short passage on the making of baked Alaska. In the second sentence of the passage, they heard that the ice cream melts in the hot oven. Two sentences later, they heard that the ice cream stays hard and does not melt. Nearly half the subjects in the study failed to identify the contradiction even when they had been warned that the story was problematic. The children who did not notice the disparity seemed to be concentrating on the soundness of each individual statement rather than on the sense they made in total (Markman, 1979, cited in Siegler, 1986, pp. 242–243). Their monitoring of their own understanding differed in kind from that of older children and adults.

But how does monitoring relate to language? From about 2 years, children are able to correct their own language errors indicating use of a language monitor that compares their utterances with what they know of language. They apply this monitor to their own pronunciation, vocabulary choices, and grammar. As we also saw in Chapter 3, they monitor what they hear, rejecting adults' infantile pronunciations when they fail to correspond to those stored in memory. Once children begin school, they begin to apply the same kinds of monitoring to their reading, eventually learning to monitor their comprehension of what they are reading and to intervene, much as our television watcher did, when it is found wanting. In general, the ability to monitor one's own comprehension marks an important distinction between good and poor readers. More mature and better readers do frequent comprehension checks and go back and read again if they find their understanding wanting. Ironically, less able readers, who could benefit most from such rereading, seldom do so.

Finally, we come to the place of content knowledge in memory development and its relationship to language. The more children know about the world, the easier it is to find conceptual pegs for new information. Actually, content knowledge influences memory in at least two ways. It affects the amount of information recalled as well as what is recalled. Take, for example, two women attending a cat show together. Both have seen cats, of course, but one has never been to a cat show before, never owned a cat, and prefers dogs. The second woman has two cats of her own, has always had at least one cat, and has attended many cat shows. The second woman will be able to recall more about what she has seen and different information than the first. While the first woman might report going to a cat show and seeing a lot of cats, some with long hair and some with short, some white, some black, and some striped; the second woman is more likely to recall seeing a prize-winning, flame-point Himalayan and a lilac-pointed Siamese and the fact that there were only three Burmese when normally she would expect to see at least a dozen. The content knowledge that the second woman has about cats has provided an organizational framework to facilitate her storage and recall of the information surrounding the cat show.

The availability of background content knowledge sometimes leads to the recall of details which, although plausible, never occurred in fact. In the act of reconstructing a sequence of events surrounding a baseball game, a person knowledgeable about baseball may recall that there were four batters in the third inning and that the first one struck out. In attempting to explain the remainder of the inning, she may report that the second batter was walked and the next two struck out when, in fact, the second and third *both* walked and the fourth hit into a double play. Either sequence of events is plausible, and because she has the framework of the rules of baseball and prior experience watching the game, she constructs a perfectly conceivable but inaccurate account. A person unfamiliar with baseball would not make such a mistake; neither would she recall as much about the game.

The role that language plays in content knowledge is twofold. First, it is the medium through which children acquire much of their knowledge about the world. Second, it facilitates the formation of organizational networks, which not only make this knowledge more readily available but make possible the integration of new, related items. We have already seen in our discussion of memory strategies that language plays a central role in categorization. The ability to categorize makes it possible to store and retrieve *more* information, thus improving memory.

Language, Memory, and the Child's Perspective

In the previous section, the questions under discussion were what capacities change in the process of memory development? And what is the role of language in those changes? These are adult interpretations of the issues, not child interpretations. Indeed, infants would be quite surprised to learn that at such a tender age they are engaging in such esoteric activities. It is likely impossible that we will ever know just what children's perspectives are on any aspect of growth in the very early years. However, it is important that we try to understand what actually happens from the child's perspective while these important changes are taking place.

Put another way, the questions are: What are children doing while the basic capacities, memory strategies, and metamemory develop? And how does what they are doing contributes to that development? Children's auditory discrimination becomes attuned to the native language at around 6 or 7 months of age. It is unlikely that they are conducting acoustic experiments on themselves. Rather, they are engaging with their mothers, fathers, or others in a variety of language activities. A recording of Janet's mother talking to her when she was not quite 6 months old illustrates the kinds of language experience that infants have:

> And what would our princess like to wear this morning? How about this purple jumpsuit? Do you like purple? Yes. This is definitely purple, isn't it? Okay. You'd rather play

with that one. Okay, why not? You play with it, and I'll put this yellow one on you in-stead. That's Daddy's favorite color. Daddy? You like Daddy don't you? Well, he'll really like this outfit, won't he? You sure are happy this morning. What's making you so happy? (She picks up Janet's stuffed mouse named Mealey.) Is Mealey happy, too? Why do you think Mealey's so happy? 'Cause he loves Janet.

Although her mother has done all the talking in this interchange, it has, along with many similar ones, taught Janet that the language noises she hears are purposeful, communicative, and that they are associated with pleasurable events, particularly the society of other people.

Similarly, what concerns children as they make associations between objects and labels is not the increased memory capacity nor even the enlarged vocabulary that re-sults. They are consumed, instead, with a lively and eager curiosity. They want to know what the things in their world are called, and when they find out, they rehearse or prac-tice them until they can remember them. Most likely, they don't practice in a conscious effort to remember, but because playing with language in this way is fun. They engage in rhyming word play because it is fun to do and as a way of actively exploring the char-acteristics of the language they are beginning to learn. That they are also developing verbal elaboration strategies that will increase memory is of no consequence to them. At this very young age—even before the first birthday—children are already taking charge of their own learning, and this is a fact that we should always keep in mind.

Children remain in charge as their vocabulary grows, and they begin to mark more and more meaning distinctions. As they learn that some furry four-legged crea-tures are cats and others dogs and that certain features distinguish them, children are not aware that they are also developing another memory strategy. They are learning which distinctions matter in their world. Acquiring content knowledge helps them to organize their experience and to retrieve it more easily, but they don't do it for that reason. In organizing their experience, they are trying to discern meaningful or-der in their worlds. Their curiosity and need to understand the world lead them to work out the distinctions that are relevant to it.

Language, then, is central to the growth of memory, which, in turn, is central to children's cognitive development. From children's perspective, language is a princi-pal means by which they come to understand and to organize their experience, in play and in all sorts of social interaction. The desire to learn and the desire to learn language are rooted in a common ground—children's active attempts to understand and make sense of the world in which they live.

THE ROLE OF LANGUAGE IN CONCEPTUAL DEVELOPMENT

There is little agreement among philosophers, psychologists, and educators as to the definition of concept. At a very basic level, most would likely agree that a concept consists of a grouping of objects, events, ideas, people, or attributes that share some similarities. Conceptualization seems to serve two functions in human cognition.

First, categorization, which is at the heart of conceptualization, is important to the development of memory. Second, concepts allow us to take our understanding beyond the bounds of our own experience. As an example, the woman in our earlier example who has never seen a flame-point will immediately know something about the animal if she is told that it is a cat and more still, if she has learned anything at all at the cat show, if she is told that it is a Siamese cat. It is easy to see that the ability to form categories is essential to conceptualization, and in turn, that the ability to conceptualize aids in the formation of more sophisticated categories. Indeed, the ability to sort aspects of the world into categories is a benchmark of both cognitive and linguistic growth. Before looking more broadly at how language and conceptual development influence each other, I would like, therefore, to talk briefly about how children learn to categorize.

Language and Categorization

The ability to organize information in a particular way, as in categories, is essential to conceptual development and to memory. Hearing new words to label new objects facilitates children's abilities to categorize the new objects. Similarly, when they learn new words for familiar objects, they are able to refine further their categorization skills. So when a child learns the word *glass* for an object that holds her apple juice, she creates an association between the object, the word for it, and presumably its appearance and function. Later, when her mother gives her juice in a cup and uses the word *cup*, she has to refine the category from "thing that holds juice" to "things that hold juice," and when milk is found in the same cup, her category definition broadens again to something like "things that hold things I drink." And so it goes. As children's vocabulary grows, so do their abilities to form categories. Would categorization be possible without language? To some degree, yes, but there is little doubt that the two work together. Kuczaj (1999) claims that children use two strategies which, taken together, constitute evidence that "language development and cognitive development are intertwined rather than isolated" (p. 153). The strategies are:

1. When acquiring a new word, search known concepts in case the word denotes a previously acquired concept. If no existing concept seems appropriate, attempt to construct a new one.
2. When acquiring a new concept, attempt to attach a known word to it.

If no word seems appropriate, look for one (Kuczaj, 1999, p. 154). Anyone interested in children's learning must also be interested in conceptual growth and theories of conceptual development. After all, what we believe about the nature of concepts shapes our beliefs about human learning:

> ... Different views of the nature of concepts lead to different expectations about the order in which children will learn particular concepts, to different explanations of why some concepts are difficult for them to learn, and to different implications about how children should be taught new concepts. (Siegler, 1986, pp. 260–261)

Psychologists' and Linguists' Views Compared

Nowhere is the importance of language to cognitive development more obvious than in conceptualization. We have only to compare psychologists' theories of concept formation with theories of semantic development to see the connections. Take, for example, Pease, Gleason, and Pan (1989), writing on the categorical or semantic feature theory of semantic development:

> One explanation of early semantic development is that children acquire categorical concepts and that categories are defined by certain features. For instance, the word dog refers to a category of animals with a set of distinguishing features: they are alive and warm-blooded, have four legs, bark, and are covered with hair. According to Eve Clark (1974), when a child learns a new word, it is in the context of a specific situation: the word dog may at first be understood to apply only to the child's own dog. Only later comes the understanding that other creatures may also be called dog as long as they share the small set of critical features that uniquely define the category. (p. 105)

Their example of how semantic feature theory might work bears a striking resemblance to Siegler's (1991) description of a theory of conceptual development known as defining-features representations:

> Defining-features representations are like the simplest and most straightforward dictionary definitions. They include only the necessary and sufficient features that determine whether an example is or is not an instance of the concept. (p. 213)

These two authors, though writing from different perspectives, are describing the same thing; the first is merely focusing on language as the medium by which concepts are represented. It should be noted, however, that although many linguists and psychologists have written about children's representing concepts in terms of defining features, there is by no means universal agreement that very young children are capable of representing concepts in this way. Piaget was one theorist who believed that young children categorize on the basis of themes—a dog and a bone might be put into the same conceptual category because dogs eat bones—and that the nature of conceptual development lies in their learning to conceptualize on the basis of shared characteristics.

An analogous parallel occurs between aspects of probabilistic representations in conceptualization theory and prototypes in language acquisition theory. In conceptualization theory, the probabilistic view holds that some objects may be perceived as better examples of a particular conceptual category than others. People may view Persians as better examples of cats than Manxes, apples as better examples of fruits than raisins, and steak as a better example of meat than chopped liver. The reasons why they have these preferences are that they consider the properties required for an object to belong to a certain conceptual category and choose as best the one that has the most. Thus, a Persian might be considered a better example of cat on the basis of its length of hair and length of tail; on the basis of these features, the probability is higher that the Persian is a cat than the Manx.

There is an echo of this reasoning in the description of the prototype theory of semantic development: "Yet another theory suggests that we first acquire concepts that are protypical, or the best examples of the categories we are learning" (Rosch & Mervis, 1975). Rosch and her colleagues have shown that we all share the view that some members of a category are much better representatives, or exemplars, than others. A German shepherd is a better dog than a Chihuahua; a robin is a better bird than a chicken. According to prototype theory, children acquire these core concepts when they acquire meaning and only later come to recognize members of that category that are distant from the prototypes (Pease, Gleason, & Pan, 1989, p. 105).

There is also a parallel between the nature of children's development as it is seen within an exemplar-based representational view of conceptualization and language growth that proceeds from lexical to rule learning. Those who believe in exemplar-based representation believe that children store numerous examples of objects and events as they occur in life. When they encounter a new object or event, they compare it to other examples in memory to determine whether the new object or event matches stored examples or the exemplar-based representations they may have created from stored examples. Under this view, development would consist of moving from exemplar-based representations to the learning of rules or regularities. Indeed, research has shown that 7-year-olds learn more effectively under conditions that encouraged them to pay careful attention to particular examples, and 10-year-olds learned equally well under this condition and under the condition that promoted rule learning (Kossan, 1981).

Both linguistic and interactionist theories of language acquisition would claim that while children may begin by learning individual words and their meanings and, possibly, that early sentences are learned as wholes, language acquisition cannot progress until the child begins to learn the rules for putting words into sentences. They would cite as evidence the fact that the number of potential sentences that can be understood and produced is infinite and that no one can learn every exemplar sentence in a language.

The similarity between theories of concept formation and those of semantic development is not merely serendipitous. The first words that children acquire and the use to which they put them provide a mirror on the concepts they are acquiring. More likely than not, language influences those concepts. Certainly there is evidence that people "find it easier to make a conceptual distinction if it neatly corresponds to words available in their language" (Crystal, 1987, p. 15). It would follow, then, that children's increasing facility with conceptualization corresponds to their increasing facility with language.

Language and Conceptualization from the Child's Perspective

In the lives of children, language and the ability to conceptualize provide a means for them to extend their understanding beyond the bounds of their own experience. Although it is possible to understand an idea or a concept without being able to put it into words, it is the very act of putting it into words that clarifies and makes understanding precise.

Attempting to verbalize a "fuzzy" idea serves to crystalize both what we know and we what we do not—our understanding and our ignorance. Most of us are aware of the former—Donald Murray has often said that he writes to find out what he knows. The latter notion of revealing ignorance is, perhaps, less familiar, yet learning involves, in Margaret Donaldson's words, "a simple realization of ignorance" (1978, p. 76). Implicit in the notion of wanting to know is the awareness that we do not. There is no better way of capturing that awareness than to try to put into words an idea or a concept of which we have imperfect understanding. In a real sense, then, children talk their way to understanding. This is true of learning in general and of language learning in particular.

Children begin to talk long before they are masters of the language and it is through talk that they acquire the skills to *become* masters. In their early talk, we find not only evidence that they practice or rehearse the language they are learning but evidence that they are actively engaged in the figuring out of the system that is language. A dialogue between Shelly, a child of 3;6, and her mother illustrates:

> **Mother:** *It's cold outside. Let's put on your pants.*
> **Shelly:** *Where?*
> **M:** *There, on your bed.*
> **S:** *Pants? No, only pant. One.*
> **M:** *Oh, I see. No, these are called pants even though there's only one of them.*
> **S:** *Why?*
> **M:** *I don't know. Maybe 'cause there are two legs.*
> **S:** *Oh. Pantlegs.*
> **M:** *Very good!*

In this exchange, we see that Shelly has acquired both the concept and the language to express the plural. However, her understanding is not perfect, and so she assumes, quite reasonably, that because *pants* sounds plural, it must *be* plural. She is initially unaware of her ignorance, but once her mother explains the error, she readily incorporates the explanation into her vocabulary and to her comprehension of the rules for plural formation. Perhaps the most important point to be made here is that Shelly does not wait for someone to instruct her in the ways of language; she gets on with the business of learning it at the same time as she learns about the world around her.

THE ROLE OF LANGUAGE IN THE DEVELOPMENT OF ACADEMIC SKILLS

Reading and writing rely on a specific set of cognitive skills, including attention, memory, symbolic thinking, and self-regulation. As children learn to read and write, they continue to improve these skills, making them more purposeful and deliberate. For example, deliberate attention is required to differentiate between letters—even if they look alike—and to isolate specific portions of a word for encoding or decoding. Children must remember previous words as they decode subsequent words in a sentence. If they do not make a purposeful attempt to remember, they cannot extract the meaning from the sentence. Writing and reading require an understanding of symbols; thus, if children cannot think symbolically, they cannot learn to manipulate letters and words. Finally, children must be able to self-regulate so that they can monitor their own understanding of print, abandoning ineffective reading strategies and moving on to more effective ones (The Early Literacy Advisor, 2002, General Cognitive Skills section).

Although a great deal of children's academic thinking develops during the school years, it has been estimated that one-third of their academic skills are attained before age 6 (Yardley, 1973). How language serves to shape children's academic thinking is thus of utmost concern since this is the time during which the foundations for their future success in school are laid. Before they begin formal schooling, children have a great deal of experience in learning. In fact, in some ways, very young children may be at an advantage because, as Alice Yardley observed, having no words, they are "protected from being told what to learn and how to learn it" (1973, p. 16). When their children confront a problem or puzzle that presents a learning opportunity, wise parents refrain from providing too much help and thus depriving their children of the rewarding experience of finding a solution independently. Whether the problem is putting the shoe on the appropriate foot, fitting a round puzzle piece into its proper space, or figuring out the mechanics of a zipper, the parent who insists on telling the child how to solve the problem, or worse, solves it for him, takes away the experience of learning.

Fortunately, childhood abounds with such opportunities and even children with over-helpful parents will find a great deal to learn and will develop a great many strategies for doing so. Much of this learning is related to the subjects they later encounter in school because their parents have actively taught them, they have watched educational television programs such as *Sesame Street* and *The Electric Company*, or in some instances, they have found their own resources for learning. Three areas in which they have learned a great deal about how to learn are reading, writing, and arithmetic.

Early Learning of Mathematics

Most of today's children know how to solve addition problems with sums lower than 10 before they enter school. One of the strategies that preschool children use is to choose the larger of the two numbers to be added and count upward from it the number of times indicated by the smaller number. Thus, a child adding three and five would begin with five and count up three—*five, six, seven, eight*. Notice that the ability to apply this strategy rests in memory and in language. The child has to be able to remember the strategy and then, in essence, rename one as six, two as seven, and three as eight. This is not the only approach children use, however. Sometimes they simply put up their fingers and count on them, and other times they simply recall the answer from memory.

Children also use counting strategies in solving subtraction problems: either counting up from the lower number to the higher or down from the higher (counting down the same number of times as the lower number). Which of the two strategies they use seems to depend on which requires the fewer "counts." For the problem, 6 - 2, for example, children would likely count backward from six, two counts since this is easier than counting upward from two to six, which would require four counts. For our purposes, what is interesting about these early strategies is that they all require the child to count, and counting is not possible without language. It is not unwarranted to claim, then, that children's early mathematics ability resides in language.

What kinds of experiences do preschool children have with learning mathematics? During the latter years of the 1980s, a number of disturbing reports appeared in the press of "Yuppie" parents who transferred their own ambition to their children and enrolled them in high-pressure academic preschools or engaged them at a tender age in such questionable educational practices as superlearning. While it may turn out that these early enrichment programs did in fact produce children who achieved superior marks in school and entrance to Harvard or Oxford, we have to wonder about the cost to the child of a lost childhood. Happily, such high-pressure programs are not necessary; in the course of a normal childhood, children develop a natural interest in numbers. From the time the infant notices that the cookies have been eaten and observes *No more* or *All gone*, the foundations for numeracy are established. Later, the addition or subtraction of objects within their own worlds of experience—blocks, small wooden people or animals, finger puppets—propel children along the path of counting, which leads eventually to addition and subtraction. Parents need not "teach" basic arithmetic to their children—for example, drill the sums, requiring children to memorize one plus one is two, two plus two is four, etc. In fact, they may impede the child's own problem-solving skills by doing so. All they need do is to encourage their children's natural curiosity and, possibly, to play counting and rhyming games with their children. By doing so they will be, in a real sense, laying the foundations on which later success in school mathematics will be based.

Mathematics is not the only academic skill that children have begun to acquire before they start school. It is only one of the three Rs considered to be the rudiments of academic learning. Reading and writing are rudimentary not only as subjects in their own right but because they are essential to success in almost all subjects children encounter during their 12 or 13 years of formal schooling. A number of researchers have established clearly that children learn a great deal about both before they get to school.

Early Learning Associated with Reading

Learning to read can be thought of as an evolutionary process that begins shortly after birth:

Children first construct concepts about books and how print works, and then begin to attend to aspects of the print that surrounds them. This is followed by growth of phonemic awareness and acquisition of phoneme-grapheme knowledge. As children construct knowledge about print and the relationship between print and speech, they also are building oral language skills that support their progress as they encounter the demands of first grade and begin to move into conventional forms of reading and writing. (Dickinson et al., 1993, p. 376)

When we are talking about the role language plays in early learning, what we are *really* talking about is the *speech* in children's early reading. Shortly we will see that it does play an important role, but before we can fully understand what that role is, we need to have a broader understanding of the reading process. To understand the nature of children's early knowledge of and about reading, we could take one of two broad approaches. We could attempt to describe the roughly chronological stages of the reading process (i.e., what children typically know and do at a particular age), or we could break the reading process down into a number of component skills and describe the learning associated with each. For our purposes, it is most revealing to do the latter, focusing in particular on letter perception, phonemic awareness, word identification, and the processes involved in the comprehension of larger prose units. The question before us, then, is: What is the nature of children's knowledge of these components of reading before they begin school and how did they come by it?

To begin with, a great many children do learn to read before they begin school. By reading I mean not only word identification of the type they learn on *Sesame Street* but also the ability to recreate meaning from printed text whether that text be a sign in a grocery store, a toy advertisement, or a children's book. My elder son began to identify individual words well before his third birthday. Noticing his interest in the words on *Sesame Street*, I placed large-print labels on many of the more common objects in the house but made no further effort to teach him to read. He learned the associations very quickly and by the time he was just past 3 was sounding out the words in his own books that I had been reading to him for some time. He already knew the stories the books told and had learned from *Sesame Street* that letters had sound equivalents and had put the two kinds of knowledge together. He had, in essence, taught himself to read. My experience with my son is consistent with what research has to say about early readers: The factors that determine whether a child will learn to read before schooling are the degree of interest the child has in reading and the degree of interest the parents have in reading as demonstrated by their reading to the child, reading for pleasure themselves, and having plenty of reading materials available in the home (Durkin, 1966).

Even children who do not learn to read before they begin school know a great deal about the process of reading. It is as though they have been getting ready to learn to read since birth. They have acquired certain abilities that are necessary to reading ability. These cognitive correlates of early reading ability include the perception of letters as being distinct from other kinds of marks, drawings, and squiggles that one might encounter in the world and as being distinct from one another. Marking these kinds of discriminations is a complex perceptual task, requiring children to learn which curved, horizontal, vertical, and diagonal lines are meaningful and which only incidental. Both parents and educators have pondered the question of whether teaching children the names of the letters helps the children learn to read. The research evidence is not clear on the subject. On the one hand, DeHirsch and colleagues (1966) found that children's ability to name letters predicts their reading achievement through first and second grade and into third. On the other hand, there is no evidence that there is a causal relationship between the two: It may be the case that children who learn letter names at a young age do so because they have an interest in words and this same interest makes them better readers. But if interest is such an important factor, and we saw earlier that both the parents' and the child's interest correlate positively and strongly with later reading ability, then it would seem that teaching children the names of letters might be beneficial.

Another cognitive correlate of reading ability that preschool children attain is phonemic awareness. However disparate their views of the reading process, most experts agree that *some* degree of sensitivity to the fact that words consist of individual sounds is important to successful reading. Children learning to read English and other alphabetic languages must understand, at the least, that words consist of letters and those letters represent separate sounds that may also exist in other words. Evidence is mounting that the kind of phonemic awareness that is most helpful is that of onsets and rimes (see Chapter 2 and Chapter 10), but there is no compelling evidence that children's understanding of phonemic awareness need be much more sophisticated than this. The reason is that the ability to divide a word into its component sounds is the converse ability to the one required in reading, which is to blend the sounds together to form a sequence of sounds that is sufficiently familiar to permit word recognition. It *is* clear, though, that word recognition is essential to the task of learning to read.

What strategies do preschool children develop that enable them to identify words? Word recognition is a necessary prerequisite to reading, and it is a complicated process to describe. To simplify the procedure greatly, children must examine the printed words and then locate the corresponding entry from long-term memory. Whether they use a phonologically based method or a visually based method of retrieval, this aspect of the task is the same. Using a phonologically based method, they will first recode the printed word into a sequence of sounds and search for a corresponding sound sequence. Using visually based retrieval, they will search for a visual match, skipping the sounding out stage. Children who are especially adept at phonological retrieval will not need to recode the entire word, and even children who normally adopt a visual procedure may occasionally recode the first letter or two of a word.

Although these two methods of retrieval correspond to two approaches to reading instruction, the phonics-based and the whole-word, there is evidence that without instruction children genuinely differ in the strategy they prefer. The traditionally held belief that children begin by sounding out words and then graduate to visual recognition is simply not true for all children. Obviously, many children need to begin with phonological recoding; others recognize the word on the basis of its visual configuration and the context. On confronting the word *stop*, for example, one child may assign a hissing noise to the first letter, a voiceless alveolar stop to the second, and so on until a pronunciation is reached that corresponds with one already in memory. Another child may learn the word *stop* by making the association with the red hexagonal sign on which it usually appears. In order to become efficient and fluent readers, all children must eventually abandon phonological recoding as a general strategy although it may be reactivated as a back-up strategy when others fail. To illustrate that even proficient readers use a phonological attack strategy when confronted with unfamiliar words, we have only to consider our own behavior with unfamiliar words. If we encounter the pseudoword *grane*, for example, and search our memory on the basis of the visual information alone, we will fail. What we do instead is assign it a pronunciation on the basis of our knowledge of sound-symbol correspondence, and then search for a match. We then conclude that it is a misspelling of *grain*, a mistyped version of *crane*, or simply a nonsense form, depending on the context. A phonological strategy is available in problem situations such as this, but it is too inefficient as a general strategy, and children who rely on it exclusively will never become proficient readers.

In order to become proficient readers, it is necessary that children acquire more than letter perception skills, phonemic awareness, and word identification strategies. In order to become true readers, they must be able to recreate meaning from printed text. Although we use the word *comprehension* to refer to this ability, it is not meant to convey a passive process. On the contrary, reading comprehension is likely one of the most cognitively active and complex activities in which we engage. It is also one of the most important in the lives of young children. To a very large degree, success in reading comprehension will predict children's success in school, but just as important, it will give them the means for developing and pursuing new interests for the rest of their lives, to escape boredom, and to acquire a vast amount of information about the world around them and about worlds they may never experience directly. What occurs during the preschool years that serves to shape children's facility to comprehend text?

To answer that question fully is beyond the scope of this book, but it is possible to describe the basic processes involved in comprehension. Notice that in the last sentence, I wrote *comprehension* and not *reading comprehension*. That is because reading comprehension is not an isolated cognitive phenomenon. It involves many of the same processes as listening comprehension. Both listening and reading require us to form and integrate propositions and to draw inferences about what is read or heard and to relate it to what is already known. The fundamental difference between listening and reading comprehension is that in reading, the reader must be able to identify individual words, which makes possible the identification of propositions. Perfetti (1984) has postulated two broad components of text comprehension. Local processing refers to "those processes that construct elementary meaning units from text over a relatively brief period" (p. 33). He includes as local processes the identification of words (lexical access) and the building of propositions (proposition assembly). Text modeling:

> refers to the processes the reader uses to combine local processes with knowledge about concepts, knowledge about inferences (inference rules), knowledge about the forms of texts, and general knowledge about the everyday world ... to form a representation of the text meaning. It is this representation that the reader consults at some later time to recall or to answer questions about what has been read. (p. 40)

As an example, let us consider how a proficient reader might come to understand the following sentences:

1. Joe and Jen went to a used car lot.
2. They waited for a salesman to appear.
3. After awhile, they began to look around for themselves.
4. They spotted a blue truck sitting in the shadows.
5. Just as they approached the truck, a smiling man appeared.

Using local processes the reader would construct a rudimentary level of meaning. To begin with, the reader would have to have some kind of recognition and retrieval system to match the words on the printed page with the words stored in memory. Also, the reader would have to select the contextually appropriate meaning for words with more than one meaning. *Lot* in the first sentence is a good example. Its position in the sentence as well as the meanings of the words around it will lead the reader to discount the "large number" lot in favor of the "plot of land" lot. Locating, or encoding, the individual words permits the reader to encode the elementary units of text, propositions. The first sentence in the example has eight:

1. Joe exists.
2. Jen exists.
3. Lot exists.
4. Cars exist.
5. They go to the lot.
6. They go at some time in the past.
7. Cars are located at the lot.
8. The cars are used.

Ignoring the fact that the eighth proposition probably contains at least one other proposition, these are the basic meaning elements that the reader has to encode. Each sentence consists of a number of such propositions; therefore a text can be said to comprise a set of propositions embedded in a set of sentences. The next step in the local processing of these sentences is to assemble and integrate the propositions for longer-term memory. By *integrate*, it is meant the combining of "successively occurring propositions with each other" (Perfetti, 1984, p. 38). The eight propositions of the first sentence must be integrated with each other and then with propositions in successive sentences. A number of conventions of writing facilitate the reader's doing this. One is the use of pronouns. Notice how *they* in sentences two through five serves to link these sentences to each other and to the first sentence, which carries the referent, *Joe* and *Jen*. Another is the use of the definite article. When the truck is first introduced in the fourth sentence, the indefinite *a* is used. When it appears again in the fifth sentence, the use of *the* reminds the reader that he already knows about the existence of this truck. The definite article is used in a different way in the fourth sentence where we find the truck sitting in *the shadows* even though there has been no previous mention of shadows. In this case, the definite article serves as a signal to the reader's inferencing mechanism. If the reader knows that lots *can* have shadowy places, then the proposition is integrated easily with the others. As Perfetti (1984) puts it, "... integrative processes depend on linguistic triggers and the accessibility of linking propositions in memory" (p. 40). In very young children, these triggers and links are largely based in their experience of oral language.

We have not yet achieved comprehension of our short text, though. A useful way of demonstrating the non-local or long-term comprehension process is to reconsider the five sentences we saw earlier. As I write this paragraph, those sentences no longer appear on my computer monitor—I have typed three or four screens beyond them. I shall now reconstruct them from memory and see what variations occur:

1. Joe and Jen went to a used car lot.
2. They were looking around.
3. They didn't see a salesman present.
4. They saw a blue truck sitting in the shadows.
5. As they approached the truck, a smiling salesman appeared.

In my recall of the passage, I correctly reproduced only the first sentence, but I did reconstruct the propositions in the other sentences more or less correctly. Notice that I included a proposition not included in the original, namely that the man who appeared was a salesman. This is an inference that was made possible by my knowledge of the world of car lots. My comprehension of the passage, then, resulted from the three local processes combined with my general knowledge about the everyday world.

It does not sound like a very complicated process, but in fact it is. What has to develop in the young child to make reading comprehension possible? Siegler has suggested that it is a product of five different processes. First, children need to be able to recognize and identify words quickly, with minimal attention to the task and while simultaneously attending to higher-level tasks. This is called *automatization of lexical access* and means simply that the child must be able to recognize words without conscious effort. Second, children's short-term memories need to expand so that they can remember longer and longer pieces of text. The ability to remember what they have just read is important because it makes it possible for them to integrate previous propositions and to draw inferences among them.

The third dimension of development that children must undergo in order to become proficient readers has to do with background knowledge. Specifically, as children learn more about the worlds in which they live and learn to structure that knowledge in some coherent way, they stand a chance of becoming better readers. As an example, children who are familiar with the standard organization of fairy tales can recall new fairy tales more easily than children who have never heard fairy tales. When it comes to reading an unfamiliar fairy tale, the child who knows how they are structured has a head start on comprehension over the child who does not know. This is true of other types of reading as well. The child with experience of how knowledge is organized for the particular reading task will fare better than the one without.

A fourth area in which children must develop if they are to become successful readers is in monitoring their comprehension. Researchers have demonstrated that better readers within all age groups are the ones who monitor their understanding of the text they are reading and adopt strategies for dealing with any problems they have. These strategies include returning to the source of the problem, correcting words they have identified incorrectly, slowing down, or creating concrete examples for abstract characterizations (Baker & Brown, 1984; Clay, 1973; Forrest & Walker, 1979).

The fifth facet of development that drives reading comprehension is children's increasing ability to adapt their reading strategies to the demands of the particular task. Different types of reading require reading strategy. As adults, most of us can read a novel in a busy airport or even in front of the television set. Most of us probably could not read a chapter from a university-level physics text in the same setting. Moreover, if we *tried* to read the physics text in the same way as the novel, we would likely not understand or remember very much of what we read. This is because our strategies for comprehending different kinds of text depend on our purpose and on the way the material is structured and presented. Different material makes different demands on us as readers. The ability to adjust our reading behavior to those demands is a significant part of our development as readers.

Very similar cognitive processes operate as we listen to oral language and similar kinds of cognitive development must occur to make us proficient listeners. The fact that listening and reading comprehension have so much in common has led parents and educators to raise the obvious question of why so many children fail to become proficient readers. In their quest for an answer, it has also led many of them to concentrate their attention on that aspect of reading comprehension that most notably differs from listening comprehension, namely lexical access or word identification. Following such reasoning, a reading teacher's thrust would be word-attack skills—if the children can identify the words, they can create the meaning. And for some children this *seems* to be the case. Unfortunately, such reasoning ignores a number of other differences between listening and reading. Children, from birth, have been exposed to oral language being used for communicative purposes. No attempt was made to teach them to listen and the internal knowledge structures (the general knowledge about the everyday world necessary to comprehension of oral or written text) were built at the same time as the language was being created. From birth, they have known the structure of talk and the purpose of talk and no one ever expected them to participate without knowing those things. For some children, there is a genuine difference with reading. If they have not had direct experience with reading, they may not know about the forms of text, the world of text, or the kinds of things that are written about. They have general knowledge about the everyday world, but this may not be enough to see them through the reading comprehension process if they are lacking in the other kinds of information needed to construct a "text model." If we think of words as blocks and the task of reading as building a castle from blocks, then the problem is easy to see. Having the blocks is essential, but unless you know what a castle looks like, there is little hope of succeeding in getting it built. No amount of block identification activity will help, but some pictures of castles or some kind of building plan for a castle would help a great deal.

Most children *do* become proficient readers, eventually, and the foundation for their success is laid in early childhood. It is a simple fact of human nature that most people like to do those things which they are good at doing. Children who have learned to love stories from infancy and who have developed an avid interest in print will succeed as readers *unless* the educational system somehow manages to negate all the positive influences of those early years. We will see in a later chapter that this is entirely (and unfortunately) possible. For now, we shall turn our attention to the other side of the reading coin, writing.

Early Learning Associated with Writing

On a number of occasions, Donald Graves has remarked that learning to write should be as easy as learning to read. When we think about their obvious relationship to one another, reading and writing would seem to be essentially mirror images of each other. And perhaps they are. We simply do not know as much about how children learn to write as we do about how they learn to read, although fortunately, researchers are beginning to study young children's writing. They are beginning to find that it makes many of the same demands as speaking, but it is in some ways more demanding.

The business of committing to paper a first draft, whether it be a story told by a 6-year-old or a term paper written by a university student, requires a complex network of interactive processes. In both cases, the writer faces the demands imposed by unfamiliar topics and by multiple goals as well as the mechanical chore of getting thoughts recorded whether to paper or computer memory. Both the child drafting the story and the university student drafting the term paper must begin by retrieving information stored in long-term memory, information relevant to the topic at hand. If the idea for the story (or the term paper) is the writer's own, he has a slight advantage over the writer who is assigned his story or term-paper topic and may have little relevant material stored in long-term memory on which to call. Even when there is information stored, the writer may not have it conveniently organized and may have to pull it from diverse regions of memory. A paragraph from a first-year university examination paper and a story written by a child in third grade illustrate:

> Linguistics is the study of language. It is a popular course at many universities and is useful for people studying to be teachers, daycare workers, social workers, doctors, lawyers and dentists. One branch of linguistics which is widely studied is psycholinguistics. This is quite unlike historical linguistics

which almost nobody studies anymore and would not be useful to daycare workers, social workers, doctors or dentists but might come handy for very old teachers and lawyers. And historians, of course. People who study linguistics are called linguists. They know a lot about languages but do not know how to speak them.

This student was obviously unprepared for the topic demands of this exam and was forced to pull from his long-term memory every bit of information he could about linguistics. The child who wrote the next passage solved a similar problem in much the same way:

About Deserts

Deserts are hot places wear the wind blose. Not very many peple liv on deserts. Kaktus and tubble weeds grow and maybe some animals but I don't no wich ones. There is a big desert somewear in California and another one in Sehaira, but none in Nova Scotia. The End.

A second demand made on the writer is to formulate goals, or plans, and to keep them in mind long enough to complete the draft. We can see the difficulty with planning in the child's piece on deserts. It is organized in the sense that all the sentences relate to the title: "About Deserts." There is little connection between any of the sentences except that they relate to the title. (Unfortunately, this is true of the university student's paragraph as well!) Apparently, this kind of organization is typical of children in second through fourth grade (McCutchen & Perfetti, 1982) and demonstrates their difficulty with keeping track of both the point of the topic sentence and the details of other sentences. The result is that their writing sounds more like a list than exposition, narrative, or description.

Finally, the process of drafting makes complex mechanical demands on children. The job of coordinating small fingers to form letters and getting them ordered into words demands so much attention that children may lose track of what they want to say. Research has shown that when children are permitted to dictate their stories rather than write them, they write better quality stories (Bereiter & Scardamalia, 1982). In brief, children's writing ability, where ability consists of being able to tell a story or form a coherent description, is underestimated if we consider only the words they write down. Their sense of story, developed in early childhood, will carry them a long way if they are freed, in at least some writing tasks, from the mechanical demands of writing.

Language and Academic Skills from the Child's Perspective: Six Characteristics of Children's Preschool Learning

It is adults, not children, who categorize some learning as academic and other learning as not. For children, it is all part and parcel of the same thing, and it is driven by their natural curiosity in the context of real problems. Margaret Voss (1988) relates a story of her son's early learning about reading that makes this point clearly:

> One summer afternoon just a month before his third birthday, Nathaniel sat at the picnic table in our backyard. He had just enjoyed a treat, a jar of apple blueberry baby food. As I turned the jar to examine the label, wondering if I'd just given my son some added sugar, Nathaniel suddenly proclaimed, "Make way for applesauce." Amused and confused, I asked, "What?" "Make way for applesauce," he repeated, pointing to the label. Then he reached out and ran his fingers underneath some words, just as I sometimes do as I read book titles to him. He continued, pointing to and reading one word at a time: "it say, 'Make…way…for…applesauce.' " (p. 272)

Nathaniel had obviously worked out from his previous experience that print says something—Voss reports that she had been reading his current favorite *Make Way for Ducklings* over and over. But he also knew that the print on the label likely related to the contents of the jar, which he also knew. He extrapolated from his prior experience in trying to make sense of a new one. Nathaniel had begun to teach himself to read more than 2 years before the schools would get their chance.

Parents and educators, not children, insist on dividing and packaging learning. But before they get to school, children have learned a great deal in general, and they have learned a great deal about learning. Several centuries of research has provided no small amount of insight into the nature of children's early learning, but we hardly need review it all to make some common-sense observations about what goes on in children's worlds as they build their world views, which to adults is the basis for their academic learning.

Six characteristics of children's preschool learning are of particular importance to teachers of children:

1. *Children's learning progresses according to their degree of readiness.*   The degree of physical, cognitive, emotional, and social maturity that children have attained governs what they learn and when. The most obvious example is language itself. It does no good for a mother to coax and coach her 1-month-old son to say *Mama* or *Dada*. The child has not yet achieved sufficient motor control over his articulators to produce the sound reliably. He has not the memory capacity to make the correct associations or to reproduce the correct sequence of sounds reliably. Neither will he be able, 6 months later, to produce three- or four-word sentences, no matter how much teaching occurs, which brings us to another characteristic of early learning.

2. *Young children are, for the most part, in charge of their own learning.*   This is not to say that they know they are in charge, but simply that they determine what and when they will learn. These decisions are governed, in part, by maturity but also by their natural and robust curiosity about the world around them. My older son, Kerry, could put together wooden jigsaw puzzles with several pieces well before his second birthday. Initially, he was driven to try to put the puzzles together by his desire to see the picture as a whole and, I suspect, by an equally compelling desire to find out if he could do the task. By the time he was 3, he had taught himself to read by watching *Sesame Street* and by repeatedly asking me to identify words in his books, on signs, and everywhere else he saw them. Figuring out the relationship between the sounds of words and their written form was very likely another kind of puzzle that he needed to solve.

My other son, Christopher had no interest in the puzzles, possibly because he had seen his brother playing with them so often and knew too well what they were supposed to look like, but long before his second birthday, he wanted to learn to count. He insisted that I count his fingers, my fingers, his toes, books on his shelf, plates at the table, all sorts of things over and over. He would repeat after me, *one-two-three* at first and gradually into the 10s, 20s, and 30s. This child, incidentally, went on to achieve a near-perfect score on the math SAT some 15 years later. Chris decided not only what he was going to learn but how he was going to learn it. In this he was not unusual. Children are born with curiosity and the drive to satisfy it is the essence of learning.

3. *Play plays an important role in children's learning.*   A great variety of learning occurs as children are playing. Playing on swings, monkey-bars, tricycles, wagons, and even on stairs helps them to acquire gross motor skills and bodily coordination. Playing with smaller objects such as the puzzles Kerry loved or pencils, crayons, or small blocks helps them to develop fine motor skills as well as eye-hand coordination. Play is also significant to academic learning. Parents who play games with children to keep them from getting bored are providing more opportunities for learning than they realize. When they play rhyming games, I spy, read road signs or license plate numbers, or count red cars and white cars, they are providing occasions for children to sharpen their recognition and discrimination powers and providing experiences important to literacy. All children play pretend games and benefit from them in at least two ways. First, they are wonderful for the imagination, giving children opportunities to think about the past and to integrate it with the future. Second, fantasy games provide important opportunities for children to use language that is not bounded by the present—they begin, in short, the process of decontextualizing language, of using language that does not refer to real objects in present time.

4. *The role of parents in early learning is facilitator, not instructor.*   As much as I might be tempted to do so, I cannot take credit for my older son's ability to put together puzzles or the fact that he was a very early reader nor for my younger son's learning to count. I helped, of course, but with both children, my job was to sense their readiness (though they made it fairly obvious), provide the help they requested, and provide a number of different materials that would help them to extend their understandings—different kinds and progressively more difficult puzzles for Kerry and an abundance of things to count for Chris.

Perhaps the most important contribution parents make to children's early learning is as partners in daily interaction. Whether the activity be routine, such as washing hands and putting on pajamas, or special, such as decorating a birthday cake or trimming the Christmas tree, the dialogues that occur between parents and children are the means by which children learn. The very first thing they learn, as John Holt (1989) points out, is that speech has purpose:

> Children get ready to speak by hearing speech all around them. The important thing about that speech is that the adults, for the most part, are not talking in order to give chil-

dren a model. They are talking to each other because they have things to say. So the first thing the baby intuits, figures out, about the speech of adults, is that it is serious. (p. 10)

Once children have learned that the talk around them is purposeful, parents begin to play another role in their dialogues with their children. That role is not as teacher so much as it is facilitator. Gordon Wells (1986) explains:

> meaning making in conversation should be a collaborative activity. But where there is a considerable disparity between the participants in their mental models and their linguistic resources, the more mature participants to make adjustments in order to make collaboration possible. (p. 89)

Parents, as the more mature participants, make those adjustments that make meaningful dialogue possible. If they are wise they do so not by appropriating the child's conversation as their own or by interfering with the child's attempts to make meaning but by holding the conversational doors open in an effort to understand the child's intended meaning. Parents who understand that their own perspective, their own knowledge, cannot be transmitted directly also understand that their role is to gently guide their children as they rebuild the world for themselves.

5. *Interaction is essential to children's early learning.*   This was the principal theme of Chapter 8. We return to it here. Children are not passive participants in the business of learning, vessels awaiting someone to pour in knowledge. Possessed of a boundless curiosity, they eagerly seek answers, test hypotheses, and reconfirm those hypotheses as they essentially reconstruct the world through their own experiences.

In the simple act of questioning, children find out what they need to know, extend their knowledge, and open themselves to new ideas on which to build. Consider the following exchange between Matthew, age 3, and his father:

Matthew: *What that?*
Daddy: *Screwdriver. It's called a screwdriver.*
M: *What do?*
D: *Well, I'm using it now to put this thing—see it, it's called a screw—into the wood here so horsie's head won't fall off.*
M: *Horsie head. What that? (Again asking about the screwdriver.)*
D: *Srewdriver.*
M: *'tew… (he falters).*
D: *Screw driver.*
M: *Tew diver.*
D: *Good.*
M: *Tew diver. Tew diver. Here? (He points to a screw holding on one of the wooden horse's legs.)*
D: *Yes. That's a screw. I can use the screwdriver to take the screw out. (He begins to remove the screw.)*
M: *Tew diver. Out.*
D: *Right. It takes the screw out, too.*
M: *(Watches his father loosen the screw.) No!*

> **D:** *Don't worry. We'll put it back again. (Begins reversing the screw.)*
> **M:** *Tew diver. In.*

It is doubtful that Matthew fully understood his father's explanation, but in this situation, he discovered a new label for something in his environment. He doesn't have to wait until he has perfect understanding (or pronunciation!) of the word to use it. As he uses it in a variety of contexts, its use will be refined. That refinement will come in dialogues similar to this one in collaboration with adults. But, of course, in this and other such dialogues, Matthew has learned far more than single words. John Holt (1983) points out that word learning may come nearer the end of children's language learning than the beginning. Before they learn words, children learn:

> ... the large idea of communication by speech, that all those noises that come out of people's mouths mean something and can make things happen. Then, from the tones of people's voices and the contexts in which they speak, ... a very general idea of what they are saying, ... Then they begin to intuit a rough outline of the grammar—i.e., the structure—of the language. Finally, they begin to learn words, and to put those words into their proper slots in the very rough models of grammar which they have invented. (p. 93).

There is an important distinction to be marked here concerning what children learn in dialogue with adults. It is not possible for an adult to pass along a whole, perfectly formed word meaning or concept to a child. What is passed on is the infrastructure that, in continuous interaction with adults and other children, children will build upon. Sometimes, children show a great deal of creativity in the language constructions they build, creating forms or categories that bear little resemblance to those accepted by the adult community. John Holt (1983) relates another story of a child named Jackie, a 2-year-old, who had created in his mind a class of objects that we would call "dry, crumbly things to eat—cookies, crackers, dry toast—to which he had given the name 'Zee.' Neither his father nor his mother knew how he had come to pick that word.... Clearly the baby had decided for himself that it was a good name for this class of things" (p. 91).

This child had created a category that does not exist in his native language and a word to label it. Such behavior should suggest to us that the role adults play in children's language is not and should not be to teach language. In the dialogue between Matthew and his father, we saw an honest, companionable exchange with little if any covert teaching going on. Let's compare it with a dialogue between Barbie, age 2;10, and her mother:

> **Mother:** *Do you want peanut butter or cheese today?*
> **Barbie:** *Peanut butter.*
> **M:** *And jelly or —*
> **B:** *No jelly.*
> **M:** *You don't want jelly. What do you want?*
> **B:** *Fuff.*
> **M:** *Marshmallow fluff?*

B: *Yep. Fuff.*
M: *Can you say "marshmallow"?*
B: *No.*
M: *Sure you can. Try. Marsh - mal - low.*
B: *Mawo.*
M: *Good. Marsh - mal - low.*
B: *Fuff.*

This dialogue differs from the one between Matthew and his father in one important way: Barbie's mother takes advantage of the opportunity to do a little language teaching. In this instance, she isn't very successful, but we have to wonder whether such thinly disguised attempts to teach language to young children are good, bad, or necessary. Barbie herself shows that they do little good, and John Holt (1983) points out that "billions of children learn to speak who have never been spoken to in this way" (p. 96). Therefore, we have to consider the strong possibility that surreptitious teaching is a waste of everyone's time. If children do not benefit from it, then we must next decide whether it may do harm. Probably not, but there is at least a slight possibility it does for the simple reason that if children find talk useless or uninteresting, they might not bother with it, and that could be detrimental to their learning it.

What, then, is the role of dialogue with adults in children's language and learning? To answer this, we need to look at the adult's role not as *talker* but as listener. Parents who work very hard at understanding what young children say to them contribute very significantly to their children's learning. Children catch on quickly when people aren't really paying attention, and if they too frequently have the experience of not being able make themselves understood or to get a response to their overtures, they may conclude that there is no point in even trying to make themselves understood. Parents who persist in trying to understand children's attempts to communicate and make sense of the world will foster in their children a positive attitude toward language and learning. Finally, Holt captures the essence of the role of the adult when he says that if children find talk to be honest, companionable, and fun, then they will want to do it and will learn to do it. Talk related to activity, talk about things of significance to children, talk introduced by children—all kinds of *real* talk—inspire children to figure out how to do it.

6. *Learning is embedded in the process of socialization.*   Children's lives are not like school curricula. They are not divided up into components and assigned different periods of time—an hour to work on motor development, half an hour for memory development, 20 minutes for hygiene, and an hour and a half for socialization into the family and community. Their learning occurs in an unfragmented whole as part of the process of acquiring full membership in the local society of the family and community. Humans are social animals; they live in groups, and children's early learning is directed toward achieving group membership. They don't learn to say words because it is biologically time to do so or even because language is part of their internal curriculum. They learn language because that is the means through which people connect with one another. From the perspective of children, their preschool years are spent not in learning words, improving their memory, learning concepts, or acquiring the bases for academic learning but in learning to become like the people around them.

Technology and Academic Achievement

This is an extremely difficult subject to explore for the simple reason that, paradoxically, we know little but our knowledge is growing so rapidly that what I write today may well be out of date by the time you read these words. In my generation, parents and teachers began to worry about the effects of television on our academic achievement, and especially on our reading ability. My sons' generation proved that there was some reason for concern as we saw reading scores plummet with the increase of viewing hours. Of course, many other factors must have had an impact, including changes in the methods used for teaching reading in the schools. Nevertheless, teachers are in almost universal agreement that television viewing is problematic for children's developing reading skills if they are watching television rather than reading. To learn to read, children must read and not just in class where there is only a modest amount of time available to spend in reading practice. An additional problem is that parents themselves watch more television and thus are less likely to model reading behavior, or most significantly, read to their children. It is all too easy to pop a video into the VCR and let children entertain themselves through this rather passive medium.

The computer revolution, on the other hand, and in particular the growing popularity of the Internet, is having a different effect, one that just may be beneficial to reading skills. A 1998 study showed that adults with Internet access spend less time viewing the news and more time reading it *on the Internet*. The same researchers also report that "new online users increasingly come from lower and middle socio-economic groups which are heavier than average television watchers" (The Pew Research Center, 1998). Although these findings do not specifically apply to children, they do suggest some reason for optimism, if for no other reason than much online activity requires both reading and writing, and that children tend to adopt the behaviors of their parents.

On the whole, I am optimistic that the Internet will have a beneficial effect on reading and on education in general. I agree with Bertram Bruce's observation that the Internet represents an *additional* kind of literacy. In other words, the medium of the Internet will not replace the traditional kinds of literacy (just as television did not replace radio). "Instead of replacing one kind of literacy with another, we add to our repertoire" (Bruce, 1998). The truth of this assertion is found in the current text. Throughout, I have augmented my traditional library research and reading with sources from the Internet. Preschool children are not researchers, but they are increasingly exposed to and participating in the world of the Internet. With parental and teacher guidance, this can be an important addition to their tool kit for becoming lifelong readers and lifelong learners.

CONCLUSION

In this chapter, we have examined the interactive development of language and cognition. In particular, we looked at the development of memory, conceptualization, and academic thinking and the role language plays in each. Throughout, an attempt was made to understand the relationship between language and learning from the child's point of view. Out of all these discussions came six characteristics of children's preschool learning—characteristics that should serve as reminders to educators planning curricula and teaching methods, so they will not create a disconnect between children's preschool and school experiences. In the next chapter, we examine language and learning in the environment of the school from the perspective of what is and what can and should be.

For Further Study

1. Read the following list of words twice and then close the book and attempt to repeat them. Which words did you not recall? What strategies did you adopt to remember the words?

cook	joyful
data	acne
boy	tonic
book	gymnasium
matches	caldron
sugar	rabbit

   See how many of the words you can remember one day later.

2. Repeat the same exercise with the following list, only this time write down the words first and then try to recall them without looking. Were you more successful than in the previous exercise? Why?

misery	cup
cape	Romania
tuna	juice
picture	market
secretary	anger
dust	convention

3. What is the role of motivation in learning to read?

4. Sir Edmund Huey once observed that "an understanding of all that is involved in the reading system would be 'the acme of a psychologist's achievement'" (Dickinson et al., 1993, p. 377). Explain what you think he meant by this statement and why he believed it was true.

5. To what degree can reading be thought of as socially interactive?

6. How do you think the process of learning to read differs in a child who has a significant hearing impairment? Use the Internet to find out what research has to say about this question.

For Further Reading

Bialystok, E. (1991). *Language processing in bilingual children*. Cambridge, MA: Cambridge University Press.

De Boysson-Bardies, B. (1999). *How language comes to children*. Cambridge, MA: MIT Press.

Bowerman, M. & Levinson, S. C. (Eds.) (2001). *Language acquisition and conceptual development*. Cambridge, MA: Cambridge University Press.

Falk, J. S. (1999). *Women, language and linguistics*. New York: Routledge.

CHAPTER TEN

Schooling and Language Growth

An item in the local newspaper recently was entitled "Dick and Jane haven't a hope, the way kids are taught today" (McMartin, 2001). The article was not based on scientific research but on interviews with teachers and teacher educators, and it reflected the general dissatisfaction in the public and among educators that there is something very wrong with our literacy levels as well as the growing tendency to blame the way reading and writing are taught. I am coming to the view that there *is* something wrong with reading instruction, and whatever the reason, it is not because we have not studied the problem carefully and steadily over the last several decades. Much of our attention in this chapter will be directed toward reading and writing and what can and should be done in schools to make those skills grow to their full potential in each and every child.

Researchers who study language acquisition tend to concentrate on infants and young children. The unofficial canon is that by the time they reach school age, children have learned most of the language they are going to learn. There is no argument that they have mastered major feats of phonology, morphology, and syntax and have an impressive vocabulary. These are magnificent accomplishments, but the task has not ended. Teachers know that children have a great deal more language to learn, both oral and written. When they come to school, children begin to build upon their experience as language learners, but that experience will only carry them so far because, as we have seen, there are fundamental differences between the language of the home and the language of the school. The former is, for the most part, grounded in tangible reality while the latter tends to be more closely linked to the abstract world of concepts and ideas.

At the end of the last chapter, six characteristics of early learning outside school were outlined. If we were to condense those characteristics into a single observation, we could do no better than to borrow from Gordon Wells's (1986) fine book *The Meaning Makers*:

> In the preschool years, ... talking and learning go hand in hand. Children talk about the things that interest them and try to increase their understanding; and, for much of the time, their adult conversational partners sustain and support their efforts, seeking, where appropriate, 'to add a pebble to the pile.' What is characteristic of such learning is that it is spontaneous and unplanned and, because it arises out of activities in which one or both of the participants are engaged, it is focused and given meaning by the context in which it occurs. (p. 67)

In his book, Wells makes direct and systematic comparisons between children's language and learning in the home and in the school, his principal argument being that the mismatch between the two goes a long way toward accounting for the lack of success that some children experience.

THE ATTITUDES OF SOME EDUCATORS

The business of teaching and of planning educational curricula should be governed by two fundamental questions: What is the nature of human learning? And what is the best way of teaching to facilitate that learning? It is probably important to ask a third question as well; What is to be learned? Certainly, in teacher education programs, various forms of those three questions form the bases of the curriculum, although the degree to which they are answered is arguable. To some degree, what is to be learned is historically and societally constrained and largely outside the control of individual teachers. That is, the larger decisions about what to teach are generally not made by teachers. They do have some control, however, over the specifics of the curriculum—the day to day lesson plans, for example—as well as how to go about teaching it. For our purposes in this chapter, we will concentrate on the first two questions. Refining the questions slightly, educators should be asking what *experience* of learning children bring when they begin school and how educators can build upon that experience in preparing for the next stage of children's education. In other words, it would make sense if we thought of schooling not as the beginning of education but as the next stage in a process that began 5 or 6 years earlier. With regard to language learning, and literacy in particular, we would think of the school years as providing new opportunities for children to acquire more language and more uses for their language, to grow in and with their language.

Some educators might view education exactly in that way, but they are likely in the minority, or so educators such as Gordon Wells, John Holt, and Judy Lindfors believe. Indeed, I would claim that most teachers of elementary school children assume the canonical view that equates education with schooling.

When children arrive at school, things begin to change. Now a child is one among many, known by teachers in ways less intimate. A child is no longer known in her entirety; it is as if her life history begins again when she walks through the classroom door. (Kuschner, 1989, p. 45)

The first day of school has always been a momentous occasion, one most of us remember even after the passing of several decades. In the past and for some children, the significance of the occasion may have resided in the fact that school marked the beginning of separation from home and parents. It remains a noteworthy event for children today, even though many children have already spent a number of years in day care or nursery school. As David Kuschner says of his daughter, Emily:

Somehow my daughter knew that there was something special about going to kindergarten, that there was something special about starting school. Even though she had attended a day care center for two years, knew what it was like to move through activity times and learning centers, knew what it was like to have "school friends" as something different from neighborhood friends, and knew what it was like to have teachers, she had it in her mind that kindergarten would be different.

... I don't know when or how she had learned about school, but somehow she knew it would be different. And she was right. (Kuschner, 1989, p. 44)

Schools take responsibility and credit for all manner of new learning, chief among which is literacy, even though many children know a great deal about reading and writing when they arrive at school. All in all, we carry on as though learning is what begins when the child first puts a tentative foot inside the classroom door, as though children's minds are blank slates to be written upon or soft clay to be molded. Despite the fact that there may be much writing and molding yet to be done, children arrive at school neither blank nor unformed.

Change the Child

It is just common sense to assume that children who are comfortable in the school setting, who do not find their daily activities to be much different from those they have engaged in at home, will adapt to school more easily and be more successful. This is an assumption shared by schools and parents and born out by research. Both Heath and Wells show rather conclusively that schools are essentially middle-class institutions, and the children who best succeed there are those from middle-class homes with middle-class values. Educators have known this for a very long time, and although they are to be commended for their efforts in creating equal educational opportunities, the response has been dubious. Most educators are likely unaware that their response is not, and has not traditionally been, to change the school in any fundamental way, but to change the child. Rather than to make the school environment (over which they have nearly complete control) more welcoming, educators choose to try to change the child. The evidence abounds. Programs such as Head Start have traditionally concentrated on compensating for or overcoming sociological disadvantage (read "Change the child") rather than on changing the school.

This is a totally unreasonable attitude for a number of reasons. In the first place, such solutions view the child as having a deficit. I find this to be objectionable in itself because it makes assumptions about the home that we usually cannot confirm, and because it lets schools off the hook a little too easily. Even if it were true, from a practical perspective, we cannot undo the home experience of the child, even if such action were necessary or defensible. The attitude also ignores what we have discovered in the past decade about sociocultural bias. As David Dillon (1989) writes in an editorial for an issue of *Language Arts* dedicated to home-school relationships:

> ... there are different kinds of literacies characteristic of different cultural, religious, and especially socioeconomic groups. Being literate according to the norms of one social group does not mean being literate within another social group. (p. 7)

He also points out that research hasn't even begun to address the effect this kind of thinking has on non-mainstream children. We only have to look at the disproportionally high referrral rates of Native American (First Nations) children to special education classes or the high incidence of misdiagnosis of learning disabilities (Bailey, 1994) to realize that our first response is almost always to fix the child. It is telling that researchers have to point out that a change in attitude and expectation among all parties to the educational enterprise—parents, community, and educators—is required if Native American children are to have anything approaching equal educational opportunity (Bailey, 1994). However, experienced and sensitive teachers have always known this. They could tell us that thinking about education in such a narrow way means that we fail to take advantage of the assets, the experience children already have of the world and of learning, and makes the job of teaching harder rather than easier. In short, the direction of educational thinking has traditionally been on preparing children for school rather than on preparing schools for children and it has resulted in failure for too many children.

Change the Language

When educators set about to change children, one of the first things they identify as needing change is their language. Sometimes, misinterpretation or misapplication of sociolinguistic theory is to blame. In the 1970s, a British sociolinguist named Basil Bernstein hypothesized the existence of two kinds of oral language. The first, called the elaborated code, was the language used in formal situations (such as school) and was characterized by complex syntactic and stylistic conventions. It was considered to be the language for representing abstract thought, its meaning created by linguistic means alone. The other, called the restricted code, was used in informal situations and was characterized by a simpler stylistic and syntactic range and a restricted vocabulary. It was also thought to rely more heavily on accompanying context (e.g., situation and gestures) to make its meaning clear and to be incapable of expressing abstractions. Bernstein's observation that middle-class children have access to both codes and that some lower-class children may have access only to the restricted code led many educators to take the view that children from lower socioeconomic classes have a language deficit that must be overcome if they are to succeed in school.

The hypothesis has largely been discredited now, in part because of the work of Labov (1982) and Wells (1986). Labov demonstrated that the so-called restricted code is perfectly adequate for expressing abstract concepts. More recently, researchers have shown concrete differences between the discourse style of non-mainstream children and that of teachers and middle-class white children. A number of studies (Wells, 1986; Heath, 1983; Lindsay, 1992; Michaels & Cazden, 1987) have all examined one aspect or another of the relationship between children's sociolinguistic background and the language of the school. Attempting to discover precisely what it is about the language of the school that makes it relatively "unlearnable" for non-mainstream children, researchers have found that one of the chief differences lies in narrative style. Black children and Native American children (*First Nations* children in Canada) tend to use a style of narrative discourse termed *topic associating* as opposed to the *topic centered* style favored by white teachers and middle-class white children. There are, in fact, many different styles within the broad category of *topic associating*, and it would be a mistake to assume that all native children or all minority children acquire the same discourse style. The point is that the topic associating is different from the topic centered discourse style of middle-class white children. This style typically features tightly organized plot structure—a beginning, middle, and end—with lexical devices (*and then, because, and so...*) providing cohesion to the narrative. A topic associating discourse style is marked by "frequent shifts without explicity lexical markers" and cohesion provided chiefly through intonation (Lindsay, 1992, p. 205). Since most published stories for children are topic centered, it is easy to understand why Gordon Wells's study, and many others, have shown that children who have engaged in the school-like activities of reading and storytelling, and whose narrative styles more closely match the teacher's, are most successful in school. This research points educators in the right direction, but it is a direction that is usually ignored. Rather, the research is used as a justification for the less than stellar achievement levels of non-mainstream children and the practice of trying to change the child's language to make it fit the mainstream. It is easy to evade responsibility for high rates of illiteracy, for example, if we can blame the children for bringing to school the wrong kind of language.

Based on his monumental and impressive longitudinal study of children acquiring language in Bristol, Gordon Wells reached what he considered to be his most important finding: "...up to the age of 5, there were no clear differences between the middle- and lower-class groups of children in their rate of development, in the range of meanings expressed, or in the range of functions for which language was used" (Wells, 1986, p. 142). In describing his findings, Wells disclosed one fact that helps to account for the tenacity of the belief that lower-class children come from linguistically deficient homes. He noted that the "half dozen or so most advanced children...did tend to come from the better-educated, professional homes" and that "the half dozen or so least advanced children came from homes where the parents were minimally educated and worked, or had worked, in unskilled or semiskilled occupations." But he was quick to point out that for 90% of the 128 children he studied, "there was no clear relationship between family background and level of language development attained" (Wells, 1986, p. 134).

The myth should be put finally and forever to rest. We can proceed in confidence that the language of the children we meet in school has served well the demands placed upon it, and there is no evidence that children from one socioeconomic class makes more demands on it than children from another. The problem is that the language of the child may differ from the language of the school, and it is the school that refuses to change. I have collected a number of accounts over the years that, taken together, constitute evidence that when it comes to children's language, some classrooms are far from being user-friendly. Incredibly, some take what seems to be an openly hostile attitude toward children's talk. Even mainstream children whose own language more closely matches the school norm find much of what happens in classrooms to be strange if not inane. They are simply better at making the necessary linguistic adaptations—they learn to play along. But not all are successful, and in this chapter, we will learn some of the reasons why.

We will look at the language of schools and in schools. Ideally, anyone interested in finding out about the language experience of children in schools will spend time in schools watching and listening. But this is not possible for everyone and, even when it is, some preparation is necessary to make the observations worthwhile experiences. This kind of background is provided, in part, by the observations of others. Some are anecdotal—the stories told by teachers and children and others who have had experience in classrooms. Others are more formal—reports of studies conducted by researchers interested in children's language growth through the school years.

WHAT'S WRONG WITH LANGUAGE IN SCHOOL

I must begin this section with a cautionary note. Finding fault is easy, but that is not my purpose. I realize that I run two tangible risks here. The first is that by selecting anecdotes to make my points about the disparity between natural language and school language, I present only the negative, when in fact I have never visited a classroom where nothing good occurred. The second is that I present a view that seems to undermine my own belief in teachers and in education. Both are dangerous, so let me attempt to control the damage before it is done.

First, even in a poor educational setting, a great deal of learning likely occurs, and that may not be apparent in the anecdotes related here. Second, *all* teachers work under conditions that are less than ideal. In recent years, salaries and benefits have improved in some states and provinces, but rarely have they kept up with relative gains in the economy. Teachers have been beleaguered by attacks on their professionalism and made the scapegoats of a political bureaucracy keen to make change (and political impact). Most importantly, classroom conditions have worsened. The demands on teachers increased dramatically in the latter half of the 20th century. As the structure of the family has become more fragile, teachers have had to assume roles and responsibilities that once belonged exclusively to families. The need to educate children to the dangers of drug abuse, protect them from abuse, act as advocates, and generally prepare them for a life that is harder and less friendly than it was a half century ago, has left teachers with less time to devote to what were once major goals of schools.

However, it's not only the additional social responsibilities that make teachers' working conditions difficult. The curriculum has changed, as well, and in almost exclusively an additive fashion. That is, governments and school boards have added to the subjects a teacher has to teach, without lengthening the school day or the school year; thus, the time available for such basics as reading and writing instruction has shrunk. As one teacher put it, "Do you want me to teach plant life cycles, animal life cycles, plant and animal characteristics, geology, weather patterns, geometric shapes and computer technology to these kids in Grades 1 and 2, or do you want me to teach them to read and write and learn simple math?" (McMartin, 2001). Teachers cannot do it all and do it well even though that is what we as a society normally expect. Because the demands on teachers are unreasonable and because they are worsening over time, we must be *very* careful not to sit in judgment on them, particularly when judgment is based on such scant evidence. That is not my intent, and I hope that I need not reiterate my support for and belief in the teachers who take on the responsibility for education but receive so little of the credit for what goes right.

Later in this chapter, we will meet two teachers who provide good, healthy experiences; the anecdotes that follow here are offered as extreme examples of how children should *not* experience language in a classroom.

"No Talking" and Other Unfriendly Signs

In 1983, John Holt wrote, "… in almost all schools, hardly anything is done to help children become fluent, precise, and skillful in speech" (p. 123). This allegation, and it is a serious one, was made toward the end of a chapter about how children learn to talk. His point was *not* to cast aspersions on schools, though he would hardly cast them bouquets either, but to identify the fundamental disparity between children's language and learning when they are left to their own devices and what they experience in schools.

A few years ago, a research assistant was observing a kindergarten class in which she recorded the following dialogue, which has been edited only slightly:

> **Teacher:** *(Pointing to a dog in a picture in a picture book.) Molly, do you know what this is?*
> **Molly:** *Yes.*
> **T:** *What is it?*
> **M:** *A dog.*
> **T:** *Very good. And what's he playing with?*
> **M:** *A ball.*
> **T:** *And what color is the ball?*
> **M:** *Red.*
> **T:** *Right. (Pointing to a girl in the picture.) What is she wearing?*
> **M:** *A skirt and blouse.*
> **T:** *What else?*

> M: *Shoes and socks.*
> T: *That's good Molly. What do you think about this picture?*
> M: *It's nice.*

At the time the recording was made, Molly was 5;6. She is of normal academic ability, and her first language is English. The teacher was not teaching Molly new English vocabulary or structures, nor was she reading a story. It is not immediately clear, in fact, just what the teacher was doing. This is, I freely admit, a radical example of bad classroom talk. Yet, for many teachers, this dialogue will be at least vaguely familiar, if not in substance then in character. The really scary thing about this dialogue is that it has not been very many years since we would have identified this as an example of a good classroom exchange and held it up as an example of how to interact with young children.

To illustrate how purposeless this talk is, suppose Molly had responded to the teacher as an adult might have if asked the same questions. The following might have transpired:

> **Teacher:** *Molly, do you know what this is?*
> **Molly:** *Of course I do, don't you?*
> T: *What is it?*
> M: *A dog. Geez! Any three-year-old knows that.*
> T: *Very good. And what's he playing with?*
> M: *Looks like a dump truck to me. Only kidding. That's a ball.*
> T: *And what color is the ball?*
> M: *Color blind, too? Fuschia with a hint of sienna.*
> T: *Right. (Pointing to a girl in the picture.) What is she wearing?*
> M: *How much longer are we going to keep this up? Whadaya think she's wearing, a barrel? She's wearing clothes. Okay, I'll play along. A skirt and a blouse.*
> T: *What else?*
> M: *Shoes and socks.*
> T: *That's good, Molly. What do you think about this picture?*
> M: *I think that girl's mother must be crazy to let her go out to play with the dog in her good clothes. No kid I know wears a skirt to school much less to play in. Come to think of it, I don't think I know anyone who owns a skirt.*

But this dialogue is fictitious. Molly did not respond in this way because she is a child and in the course of a few months in school, being subjected to talk little more purposeful than that in the first dialogue, Molly had internalized many of the characteristics of school talk. She had learned that, in school, language is unreal. People, especially teachers, talk about things that no one cares much about. She had learned that school language is decontextualized. Not only do teachers habitually talk about things that aren't there, they seem to avoid opportunities for talking about real things. In the first dialogue, the teacher didn't relate the picture to a story she was reading or make up a story about the picture or provide any real-world context at all for the child. Nor did she encourage Molly to relate the picture to her own life through talk.

Molly had also learned that people, teachers anyway, ask silly questions. Sometimes, they ask questions for which they have already determined the correct answers. Sometimes, they even ask questions that *everybody* knows the answers to and then praise the answers. *How many fingers am I holding up? Three? Very good!* Molly had learned that much school talk, devoid as it is of purpose and meaning, is easy. Once she figured out just what game the teacher was playing, it was not difficult to play along.

It is also telling to examine the dialogue from a functional perspective, which doesn't take long. Although superficially, the teacher's questions seem to request information, in fact, they do not. She already knows the answers and her questions serve only to instruct—to draw Molly's attention to a picture she probably would not be otherwise interested in. The true function of her language seems to be to control Molly's behavior, to direct it toward the teacher's unclear but likely pedagogical purpose. Beyond this, it is hard to find any other function. She is even less successful in providing opportunities for Molly to use language in different ways. Molly only responds to the questions she is asked, mechanically giving the expected responses. We cannot even claim that she is using language to inform, because both she and the teacher know that they both already know the answers. The teacher is steering Molly through a match game, checking to see if the child's answers are identical to the expected ones.

It is ironic that when children get into minor trouble at school, that trouble is so often for talking. Children learn very soon that although schools purport to value language, they don't much value *talk*, not children's talk anyway. The truth of this observation was driven home to me during a visit to a southern California school a few years ago:

> A Canadian teacher, a former student of mine, had been hired to teach ESL in a junior high school, considered by the local Board of Education to be one of the best in the area, a model school in many regards. While I was there, the young teacher took me to visit a number of classrooms, but one stands out in my memory. The room was filled with bright, colorful travel posters of exotic places. A VTR and monitor stood in a prominent place in the front of the room and every piece of furniture, every object in the room was labelled with its name in clear black letters on a white card. What I remember best, though, was the largest sign in the room, placed above the blackboard in letters about nine inches high. In this ESL classroom where the purpose was to foster children's language learning, the sign said "NO TALKING."

We shouldn't assume that there was no talking in that classroom, for most assuredly there was. This brings us to another problem with classroom talk, and a very serious one: The people who would most benefit from honest, purposeful talk are the ones who get the least opportunity to do it. Teachers don't need the practice; children do. But they get little of it in the worst situations and not nearly enough in the best. We don't need research studies or even samples of classroom talk to tell us that this is true. We only have to consider the normal protocol of the classroom. For the most part, it states that children talk only to the teacher and only when requested to do so.

Teachers "Value" Talk

The message on a "No Talking" sign seems unambiguous, but it may not be clear. Every time a teacher asks a question to which there is only a single correct answer that she will accept, she is sending the message that a child's talk is important only if it fits her expectations. It is in this sense, that teachers "value" talk—they *evaluate* it. When he makes a value judgment about a child's language, as he does when he tries to correct it or change it, a teacher is telling the child that her talk doesn't count. The message is sent in myriad ways. The following dialogue that a student teacher recorded tells a wonderfully revealing story about children with dialect differences that underscores my point:

> A teacher in a Western Canadian school had a number of minority children in her grade-one class. Among these children were represented three different aboriginal languages. One of the children, Bob, was a native speaker of English, but it was a non-standard dialect since he had learned it on the Reserve from his parents and their generation who were not native speakers of English. The teacher was of the misguided opinion that these children needed ESL and thus, her lessons sometimes had that flavor. One morning a few days after the beginning of school in September, the teacher was "teaching" the names of items of clothing, and the following occurred:

> **Teacher:** *(Pointing to her shoes.) What are these called?*
> **Child 1 (Bob):** *Shoes.*
> **T:** *Right. And what do you wear with shoes?*
> **Bob:** *Socks (pronounced "shocks"). I gots green ones.*
> **T:** *Those are 'socks' Bobby. Can you say 'socks?'*
> **B:** *Yeah. Shocks. I got shum blue ones, too.*
> **T:** *Some blue what?*
> **B:** *Shocks.*
> **T:** *No, say "socks." Those are "socks" not shocks.*
> **B:** *Das what I say. Shocks.*

By this time Bob, and probably the other children as well, wondered why they were dwelling on such an inane topic. Surely there was no one left in the class who didn't know what socks were. This teacher made several mistakes but chief among them were the assumption that talk in the classroom would serve *her purposes* and that *she alone* was the arbiter of correct pronunciation. This teacher should have counted herself very fortunate if Bob ever ventured to speak again. Why would he? This anecdote, like the earlier ones, is extreme in illustrating its point. There are, however, thousands of dialogues each day between teachers and students, and many of these are characterized by dishonesty and manipulation.

Dishonest and Manipulative Talk

By dishonesty, I do not mean that teachers tell children lies, and by manipulation I do not mean to suggest that teachers consciously manipulate children's behaviour to selfish ends. Rather, I mean any kind of unnatural classroom talk that is directed toward pedagogical ends and not toward communication with children. Some see this kind of talk as epidemic in classrooms. As John Holt (1983) writes:

> … if we think that every time we talk to a child we must teach her something, our talk may become calculated and fake, and may lead the child to think, like so many of today's young people, that all talk is a lie and a cheat. (p.107)

We saw this kind of dishonesty in the dialogue—it could hardly be called conversation—between Molly and her teacher. It isn't necessary to call upon such extreme examples, however, to make the point. We have only to consider the false tones that primary teachers sometimes adopt when talking to children or the fact that we plan so much of our talk to lead us down some pedagogical path.

A number of researchers have described this "pedagogical register" or "teacher-talk register." Heath has observed that it uses higher pitch than other speech registers and has exaggerated enunciation and intonation patterns (Heath, 1978, cited in Roller, 1989). Cazden has mentioned "the myriad expressions of control; the prevalence of 'testing' questions; the use of boundary markers such as *now, well*, and *okay*" (1987, p. 31). We have all heard this kind of teacher talk, and if we recognize it, we can be certain that children recognize it as well. They may not make quite the same judgments about it, but with enough exposure, they must surely come to understand that it is different from the registers used when two people are engaged in an honest conversational exchange. The pedagogical "register proclaims not that 'we are talking together,' but that 'I am teaching you'"(Roller, 1989, p. 497).

Teacher talk also reveals itself as dishonest when it is directed toward a pedagogical point and entirely controlled by the teacher. Cathy Roller provides a good example of this kind of talk and of the pedagogical register in use in the following example:

Teacher: *The first question I'd like to ask you about today is whether or not you've participated in a science fair or some kind of contest where you had to make something. Think for a minute. How did you feel when you were entering this contest? Give me a low signal when you're ready to tell about your past experience. OK, C1.*

Child 1: *When I was in Cub Scouts we had to make a robot out of boards, bottle caps, and (unintelligible). At first I though I was going to win, but when I got to the judging I saw other things that were a lot better than mine.*

T: *While you were constructing your robot you thought you probably would win. Were you nervous?*

C1: *No.*

T: *Not too nervous. Who else has been in a contest like that?*

Child 2: *I was in the same thing. I wasn't, I got it done. I knew I wouldn't win anything.*

T: *Uh, huh.*

C2: *Turned out I was sick that night so I never got to take it in.*

T: *You never got to take it in. C3, have you ever entered a contest or something like that? Some other kind of competition maybe, where you're up against other people and they're doing the same kind of thing you're doing? C4?*

Child 4: *In fourth grade where we had a Valentine party. We had to make these boxes. When I first made it, I didn't think I was going to win at all because I just got some old things and put it together so.*

T: *What kind of box was it?*

C4: *Just a Valentine's box in fourth grade where we used to put our envelopes into.*

T: *Uh, huh. I can remember doing that in school too. C5? Have you ever entered a competition?*

Child 5: *There was a Halloween where you had to color a picture in or draw it. I entered it but I didn't win anything.*

T: *How did you feel?*

C5: *I didn't really care.*

T: *You didn't care whether you won or not. Well, in the story today is a girl named Maria, and she's entering a science fair, so she has to have a pretty elaborate project. How do you think she feels? Just think about it a minute. The importance of the project. C3?*

Child 3: *I think she feels really nervous.*

T: *Nervous. C4, how about you?*

C4: *She's anxious.*

T: *OK. Let me get some of these words down. I like these words. Nervous, anxious (writing on board). Anybody else? C1.*

C1: *Scared.*

T: *Scared. C5, do you agree with those?*

C5: *Uh, huh.*

T: *Is that what you think she probably will be feeling? OK. (Roller, 1989, pp. 495–496)*

This is an excellent example of talk that scores of teacher educators in the past touted as good teacher talk, and as good preparation for the basal story to follow. After all, as Roller pointed out, the "teacher initiated the discussion, directed the turns, and, after each child's response, commented" in relentless pursuit of her teaching point which was, we can assume, to relate the children's prior knowledge to the reading they were about to do (1989, p. 496). There was a time when some teachers believed this was as it should be. But is it? Admittedly, it is not as bad as the talk that occurred between Molly and her teacher, but we have only to look more closely at the interchange to see that it is highly controlled and manipulative in a number of ways.

First, it was carried out according to the teacher's agenda. She had a purpose, and she manipulated the children's talk to that purpose. She initiated the turns, decided when they were completed, and controlled what would be talked about. The teacher conveniently ignored the fact that some of the children's honest responses did *not* lead them in the direction she wanted them led (most of them reported feeling no nervousness or anxiety) for it did not matter. She soon wrested control of the talk back and called on another child who might give a better response.

Second, it was conversationally dishonest. No adult would stay around very long to talk to someone whose only contribution to the conversation was to repeat what was last said and then turn to someone else. The repetitions of the children's responses served no purpose whatever. Had they elaborated or expanded the children's language (and this is likely what the teacher *believed* they did), they would have served some purpose. But they did not. Third, the exchange was dishonest in the sense that although it pretended to draw out children's experiences, it did not do so in any meaningful way. As Roller observed, even though the teacher directed many questions at the children's experience, she also controlled the bounds of the communication. She determined what was appropriate for discussion and made it clear that what was appropriate was what she wanted to hear (Roller, 1989, p. 497).

This excerpt demonstrates another difficulty with classroom talk. Even if honesty, directness, and high interest for the children had characterized the discussion, it did not provide much opportunity for each child to talk. Instead, the children formed a captive audience, witnesses to the teacher's controlling language. She used language to accomplish her own agenda, ostensibly providing opportunities for children to engage in meaningful talk but in fact setting severe limits on the language they used.

Teacher Talk Is Teacher Talking

At home, most children have ample opportunity to talk even if they have to share the time with a number of siblings or members of an extended family. But that changes when they get to school. As Cazden notes, "In the classroom, the group is larger than even the largest families gathered at meals, and so getting a turn to talk is much harder...." (1987, p. 31). Children need to talk and, for the most part, teachers do not, yet we can see that teachers do most of the talking. In the excerpt just given, we saw a teacher dominating the proceedings, but a closer examination gives us some idea about the impact of that domination on the air time accorded individual children. We don't need a sophisticated analysis; we can get a rough indication by comparing the number of words uttered by each speaker. Table 10.1 shows the proportion of talk attributable to the teacher and each child measured in words.

Table 10.1 Proportion of Teacher Talk

Participant	Total Words	% of Total
Teacher	288	62.3
C1	48	10.4
C2	33	7.1
C3	6	1.3
C4	59	12.8
C5	28	6.1
Total	462	100.0

We see that, even in comparison to the total amount of talk allowed the children, the teacher gets the lion's share with more than 62%. When we consider what this means to each child, the picture grows even darker. At best, C4 generated a total of 59 words for just under 13% of the total talk.

When he directly compared language of the school with language of the home, Gordon Wells found that the number of child utterances directed to an adult was nearly three times greater at home than at school and that children initiated conversation nearly three times more often at home than at school. The number of child speaking terms per conversation was greater at home, by a ratio nearly two to one, but the most telling of the results were these:

- The proportion of display questions directed by an adult to a child was seven times greater at school than at home. (These are questions that do not request information but provide an opportunity to display knowledge, such as *What color is the ball?* asked Molly by her teacher.),

- Adults used language to extend children's meaning twice as often at home as at school, and similarly,

- By a proportion of two to one, teachers develop their *own* meanings more than parents do when talking to children. (Wells, 1986, pp. 67–94)

Teachers' domination of classroom talk costs dearly. As Wells points out, "conversation is a reciprocal activity: the more one participant dominates, the more the opportunities for the other participant to make his or her own personal contribution are reduced and constrained" (1986, p. 87). It would seem that classrooms are poor places for developing conversational skills. Not only do teachers control the amount of time children spend in talk, they also control the purposes to which it is directed. The child Molly learned very young that when school talk has purpose, it is usually the *Teacher's* purpose. She had recognized the kind of talk John Holt (1983) reviled when he wrote:

> ... The teacher does most of the talking, and now and then asks the children questions, to make sure they have been paying attention and understand. Now and then a bold teacher will start what they call a "discussion." What happens then is usually ... "answer pulling." The teacher asks a series of pointed questions, aimed at getting students to give an answer that he has decided beforehand is right. Teachers' manuals are full of this technique—"Have a discussion, in which you draw out the following points...." This kind of fake, directed conversation is worse than none at all. Small wonder that children soon get bored and disgusted with it. (p. 123)

And if they are bored, how can they be expected to learn? Much of the time, they don't. Jon McGill (1988), writing of talk in his history classroom, tells of his efforts to bring his information-dispensing talk to life:

> A recent lesson to fourth year CSE [Certificate in Secondary Education] pupils involved lengthy outlines of the origins of trade unions. Though I specifically wanted an information giving lesson I also wanted to entertain. Though I conveyed the information using dramatic language, role play and gesture, I was nonetheless left feeling that, in summa-

rizing the lesson, students would see it simply as the teacher having talked—and remain unimpressed by the pyrotechnics which tried to disguise the fact. The next lesson with these pupils demonstrated that they retained little except the drama and the display. What I said was of little impact and during my "exemplary" lesson, they had said little. (pp. 78–79)

Claire Staab (1991) reported results of a study which showed that in the third-grade and sixth-grade classrooms she studied, 78% of class time was devoted either to the teacher talking or to quiet time. This research showed that although 98.5% of the participating teachers professed to believe that "oral language should be a way to learn all content areas," in practice the oral language tended to be their own (p. 44). Staab also found that her results were essentially the same as those reported 20 years ago, suggesting that all the research and writing about the importance of talk in classrooms has had little effect.

Teachers talk and, sometimes, children listen. Even less often, it seems, they learn. The same tale is told in thousands of households each day as children return home from school to be asked the time-honored question, What did you do in school today?

> **Parent:** *What did you do in school today?*
> **Child:** *Nothing.*
> **P:** *Surely, something happened.*
> **C:** *(Thinking about it for a moment.) Nope.*
> **P:** *Nothing at all?*
> **C:** *No. The teacher talked a lot. And Mary Beth got in trouble.*
> **P:** *What did the teacher talk about?*
> **C:** *I dunno. Stuff.*
> **P:** *What did Mary Beth get into trouble for?*
> **C:** *Talking to Peter and me. She was telling us about how her brother broke his foot. You know James? Well, he went skiing for the first time ever and....*

Teachers will have to learn to value children's talk, genuinely, before they will be able to break out of the mold of talking too much and with too little meaning.

School Talk Is Homogeneous

Talk at home is unstructured and relatively free. Parents do not schedule time for conversation, although they may schedule time for a bedtime story. Conversation happens as the people in the household go about their daily activities. Similarly, most children are exposed to a wide variety of talk—numerous dialects and numerous purposes. Dillon (1980) describes the kinds of language a child encounters in the simple act of getting ready for school in the morning:

> Susan's grandmother, who lives with them, tells Susan that her lunch is in the ice box. Susan is in a hurry as she gets it, and her mother calls after her, "Susan, close the refrigerator door." As she stops to do this, Susan hears the morning weather report. It's an interview of a New England resident and sounds something like "The stawm dumped a lawt

of snow heah," and she wishes her own Midwestern town would get some snow soon. She meets her friends on the way to school and greets them one by one. "Hey, what's up?" "Boy, sure is cold!" "Think it'll snow?" As they approach the school, the children meet the principal. "Good morning, Mr. Lawrence," Susan says. "How are you today?" He responds and heads for his office as Susan and her friends hurry to class. (pp. 29–30)

In the course of a few minutes, Susan has been exposed to variations caused by language change over time—her grandmother uses *icebox* and her mother *refrigerator.* She hears and has no difficulty understanding the regional dialect on the broadcast news. She switches easily to the subject and vernacular of her peer group and, when she gets to school, to the more formal requirement of greeting the principal. She hurries to class where she will find *some* variation among her classmates, but chances are that the language she encounters there will be somewhat more homogenized than the language of the home, not only because the teacher does most of the talking but because schools sustain their own brand of language.

Most schools perpetuate a variety of English they call the standard dialect. Even in schools that have dropped the notion of a standard, preferred, or educated dialect, there is still a high degree of conformity. This is true in part because they mostly hear teachers whose speech has likely been sanitized as they acquired the education needed to become teachers. I live in a part of Canada where the residents have a readily distinguishable dialect. Yet, a few years ago, when a colleague I had known for many years revealed that she was a native of this province, I expressed surprised. She did not sound like a Newfoundlander. "No," she replied. "My mother was an English teacher, and she made sure that I grew up speaking 'properly.'" I have heard similar stories and recall my own attempt to lose my Ozark dialect and adopt the New England norm of the New Hampshire university that I attended as an undergraduate. The pressures of the educational system are toward linguistic standardization of a type that *may* lead to greater understanding but also leads to feelings of inferiority and exclusion by those who do not happen to conform.

In the second place, there is a sameness to the kinds of things talked about in classrooms. Routines and rules by which classes are conducted and which teachers talk about are essentially the same throughout English-speaking North America. Many language programs are organized to correspond with the scope and sequence charts detailed in the teachers' manuals accompanying basal readers, yielding even more conformity of language and limiting what is talked about.

Third, as we have seen in a number of different examples, school talk seems to be restricted to a very few functions. Staab's (1991) study, while not directly addressing language function, in identifying the fact that teachers did most of the talking, provided strong clues about the nature of the talk. Indeed, teachers spent 49% of the total class activity time talking, mostly lecturing, or instructing, so we can presume that the most commonly used function was the informing function. They spent an additional 29% of the total time in "asking students to work quietly and independently," thus giving a good indication of the other kind of language which dominates classrooms—the language of getting things done, that is, controlling language, or to use Halliday's term, instrumental language. Of the 22% of time left for students to talk, 15% was described as "informal talk," leaving 7% for all the other kinds of talk in which children might engage.

Fourth, and this is perhaps the most frightening and depressing aspect of homogeneity, schools often assume through the language of teachers and the teaching materials they choose that all children have the same background, interests, and experience of language. The individual child, the private person known wholly to her parents, becomes the recipient of a preplanned and largely prepackaged school curriculum. Even if they pay lip service to the facts of individual variation among children, schools are only rarely able to respond in ways appropriate for all children. It is a very strong claim, but one that is supported if not directly then at least obliquely by the research evidence, that one of the chief reasons for children failing in school is the fact that schools make this erroneous assumption. In fact, recent research suggests that the language of instruction and the types of materials that might be appropriate are largely dependent on the needs of individual children, particularly when they are outside the mainstream culture. Homogeneity of classroom talk is, thus, not only unnatural, it is particularly detrimental to non-mainstream children.

School Talk Intimidates

Perhaps one of the reasons that the first day of school is such a momentous occasion is that the oral culture of childhood has spread the word that school is a pretty frightening place to be. We may wonder from our adult perspective how this can be so given all the efforts we make to create comfortable, safe learning environments. But from the child's perspective, the temporary feeling of safety may be lost when we challenge his ownership of knowing.

> Although it has been 20 years since the incident occurred, I remember clearly the day my older son came home from first grade in tears, a grimy worksheet crunched in his fist. When I asked him to show it to me, the cause of his distress poured out. "I got minus," he sobbed, pointing to the mark at the top of the page. (The teacher used a plus, minus, check system to indicate that the work was excellent, deficient, or satisfactory, respectively.) "And I did it right!" he sobbed.
>
> I looked at the worksheet. There was a capital letter *D* at the top and the directions to circle all the items pictured which began with the letter *d*. Kerry had dutifully circled the first two, a dog and a door, but had stopped at that point. "I think your teacher expected you to circle *all* the things which start with the *d* sound. Why did you stop there?" "Because I knew how to do that."

At age 6, Kerry had assumed that school was for learning to do things he didn't already know how to do. Once he had worked out what he was supposed to do with the worksheet and that he knew how to do it correctly, he abandoned the project and turned his attention to something he didn't know. He may have turned to a science fiction book borrowed from the school library or one that he had borrowed from his father's bookshelf. He had failed in school because he chose to read instead of circling ducks. His learning at school had come into conflict with his previous experience of learning at home.

Parents tend to respond to the child's meaning and rejoice in each indication of progress. The role of the teacher is generally different: There is a strong demand for correctness, and teachers tend to view errors as failures rather than partial successes. The responsibility for effective communication and for progress falls upon children. Those who do not succeed may be labeled as being lazy, slow, or even disabled...." (Zutell, 1980, p. 19)

Kerry was in almost continual trouble at school that year—for talking, for not finishing his worksheets, and for not participating in his reading group. When I went to school to discuss his problems with his teacher, she opened our conference by saying, "I'm very worried about Kerry. He's a bright little boy, but he's having such trouble in reading." I smiled. Had she told me he was having trouble in music or art, I would have assumed that he had inherited my ear or his father's eye; but, this is a child who had taught himself to read before he was 3 years old. At home, he was reading stories from the newspaper and sixth-grade-level science fiction, but at school he couldn't read. What his teacher was really saying, of course, was that he wasn't doing the activities deemed appropriate during the time allotted to reading. Chances are these had little to do with real reading, for Smith (1975) was likely right in his estimation that in every hour assigned to reading instruction in the elementary classroom, children only spend about 4 minutes actually reading (cited in Zutell, 1980, p. 19). He didn't mention circling ducks, but my student teachers tell me that children still spend a significant amount of time in worksheet activity during the time officially designated for reading. Staab's (1991) study, though not directed precisely to this question, showed that children in third grade and sixth grade spent about 15% of their time in activities designated as reading. But more than 40% of this time was taken up by the teacher talking. Children spent 47% of this time in "quiet classroom" activities that surely included reading (although the researcher does not indicate how much of this time was actually spent reading). Estimating generously that 90% of the quiet time was spent in reading, the figures would translate into very few minutes per day.

It would seem that Kerry was one of many children Jerome Bruner was talking about when he said that "much of what we do and say in school only makes children feel that they do not know things that, in fact, they knew perfectly well before we began to talk about them" (Holt, 1983, p. 95). When we lead children to mistrust their own knowledge, then we are using language to intimidate. When we demand that they circle ducks to prove they know certain sound-symbol correspondences, we show that we have lost touch with the real business of education.

School Language Is Disembodied

At home, children's language is grounded in the reality of family life. They have parents and sometimes siblings who support in myriad ways their attempts at communication and thus their learning of language. Learning in the home is characterized by demonstration and performance. Children watch their fathers bake cookies or fix tires and ask questions, as we have seen in earlier chapters. In watching and assisting, they learn various kinds of skills and the language associated with them. When they get to school, however, children are instructed in how to do things and then get to practice doing them.

That instruction and practice differ from demonstration and performance is easy to establish. Take reading for example. We found out earlier that children who learn to read at home learn by demonstration—they see parents and older siblings getting meaning from print—and by performance—remember "make way for applesauce." At school, rarely do children witness the teacher reading for her own purposes. When they do witness the teacher reading, no one seriously believes that it is part of the reading lesson. No, teachers tell students what to do in order to be able to read and then children do their reading, except that doing reading is seldom reading. Word attack skills, spelling lessons, handwriting practice, and a myriad of other language activities come between the child and the reading. Language is no longer the medium; it has become the instructional message. That we routinely disembody language is implied in John Holt's lesson on the teaching of reading:

> What we must do in helping anyone learn to read is to make very clear that writing is an extension of speech, that beyond every written word there is a human voice speaking, and that reading is the way to hear what those voices are saying. (Holt, 1989, p. 31)

What Holt suggests is, essentially, that we embody the language of print. We would do well to consider that advice in all our teaching, for it is not only in the teaching of reading that we separate language from reality. Too often, for example, we talk about numbers and their properties rather than demonstrating them with real countable objects and allowing children to do their own manipulations with them.

We can learn a valuable lesson from second language immersion classes in this regard. When children do not understand the language of instruction and when the teacher is responsible for teaching not only the content but the language as well, she cannot talk about numbers in the abstract. She cannot say, "If I have two oranges and give Peter one…" and expect the children to understand what she is saying. And if they do not understand what she is saying, they will not understand the subtraction problem she is presenting. Rather, she must use visuals—she must demonstrate the concept with real oranges and real people in real time. Immersion teachers routinely rely on concrete objects and on demonstration to make themselves understood. In the process, the children learn not only the content but the language simultaneously because the language of numeracy is embodied in the concepts of numeracy.

LANGUAGE IN SCHOOL: THE POSITIVE SIDE

Earlier in this chapter, I painted a rather bleak picture of language learning in schools. If I were to end the chapter here, I would leave readers with the impression that schools are language deserts where the only children who flourish are those who are nurtured in the oasis of the home. That would be patently unfair. There are fine schools in North America populated with children who are thriving in an environment rich in language and language learning opportunity. Many of these schools have embodied in their curriculum and teaching methods the principles of whole language. In such schools, teachers have taken a critical look at their practice, found it wanting, and in response have embraced a new ideology and its corresponding teaching practices. They have accepted and acted upon the truths about language learning that we have learned already—that children learn language best when it is used for real purposes and when teachers refrain from fragmenting it into meaningless pieces or isolated skills. This was the belief that underpinned whole language.

Whole language was one of the more controversial trends of the last two decades. When the tenets of whole language—and it isn't really a method so much as a belief system—were implemented in a sensible manner, it was a successful approach. Unfortunately, there was also a great deal of educational malpractice perpetrated in the name of whole language. Teachers or educational administrators who have not fully understood the concepts supporting whole language practice have sometimes used it as an excuse for a type of pedagogical *laissez-faire* that has not had the desired effect on children. A number of educators have expressed the fear that "some whole language teachers, in their efforts to avoid interfering with children's natural development (Walkerdine, 1986), construct a *laissez-faire* approach to literacy instruction that, in effect, withdraws teachers' support for students' learning" (Dudley-Marling & Fine, 1997, p. 257, citing Dudley-Marling & Dippo, 1991). But where whole language practice has been true to its definitions and principles, the result has been beneficial to children's language development in school.

Whole Language Defined

What, then, is whole language? First, to reiterate, whole language is not a method of teaching reading and is not associated with any particular set of practices, although practitioners undoubtedly engage in certain common routines and practices. Although there are likely as many definitions as believers, the definition provided by Froese in his introduction to the text he edited entitled *Whole-Language, Practice and Theory* (1990), is a representative one: "We define whole-language as a child-centered, literature-based approach to language teaching that immerses students in real communication situations whenever possible" (p. 2). Note that a great many teaching methods would be entirely compatible with that definition, but the important point is that the belief expressed in that definition has the potential for profound change. The approach is *child-centered*; so is the language situation in which most children have been successful language learners. The approach is *literature-based*; children who learn to read are those who are read to, and the stories and books that they hear are chosen for their interest and appeal, and not for the sequence and scope of vocabulary or language structures. The approach immerses children in *real communication situations*; before school, children learn language by talking to people about real events and objects in familiar environments.

Whole Language in Practice

Definitions are useful as broad indicators of an approach to language teaching and learning, but they provide few insights into what actually happens in practice. How do the lofty goals implicit in the definition get realized in classrooms full of children? To answer the question, we will visit the classrooms of two teachers who claim to be practitioners of whole language and find out how they translate a set of principles into classroom life. We can't stay long in either class, but even a little time will give us some insights into whole language in practice.

Teacher #1, Mary Kennedy, Calgary, Alberta.   Mary Kennedy teaches second grade in an urban school in Calgary, Alberta, a city of approximately 750,000 located in the foothills of the Canadian Rocky Mountains. There are 24 children in the class, and only 8 are native speakers of English. Of the remaining 16, 8 are beginners and the other 8 are at various levels of proficiency ranging from low intermediate to advanced. These children come from a variety of linguistic and ethnic backgrounds— Sarcee, Chinese, Vietnamese, Korean, Polish, Spanish, and Thai.

The classroom is a warm and inviting place to spend the day. Colorful labels are stuck almost everywhere, a particular help to the non-native speakers just beginning to learn spoken and written English. There are bright displays of the children's art work and a listening center with dozens of audio tapes and corresponding books. In one large corner of the room is the library where dozens of children's books are arranged for easy access and chairs and large floor cushions invite children to linger and read. In a prominent position in the reading area is an oak chair similar to the one that sits behind the teacher's desk (where I've never seen Ms. Kennedy sit). This oak chair has stretched across its back a blue banner with gold letters identifying it as the "Author's Chair." From this chair, children read their finished work to others in the class. For sharing earlier drafts, they work in other parts of the classroom, usually the tables where they write, but for the premiere of the published work, the authors come proudly to the author's chair.

Every morning begins in exactly the same way. For the first 15 minutes or so, Mary reads to the children. She reads a book from the classroom library, one from the school library, or one which she or one of the children has brought from home. The book may be a Big Book, a brightly illustrated book, or even one with few pictures or illustrations. Her main criterion for selection is the children's interest, and so she quite naturally lets them choose the books at least part of the time. Whenever she reads to the class, Mary turns on the tape recorder. She does this so that, at a later time, children may listen to the story again. All the children enjoy listening to the story at the listening center, but perhaps the most noteworthy benefit is to the non-native speakers, many of whom cannot yet read in English. These children are often found at the listening center listening to the tape as they follow along in the book, thus closely replicating the experience of being read to by an adult.

After Mary finishes reading the book, the children talk to her about the story. She actively seeks their reactions and usually refrains from judging their input. The following dialogue is typical:

Mary Kennedy: *Michael, I noticed that you were laughing a lot during the story. What did you find funny?*

Michael: *The way they all got stuffed into the mitten! My mitten is too little!*

Laura: *One time my kitty tried to get in my mitten and she got her head stuck. It was funny the way she tried to get out but couldn't.*

M. K.: *It would be funny, wouldn't it, to see lots of little animals trying to get into one little mitten?*

YanHua: *(Holding up a child's glove.) This?*

M. K.: *That's very like a mitten, YanHua. It's called a glove. (She turns and writes the word on the paper chart beside her.) Glove. Can you say that?*

M: *I've got mittens. I'll show you! (He leaves the group to go to the coat room.)*

M. K.: *Michael's going to get his mitten to show you, Yan Hua. While we're waiting, I was wondering if someone else wanted to share how you felt about the story?*

Gi Ping: *Me! I like 'quirrel!*

M. K.: *What did you like about the squirrel?*

GP: *Look funny. Not like real 'quirrel.*

M. K.: *No, you're right. He doesn't look much like a real one, does he? Oh, here's Michael with his mitten. That's a bright color, isn't it?*

M: *My grandma made it for me! See?*

The talk here is genuine; it has not been contrived by the teacher to make *her* point, and it is of interest to all those who take part. It is also allowed to range, as natural conversation frequently does, from topic to topic as attention shifts focus. Notice that it is functionally rich talk. In contrast with some of the examples earlier, we find here informing talk used genuinely—when Mary asks Michael what he finds funny, for instance, she doesn't already know the answer—as well as talk that helps foster language for meeting social needs. In this discussion with the children, she is also providing them with opportunities for projecting into the experiences of the animals stuffing themselves into the mitten.

Ms. Kennedy organizes her teaching around themes, and she integrates the entire curriculum into those themes. Science, arithmetic, language arts, social studies, art, and music are all focused on a single theme, be it dinosaurs, rivers, Christmas, winter, or outer space. The children never seem to get bored with this approach. On the contrary, they seem to enjoy the opportunity to concentrate on a particular subject and not to have to experience the frustration of becoming deeply involved with a subject only to have the teacher suddenly pry them away because it is time to do something entirely different. One of the reasons for their high interest level is that they are consulted on the choice of themes. Sometimes Ms. Kennedy offers them a choice from several and at other times the children offer their own suggestions. One year when the children wanted to include "transformers" as one of their themes, the teacher-pupil roles were reversed for a time as the children supplied much of the information and ideas for activities needed to develop the theme fully.

Writing has a central place in the classroom lives of these second-grade children. They have each written something about each theme. Some themes, such as Christmas, generate books that may be short novels or collections of stories, poems, and drawings. Others generate shorter pieces—whimsical couplets, limericks, or even riddles. The choice of form is left up to the children, but they write everyday, sometimes for an hour or more. A good illustration of the sophistication of the written language that the children in this class produced after only a few months is the book written by a Vietnamese girl named Doan (pronounced to rhyme with Joanne). Doan had been in Canada for only 18 months when she wrote the three-chapter story reproduced here:

The Little Rabbit Princess Named Lindary

Chapter One

Once in a dark, dark forest there lived a young Princess Rabbit. She was only two months old when her grandpa and grandma died. Her mother, the Queen had eighteen kindly witches and two wicked witches. One day it was Princess Rabbit's birthday. Her friends, Tung the bobcat, Tyson the tiger, Thuy the owl, Que the cat, Quy the dog and Tammy the pig, all went to Lindary's hole house. They played hide and seek, tag and frozen tag. They ate icecream, carrots, potatoes, tomatoes, bugs and they drank orange juice and also they drank apple juice. They were very polite at the party.

"These friends are very kindly and wild animals," said Lindary's dad the king. Soon her birthday was over. Her friends went home.

Chapter Two

It was 19 years later and her mother the queen and her dad the king died at last. Her mother and father died because they were too old. She lived alone in the hole.

It was Christmas. One frozen winter day she went up the hole to get a small pine tree to fill in the hole house. But she couldn't carry the tree because it was too heavy for her.

So she called to some of her friends Tung bobcat, Tyson the tiger, Thuy the Owl, Que the cat, Quy the dog and Tammy the pig. They tried to carry it. At last they got it in the hole. They celebrated Christmas the other day.

Chapter Three

Soon Lindary was 20 years old. Just then she met a Prince rabbit and Lindary talked to the prince but while she was talking to the prince, the prince replied, "I want to marry you." "So do I" answered the rabbit princess. The next day they got married and they lived happily every after.

The End

Teacher #2, Colleen Maguire, Halifax, Nova Scotia.   Ms. Maguire teaches third and fourth grades in a neighborhood elementary school located within view and easy walking distance of the Bedford Basin. Split grades are not common in this district any longer, but a few remain and Ms. Maguire says that she enjoys teaching the third/fourth split. She teaches all subjects in the curriculum although an art teacher comes once each week to supplement the activities planned by Ms. Maguire. She teaches music herself because music is important in her life. She has made it an important part of the children's daily lives as well.

Each morning after the children arrive and put away their coats, mittens, and boots, they gather around a low table in the back of the room where Ms. Maguire has put out cartons of apple juice, orange juice, and milk as well as miniature whole-grain muffins that a local baker makes each day for the school. Most of the children will have had breakfast at home, but for those who haven't, the nutritious food is welcome. For all, it is an opportunity to begin the morning in a friendly and relaxed way. After 15 minutes, the two children who have been designated as helpers for the week put the milk and juice in the refrigerator and put the muffins away to be eaten later, while the other children select their instruments for the morning rhythm band concert.

Ms. Maguire goes to the piano to begin what has quickly become a ritual for the children. The words and music for the day's song are displayed on an overhead projector and, if the song is new to them, the children listen while Ms. Maguire plays and sings the song once, their fingers or feet tapping along with the rhythm of the piano. She then plays through the song again, explaining as she goes what each instrument is supposed to do. She is not highly directive in her explanation and often invites the children to participate when and how they see fit. Some children prefer singing to instrumentation and sing along with her.

Ms. Maguire does not introduce a new song every day; sometimes the class will work on one song for a week or more, rehearsing it, changing it, enjoying it until it is ready for performance or until they are ready to move on to another song. Performance may be for other classes in the school, for the principal or visitors, or a recording to take home for their families to hear. Though the day begins musically, it is not spent entirely in song. After the children have put away their instruments, they go to look in their mailboxes and spend the next 20 minutes or so in dealing with the morning mail. The mail is the medium through which Ms. Maguire responds to the children's writing. The writing may be in the dialogue journals the children keep with her or pieces at various stages of development which they wish to share with her. Sometimes they simply write her, or each other, letters. One morning, a third-grade girl named Beth was responding to a letter from a fourth-grade boy named Lyle. The letters are reproduced, with the permission of Beth, Jody, and Lyle, in Figure 10.1.

Once they have attended to the morning mail, the children gather around Ms. Maguire to plan the rest of the day's work. They each make a list of things they want to accomplish. Ms. Maguire joins in this activity, and everyone understands that they do not have to complete every task on the list. Everyone tries, however, and most do

Figure 10.1 Beth
and Lyle's Notes

November 21, 1990

Dear Beth,
         I want to tell
you a secret but Jody told
me not too. Will you promise
not to tell if I tell you?

         Your Friend,
              Lyle

P.S. It is about Jody.

Thursday, Nov 22, 1990
Dear Lyle,
I don't want to know any
secret about Jody because
I think you probly made
it all up. Jody is my friend
and she tells me all her
secrets so you don't know
anything that I don't
know anyways. Did you
know we got a new puppy?
Yours truely,
Elizabeth A. Barnes

succeed in finishing the work they've established for themselves. Beth made the following list for November 21, 1990:

Beth's Things "TO DO"
1. Finish picture of UFO.
2. Write poem to go with picture.
3. Listen to story about space monsters. (Ms. Mcguire tape records the stories she reads to the children so that they may listen to them later.)
4. Recess!
5. Work on math log.

Other more structured activities occur in the children's day. On this day, for example, the children were working on problems related to the distances between the earth and the planet from which the UFO in a story they had read had come. Ms. Maguire worked through one problem with the class, and then they referred back to their math logs for assistance in completing the rest. For most children, the math log was a reflective account of the process of mathematics as they experienced it in the classroom. It was a combination of notes about how to reach solutions and editorial comment about the difficulty or the mental processes they used to find them.

Ms. Maguire's class might not seem like a typical whole language class, whatever that might be. Descriptions of whole language classrooms rarely include lengthy accounts of music activities. But Ms. Maguire's class is a whole language classroom in an important sense: Her concern is with the *use* of language and not with the *practice* of language. In songs and in the talk that goes on about songs and performance, children are not just rehearsing for communication; they are communicating. In making their "To Do" lists, they are using language for a real purpose, but even more importantly, they are taking charge of their own learning. In keeping their math logs, they are using language for learning, for monitoring their own experience, and for recalling past solutions to problems.

Whole Language in (Mis)practice

The debate among language teachers is not only about whether or not to adopt whole language. Among those who profess to believe in whole language, there is a great deal of variability in what they believe, in how they actually teach, and in the class activities in which their pupils engage. In her foreword to *Portraits of Whole Language Classrooms* (Mills & Clyde, 1990), Virginia Woodward acknowledges the misconceptions surrounding whole language pedagogy. She quotes the observations of a number of educators to illustrate that the approach is widely interpreted. Four of the remarks made by different educators reveal the spectrum of conceptions about whole language and suggest the breadth of practice they mandate. The four are:

1. I do whole language; I use Big Books.
2. It seems like whole language is just glorified language experience.
3. We do whole language activities of Fridays.
4. Whole language is what good teachers do naturally. (Mills & Clyde, 1990, p. ix)

Closer examination of these observations, selected but not unrepresentative of those held by a great many educators, say much about the assortment of practices that take place in the name of whole language.

1. *I do whole language; I use Big Books.*   Using Big Books is certainly consistent with whole language. They allow what Judith Newman refers to as "shared reading..., an important component of a whole language curriculum." She continues:

> The enlarged books allow the teacher to create an intimate atmosphere with a number of children at once. The large book sets a stage for involvement with both the story and the print since the children are all able to see what's on the page as they listen to and watch the teacher read along. It is through such shared reading that children begin to understand how print and meaning are related. (1985b, pp. 62–63)

But does using Big Books mean that a teacher is using a whole language curriculum? Or, is it necessary to use Big Books in a whole language curriculum? The answer to both is no. It would be entirely possible to use Big Books within a skills-based curriculum that fragmented language into modes (listening, speaking, reading, and writing) and modes into discrete skill areas (writing into printing, handwriting, spelling, sentence construction, paragraph construction, etc.). On the other hand, it is quite possible to take a whole language approach even with young pupils and not use Big Books. Teachers without the budgets to buy a great many Big Books have managed very well using a number of alternatives. Moreover, whole language is implemented in the higher elementary grades where Big Books would not be appropriate. The important thing is the shared experience of reading, which can be accomplished in a number of ways.

2. *It seems like whole language is just glorified language experience.*   Again we have a practice that is consonant with a whole language curriculum but does not define it. Language experience may be incorporated into a whole language curriculum because:

> Language, whether oral or written, is learned through active "play" with language, through experimenting with different ways to express ideas, and exploring relationships between the children's language and their knowledge. Language experience stories evolve from the children's interests and activities.... Language experience stories are an excellent tool for helping children makes sense of written language because they emphasize the importance of the connection between a reader's experiences and written language. (Newman, 1985b, p. 62)

Although it might be argued that language experience is one of the cornerstones of whole language, there is a great deal more to it than language experience. Moreover, it is possible to use language experience activities in ways that are fundamentally incompatible with whole language. For example, I once visited a classroom in which the teacher used language experience, in her words, "to teach reading," and allotted it a set period of time. But once reading instruction time was over, the children turned to their "language" activities, an unrelated lesson on antonyms. This teacher did not use Big Books, sustained silent reading, or any of the other practices commonly associated with a whole language curriculum.

3. *We do whole language activities on Fridays.*   We can only wonder what happens the rest of the week. Clearly, this teacher has no understanding of what whole language is and why it works. Perhaps it is better for a teacher to practice whole language one day a week than not at all, but it is a little like following a 1,000 calorie diet on Monday and eating indiscriminately the rest of the week. Children may enjoy the Friday activities more, and they probably won't do any harm. Neither will they contribute much to their language learning.

4. *Whole language is what good teachers do naturally.*   In the second edition of this book, I wrote "this is my favorite, partly because I wish it were true." Now, I am convinced that it is true, or at least it is if we change "good" to "effective." Although I'm not at all sure that what I mean is what the person who made the comment meant, I do believe that effective teachers know that language teaching and language learning have much in common and plan their instruction accordingly. If a teacher learns about how children learn and function in language in other settings and works out ways to incorporate that prior learning into the learning of literacy, then that teacher is practicing whole language whatever label she might put on it. By the same token, there are effective teachers who use methods that might be largely inconsistent with typical whole language practices; these other methods work because the teachers are so committed and dedicated to the method and to the children they teach. What was intended by the statement "whole language is what good teachers do naturally," however, was very likely the *laissez-faire* attitude I mentioned earlier, one that is dangerous because it gives the teacher license to do nothing.

These four observations have served to crystallize the divergence there is in how educators think about whole language. Collectively, the four remarks indicate misunderstanding about what whole language is. Even among teachers who *do* understand it, there are vast differences in the classrooms they inhabit. The description of the diversity is beyond the scope of this book, although we saw in the last chapter brief sketches of whole language in practice and will get glimpses into the approach again in Chapter 11.

Whole language is not the only teaching practice on which educators fail to reach agreement; it is simply the current one and the one that has received the greatest amount of attention in recent years. It is discussed here because it is also the approach to language teaching that is most consistent with our best understanding of how language acquisition occurs. Since a teaching approach should be informed by both a theory of language and a theory of language learning (Richards & Rodgers, 1986), then whole language merits special consideration in any book on language acquisition that encompasses the school years.

The Debate: Whole Language or Phonics

An issue that was once of concern only to elementary school teachers and a few academics is now being hotly debated in the public press. Proponents of **phonics** methods point to test scores and to the results of research studies showing that children who are taught specifically about the alphabetic code are better at decoding than children who are not. They point to research showing that fluent readers with good comprehension skills are almost always good decoders. In the public debate, this is a compelling argument. Good readers can decode; hence we should teach children to decode. The fallacy of this argument is easy to uncover. No model of the fluent reader is particularly useful as a description of how she got to be a fluent reader. A thorough catalogue of a competent reader's skills does not map the path between illiteracy and literacy. A good reader, for example, is good at prediction—the next word, the next sentence, the rest of the story. And yet, no one would seriously suggest that prediction be taught as an initial strategy for beginning readers—certainly not the *only* strategy. Even proponents of phonics-based instruction concede this point. Answering their critics' observation that children learn print relationships by reading real, continuous text, Foorman and her colleagues (1997) concur, observing that "there is a period during beginning reading instruction when all children benefit from practicing letter-sound connections in decodable text." This brings us to the second problem with the argument, that of exclusivity.

Both the scholarly literature and, particularly, the popular media polarize the issue: phonics *or* whole language. In fact, responsible educators will admit that neither approach is right for every child in every situation if it is the only one used. Inherent in the definition of whole language, in fact, is the recognition that individual children differ in ability, interest, and learning style. Teaching sound-symbol correspondence is entirely compatible with whole language so long as it is balanced by other more natural language activities. Barbara Foorman and her colleagues at the Universiy of Houston provide very strong evidence that children who receive "direct instrucion in the alphabetic code" are significantly better at reading comprehension than are children who are taught using a mainly literature-based approach (1997). The NICHD (National Institute of Child Health and Development) is even clearer. Synthesizing the research conducted at 41 sites in the United States, the NICHD has concluded that it is critical that children be taught "the alphabetic principle" in order to prevent or remediate reading failure. They do not, however, advocate "code-*only* instruction, a focus on skill worksheets, skills taught in a disjointed manner, or skills taught only in isolation" (Mathes & Torgesen, 2000, p. 5). Conversely, NICHD researchers do not support depriving beginning readers of authentic literature. "What they, as a group, do advocate for is balance" (p. 6). We can only hope that the argument has run its course and that teachers can get on with figuring out the best way to provide instruction that ensures that every child will learn to read to his or her full capacity.

Even though the debate should be over, there is no indication that it is. Whole language continues to be the subject of a great deal of public commentary. Partly as a result of a general movement toward accountability of the public schools to the society that supports them and partly as a result of a broad societal concern with literacy, whole language has come under attack as an educationally soft approach to teaching. Among the more vociferous critics are some parents and business leaders who argue that the schools are not doing an adequate job in what *should be* their fundamental task, the teaching of reading and writing. They blame whole language teaching and argue for, indeed *demand*, a return to phonics.

Those who carry the standards banner highest, who proclaim accountability loudest, tend to blame whole language and other child-centered approaches for what they consider to be a crisis in education. They equate standards with basics and basics with reading, writing, and arithmetic taught by traditional methods such as phonics. What many fail to realize is that would-be reformers have a tendency to recall a standard of achievement from the past that, in fact, never existed. In other words, close analysis of the test scores reveals that as retention rates improve, children who once would have dropped out before writing the tests are now writing the tests. They bring down the overall average, that's true, but they are accomplishing far more than their counterparts several decades ago. Let's take an actual example. A school district in the province of Newfoundland and Labrador has typically had some of the lowest reading scores in Canada as measured by the Canadian Test of Basic Skills. During the last 20 years, the scores have shown only a modest improvement, yet, during the same period, the retention rate has improved dramatically. Where the drop-out rate was once 85% (before 12th grade), it is now only 15%. More children are learning more, but the gross measure of the Basic Skills test does not show the gains. We must also remember that the demands placed on literacy are greater than ever before while the time to teach reading and writing has shrunk. As the demand for other relevant subjects has increased, teachers' time has been taken away from literacy instruction. One teacher notes that the growing complexity of modern life has led school officials to design:

> a curriculum that tries to teach *everything*, that tries to be not just instructional, but empathetic, in the fuzziest, airy-fairiec sense of the word. Thus, you get Grade 1 kids not only being asked to learn how to read, but to "describe their roles and rights" (Politics and Law) and to "demonstrate a willingness to identify their personal attributes, skills, and success" (Personal Planning). You don't go to school any more to learn how to spell *cat*; you go to get self actualized. (McMartin, 2001)

Moreover, as teachers' time has been increasingly devoted to roles once held by parents, social workers, and others in the child's community, they have had less time to spend in teaching basic literacy. Furthermore, the society has changed in ways that impact schooling fundamentally. Children spend more time watching television than they did in the past, for example, as well as playing computer games. This is not to blame the child, but only to say that gross measures do not give a very clear indication of the true state of literacy or the best method of achieving it. Nevertheless, a substantive debate is being waged over whole language, and it is not likely to be resolved in the foreseeable future despite the very sensible position put forward by NICHD researchers on the need for a method that takes the best from both approaches.

SIX CHARACTERISTICS OF LEARNING: A COMPARISON

This chapter began with a statement from Gordon Wells that served to crystallize the six characteristics of children's preschool learning from Chapter 8. In the following pages, we see that there are still many schools which are a long way from reproducing these characteristics. Let us now return individually to those six characteristics to see how each fares under the harsh scrutiny of the classroom lights.

1. *Children's learning progresses according to their degree of readiness.* I am certain that there are schools that can make this claim, but I am equally certain that many more cannot. Some engage in educational practices that purport to recognize and provide for individual children's needs. But even some of these are bastardized. A good example is the notion of reading readiness. This term *should* imply that children learn to read when they are ready to learn. But in practice, it has come to mean that the school has to *do* something to children to get them ready. As John Holt (1989) pointed out in *Learning All the Time,* one of the more foolish notions advocated by educators was "that the way to get children 'ready to read' is to show them a lot of books full of nothing but pictures and ask them a lot of silly questions about them.... What children need to get ready for reading is exposure to a lot of print. Not pictures, but print" (p. 10).

The simple fact of the matter is that well-intentioned educators find it difficult if not impossible to tailor educational practices in accordance with individual children's readiness to learn. One of the reasons for this difficulty is that most schools are still organized around a common curriculum for each grade, a narrow range of instructional modes, and a limited variety of materials. It is not difficult to understand why schools organize themselves in this way; they are institutions charged with the responsibility of educating large numbers of children within a finite time and budget. That they would attempt to regularize the task in some way is understandable. But the regularization of schools means necessarily that learning cannot proceed according to the child's degree of readiness but must proceed according to some predetermined syllabus.

This is not the case in whole language classrooms. The goals of whole language are entirely consistent with the fact that children proceed according to their degree of readiness. Whole language is, after all, child-centered, and it would be impossible to have a child-centered curriculum that set rigid goals and dictated means for achieving them. The goals of whole language tend instead to be more flexible—to help each child continue to grow in language in the way and the time that best suits him or her. Whole language practitioners recognize that there are many ways for children to achieve those goals and that they will do so according to their own developmental schedule. Comparing whole language practice with this particular characteristic of children's learning results in a close fit, one that can be seen even on a daily basis. For example, it was Beth's decision to put "write a poem" on her "To Do" list, and because it was her idea and she was ready to carry it out, the experience was likely more satisfying for her than it would have been had the assignment been handed down by her teacher.

2. *Young children are, for the most part, in charge of their own learning.*   If schools are unable to respond to children according to their individual level of readiness to learn, it is to be expected that they will be unable to provide environments that permit children to take charge of their own learning. Allowing children to decide what they want to learn and how they want to learn it requires a great deal of faith in children's desire to know and it requires the relinquishing of control, or as John Holt would have said, the *illusion* of control.

First, it is easy to understand why educators would doubt children's ability to take charge of their own learning. Schools take away children's independence as learners and then complain about the results. Holt recognized this phenomenon in a number of his writings. Describing a child's learning when left to his own devices, he wrote of a boy learning to write who was not content to repeat his successes but kept moving on to harder tasks, setting himself on increasingly difficult tasks. Generalizing to other children, Holt (1989) wrote:

> This is what all children do as they grow up—until they get to school. What all too often happens there is that children, seeing school challenges as threats, which they often are— if you fail to accomplish them, you stand a good risk of being shamed …—fall more and more out of the habit of challenging themselves, even outside of school. (p. 17)

Second, to permit children to set, meet, and evaluate their own challenges, schools—and teachers in particular—must be willing to relinquish absolute control of learning. That kind of control is an illusion anyway since it is quite impossible to determine what another human being will or will not learn. We *do* have control of curricula, materials, and the mode of teaching, but we are deluding ourselves very seriously to believe that we can truly control what children learn. So why not give up the illusion and begin to let children, who are not inexperienced at the business of learning and who are the true experts on how they themselves learn, guide their own learning?

This is, of course, exactly what whole language classrooms have done. We saw in the snapshots of Ms. Kennedy's and Ms. Maguire's classes children taking charge of their own learning—writing their "To Do" lists, reading and writing letters from their mailboxes, keeping in their math logs whatever they thought would help them to remember, deciding what kind of response they want to make to a story they have heard in class, or helping to choose the theme they will study next. An incident that I observed in Ms. Kennedy's class one day illustrates that even practices that might not ordinarily be thought of as consistent with whole language principles may, in the environment of whole language, reveal children to be in charge of their own learning.

One little girl named Jill was highly resistant to invented spelling. She had observed the consistency of the spelling in books and, quite of her own accord, wanted her writing to be right. Frustrated with her attempts to spell *through*—she had tried *thru, thoug, tough,* and *thrugh*—she finally asked Ms. Kennedy: "Wouldn't it be easier if you just *taught* me how to spell?"

Jill's point is a good one. There is a danger that in our zeal to adopt whole language we overlook the need of some children to be taught in more traditional ways. That is a danger inherent in any new educational practice—that established methods will be abandoned in favor of newer ones even though, for at least some children, there may be merit in the older methods.

3. *Play plays an important role in children's learning.*   Part of the hidden culture of schooling is the idea that school is serious business. Children such as Emily (p. 255) know this to be the case before they get to school. It is one of the things that makes school different from kindergarten. They learn when they get there that recess is not just an opportunity to get a breath of fresh air; it is *the* time for play and represents a distinct break from the hard business of schoolwork. That learning and play might happily coexist is an alien notion to many educators, particularly those who put up "No talking" signs.

It is hard to imagine how classrooms in which "No talking" is an important rule of behavior could possibly value play as a medium for learning. How can children play without talking? It is equally hard to imagine how teachers who need to control and manipulate talk to their own purposes could place any educational value on the talk that children do for *their* purposes. In contrast, the tenet of whole language, which emphasizes immersing children in real communication situations, is entirely consistent with this characteristic of children's learning. What could be more natural to a child than play?

4.   *The role of parents in early learning is facilitator not instructor.*   When we transport this characteristic from the home into the school situation, the obvious parallel is for the teacher to act as facilitator rather than director of learning. Yet, in example after example earlier in this chapter, we saw that this was not the case. Many teachers attempt to control learning from the curriculum planning stage right through to manipulating children's talk to push them toward a particular teaching objective. We saw the teacher-as-director in Molly's dialogue with her teacher and we saw it again in Jon McGill's history account of the information-dispensing talk in his history class.

The model of teacher as instructor is deeply ingrained in our culture. Our entire pedagogical history is of the teacher as the giver of information, the holder and grantor of wisdom. To abandon this view of the teacher's role means bucking 2,000 years of tradition. Even teachers who want to change may find it very hard to give up the notion of teaching as the dispensing of information. After all, they went to university for 4, 5, or 6 years to learn all that information; surely it's their duty to teach it to someone else. It takes a great act of faith, or as Ms. Kennedy put it "many years of experience. I don't know why it took me so long to give up the old ways since my better judgment told me years ago that they weren't working anyway." Mary's conversion began before the label "whole language teacher" existed and was completed when she went back to university for graduate study and learned that her instincts were consonant with a change that was taking place in language education.

Relinquishing control of and thus some of the responsibility for learning to the child is at the heart of whole language thinking. Teachers who create the kinds of environments conducive to learning and to wanting to learn are playing a role that is every bit as important and a great deal more effective than teacher-as-instructional-director.

5. *Interaction is essential to children's early learning.*   Before they come to school, children learn their language and most other things they know through their interactions with people and the environment. In school, they continue to learn through interactions, but the quality of those interactions may not compare with those of the home. We saw in many of the earlier anecdotes in this chapter that children's interactions with teachers are often contrived by teachers toward a particular goal established by teachers. The fact that some teachers believe that all their talk must be directed toward a pedagogical end is evidence that their interaction is suspect. We saw and heard in the register adopted by some teachers and in the asking of questions that both teacher and child know not to be real questions, a falseness that disclosed the truth of their intent. Teachers were trying to teach language. These behaviors do not constitute true interaction.

In contrast, we saw in the two whole language classrooms a quality of interaction that was similar to that which occurs in children's homes. We saw and heard teachers not attempting to teach language but talking with children honestly, in real voices, and toward purposes that had legitimacy for both teachers and children. When Ms. Maguire wrote letters to the children in her classes and responded to their letters to her, when the children in Ms. Kennedy's class told her what they liked and didn't like about the stories they heard and when Ms. Kennedy declined to pass judgment on those opinions, we were witness to productive interaction. Because it is partly defined by its emphasis on real communication for real purposes, the whole language approach should always result in quality interaction between teachers and children. And where there is quality interaction, there is more likely to be learning.

6. *Learning is embedded in the process of socialization.*   Doubtless, there are many reasons and many conditions under which humans learn. During our earliest years and, if we are fortunate, throughout our lifetimes, we learn for the sheer pleasure of it, for the delight in knowing something previously unknown. But our learning is also driven by more pragmatic drives—the *need* to have information, knowledge, or skills for a particular purpose. It is also motivated by less obvious drives—to achieve group membership, for example. As we saw in Chapter 8, as children learn language in the home, they are being initiated into the rituals and expectations of family membership. As they venture forth into the world, they become members not only of the family but of the larger community, and a significant part of that community is the school. It is through schooling, in fact, that children in western society learn much of what they need to know to become lifelong participants in society.

It would be expected that language learning, and indeed all learning, during the school years would provide the means for socializing children to the roles of community member and citizen. To some degree, it does. The knowledge they acquire in schools takes many forms. Part of it is factual—the history of the nation in which they live, its system of government, its laws. These facts provide the basis for citizenship just as the facts of mathematics provide the basis for their coping with the worlds of finance and science. What they acquire in school also includes linguistic knowledge that cannot be quantified as a list of facts. I suggested earlier in this chapter that the lessons they learn about language may not be the ones we want them to learn. When their talk is not valued, children may well internalize a rule to the effect that some people's talk, namely those in positions of authority, is more important than other people's talk, namely those not in power. When they witness the use of language to manipulate their own behavior, they learn the power of language to corrupt. When they experience the homogenized talk of the school, children may fail to develop appreciation of the linguistic diversity that does not divide us but helps to identify us as individuals and as distinct groups within the larger English-speaking society. When their talk is channeled and controlled as it so frequently is in school, they risk losing the spontaneity and whimsy that is the stuff of verbal creativity. These are the lessons taught, perhaps unwittingly, but too often and by too many schools. But not by all. In some schools, as we saw earlier, language is not scheduled into the school day as a subject to be dissected, analyzed, or memorized. Rather, it is part of the process of children's learning and part of the process of their joining the community of educated people. These rather lofty-sounding goals can be accomplished. To do so requires teachers and children who communicate with one another and share responsibility for growth in language and in learning.

For Further Study

1. Claire Staab found that women teachers provided "significantly more opportunities for students to speak formally than did male teachers." Speculate on the effect this likely has on both male and female children.

2. Gordon Wells and Shirley Brice Heath have demonstrated that the progress of non-mainstream children may be hampered "by the difference in the ways in which language is used and questions are posed in homes and schools" (Commins, 1989, p. 29). What can the primary school teacher do to ensure the success of children from these homes?

3. When whole language is the subject of public debate, critics frequently attack invented spelling, in particular. Why do you think this is true? What defense can you mount for invented spelling?

4. Find a recently published critique of or attack on phonics instruction and write a rebuttal.

5. Think about the impact on literacy and list at least three reasons for *and* against having computers available in the primary classroom.

6. See *http://www.nichd.nih.gov/reading.htm* for a complete account of NICHD research on the teaching of reading.

For Further Reading

Adams, M. J. (1994). *Beginning to read.* Cambridge, MA: MIT Press.
Chall, J. S. (2000). *The academic achievement challenge.* New York: Guilford Press.
Fennimore, B. (2000). *Talk matters: Refocusing the language of public schooling.* New York: Teachers College Press.

CHAPTER ELEVEN

Intercultural Communication

Communication breaks down. It happens every day in every medium in which we communicate. It breaks down any time there is a difference between the message that was intended and the message that was received. Sometimes, the differences are trivial enough that the miscommunication goes unnoticed or does no real harm. Other times, the results can be devastating or just comical. One television commercial running for a cellular telephone company shows the impact of imperfect transmission. A football coach has instructed his manager on a cell phone (not the one being advertised), to "Make sure there's a back up for O'Neil." The coach is more than a little distressed when he sees, as we do when the camera zooms out, a football field, players, and in full evening dress, The Captain and Tennile.

A friend of mine recounts the following miscommunication with her partner. They are in a car having just left home for a shopping expedition:

Husband: *Got any bread?*
Wife: *Some.*
H: *Enough?*
W: *Well I was planning to get more.*
H: *How much have you got with you?*
W: *With me? Why would I have it with me?*
H: *Duh? Because we're, like, going shopping…?*
W: *Yes, and I just said I was going to buy more.*

At this point, it was clear to both parties that he was using an argot that she did not use. Had this same conversation taken place in 1970, when *bread* was a colloquial term for *money* or *cash*, the breakdown wouldn't have occurred. When my friend relayed the story to me, she rolled her eyes as she admitted that he still uses *pad* to refer to one's residence. My friend's husband usually manages to communicate fairly effectively across the decades but in some instances, as in this one, the intent of his communication is not immediately clear. There are many different kinds of miscommunication, but the basic reason is always the same: The message is sent by a human with one set of understandings, contexts, and assumptions and received by a human with quite another set.

Even when people share the same background, speak the same language, and have the same intention during the communication, the possibility of miscommunication abounds. Sometimes, it is a problem of ambiguity inherent in the language. Newspaper headlines provide excellent examples of how **communication** can go awry. Consider the following actual headlines:

1. Two sisters reunited after 18 years in checkout line
2. Farmer Bill dies in House
3. Drunk gets nine months in violin case
4. Iraqi head seeks arms

The source of the ambiguity and potential miscommunication in these headlines resides in the abbreviated form of the language, in word order (in number 1), and the lack of context. In the case of the second and fourth examples, the ambiguity resides in the dual meaning of certain words—*bill, house, head,* and *arms.* It is even arguable that the headlines are deliberately misleading to entice the reader to read the entire article, and indeed, the miscommunication is easily resolved by doing so.

Other miscommunication occurs when the participants in a dialogue have different assumptions, often about the purpose of the communication. An old joke illustrates:

> A college senior took his new girlfriend to a football game. They found seats in the crowded stadium and were watching the action. A substitute was put into the game and as he was running onto the field to take his position, the boy said to his girlfriend, "Take a good look at that fellow. I expect him to be our best man next year." His girlfriend snuggled closer to him and said, "That's the strangest way I ever heard of for a fellow to propose to a girl. Regardless of how you said it, I accept."

All these examples of a failure to communicate effectively occurred even though the participants share a common culture. When speakers come from different cultural backgrounds, the chances for miscommunication are even greater. Sometimes, the effects can be felt around the globe. Glaser summarizes Cohen (1991, p. 126) in the following example:

> Cultural differences can sometimes mean that signals are missed, which can cause delays and missed opportunities. For example, many such signals were missed by American diplomats in the early days of U.S.–China reconciliation. Cohen points out that "U.S. observers entirely missed the most significant Chinese signal of reconciliation of all in the

1970–71 period." In October 1970 Chairman Mao invited an American author and journalist to stand next to him atop the Gate of Heavenly Peace. While this gesture seems obscure to American diplomats, and hence they did not respond to it, the symbolism was clear to the Chinese, who expected a significant response. (Glaser, 1998)

World politics might look very different today had those signals not been missed. Most of us, however, will never have to be directly concerned with the effects of cultural miscommunication on that scale. But as educators, we have what may be as great a responsibility because communication breakdowns in the school setting lead to failure.

We saw in the last example that communication involves more than language, and in some cultures, language is no more important than non-linguistic ways of communicating. In this chapter, we will examine certain aspects of culture and communication in an attempt to foster some understanding about cultural differences and to raise sensitivity to the impact of these differences in multicultural classrooms.

SEEING THE WORLD THROUGH
DIFFERENT LENSES

Three people from different parts of the world are gathered at a shopping mall in an affluent suburb of Los Angeles. They are standing together in the parking lot, looking past the parking lot toward the well-lit mall. Each person has normal vision and they are standing close enough to one another that what they see is exactly the same. But is it? One of the visitors sees the cars and shakes his head at the quantity of the earth's resources that are used in creating and maintaining these expensive machines. Another looks at the people getting into and out of the cars and wonders why there are rarely more than two people in any of them. Where are the families? The third doesn't appear to notice the cars and looks straight ahead, wondering whether the sale has started at the Gucci boutique. What they perceive is conditioned by their experience and by their values, which are a result of the belief systems held in their respective cultures. Samovar, Porter, and Stefani use a more familiar example—the moon. They point out that even though the physical sphere that we know as the moon looks pretty much the same from wherever it is viewed, Native Americans see a rabbit, many Europeans see a man, and Samoans see a woman weaving (1998, p. 56). Similarly, "whether we feel delighted or ill at the thought of eating the meat of a cow, fish, dog, or snake depends on what our culture has taught us about food" (p. 57). We all have essentially the same sensory and cognitive apparatus, and yet we perceive things very differently.

We cannot, in the course of this chapter, possibly describe every culture's view on every aspect of the world. For one thing, there are too many cultures and the world is too complex a place, but even more importantly, it would not be terribly useful to do so because any particular value held by a particular culture may not be held by every member of that culture. In other words, a great deal of individual variation occurs within cultures. Nevertheless, it is useful to look at culture in some broad strokes, particularly those aspects that have to do with the ability to communicate in multicultural classrooms. We begin with some assumptions about the dominant American culture and then go on to look at each one of those and the difficulty it might pose for one or more other cultural groups.

As an American-born Canadian, I might jeopardize my Canadian citizenship for saying so, but American culture dominates English North America, and although there are some differences between Americans and Canadians, Canadians will at least recognize the strong influence exerted by the U.S. cultural patterns. Indeed, all of these patterns have currency in Western societies, but they are most strongly represented, in my observation, by the United States. I have chosen five dominant patterns or values to explore: individualism, equality, competition, materialism, and science and technology.

Probably the most significant of these is *individualism*—some would even say "the cult of the individual," but it is hardly a cult, so deeply ingrained is the Lockeian notion that the individual is the basic unit of nature. From stories of the self-made man to homilies such as "If you want a job done right, do it yourself," the belief in the individual to shape his or her own destiny and in his or her right to do so is probably stronger in the United States than anywhere else. I would suggest that this is the underlying pattern that has kept the United States from creating a public health system such as those that exist in Canada and in Great Britain. It also underlies the gun laws, or lack thereof, and explains why so much airtime was devoted, following September 11, to people talking about tolerating the loss of their rights necessitated by greater airline security. I recall thinking that I could simply not imagine this discussion ever taking place in Canada, England, Israel, or any of the other countries in which I have spent time. Even though individualism is valued in those countries, there is a somewhat more balanced view that the safety of the society takes precedence over the rights of the individual, whether the subject be airline safety or gun ownership.

Individualism is also at the heart of the notion of *equality*. Although hierarchical structures do exist within the society, there is also the underlying belief that everyone has an equal chance of attaining a higher status. The belief that anyone can grow up to be President, the belief that one has only to work hard enough to accomplish any dream—these are part and parcel of the equality of opportunity belief that underlies the American meritocracy. Equality as a value is also seen in social relationships. In families, for example, members tend to be treated equally, children and adults have more nearly equal status than they do in many other societies. Formality is not important between parents and children.

Closely related to individualism is the value placed on *competition*. From the cradle, we are evaluated in terms of others. As I write these words, we are being inundated with lists—the top-10 models, the 10 best-looking people in the world, the top-10 news events of the year, the 50-best movies, the 5 best-selling cars in America, and on and on and on. To be the best, not in terms of some absolute ideal, but in relation to those around us is a value that is largely accepted without question in many aspects of our lives. It is one, however, along with individualism, that often causes problems for Americans as they interact with people of other cultures at home or abroad.

Another cultural pattern often identified with Americans is *materialism*. It is not necessarily that material objects are the most important thing in the lives of Americans; rather, it is their assumption that people have the right to be physically comfortable and that to some degree a person's value is judged by the value of his or her goods. Materialism as a value shows itself in the assumption that many Americans have that the rest of the world is jealous of their standard of living. The truth is that some are; many are not.

Related to both individualism and materialism is the esteem in which *science and technology* are held. The relationship is not so much in the material comforts that these can provide but in the belief in tangible reality that underlies both materialism and the near-worship of science and technology. "Very broadly, this emphasis on science reflects the values of the rationalistic-individualistic tradition that is so deeply embedded in Western civilization" (Samovar et al., 1998, p. 64). Individualization, equality, materialism, and faith in science are cultural patterns of the United States and much of Western society.

In identifying a few of the cultural values that Americans hold, my intent is not to judge them but to point out that each of them is an alien value or pattern in some cultures. Not all cultures view the individual's rights as being as important as those of the collective; not all cultures share our assumptions about equality, accepting that there may be rights or privileges accorded some members of the society on the basis of their hierarchical place in that society; not all cultures seek answers in science or view scientific progress as a positive value; and certainly not every society shares our acceptance and, indeed, expectation of materialism. Every value that dominant American culture has is alien to someone. Let's consider each value in turn.

PERSPECTIVES FROM OTHER CULTURES

Individualism is one of the values that Hofstede has identified as having a significant impact on behavior in all cultures. It is not helpful to think about individualism, or indeed any other cultural value, as an absolute. Rather, it is useful to think about a continuum with, in this case, individualism at one end and collectivism at the other. A number of anthropologists and sociologists have constructed taxonomies for examining cultural dimensions. Hofstede is one of the best known. In societies that tend toward the individualism end of the scale, people's personal goals take precedence over their loyalty to groups to which they may belong. They change group membership (employer, church, club, or less formal social group) as it suits their personal needs. Each person is believed to have the right to his or her own property and opinions and responsibility for their own decisions. According to Hofstede, societies that rate the individualism scale include the United States, Canada, Great Britain, Australia, New Zealand, and the Netherlands (Hofstede, 1980, cited in Samovar et al., 1998, p. 67).

At the other end of the scale are societies that put greater emphasis on the views, needs, and goals of the group than the self. In these societies, identity is based on social systems, and individuals are dependent on groups for survival. These groups may be extended families, clans, or tribes. Societies that tend toward collectivism include Pakistan, Venezuela, and Colombia (according to Hofstede), although Triandis has estimated that 70% of the world's population lives in cultures that value collectivism (1972, cited in Samovar et al., 1998). It is not surprising, then, that some cocultures within the United States exhibit the same value. Both African Americans and Mexican Americans exhibit many of the same cultural patterns associated with collectivism.

Competition goes hand in hand with individualism in the United States. For all our lives, we are ranked, graded, classified, and found better or worse at something than those around us. Most of the grading systems used in schools as well as standardized tests have a competitive assumption built into them. There is something of a paradox in this value, given the strong distaste for unequal power, but the explanation may lie in the assumption that everyone has an equal chance to the best. Competitiveness does not co-exist with individualism everywhere. The Japanese, for example, rate in the mid to high range on the collectivism scale of cultural values but, according to Hofstede, lean more toward the "masculine" traits of ambition, achievement, and the acquisition of money than do the Americans, British, or Germans.

Often the competitive spirit is directed toward materialism. Indeed, the values of individualism, competition, materialism, and even equality are so tightly woven into the fabric of American society that it is difficult to talk about any one of them in isolation from the others. It is very difficult for materialistic societies to see themselves in the same way as those who put less value on possessions. It is not the case, as many people assume, that everyone would want to live as Americans do. It is true that there are many societies on the planet with similar values, but there are also large numbers of people for whom the accumulation of personal wealth is as alien a concept as moonwalking.

When we talk about equality, we are talking about a society's tolerance for power being distributed unequally. At the equality end of the spectrum, there is relatively little tolerance for the unequal distribution of power. At the opposite end of the spectrum is acceptance of uneven distribution of power and, thus, a more rigid hierarchical structure. In addition to the United States, societies that tend toward the equality end include Canada, Israel, the Netherlands, New Zealand, Norway, and Denmark, among others. Toward the other end of the spectrum, with more rigid hierarchies dominating social structures, are the Phillipines, Brazil, India, Venezuela, Mexico, and Yugoslavia.

It is not surprising that societies that value individualism also value science and technology; both spring from the rationalistic-individualistic tradition that has been so much a part of Western philosophy from John Locke to Rene Descartes to Bertrand Russell and even Albert Einstein. Western societies, to a large degree, believe in science and its ability to solve all of human problems, whether that science be applied to pharmacology, alternative energy sources, anti-terrorist defense, or indeed, more and better possessions to improve the quality of life.

IMPLICATIONS FOR INTERCULTURAL COMMUNICATION IN THE CLASSROOM

Sonia Nieto makes a point in her fine book, *The Sociopolitical Context of Multicultural Education*, that I have often thought about but never articulated so clearly:

> Many teachers...do not want to acknowledge cultural or racial differences. "I don't see Black or White," a teacher will say, "I see only *students.*" This statement assumes that to be color-blind is to be fair, impartial, and objective because to see differences, in this line of reasoning, is to see defects and inferiority. Although it sounds fair and honest and ethical, the opposite may actually be true. (2000, p. 138)

It is true because cultures are different, children are different, and to treat them otherwise is to perpetrate a gross injustice. The Supreme Court of the United States recognized the error of this kind of thinking in the landmark Lau decision in 1974. A case had been brought against the San Francisco School Department by parents of Chinese-speaking students who alleged that their children were not being provided with an education that was equal to that of their English-speaking peers. The Department countered with the assertion that they were providing exactly the same education to everyone. The high court reasoned that the argument was specious; because the Chinese children could not understand the English language, the instruction was of little value to them and the Department was not thus providing anything like an equal education. It's a little like going into an isolated region in Africa, taking valuable resources from the inhabitants, paying them in a currency that they cannot use, and then declaring the deal fairly done. In education, as in most matters, equal does not mean the same. In order to provide an education that is equally available to all children, there is a great deal that must be taken into consideration.

In the United States, more than one-third of children in elementary schools are from minority cultures, but the population of teachers does not reflect this mix, remaining prominently from the dominant culture. Classrooms are made up of individuals, but the relationship among those individuals is perceived differently by members of different cultures. To the member of the dominant North American culture, and perhaps to the teacher, the class is comprised of 25 individuals, all with individual abilities, rights, and objectives. But some members of that class might view the group as having a common goal and view the accomplishment of the group as being more important than the accomplishments of individuals. The U.S. belief in individualism carries with it the value of assertiveness. As Samovar and his colleagues (1998) write:

> The many signs of assertive and aggressive behavior in our culture, like all aspects of culture, did not develop by chance. A culture that has a long history of valuing nonconformity, individualism, competition, and freedom of expression is bound to encourage assertive behavior. (p. 83)

It is inevitable, then, that behavior that is considered normal and acceptable in the dominant culture will seem overly aggressive, possibly rude, and unmindful of the welfare of the group to members of cultures who do not share this value.

In terms of communication, the stage is set for problems. I recall giving my first presentation at an international conference. Members of the audience were primarily from Asia and, in my view, showed little interest in my remarks. Afterward, I was surprised when a distinguished Taiwanese professor came up to compliment me on my remarks and even more surprised when he apologized for our Israeli colleagues who had entered into a lively discussion at the end. I, of course, had not been offended by the Israelis' interest so much as the Taiwanese silence. The same kinds of misunderstanding can occur in the classroom, and the wise teacher is mindful of the possibilities.

Societies that tend toward collectivism as opposed to individualism also value harmony, particularly in group situations. For example, when doing business in Japan, Western business people need to understand that interpersonal harmony is very highly valued, and that a business meeting is no place to deal with controversial matters. These are to be dealt with in advance of meetings in one-to-one negotiating sessions that follow careful rules to avoid offending behavior. Japanese children may be reticent to engage in discussions of controversial subjects or the kinds of debate that typify many North American classrooms. China places a similar view on harmony, and this value has its roots in Confucianism, which considers harmony to be the goal of human existence. The North American classroom, with its jumble of children competing with each other for attention and achievement, might seem a very strange place to a child who has begun his or her schooling in another culture that placed a higher value on harmony. Similarly, children from cultures that value mysticism and intuition may experience discomfort with the nearly exclusionary belief in science and enquiry. In this value, as in all others, teachers have to be alert to the conflict between the value system of the home and the value system of the dominant majority in school or, indeed, among the many value systems represented in the classroom.

Because Americans like and expect to be treated as equals, intercultural conflict may arise when they interact with members of cultures who do not share that value. Children from societies who accept a less even distribution of power would be far less likely to interrupt the teacher, for instance, accepting the teacher's power over them more readily than children from the dominant culture. They are also likely to ask fewer questions, fearing that their questions will be seen as disrespectful of the teacher's authority. For the same reason, Asian children tend to avoid eye contact with teachers because that is seen to be disrespectful. American children, in contrast, are brought up with less respect for authority and believing that eye contact shows respect. One of the principal manifestations of the value is informality—using first names with strangers is something that the Chinese, for example, find very odd.

I mentioned earlier that not all cultures share the same positive view of competition. One of the biggest dangers for miscommunication is in the assumptions teachers might make about some children as "lacking in drive" or "without ambition," negative traits in the dominant culture. From their perspective, members of cultures who value the more "feminine" traits of nurturance and caring find the dog-eat-dog attitudes in the United States to be cold, calculated, and selfish. Again, the potential for misunderstandings in the classroom abound.

It is impossible to prepare for all eventualities and to prevent all forms of cultural misunderstandings. There are many dimensions of cultural values that I have not touched upon—attitudes toward progress and change, tolerance for uncertainty, a past versus a future orientation, and the relationship of humans to their natural environment are a few other values upon which cultural groups may be differentiated. At the end of this chapter are recommendations for further reading on this subject. My intent here has been to suggest a way of thinking about cultural differences and, most importantly, the necessity to do so. In the next section, we will see how cultural differences may manifest themselves in three areas of classroom life—learning styles and preferences, communication styles, and school achievement.

CULTURE AND LEARNING STYLES

Learning style refers to the way in which learners receive and process information. Some of us are visual learners, needing to see something in writing in order to remember it. Others are auditory learners and the spoken word is sufficient. Some of us use both learning styles depending on the situation. For example, I will trust my memory if the subject under discussion is of high interest or relevance, but will take notes if it is not or if it is highly technical. Some learners are primarily kinesthetic learners, needing to touch, manipulate, and move in order to learn. Some learners are more active and some more reflective. We have a tendency in North America to assume that a child who is not actively participating is not involved with what is happening in the classroom, is not learning. This is a false assumption, of course, since many learners prefer to listen and reflect—to learn before doing.

Discussion of learning styles or preferences sometimes takes place within the context of *multiple intelligences*, a term used to refer to the different ways of demonstrating intellectual ability. Howard Gardner (1983, 1993, 1997, 1999) has identified eight different types of intelligence, each possessed in some degree by most people, and has demonstrated that people differ in the specific pattern of intelligences that they possess. Gardner identifies:

1. Visual/spatial intelligence, or the ability to perceive things visually. People who are good at word-search puzzles, jigsaw puzzles, sketching, painting, design (whether interior, floral, or architectural!) are demonstrating this intelligence.

2. Linguistic/verbal intelligence, or the ability to use language effectively. People who have linguistic/verbal intelligence like word games, rhyming, storytelling, and reading.

3. Logical/mathematical intelligence, or the ability to reason logically, compute, and manipulate numbers. People who have logical/mathematical intelligence are good at problem solving, categorizing, and conducting experiments.

4. Bodily/kinesthetic intelligence, or the ability to control bodily movements and to handle objects skillfully. This kind of intelligence manifests itself in dancing, athletics, crafts, sculpture, or woodworking.

5. Musical/rhythmic intelligence, or the ability to appreciate and to produce music. People with this kind of intelligence tend to be able to sing, to write music, to play an instrument, and to have perfect or near-perfect pitch.

6. Interpersonal intelligence, or the ability to relate to and understand other people. People with this kind of intelligence are generally able to understand things from another's point of view and to communicate both verbally and non-verbally.

7. Intrapersonal intelligence, or the ability to be self-reflective and self-aware. People who are strong in this type of intelligence tend to recognize their own strengths and weaknesses and understand their relationships with other people.

8. Naturalist intelligence relates to our recognition and appreciation of the plant and animal kingdoms that make up the natural world. People who are strong in this type of intelligence tend to be drawn to and to react to animals and to be impressed by natural phenomena—whether the Grand Canyon, a hurricane, or snow falling in perfect silence on majestic pine trees. The person with naturalist intelligence is likely to be good at identifying and growing various plants or at working with animals and use these abilities productively in farming, forestry, or veterinary science, for example.

Individuals differ according to the particular profile of intelligences they possess, and there is as much variation among people within cultures as between. The notion is important to multicultural education, though, because it reminds us that the traditional assumptions about intelligence underlying formal education (i.e., valuing linguistic/verbal and logical/mathematical intelligences above all others) are going to result in even more unfairness given the additional dimension of cultural difference. The profile of intelligences that a learner possesses influences the style of learning that each individual prefers.

Learning style is influenced by many other factors—by the previous interaction a child has had with mother or other caregiver, by the values and attitudes taught in the home, and by prior experience in learning. Even if it were possible to associate learning styles with particular culture, however, it would probably not be desirable. Sonia Nieto (2000) makes an excellent point about the dangers, citing a particular example of a little knowledge being a very dangerous thing. Aware of research showing that Hispanics value cooperative over competitive approaches, teachers engaged in practices that were clearly discriminatory:

> … in integrated classrooms in which Hispanic children were present, teachers seldom granted them solo performances in plays or leadership activities in other situations. Teachers rationalized that Hispanics would be more likely to feel uncomfortable in the limelight or in leadership roles. They also reasoned that Hispanic children liked to share books because of their preference for working cooperatively. (p. 143, citing research by Flora Ida Oritz, 1988)

The teachers may have had good intentions, but the faulty interpretation or the over-generalization of research data to the teaching situation resulted in practices that discriminated against Hispanic children.

So what are teachers to do? Ignore research? Treat everyone the same? There's no doubt about it—it's difficult to make the right decisions. In the previous example, the teachers would have done well to consult with the children and let them participate in the decision. The best advice I can give is, first, to be sensitive to the possibility of different learning styles in all children and learn from them. Over time, you will see certain patterns emerge, perhaps related to culture, but it would be a mistake to assume that the next child you encounter will have the same learning preferences as the last four or five or six from the same ethnic group. Second, try to create the kind of classroom that makes it possible for learners to succeed whatever their learning style might be.

Culture and Communication Styles

The way in which children interact with each other and with their teacher in the classroom is largely determined by their communication styles, which are, in large part, determined by culture even though there are strong individual differences within cultures. Effective classroom interaction is essential to education, and communication style is an important variable. I have written throughout the book that there is often a discontinuity between the language of the home and the language of the school. When the language of the school is other than English and the culture is one not shared by the teacher or a majority of the children in the class, there is a risk of low achievement. Shirley Brice Heath studied the home and school language of African-American children in the Carolinas during the 1970s. Her work showed that children suffered in school because of the different ways of using language at home and the predominantly white teachers in the schools. The children she studied were not accustomed to the ritualized and somewhat artificial uses to which language was put in the classroom (remember the examples from Chapter 10), and the result was frequent breakdowns in communication. Heath guided the teachers to ask questions in different ways—to modify *their* behavior rather than try to modify the children's—and helped to close the gap between the two worlds.

Ray McDermott has suggested that, in classrooms where children from the non-dominant culture are taught by a teacher from the dominant culture, "communication breakdowns happen simply by virtue of each group behaving in ways their subculture sees as normal" (Nieto, 2000, p. 144 citing McDermott, 1987). Too many of these breakdowns and children become frustrated, motivation is threatened, and learning jeopardized. To use an example, when teachers in the dominant culture ask questions, they wait for only a short time for a response. Yet, such a practice may disadvantage aboriginal children whose culture encourages deliberation before speaking and thus may take longer to respond. Teachers will mistakenly assume that the long silence means that the children don't know the answer.

They will make similar mistakes if they are unaware of other culturally determined facets of communication—the wrinkling of the nose that Puerto Rican children do to ask "what?" or to indicate that they don't understand, or the raised eyebrows used in some native cultures to indicate "yes." They may not understand that when scolded, "Puerto Rican and Mexican children may avoid eye contact with adults as a sign of respect and shame" (Chisolm, 1994, p. 4). All of these behaviors are part of the patterns of communication styles that children bring to the classroom, and it behooves teachers to learn as much as they can about the cultures of the children they teach. We cannot, of course, learn everything about all cultures, so it is especially important to stay open minded and to question the assumptions we make and the conclusions we might draw from behavior we observe. We must remember that culture can, often in subtle ways, interfere with learning (Nieto, 1994, p. 146).

Culture and School Achievement

A poignant example of the effects of **cultural discontinuity** is described by Richard St. Germaine in his account of a study of Canadian Sioux students conducted by Wilson. These students had attended a reservation school through elementary school, but when it came time for high school, they were bused to a city school. Teachers in the reservation school described the students as "having high expectations, as being attentive and interactive with teachers." The children also received good test scores and grades. This changed when they entered "the large, predominantly White high school." There, they suffered "racial prejudice, isolation, low expectations of teachers." They failed; 18 out of the 23 students involved in the study dropped out between 10th and 12th grade. Wilson's study attributes the failure of the Sioux children to "cultural discontinuity.... In the reservation classrooms, small groups of students were observed sitting at circular tables with the teacher moving freely about the room, making contact with students." The high school classrooms were arranged as most high schools are with everyone facing the teacher. The previously successful Native students sat in the back of the classrooms and were mostly ignored by their white peers (Wilson, 1991, cited in St. Germaine, 1995).

Cultural discontinuity was also offered as one cause of the high drop-out rates in Alaskan Indian populations. As a result of a court ruling in the 1970s, small village high schools were established in Alaskan Native communities. While most reports admit that the schools are limited in their ability to offer an extended curriculum or provide extracurricular activities, they also acknowledge that the drop-out rate has improved substantially. Keeping students close to home and providing an educational environment that is more congruent with their cultural experience has paid off (Kleinfeld, 1985; Deyhle & Swisher, 1997; Swisher & Hoisch, 1992).

Earlier in this chapter, I described how Americans tend to be less formal than many other peoples. Although classrooms are more formal than some other situations—family dinners, for example—to learners from cultures that have greater expectations of formality, the informality of the American classroom must come as a shock. Nieto describes a hypothetical Vietnamese child, newly arrived, as feeling "extremely off balance and uncomfortable in a classroom environment in which teachers are informal and friendly, students are expected to ask questions and speak in front of the class..." (2000, p. 147). She goes on to present a case study of a Vietnamese child who does *not* have this reaction, and indeed it has been my experience that only about half of the Vietnamese children *do* react in this way. The point is important, though, for obvious reasons. When I lived in Newfoundland, I made numerous trips to Labrador to meet with teachers working in Native schools there. These teachers reported that it took them awhile to understand that the children in their classes did not respond well to requests to perform individually or even to work alone on class assignments. These demands of the classroom were inconsistent with the cultural patterns they experienced at home. The message is clear: The greater discontinuity between home and school, and the less effort the teacher makes to accommodate the learners, the greater the danger for educational failure.

Assumptions are always dangerous, and no more so than when we make assumptions about things we know little about, especially culture. A popular view, almost an urban myth, among educators and the general public is that South Asian students are remarkably successful in school *because* the cultural values of South Asians stress the importance of education. This may or may not be true; what *is* true, however, is that studies in the United States have shown that 87% of South Asian fathers and 70% of mothers have a university degree or higher (Kim, 1997, cited in Nieto, 2000, p. 148). Compare that with the educational attainment of North American parents or Canadian parents as a whole—31% and 40%, respectively, have university degrees or higher—and another picture, or at least another possibility, begins to emerge. Remember, too, Gordon Wells's finding that the educational attainment of the mother was the best predictor of school success in the child. In other words, for many South Asian children, the discontinuity between home and school is lessened by the fact that their *parents* value education and not because their culture values it, or at least, that is what the available evidence suggests.

SOME EASY AND SOME NOT-SO-EASY FIXES

The problems are difficult and the solutions more so. We have a duty to provide every child in every class we teach with every possible opportunity to succeed. We need to eliminate the barriers and make schools more accepting of the diversity that defines the societies in which we live—accepting *and* accommodating. From the experience of schools and teachers that have made progress in dealing effectively with cultural diversity, I have identified a number of principles and practices that will guide us in creating the classrooms that acknowledge and celebrate cultural diversity, that reduce the opportunities for miscommunication, and that increase children's chances for success. The following suggestions are intended to help to meet those goals by increasing cultural competence:

1. Become a student of the world. There is a great deal to be learned about other countries and other perspectives by reading history and current events.
2. Spend a few minutes each day learning something about a culture other than your own. The Internet makes this easy and fun. If you are a teacher with children from other cultures in your class, take their cultures as a starting point.

3. Become more aware of your own beliefs and how they are culturally determined.

4. Don't make assumptions and don't be afraid to ask. A little knowledge truly is a dangerous thing, as we saw earlier in this chapter. Don't assume that you know the reason that a child is struggling—dig deeper and find out. A good source is your community's immigrant assistance society.

5. Learn about the contributions of people from other countries to your own country's history. If you are to have a multinational perspective, you must understand the role played by cultures other than the dominant one in the shaping of your country's history.

6. If you are not a student of world history, read a good text book. Read two, one on European and one on non-European history. It will give you perspective.

7. If possible, take a course on cultural diversity. There are many available, some on-line.

8. Learn a foreign language. You don't need to become proficient, but you do need the experience of trying and experiencing first-hand the effect culture has on language.

9. Learn to look for cultural bias in teaching materials and methods. This includes technology. Technology is not culturally neutral; software reflects the bias of its creator.

10. Read on the subject of equity in education. There is a vast literature and it provides a perspective from which to reflect on our own practices.

11. Read about bias in tests and other assessment tools and look for alternative forms of assessment.

12. Schools should be kept small; if that is not possible, teachers need to find ways of creating small spaces populated by a small number of people within the larger setting. Find out about other ways of organizing schools to create friendlier environments.

13. Encourage bilingual programs or foreign language programs in elementary schools; everyone learns from them. Even if the children of the dominant culture never completely master another language, the experience of trying to learn makes everyone more sensitive to the experience of cultural minorities.

14. Expect high achievement from everyone in your class; don't write off any child.

15. Be open-minded.

CONCLUSION

The title of this chapter may have led readers to expect something very different—perhaps a discussion of common grammatical or pronunciation errors made by non-native speakers. Originally, that was my purpose. I had intended to provide a number of vignettes illustrating how communication failed because the two communicators came from different cultures. My intent, however, changed as I realized that I was inadvertently obscuring the larger issue, that of school failure. Thus, I have looked more broadly at the issue of culture and schooling. Communication, though, still lies at the heart of the matter: Communication breakdowns occur because a speaker and listener, or writer and reader, can never be wholly congruent. No matter how much they may have in common, as different individuals, they each have a different set of experiences and expectations. These differences may be even more profound when different cultures are involved, and so the purpose of this chapter has been to examine some of our notions about culture and its impact in the classroom. Misunderstandings, faulty assumptions, and blind ignorance all contribute to communication breakdown, and communication breakdown results in educational failure. It is something we cannot afford.

For Further Study

1. The Internet provides many examples of communication breakdown. From that source or from your own experiences, find several illustrating breakdown of communication in e-mail. Provide an explanation for the breakdown where possible.

2. Look up *additive bilingualism,* and describe how it might address the cultural discontinuity described in this chapter.

3. Find examples of gender differences interacting with culture to produce miscommunicaton.

4. How will being open-minded help teachers develop cultural sensitivity?

5. The author uses the term *cultural competence.* What do you think is meant by that term?

6. What do you think should be added to your preparation to become a teacher to give you cultural competence?

7. Can you think of any advantages to being "color-blind?"

For Further Reading

For further information about multiple intelligences, see *http://adulted.about.com/library/weekly/aa061400a.htm.*

For a very readable and cogent discussion of culture in the elementary classroom, see Sandy Kaser & Kathy G. Short's (March, 1998) article "Exploring culture through children's connections," *Language Arts, 75* (3) pp. 185–192.

For an example of curriculum based on nonverbal communication, see Virginia Vogel Zanger's (1993) book *Face to face communication, culture, and collaboration,* (2nd ed.). Boston: Heinle and Heinle.

CHAPTER TWELVE

Language and Learning: Eliminating the Cultural Discontinuity

In earlier chapters, we explored the nature of language acquisition in early childhood and throughout the school years in both monolingual and bilingual children. We looked at children's experience of language learning in the home and in the school, and we explored the differences. In the last chapter, we saw that those differences, or the way in which schools deal with those differences, can cause a serious discontinuity in the child's experiences of home and school. My purpose throughout was not to attack or defend a particular teaching method or practice but to reflect in such a way that would help teachers to reach rational and effective decisions about children's language and children's education. To reiterate what I have said so many times, the task of the teacher is to provide the learning environment in which every child can succeed. It is a formidable task, to say the least, and it would be foolhardy of me to attempt to tell teachers or prospective teachers how it might be accomplished. Every class is different from every other. Nevertheless, I believe that we have learned enough about language acquisition, about children, about schools, and about teaching to reach some conclusions about how to approach the job.

ELEVEN PRINCIPLES FOR
RECONCILING DIVERSE VIEWS

At this point, it might seem that the task of the teacher simply cannot be done. There are just too many masters to please—the researchers and theorists who tell us how language is learned (even though they seem rarely to agree among themselves); the parents of the children in school who may have their own ideas about their children's learning; the larger community, which consists of a variety of interest groups, including those of business and industry; and other educators who influence teachers' attitudes about language teaching as well as what goes on in the classroom. Indeed, the job is a monumentally difficult one and one to which few people are well suited, but it can be done. The purpose of this chapter is to extract and synthesize from the previous chapters not a teaching method nor even a formula for finding one, for these are things that all teachers must do for themselves, but a set of principles that are intended to assist teachers in reconciling the disparate views—in pleasing the different masters.

There are eleven of these principles. The first seven address the issue of reconciling theory and practice, specifically what we know about language acquisition in the home and school and how that should inform our teaching. The next three are concerned with how to deal with the divergent views of the other communities who are stakeholders in language education policy, and the final one synthesizes the issues and discussion so far into a single maxim.

Principle #1: There Are Many Right Ways to Teach

We saw in Chapter 3 that there are a number of competing theories about how children acquire language, and that there is no one that accounts for all the available data nor answers all the questions that parents, researchers, or teachers might ask. Fortunately, as teachers, we do not have to construct a theory of language learning so the fact that these disparate theories cannot be readily coalesced into a single theory of language learning need not concern us greatly. We are more concerned with the facts of language development and how these inform our teaching practice. Since there is no single theory that accounts for all the facts of language acquisition, it is not surprising that there is no single theory of language teaching and that there are many ways that work.

Consistent with our best knowledge about language acquisition, there are a number of ways of planning for children's language development in the school years. The facts of language acquisition do not dictate any single method, although they would constitute strong evidence against some, such as the rote learning of vocabulary items out of context. The important thing is to remember to incorporate our best information about language acquisition into all language activities for children. That information includes the five attributes of language set forth in Chapter 1: Language is linked to cognition, language is natural, language is culturally bound, language has structure, and language has many varieties. It also includes the following attributes about language learning that were discussed in later chapters.

Children Learn and Use Language in a Social Setting

Children do not learn to talk in isolation. Social interaction provides the motivation, the opportunity, and the models for language learning. Children are most successful in all aspects of language learning if they are full participants, that is, if parents and teachers talk *with* rather than *to* them and join with them in reading and writing activities. In Janet, Quy, Lucy, Jani, and Michael we saw children learning language in very different circumstances. What was common to all, however, was the fact that they learned language within a setting of real use and with the encouragement of parents and teachers.

Children Need to Be "Taught" Very Little About Language

None of the children we met were taught English, yet all learned it. In the environment of their homes and communities, they had all they needed to learn language. This is not to minimize the role of the teacher in the language learning of school-aged children; rather, the role may be more usefully "seen as 'leading from behind' by supporting the language learning capabilities of students indirectly through the activities we offer them" (Newman, 1985a, p. 5). This may be a difficult part for some teachers to play, accustomed as they are to dispensing information to children. Certainly it is a very demanding role, but the demands are offstage, so to speak, as when the teacher takes the time to get to know as much as she can about all the children in her class. She does this by observing them carefully and by meeting with or writing to parents, or when she sits down at the end of the day to make her journal entries, recording the insights she or the children may have had into the learning process or making notes about one child's progress and another's frustrations. In short, when she takes the time to consider the needs and to plan for each individual child, she is teaching in a way that may not be readily apparent to a casual visitor to the classroom but that is extremely important to her pupil's success.

Principle #2: Second Language Acquisition in Children Bears a Strong Resemblance to First Language Acquisition

A corollary to this principle is, the younger the child, the stronger the resemblance. The story of Lucy's language learning provides authoritative testimony to the truth of this claim. Her acquisition was native-like in nearly every way—in part, because of her early exposure to English. The implication for teachers is that with some adaptation of materials and plans and with some extra time given, teachers can use many of the same methods for teaching ESL learners as native English speakers. This is not to say that the ESL learner should be ignored but that teachers who base their teaching on children's language needs and on good information about first and second language acquisition will usually be effective. While it is always important to consider the needs of individual children, it is not necessary to start from scratch with ESL learners. A great many techniques and activities work well for both native and non-native speakers. This is especially true of the primary grades (K–3).

In planning for the ESL children in their classes, teachers should remember that these children bring an abundance of cultural and linguistic experiences to the task of language learning. We saw in Chapter 11 how profound an effect these can have. They also bring curiosity and the need to learn English they can use immediately. It is necessary, but not sufficient, to surround ESL children with all kinds of oral and printed language; that language has to be comprehensible. Teachers who remember to use all the resources at their command to get meaning across—other children, pictures, photographs, pantomime, whatever it takes—will give ESL children the kind of input they need to begin to make sense of the new language.

It is especially important to involve ESL learners as early as possible in the same activities being done by the other children in the class. For example, when the others are writing in journals, ESL children can dictate their journal entries using whatever English they have, by using the opportunity to learn new words from the teacher to express their meanings, or by drawing or even writing in their native language (a parent or older child can usually help you to translate). Whatever the language activity the class is engaged in, it is usually possible to adapt that activity so that ESL children can take part as well.

Less Rehearsal, More Production

We should remember that in acquiring their first language, children get on with the business of communicating from the very beginning. They do not need an extended rehearsal period before they are permitted to speak in public. It is the desire to communicate and to participate in the immediate society that motivates them to learn language. This single fact should remind us of a great many things we should *not* do in school while simultaneously reminding us of a great many worthwhile activities—reading quality books and engaging in real discussion about them, and writing for a real audience, for example.

Even ESL learners need to communicate in their new language from the very beginning. Our task as teachers is not to oversee or direct their practice until they are ready to use the language but to find ways to help them communicate successfully from the first day they arrive in class. In order for them to do so, they must understand that their language need not be perfect, which means that teachers should keep in mind two corollaries to this axiom.

First, teachers should be more concerned with fluency than with accuracy. In other words, they should expose second language learners to and encourage them to use as much language as possible with little regard for correctness. Children will work out the rules in their own way in their own time, asking for help or otherwise indicating that they are ready to be taught the standard forms. Early or overemphasis on form will send the message to children that how they say something is more important than what they say, and this is not a message that is consonant with an environment that is conducive to language learning.

Second, language learning, indeed all learning, involves risk. In language learning, writing provides a good example. Even proficient writers cannot grow in their craft if they stay within comfortable modes. Journalists needs to try short stories, novels, and poems in order to expand their skills and their understanding of their art. Short story writers need to experiment with drama, poetry, and magazine articles. I remember an incident that occurred many years ago when I was a student of Donald Murray's at the University of New Hampshire. For several weeks, I had been writing competent expository pieces on a variety of safe topics. Even though he had repeatedly encouraged me to try something a little different, I stayed with a formula I knew to be successful because it had worked with countless English teachers before. Finally, in one of our weekly conferences, he wadded up my most recent effort and threw it at me. "You've demonstrated that you can write competent prose. But you're never going to get any better unless you take some risks. I don't like to tell anyone what to write about, but if you can't write something a little riskier next week, don't bother writing anything at all." I took his advice, and from that point on that I truly began to learn about writing. Many years later, I wrote a 100,000-word romance novel just to find out if I could do it. Although I'll probably never do it again, I learned a great deal about dialogue, character, and plot development in the course of the summer that it took me to write that book.

It is neither necessary nor desirable to create a risk-free environment. What is important is to create an environment in which one feels safe enough to take chances in order to optimize his/her learning. It is essential to create conditions that say to children it is all right to make mistakes, and that it is more important for everyone, including the teacher, to try than to be correct.

Principle #3: Know Why You Do What You Do

One of the major purposes of this book has been to provide teachers a basis on which to make informed decisions about their language teaching practice. We examined in earlier chapters a number of competing theories of language acquisition and concluded that each one has its strengths. Clearly, there is something that educators can learn from each one. If we learn nothing else from behaviorism, for example, we learn that children cannot learn language without being exposed to it. From the nativists, we learn that there is something unique about language, that it enjoys special status in human learning. From the cognitivists, we can take the highly significant notion that language learning involves children's active participation. It does not just seep into their heads; children do not learn by watching or listening; they have to *do* language. From the social interactionists, we draw the conclusion that language acquisition is influenced by a number of factors—physical, linguistic, and socioenvironmental. We may also conclude that because these factors differ among children, the interaction among them may produce different effects in different children. In other words, there will be certain differences among children in how they acquire language, in what they acquire and when. These insights from theory provide some help, but applying the principle articulated here means finding a specific answer each time we ask ourselves why we make a particular curricular decision or choose a language activity.

Admittedly, there may be instances when "because it works" is an acceptable answer to the question of why a teacher does a particular activity. But this answer should only be given after careful reflection about whether the method or activity really works and why. In the introduction to her fine book on whole language, Judith Newman (1985a) asserts that "the clearer we are concerning our beliefs about language and learning, the sharper our focus on what is happening in front of our eyes." She goes on to articulate the questions that she and the other researchers continually asked themselves as they prepared the book:

- What do I believe about language and language learning?
- What do I want this activity to demonstrate about reading, writing, and learning?
- Why is this a useful activity for some particular student or group of students? (p. 5)

These are questions that teachers should regularly ask themselves as they plan for the children in their classes and as they assess themselves at the end of a day or a week. It is especially important for teachers to have a clear understanding about language acquisition against which to measure their practice. They must also have well-defined ideas about language learning because otherwise it is impossible to evaluate their effectiveness as teachers. As Meredith Hutchings observed about writing in her classroom: "Only after I have identified my own beliefs about the writing process can I begin to answer the questions: What am I actually demonstrating about the writing process to my learners?" (Hutchings, 1986, p. 43).

Having examined and specified their beliefs, if teachers then find that they are habitually planning activities that are incompatible with their beliefs about language and language learning, then they should seriously reconsider their entire approach to teaching. If they cannot state their expectations or objectives or if these are frequently inconsistent with their beliefs about language learning, then they probably should abandon the activity. And surely it goes without saying that if they find that they cannot specify how an activity benefits at least some if not all the children who participate in them, then they should replace that activity with one with clearer relevance.

What this principle advocates is practice informed by research and theory. Those whose teaching is guided by a solid grounding in language acquisition and who regularly ask themselves the three evaluative questions listed previously may make mistakes, for who indeed does not, but they will make fewer. They will also be better able to correct the mistakes they do make, to learn from them, and to avoid repeating them as they proceed along the course of learning with the children in their classes.

Principle #4: Remember That Language Learning Is a Whole-to-Part Enterprise

This principle might have been included within the discussion of the second principle. Since it is rather specific and is such a vitally important concern, however, I have chosen to treat it separately. It is crucial because some of our most serious failures in education are a result of not attending to this principle. It would be tempting to blame the linguists for these communal errors in judgement. After all, as we saw in Chapter 2, their analysis of language into its component parts has been crucial to our understanding complex structure. But they did not dictate practice. It was educators who misapplied linguists' methods and their findings to language teaching. By breaking language down into its component parts and thereby rendering it meaningless, generations of teachers greatly complicated the business of language learning, particularly reading and writing, for countless children. By treating language as something separate from the child that could be done in assigned periods of time, the same teachers robbed it of its inherent appeal. By thinking about language analytically rather than synthetically or functionally, they reduced it to a series of exercises in manipulation, memorization, or worse, and many thousands of school children developed reading problems or failed to learn to write clearly. Their problems with literacy eventually resulted in the reactionary movement, which has come to be known as the accountability or back-to-basics movement.

Real language is whole and should stay that way. That does not mean that teachers should never talk about parts of language—how to spell or how to pronounce a particular word, for example. It only means that these activities should take place within a larger language context. A simple example will clarify the distinction. Teacher X spends one half hour in round-robin reading of a story in a basal reader. She follows that up with a writing exercise in which the children complete worksheets based on the reading. The worksheet has four columns headed by four words from the story. The children's task is to circle all the words in the column that begin with the same letter (or that rhyme with or have the same vowel sound as) the word at the top. Because the words at the top also appeared in the story the children read, it might appear that the worksheet phonics activity is contextualized within the larger activity of reading the story. The difficulty is that this is nominal context at best and the activity is artificial; the words were isolated from the story and studied for some reason other than the meaning they contribute or the effect they have or the children's reaction to them. In fact, it is hardly relevant at all that they came from the story. The four words do not provide a strong enough connection between the two activities to relate them; therefore, the two activities do not support each other in any way.

Teacher Y, on the other hand, takes the same amount of class time in a different way. She begins by initiating a discussion about a field trip she and the children have taken to a chicken hatchery. As they talk, she makes notes on a large flip chart, writing down some of their observations, words that aptly describe something about the trip, or their reactions to what they have seen. Together, teacher and students decide that they want to write about the trip, and they go off to their writing places to do so. Some children sit at their desks, some stay near the flip chart in the carpeted reading area, and others prefer the long table at the back of the room. One boy is writing a lengthy entry in his journal, while a girl is looking up information about the length of time it takes to hatch an egg in response to a question raised during the discussion. Another girl works on a story about the only red chick hatched in a nest of six, all the rest fuzzy yellow chicks. After she has been working for about 20 minutes, she tells her teacher she would like to read the story aloud. She begins, "Their was a mother chicken named Sandra who layd six big white eggs." Then she interrupts herself: "I know I spelled some words wrong, but I'll fix them later." And later she does. She asks her teacher: "Is that the right 'there'?" "Why do you ask?" responds

Teacher Y. "Because I know there's another one like in 'They lost their mittens.' But I can't remember which." Teacher Y then spends a few minutes on *their, there*, and *they're*, offering one or two suggestions for keeping them straight. Before she finishes, three other children are standing nearby listening. One goes away and silently makes a correction; another beams in pride that he has it right in his story.

In the second teacher's class, oral language, reading, and writing all support one another and are not fragmented in any way. The children read what they and others have written, and that writing is based on their earlier talk, which was based, in turn, on their mutual experience of visiting the chicken hatchery. All the morning's activities involve the authentic use of language and are related directly and naturally to the children's own experience—in this instance, a field trip. There is even a time for the teaching of spelling, but notice that it originates in a question asked by one of the children, a genuine question and not a demonstration question. The teacher has merely taken advantage of a teachable moment, but in doing so she has demonstrated the importance of the next principle. This need not be the only teaching of spelling, of course. I happen to believe that spelling is important and deserves more attention; I also believe, though, that reading is the best teacher followed by short, targeted spelling lessons aimed at problematic words for the children at their stage of development, which brings me to the next principle.

Principle #5: But Don't Forget the Parts

Attention to the wholeness of language and learning need not and should not mean that the parts be lost. In other words, it is important that children learn the conventions of the language, and doing so may entail for some of them paying attention to discrete segments of the language. Spelling is one example; punctuation, mechanics, and certain aspects of grammar are others. By the time children reach the upper elementary grades, they should have mastery of these conventional aspects of language use. There is evidence that they achieve this mastery in stages. Gunderson (1990) has pointed out, for example, that children go through stages of writing development that take them from the "pre-phonetic" through the "conventional or mature." Chow's (1986) study of children in whole language classes where children were encouraged to write daily in log books, but were not instructed in the conventions of writing, revealed five stages of development. In the first, the pre-phonetic stage, the children produced letters, numbers, and shapes resembling letters, apparently without understanding that there is a correspondence between the symbols and sounds or words. Next, in the semiphonetic stage, they began to use letters symbolically, to stand for words or parts of words. Writers at the third stage of development, the phonetic stage, demonstrated their awareness that letters stand for sounds and that they know which letters stand for which sounds. Invented spellings were very common at this stage, but for the most part they were rule-governed inventions. That is, children used their knowledge of the relationship between letter and sound to create their own spellings. Many times, of course, these spellings turned out to be the same as conventional spellings.

At the transitional stage, children began "to process words as visual units" (Gunderson, 1990, p. 129). Children at this stage typically continue to use invented spelling, but their writing will contain conventional patterns as well as patterns which appear irregular. They might spell *through* "though", for instance, not because they do not hear the *r* sound or know how to write it but because they are now working from a visual memory of the word and that memory is sometimes faulty. The final stage of development identified by Chow found mature or conventional writers mostly in command of the conventions of writing. The mechanics of writing had become largely automatized, leaving these writers free to write longer and more complex pieces.

Many children will proceed through these stages, achieving mastery of the conventions without requiring any overt intervention at all; they will have learned them from their own reading and writing. Others will have learned by asking the kinds of questions asked by the girl in Teacher Y's class. But some children need more help in passing from stage to stage. It may be necessary for teachers to search for or to foster actively those teachable moments during which such learning is possible.

Principle #6: A Second Language Is an Asset Some Children Bring to School

It has been all too common for teachers to think about ESL children as having some kind of deficit or limitation on their ability to learn. Labels such as LEP (limited English proficiency) perpetuate this misconception. ESL children are deficient only if we persist in looking at what they do not have instead of what they do. What they do have is a well-established and fully functional first language on which to build a second language. When we think of children as missing something, our natural tendency is to provide it. In the case of ESL learners, what we want to provide is language. We may well be tempted to tell them about or to *teach* them language, and while this might not always be a bad idea, it can lead to some disastrous practices, especially with young children. But when we refuse to think of children as lacking something and see them instead as having something very special when they come to school, then our response is not to try to correct or fill the deficit but to build on strength. We can do so with confidence. After all, we have seen in earlier chapters that the particular language the child learns at home is not as important to school success as the experience of having acquired a first language and the existence of literacy-related activities in the home. By seeing ESL children in this more positive light, it is easier to see that the same language-rich, language integrated environment that helps native speakers to acquire literacy and to further their oral language learning will also help ESL students to add English to their home language.

Principle #7: Make Sure That the Method of Evaluation Corresponds to What Happens in the Classroom

An experience I had several years ago while engaged in a collaborative research project with a second-grade teacher in Calgary underscored the importance of this principle. The teacher's class was an ideal learning environment for second-grade children. It was a whole language classroom, before the whole language concept had taken hold in Canada. Writing was a central component of her curriculum, and there were no basal readers in the room. The children wrote every day and for much longer periods than the experts claimed children of this age were capable of. They liked to write and enjoyed sharing their writing with their teacher, with me on the days I was there, and with all other visitors to their classroom. More than half the children in this class were ESL learners, and most of them beginners or near-beginners. Nevertheless, they participated fully in all the activities of the class because the teacher made the adaptations that made their participation possible. In short, this teacher was doing a commendable job.

Just after Christmas, however, the teacher experienced a minor panic attack when she thought about the fact that the children in her class would be taking a provincial examination in language at the end of third grade. This test included a traditional spelling test. The teacher began to worry that the children would not be able to pass such a test because she spent almost no time in teaching spelling. When she talked to me about her concern, I pointed out that, in the first place, the pieces her children "published" had generally excellent spelling. Besides, the invented spellings they used showed them to be well aware of sound-symbol correspondence and, in some cases, to be in that transitional phase when their spelling shows that they are developing some awareness of what the word looks like in print. She wanted to believe I was right. She even knew I was right. Nonetheless, she worried.

Finally, after a few weeks, she decided to put her mind at rest by administering a standard spelling test. She selected the words by asking the third-grade teacher about the words that had appeared on the previous year's examination and then deleting those she was sure the children wouldn't know and adding a few that she knew they had encountered. The results did nothing to abate her concern. The children did very poorly on the test, the only test they had written that year. Many of the children expressed surprise at having to do such an activity; several expressed anxiety over the outcome. The teacher talked to me again. "I really wanted them to do well just to prove that my way is as good as the skills method. What's going to happen to them when they have to write the provincial test next year?" I asked her what she was going to do. "I just can't go back to that way. They're doing so well. You've seen their stories and you've seen how eager they are when they come to school every day."

"Yes," I replied. I had listened to them read their wonderful stories. I pulled one I had copied from my desk drawer and read it aloud to her. It was a Vietnamese child's account of her neighborhood and is reproduced in Figure 12.1. "Do you want to give this up to teach spelling?"

"No, of course not, but will they be all right?"

We then talked for a long while about why the children did so poorly on the test and what she wanted to do about it. In this case, as she pointed out, the test was a completely alien experience. Imagine what it must have been like for children accustomed to spending their time writing and revising real stories to be asked to write down decontextualized, unrelated words that the teacher read aloud. These children had never had a spelling test, had, in fact, never had a formal spelling lesson. In giving them the test, she had asked them to do things with language that were unnatu-

Figure 12.1
Thuy's Neighborhood

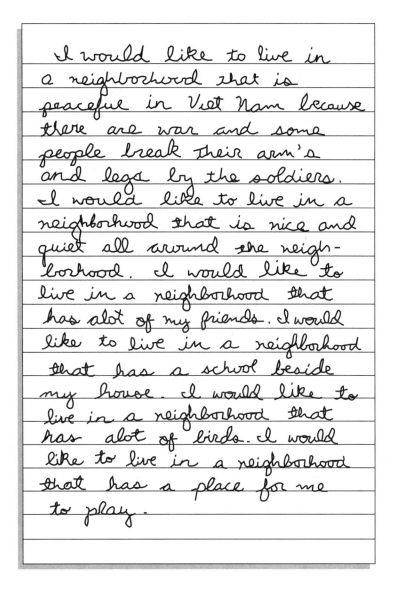

I would like to live in a neighborhood that is peaceful in Viet Nam because there are war and some people break their arm's and legs by the soldiers. I would like to live in a neighborhood that is nice and quiet all around the neighborhood. I would like to live in a neighborhood that has alot of my friends. I would like to live in a neighborhood that has a school beside my house. I would like to live in a neighborhood that has alot of birds. I would like to live in a neighborhood that has a place for me to play.

ral and outside their experience of language inside or outside the classroom. It is small wonder that they did so poorly.

"What do the results mean?" I asked. After thinking for a few seconds, she replied that they only meant that the children were not very good at performing on this particular task. It said nothing about their development as spellers or even about how they would spell those words at this time under normal circumstances. It didn't take this teacher long to conclude that the results of the test were meaningless and should not influence her decision about how to proceed with the children who, by all reasonable standards, were progressing marvelously. She decided that if she had to, she could in a very short time teach them how to take such a test, but that she would neither change her curriculum nor, until that time, subject the children to further tests of this type. She decided to put her trust in her knowledge of language acquisition and in her own experience with the children. She was right, of course, and the next year, after the third grade teacher had taken a little time to teach them how to take the test, the children performed well above the provincial average on all aspects of the language arts test. On the way to learning to write and loving to write, they had learned to spell as well.

The test in this example was a provincially mandated examination of the type that is coming back into vogue in many U.S. states and Canadian provinces. Some of these tests are constructed and scored in such a manner as to permit children to demonstrate their facility with language. Others are not; they consist of a series of unrelated questions requiring children to perform unnatural acts with language. If such tests cannot be avoided, then some time may have to be spent in teaching children how to take the tests. What is more important is that the teacher work to convince the school and the public that results of such tests reveal very little either about what children have learned or how well they have been taught.

Unfortunately, teachers may have little control over government-decreed tests. They do, however, have control over the assessment they use in their own classrooms and here it is especially important that the test match the task. As Serebrin observes of children's writing:

> We must not confuse the products of their efforts with the processes operating within particular contexts. This means that their efforts must not be evaluated by the yardstick of correct form—conventional spelling, punctuation, and sentence structure—but rather in terms of decision-making events within specific contexts. To see only their products would be to miss the significant "language events"—language users bringing all they currently know to bear upon the task with which they are faced. (1985, p. 53)

Evaluation is the part of the job that many teachers like least, yet most realize that it is a necessary part of the teaching and learning process. While a complete discussion of assessment in language education is beyond the scope of this chapter, a few observations must be made not only about what is to be evaluated but by whom. Because language is social in nature, as most meaningful language activities in the classroom involve the learner and at least one, and because we have accepted the principle that the test should reflect the task, it is also reasonable to involve the learner and possibly others in the task of evaluation. Children should be involved in making the decisions about how their learning will be evaluated, and it may be that peer evaluation will prove useful as well. Certainly, teachers should make sure that parents understand how their children's learning will be evaluated and why. They might also be invited to participate. But no matter whom the teacher involves in the evaluation process, the paramount principle to remember is the one stated previously: Children should not be evaluated in ways that are incompatible with the ways in which they have experienced learning.

These first three principles are intended to guide teachers as they attempt to reconcile the diverse views of theorists, parents, other educators, and the wider community in which they all live. But first a comment about why it is necessary to do so. First, for obvious reasons, it is desirable to create as much harmony as possible between children's homes and the school. If there is discord, then children are the ones who suffer. Most teachers realize, too, that their jobs are hard enough without having disgruntled parents to deal with. The second reason is that schools are funded by public money, and it is not in the interest of educators to have a large portion of the public dissatisfied with what they do. This is not to say that teachers should be governed by public opinion but only that they should at least take precautions not to antagonize the public and, ideally, to involve them actively in education. This is the eighth principle.

Principle #8: Involve Parents and the Community

The participation of parents in education is deemed so important today that Chapter 1 legislation in the United States requires that schools foster parental involvement activities. Involvement, under that legislation, means "helping parents understand the academic growth of their children" as well as getting them to participate in "actual reading and writing activities that support classroom learning" (Smith, 1991, p. 700). In Canada, there is a similar move in several provinces to involve parents in the operation of school. The School Council project in Newfoundland in which parents are elected to serve on a formal advisory board is a good example of such a program.

Parental participation is now deemed such a vital component of literacy education that the term *family literacy* no longer refers exclusively to the level of reading and writing attained by all family members, but to "families working together to promote mutual learning" (Nickse, 1989, cited in Smith, 1991, p. 700). One researcher, Joan Oldford-Matchim (1995), at Canada's Memorial University, has received national funding to work with schools and families on a read-aloud program to promote intergenerational literacy.

While teachers and principals should encourage parents' active participation in the life of the schools their children attend, it would be a mistake to assume that those parents who do not attend meetings with teachers or PTA meetings or who do not respond to letters sent home are disinterested in their children's welfare. A great many children are being brought up by single parents who must work, sometimes at more than one job, and shoulder the entire responsibility for their children's care. They may simply not have the time that other parents have to share actively in their children's school life. Ideally, all parents would fall into the category Snyder calls "available parents." But since they do not, it is imperative that teachers find ingenious ways of enlisting their support if not their active participation. The benefits accrue to the teacher as well as to the children. Writing of the importance of involving parents in whole language programs, Snyder (1990) says;

> When parents accept a broadened view of literacy learning, they become increasingly involved in the educative process, as models, participants and audience. Their children, as excited and achieving learners, become powerful influences for continued parental support. (p. 221)

Snyder implies that most parents participate without realizing it when they talk with their children, listen to and with them, and read with them. When teachers make the importance of these simple acts known to them, they can expect that many parents will seek to participate in other ways.

One way of involving parents is to keep them informed not only about their children's progress but about what kinds of activities are being planned for the class. If parents know ahead of time that the class is going to do a particular activity and that activity is one about which they have some specialized knowledge, they may volunteer to assist in some way. It would not be inappropriate for a teacher to send home a book with a note requesting the parent to read it aloud to the child, so long as the teacher knows that the parent is literate. If the parent is not, or if there is some doubt, then it is helpful to send home an audio tape with the book so that parent and child may share the experience of reading. If she knows that the family does not speak English, a teacher might send a child home with a book in his native language with a request that the parent and child read it together. Giving children assignments that require them to interview or talk to their parents about specific topics are also a good way of involving parents in their children's language education.

The computer age also provides opportunities for parents and children to learn together. Some Canadian schools are experimenting with programs in which the children teach their parents the computing skills they have acquired at school. While these kinds of activities have obvious benefits to both parents and children, the actual activity doesn't matter so much as the sharing.

It is especially important to try to involve the parents of minority children in the education of their children. For one thing, the teacher will have in them a valuable resource for learning about children's prior life experience. For another, it benefits children to have all the support they can get to minimize the cultural discontinuity discussed in the previous chapter.

Parents, of course, are part of a larger community, and this community is a major stakeholder in language education. Partnership between the larger community and schools is essential because full participation in the community means that one needs to be able to read and to express oneself orally and in writing, and these are prominent functions of schools. It is thus imperative that we extend our thinking beyond parents when we think about community participation in language education. Although it may take some effort on the teacher's behalf to engage the community in the life of the school, it is well worth the effort. Community members might play a number of roles that directly affect language education. Some of the more commonly used techniques are listed in Figure 12.2.

Principle #9: Don't Be Dogmatic

Teachers are professionals, and as such, we may be tempted to think of ourselves as having the answers or, at least, of knowing better than the lay community how children should be taught. Of course, to some degree, this is true, otherwise all those years of specialized education would not be necessary and we could hire teachers through the local employment agency much as we hire waiters, pizza delivery driv-

1. Invite community members to the school to share their expertise or interest with students.
2. Encourage visitors to read a favorite book or tell a favorite story.
3. Encourage repeat visits from guests the students find especially interesting.
4. Ask community members to correspond with students on areas of mutual interest.
5. Encourage community members to become volunteer tutors in the school. Senior citizens are an especially valuable resource.
6. Invite businesses to "sponsor" a class in the school. Their sponsorship may involve having their employees volunteer in the class, buying books or computer software for the class, or sponsoring or helping organize field trips.
7. Have students interview business and professional people about their reading habits, that is, what they read and why.
8. Have students interview community members for the school or class newspaper.
9. Ask businesses to display children's stories or artwork in their establishments thus providing a real "audience" for the students' work.

Figure 12.2   Nine Ways to Involve the Public in Language Education

ers, and janitors. But even though we do have specialized education and, most of us, fairly strong opinions about education, it would be a mistake to allow ourselves to become inflexible, to insist that our way is the best and only way. For one thing, from a purely practical perspective, to do so would essentially close the door on much of the community participation for which I have been arguing. For another, we would be forgetting the first principle stated. A specific example illustrates the danger.

In recent years, there has been a tendency to view whole language as providing the only way to organize the elementary school curriculum. At least, some supporters of the approach hold such a strong view. Although it is easy to understand why they would hold such an opinion, it is also easy to see how such dogmatism can backfire. I was recently conducting a 2-day materials-development workshop for ESL teachers who came together in the university's resource room to write and assemble ESL materials for their classes. In the district in which most of the teachers work, the Board of Education has made a firm and public commitment to whole language. While they have not mandated whole language for ESL classes, most of the teachers teach both ESL and English-speaking children and are familiar with the tenets of whole language. Familiar! Their devotion to whole language was so extreme that they dismissed from consideration any materials that smacked of "skills." In doing so, they denied learners the benefit of materials that were comprehensible and meaningful to them and denied themselves some important tools for managing classrooms in which students' English ability was heterogeneous.

By taking such a strong stance, these also called into question the competence of the few ESL teachers who had learned from experience that many learners need explanation and practice with certain grammar points or with spelling or with certain idioms. Finally, they risked offending (and thus losing the cooperation of) the parents of the ESL children in their classes. Many of these families have come from countries with educational systems that differ greatly from those of the United States and Canada, and their children have succeeded within those systems. They have developed certain expectations about learning, and while it is not incumbent on schools to live up to all those expectations, it is incumbent upon them to take into account the previous experience the learner has of language and of learning. Being dogmatic jeopardizes professional harmony and community participation in education.

A corollary of this principle is to be willing to compromise. It usually is possible to reach compromise on any issue without abandoning those aspects of a belief that one holds dearest. Besides, it is necessary. Most people are wary of large-scale change but will fairly readily accept small-scale change. Thus, if teachers who want to alter radically the approach to language teaching in a school but are meeting with community resistance, they should consider taking small steps. It probably will take no longer to accomplish their goals since, this way, they are more likely to have the cooperation of parents and the larger community.

Principle #10: Be Professional

Mary Ashworth (1985) pointed out that if teachers want to be taken seriously and to be treated like professionals, then they must act like professionals. With regard to establishing collaborative relationships with the community, however, certain aspects of professionalism are particularly important. One is that we become and stay informed about the community. The school's relationship with the community is a symbiotic one, and we cannot expect the community to be interested in the school if we show no interest in the community. Another aspect of professionalism, which Ashworth (1985) highlights, improves the credibility of both the individual teacher and the profession. That aspect is to engage in classroom research to support your beliefs about instruction (and possibly to modify them) and, if possible, to write articles describing this research (p. 111). Writing these articles for the lay audience and publishing them in the local press will enhance the school's profile and reputation as well as the teacher's. One teacher I know used to write an open letter to the local newspaper every week or two in which she described her own struggles with evaluation. She openly shared with the public why she felt she needed to alter the way in which children's language development was assessed and her attempts to find solutions. After a few weeks, others in the community started to write to the newspaper to make suggestions or to praise her for the thoughtful way in which she tackled what they considered a critical issue.

Principle #11: Remember That You Are Teaching Children, Not Language

A beginning teacher may feel overwhelmed by the job ahead. Even an experienced teacher, faced with ever-increasing curricular and social demands and trying to keep up with the professional literature, new theories, and new methods will be inundated by the responsibility to meet the needs of all the children in every class. The theme of diversity has prevailed throughout the previous pages. Cultural, linguistic, and individual differences have all been shown to have an impact on language and learning. This means that children come to school with individual needs that must be respected if they are to succeed. While it is not possible to structure a totally different instructional plan for each child, it is the teacher's responsibility to be attuned to the needs of each child and to attempt to meet them to the best of his ability. The teacher who puts the child's learning at the top of the educational agenda will naturally assume this responsibility.

These principles do not constitute an exhaustive list of dos and don'ts about teaching or how to reconcile the numerous views about language teaching held by individuals and groups who might be termed stakeholders in the educational process. They are instead guidelines, things to remember that might make the task a little easier. Unfortunately, following these principles will not ensure success but will improve the chances. Following them will also allow us to proceed in the knowledge that we are not compromising the interests of the principal shareholders—the children.

CONCLUSION

I conclude this book with a story that crystallizes as clearly as this one how the tenets, principles, and theories we have seen throughout the book can be realized in practice. I considered another story for this edition, but I have yet to find one that does the job so well.

The Glen Duncan School

Nestled among the lush green rolling hills of Prince Edward Island, in the country that was home to Lucy Maud Montgomery's *Ann of Green Gables*, is a neighborhood school that children still walk to each day except in the worst days of winter. It would be presumptuous to claim that it is a model school, for there are many possible models on which to base an ideal school, but in its faculty, curriculum, and practice, it represents much that is ideal. I first learned of the school when I met some of its alumni, young people in their 20s studying to be teachers at Saint Mary's University in Halifax. Some 10 or 15 years after leaving the Glen Duncan Elementary School (which is not the school's real name) these neophyte teachers recalled it fondly and told stories about their education that made it sound like a truly progressive place.

Several things struck me as noteworthy. First, it was unusual that so many of the students I encountered had attended this school. Saint Mary's admits only 40 students to the Bachelor of Education degree each year, and these are selected from between 600 and 800 applicants from across Canada. For more than one student to have attended the same elementary school is rare; three or four suggests that the university's selection process is somehow biased in their favor. Second, I have found only infrequently that university students recall their primary education at all; usually, they speak of their high school years, evaluating their experiences with what they read and see of education. But the four students I met during my years in Halifax all spoke well of their years at Glen Duncan. The account that follows is based on the memories of a young man who happened into my office on a summer day. Mark, who was a gold medalist in biology at another university before coming to do his teacher education at Saint Mary's, talked to me about his years at Glen Duncan.

Mark: *I didn't know until I started my Early School Experience [a period of observation in schools that students complete prior to beginning their student teaching] that there was anything different about Glen Duncan. But after I'd visited a few classes, I remember thinking "Wow. Times sure have changed." But when I got to talking with some of the others [students in the teacher education program] who had gone to other schools, they said that things seemed pretty much the same to them as always.*

Terry: *So what was different about Glen Duncan?*

M: *Well, in retrospect, I have to say that most of what I knew before I went to university I learned there.*

T: *That's a pretty tall claim. You learned nothing in high school?*

M: *Well, I'm sure I did. But what I mean is that at Glen Duncan I, we all, learned to learn. It's funny. I remember learning but I don't remember being taught much.*

T: *Can you explain that?*

M: *I'm not sure I can. The teachers were always there to help and to make suggestions if we needed them, but, except for one, I can't remember them standing up in front of the room talking to us, telling us about things. I remember that we used to read a lot. Most teachers would read to us at some time in the day, even when we got into the upper grades, and we always loved that. And we had silent reading periods as well when we could read anything we wanted. We wrote a lot, too. Stories, plays, newspaper articles, letters. Every day we had to write, but it wasn't a chore or anything. I really liked to write. When it was my turn to be editor of the class newsletter, I didn't like the job much. I preferred writing stories to deciding what would go into the paper and editing other people's work.*

T: *You had a newsletter?*

M: *Yes, every class had one. There were articles about what the class had been doing, what they were planning to do, that kind of thing. I remember writing the obituary for the class gerbil as well as a lot of birth announcements the year we had a rabbit for a science project.*

T: *What did you do with the newsletter?*

M: *It went home to our parents, of course, but it also went to local businesses and to the local newspaper.*

T: *Tell me about some of your other writing.*

M: *I wrote a Christmas play in fifth grade. A musical, believe it or not.*

T: *Was it staged?*

M: *No, not that one. I tried, but I couldn't get enough of my classmates interested. One girl got hers produced, though. I think that was in sixth grade. She wrote the* *play, and several of us helped write revisions and worked on the dialogue. I wrote two songs for it.*

T: *Was it a success?*

M: *Well, it didn't make it to Broadway, if that's what you're asking. But it enjoyed a three-night run in Charlottetown and was written up in the local paper.*

T: *Can you tell me anything more specific about your years at Glen Duncan? How about a typical day?*

M: *I don't think there was any such thing as a typical day. I remember walking to school most days and wondering what we'd be doing that day. I actually looked forward to it.*

T: *What might you have been doing one day in, say, third or fourth grade?*

M: *Well, after the morning routine …*

T: *What was the morning routine?*

M: *We sang "O Canada" and then had the morning news report. We had to predict one item that would be in the newspaper when it arrived later in the day. That meant that we had had to hear or see the news in the morning or talked to someone else about what was going on. We'd dictate the headlines to Mrs. Marchand—she was my third-grade teacher—and she'd write them on a flip chart and leave them until later when the newspapers came. We'd get four or five copies in the class, and we'd divide them up and comb the paper for stories to go with our headlines.*

T: *What happened after the morning routine?*

M: *Well, we'd usually settle down to our writing. We kept these large notebooks, and we could write about anything we chose but there were also certain writing assignments we had to do each week.*

T: *The teacher gave you topics to write about?*

M: *No, not exactly. She gave us tasks. One week I might have to write a letter for the class inviting someone famous to visit.*

T: *Did you send the letter?*

M: *Oh, yes, definitely. That's one of the things that I remembered when we were talking in the methods class about whole language and authentic language. Even then, most of the writing assignments were real. I already mentioned the school paper, but sometimes she would ask some of us to write a piece for the local newspaper—to collaborate on an article. Sometimes our required writing was related to other things we were studying. I remember one of my assignments was the description of one of my classmate's entries in the Science Fair. That was for the local paper.*

T: *Why not your own?*

M: *Because I already knew about my own. I guess she figured that if I wrote about someone else's I'd have to learn about it.*

T: *What would happen after writing time?*

M: *That would sometimes go on for the entire morning. Other times, though, we would work on math or science until lunch time.*

T: *What do you remember about math and science?*

M: *That it was fun, then. We used to do a lot of experiments, but before we did them, we had the most interesting discussions. She would encourage us to ask all kinds of questions and then think of all kinds of ways of finding the answers. She'd ask us "What do you think will happen if…?" or "What will it mean if…?" questions.*

T: *Such as?*

M: *Well, when we were on our way to "discovering" Archimedes' Principle—and, you know, we really thought we had discovered it?—we had designed an experiment on water displacement using a marble, a baseball, a softball, and a 12 lb. bowling ball. We thought we had it all worked out and then she asked, "What will happen if the bowling ball is the same diameter but weighs only 10 pounds?" The discussion on that was pretty animated but going no where until she asked "Suppose the ball is made of Styrofoam?"*

T: *You have very clear memories about that.*

M: *Yes, probably because I went on into science, and I've even borrowed that technique from her. But I remember the talk about science to be the most interesting thing about it. The same was true about social studies.*

T: *Oh, right, the newspaper.*

M: *Yes, the newspaper seemed to be the starting place for all our social studies lessons. The end of the Vietnam war was in the news then and we spent a lot of time trying to understand what had happened and why. We learned about other wars and talked a lot about beliefs and trade and all the reasons that countries get into wars. We learned about negotiation and compromise in our discussions based on those news stories.*

T: *Were there any children who didn't speak English when you were at Glen Duncan?*

M: *Yes, but only a few. There was a French-speaking girl who came in second grade and stayed until fourth grade and a boy who came in third grade.*

T: *What do you remember about them?*

M: *Well, there were no ESL classes. But there weren't many ESL kids either. I remember that the teacher would assign each new kid a "buddy" every week, and that buddy would help them to understand what was going on in class and on the playground. I don't remember much more except that eventually, they learned English. The girl went on to university, too. She was a biology major, like me.*

T: *Do you remember learning to read?*

M: *Not really. I remember that our first-grade teacher read to us a lot. Oh yeah, and she'd have us tell her stories, and she'd write them on a big piece of paper, and we'd read them out loud.*

T: *Language experience?*

M: *Is that what it's called? But if you're asking whether I remember being taught what sound a b makes, no, I don't. I guess I must have been, 'cause I learned to read at some point and I always liked it.*

T: *Were all your classes and teachers like the ones you've described?*

M: *With one exception, yes. There was a fifth-grade teacher who came to the school the year I was in sixth grade. She was my brother's teacher, and she* *was very rigid compared to the other teachers in the school. She gave a lot of tests and seatwork, and I don't think anyone was very happy. She left after only 1 year.*

T: *In the years since you left Glen Duncan, have you thought about why it was that that one school attracted so many fine teachers?*

M: *Actually, until I started my teacher education program, I hadn't thought about it at all. I thought all teachers were like the ones at Glen Duncan. But now I realize that they aren't, and thinking about it, I'd have to say that it was the principal who probably made the difference.*

T: *How so?*

M: *He was really special. He didn't just stay in his office the way I see some of these guys doing now. He spent a lot of time in the classrooms working with the kids. He knew all the kids in the school and their parents, too. I think the parents all liked him. He was really good at getting them involved in the school.*

T: *How did he go about that?*

M: *Well, the school couldn't afford a full-time librarian, and so he wrote to the parents.*

T: *Asking for volunteers?*

M: *Yes. I remember because my mother was thinking about working there. He wrote a long letter explaining why library was so important to the life of the school and why he had had to make the hard decision to eliminate the librarian's position. His idea was to turn the library into a community resource. He got enough volunteers—qualified ones, too—that the library could stay open three nights a week.*

T: *Was there material in an elementary school library to interest adults?*

M: *There was when he finished lobbying all the local businesses. He held an annual library fundraising drive and managed to get enough contributions to keep a good collection. Parents and former students also donated a lot of books and magazines. It was an odd assortment, for sure, but it was an interesting place to spend time.*

T: *It sounds like all of Glen Duncan might fit that description.*

M: *Yes, it was. I learned to read and to write and to think and to learn there. I'd really like to go back there to teach one day. If they'll have me.*

Mark attended the Glen Duncan school from 1972 until 1978. His recollections of his years there raise a number of intriguing questions. The first and most obvious is whether the school was special or was it typical of most others of its time. We can say with a fair degree of certainty that the Glen Duncan School would be considered special today even if measured against the strictest criteria of excellence in language teaching. That it was special nearly 20 years ago cannot be doubted. The second question is, Why? To anyone reading the chapters that preceded this one, the answers should be obvious. Nevertheless, it is appropriate as a conclusion to the book to summarize them.

Accounting for Success

Mark's account was by no means exhaustive, but it provided a window not only on the personal experience of one child, but on the curriculum, the teachers, and the principal that contributed to the school's effectiveness. While there are doubtless many reasons for its success, five stand out from reading his recollection:

1. Children participated daily in authentic tasks involving authentic language.
2. They used both reading and writing as means of discovery, as a way of learning.
3. Subject areas were integrated so that language played a central role across the curriculum.
4. ESL students were not segregated but participated fully in the life and activities of the class.
5. Education was a joint-venture enterprise whose success depended upon the partnership of the teachers, principal, and community.

It seems obvious to me that these are axioms that could guide any elementary school. This is true, I believe, not because they are profound statements of educational philosophy nor even particularly insightful statements about the nature of human learning. They are basically just common sense if we take to heart the truths about children's language and learning that we explored in the previous chapters. Let us consider the five axioms individually.

Children Participated Daily in Authentic Tasks Involving Authentic Language.
This participation began with the morning routine. In asking children to predict the stories and the headlines in the afternoon paper, the teacher was engaging the children in genuine talk in which they used language for a number of functions. The primary function was forecasting and reasoning. Children would speculate about the probability that various events would make the afternoon news, talk about causes and effects, and discuss the reasons. This daily routine would also provide opportunities for children to engage in the informing function of language in telling each other about the newscasts they had already heard. In the simple act of constructing headlines for their predicted stories, the children would have learned a great deal about the message-carrying properties of language—that some words carry more meaning than others, which can be left out—and about ambiguity that resulted when they left out too much information or the wrong information.

Later in the day, when the newspapers came, the purposeful language continued. Children read the paper, searching for stories to match their predicted headlines, and then talked about the stories they read. It is not difficult to imagine the language and the functions involved:

> Hey, look at this. Here's the story about the hurricane. (Controlling; informing)
>
> Where do you think they'd put a story about the school play? (Informing using the subfunction of requesting information)

I don't think it's here. That's strange. I guess they thought the story about the whale was more important. (Forecasting and reasoning; projecting)

Look! There's a story about the zoo on page six but I can't find anything about the aquarium. Why do you think that is? (Controlling; informing; reasoning)

As in much classroom talk, there were undoubtedly many opportunities for children to use the social language required for maintaining relationships with teacher and peers. An important point to remember was that the talk that engendered so many functional possibilities was not contrived but purposeful.

The authenticity of language use continued in the routine of morning writing. It is necessary to give children the freedom to write about whatever they want and in whatever form. That is the nature of much true writing, after all. Except for journalists who may be assigned particular stories from time to time, most writers have a great deal of freedom in deciding what and how they will write. Children were thus encouraged to write whatever they wanted, and in doing so they likely employed all five functions of language although it is likely that some were more heavily used than others. The social and projecting functions, for example, would be more heavily used in personal letters with the informing and forecasting and reasoning functions used more in letters attending to classroom business.

It is also necessary to their development as writers that children experience a variety of different writing formats. The teachers at Glen Duncan assigned tasks to provide that variety. Notice, however, that the tasks Mark remembered were legitimate writing tasks of the type that all of us might have to do in real life. They were not just realistic; they were real. This is an important distinction, I believe, because even very young children understand the difference between pretend and real activities. Like adults, they will care more about the letters they write to the President of the United States, the Prime Minister of Canada, or to Santa Claus if they have a reasonable expectation that they will be read. The more they care, the more they will learn. They will ask questions about the form their letters should take, about the way to state a thought more clearly, or the exact word they need to express a particular idea. In asking these questions and getting them answered, they engage in even more purposeful talk.

They Used Both Reading and Writing as a Means of Discovery, as a Way of Learning.
Reading and writing were not separate, independent subjects in the curriculum of Glen Duncan but formed an integral and essential component of all classroom learning. We saw in the newspaper exercise one example of purposeful reading. Mark's account does not specifically mention others, but it is perhaps interesting that he cannot recall a reading period or "learning to read" as a separate activity. He remembers his first-grade teacher's using a language experience technique, apparently with success since he became a successful reader. Later, in his account of the principal's support of the school library, he conveys a school atmosphere in which reading is a vitally important but natural part of school life.

Mark's recollection of one of his required writing tasks is telling. In being assigned to write an article about a classmate's science project rather than his own, he was forced to learn something that he might not otherwise have learned except superficially. In writing as a journalist about a scientific experiment for an audience who knew nothing of it, Mark had to understand it in far more detail than he might have had he been interested only in his role as classmate. Notice, too, that the emphasis on reading and writing did not come at the expense of oral language. Mark's account of his day is of one rich in talk. Talk about current events, about war, negotiation, and compromise; talk about science, hypothesizing, and predicting the results of experiments; talk to get the newsletter produced, to write and stage plays—this was the talk of his school years and always it was connected to reading and writing and to the real world in which he lived. All of these are excellent examples of language and learning authentically supporting one another.

Subject Areas Were Integrated So That Language Played a Central Role Across the Curriculum.   Language across the curriculum was a popular educational notion of the late 70s and early 80s, but long before that there were elementary teachers for whom this was standard practice. Obviously, it was for the teachers at Glen Duncan. We have already seen how language was linked to social studies. Reading the newspaper was the starting point for lively class discussions about current events and their causes. It is easy to imagine how much more vital these classes must have seemed than the all-too-typical history or social studies class of the "open-your-book-to-page-10" variety. Children in these classes put language to a great many authentic uses and learned about the world around them at the same time. Skeptics about the unifying capacity of language in integrating the subjects of the curriculum might argue that language and social studies are naturally compatible in ways that language and math or science are not. The teachers at Glen Duncan demonstrated the falsity of this argument.

Mark's memory of the excitement engendered by his science classes was of the talk those classes fostered. It is probably not an exaggeration to say that children learned to reason scientifically through the questions and answers raised in their discussion of scientific experiments. The hypothesizing they did before the experiment provided excellent use, not practice, of forecasting and reasoning language. Without this talk, most of the children would never have achieved the reasoning. As we saw in Chapter 9, children's language and cognitive growth go hand in hand. This is as true of the kind of reasoning required in science as it is of memory or conceptual development, other aspects of cognitive growth.

The generalizations Mark and the others had to reach as a result of their experimentation, as for instance in their discovery of Archimedes principle, were examples of informing language. The forecasting and reasoning and the informing functions are fairly typical school functions (i.e., purposes to which language is more typically put in schools), but the ways in which these functions were embodied were interesting, authentic, and memorable. It is also reasonable to assume that, in the talk that surrounded the experiments the children carried out, as well as in the talk the teacher engaged them in, there was also much use of the less formal functions of language—the social and the projecting. In Mark's case, the interdependence of language and science had a noteworthy result. It was out of the talk in which science was embedded (or perhaps it was the other way around) that grew the love of science that led to his later career choice.

ESL Students Were Not Segregated but Participated Fully in the Life and Activities of the Class. A few years ago, an elementary teacher explained to me that the ESL children in her class were always involved in the activities of the class. When I asked how they were involved, she answered, "Oh, in lots of ways. I read and they listen. And they always sit and listen while other children share the stories they've written." While I had no doubt that the children derived some benefit from such involvement, I could not help but think of the distinction Joan Kirner made between participation and involvement:

> It was Farmer Brown's birthday. The hen and the pig, who loved her dearly, were discussing what to buy for a birthday present.
>
> They found it a difficult task to think of a present for one whose material needs were few. Suddenly the hen hit on an idea, "I know," she said, "we can take her home-grown, home-made fresh bacon and eggs for breakfast. She'd love that. If we made it ourselves, she'd know we really cared."
>
> The pig thought about the hen's idea for a minute, then firmly snorted in reply, "No way am I going to give her bacon and eggs for breakfast." "Why not?" said the hen, disappointed.
>
> "Simple," snorted the pig. "You'd be involved but I'd be participating." (Cited in Potter, 1989, p. 32)

At the Glen Duncan School, the evidence points to the ESL children's participating rather than simply being involved. Although Mark could not speak from their perspective, what he did tell us of the school and of ESL learners in the school suggests that they played active roles. It is difficult to imagine that teachers who were so caring in their fostering and nurturing of language learning in the English-speaking children would forsake all their principles in providing for ESL learners. What Mark's recollection does tell us is encouraging. ESL children were not segregated but stayed in the same classroom as the English speakers. It is hard to imagine that they did not derive considerable benefit from the rich environment that Mark described.

Indeed, teachers who have insisted on their ESL children's remaining in the classroom rather than being segregated have made a number of helpful suggestions for ESL children that would be useful for mainstream students as well. Writing of the Fair Oaks School in Redwood, California, Lois Bridges Bird stresses the importance and the effectiveness of authentic language. The mostly Spanish-speaking children at Fair Oaks write real memos requesting that the furniture be repaired, they write letters in protest of government policies in Central America, and they even broadcast a half-hour radio program to the community every Friday morning. Teachers provide support and guidance but also encourage the importance of self reflection in the learning process. The freedom, support, and respect that their language program provides gives the students at Fair Oaks a sense of belief "in themselves as capable, creative learners, knowing what they need and how to get it" (Bird, 1991a, pp. 92).

Freedom does not mean that the children are not taught. But as one of their teachers, Roberta Lee, points out, they learn by doing. In producing their radio show, they have to write letters of invitation to potential guests (including the Queen of England!) as well as thank-you letters to people who appear, they have to write the scripts for the show, and learn to conduct interviews on the show. Obviously, there must be some instruction as to the form these letters, scripts, and interviews should take, but it is directed toward a real purpose that the children understand (Bird, 1991b, p. 93). Precisely because it is an authentic radio show, the language learning that it fosters will be linked to a number of subjects. Social studies is an obvious one but one can also envision a science or environment spot as well as music, drama, and literature. It is an ideal learning situation. Moreover, it is one that is ideal for both first- and-second language learners.

Education Was a Joint-Venture Enterprise Whose Success Depended Upon the Partnership of Teachers, Principal, and Community.   In order for such a partnership to work, there should be no silent partners, although it is reasonable to assume that one might speak with a louder voice than the other. At Glen Duncan, it appears that the principal was a senior partner. The fact that Mark remembered him well leads us to that conclusion. These days, it is not unusual for elementary children not to know the principal at all or to know her only as a remote figure who does paperwork, meets with parents, and perhaps dispenses discipline. For a child to remember a principal as an active member of the school, someone who spent a lot of time in the classroom and devoted his energies to improving the library, speaks well of that principal.

His way of getting parents to solve the library problem was effective because the solution brought benefits not only to the school but to the community as well. There were the indirect benefits of securing and channeling the parents' interest in the school, but there were direct benefits as well. The small community gained a stationary library where previously it had only the mobile branch from the nearby city. The library and the school became a community center where it was quite natural for parents and others in the community to find out about the life of the school. Of course, I am not suggesting that any of this made up for the loss of the librarian—for the librarian is a central figure in helping to establish a relationship between children and print. But when the principal could not save the librarian's position, he turned a potential disaster into an advantage for the school and for the community. Moreover, the incident demonstrated his understanding that the library's collection of print, visual, and audio materials was crucial to the school's functions.

Shortly after my interview with Mark, I telephoned the school to find out whether the principal was still there. It was a long shot that he would be, after nearly 20 years, but he was. So were some of the teachers who had been there when Mark attended. I went to Prince Edward Island to visit the school, and my visit confirmed that the school probably had been as unique 20 years ago as Mark had indicated, since it is still a very special place to be.

LOOKING AHEAD...

Since the last edition of this book was published, the century, indeed the millennium, has turned. The technological revolution is in full swing, and there will be no going back. There is more to know and there are more ways of finding out than ever before, and the amount of information is increasing faster than we can imagine. It is an exciting time to be a teacher and an even more exciting time to be a learner, but is also rather daunting, especially for the teacher. The generation of teachers who will read this book will help to shape educational practice in the new century; more significantly, they will help to shape human lives. They will complete the job begun at the end of the 20th century of moving education beyond the industrial age. But even in this new age, certain truths will endure. The first is that in the life of the child and in the life of the school, language is special and will remain so. It is the subject children know best when they begin school and it is the one that will largely determine their success in all the other subjects they encounter. It is the medium by which we will always communicate whether by pen, the Internet, or satellite. The second is that language requires little teaching; children will learn it if they are given the opportunity to do so. For second language learners the opportunities may have to be more numerous and more attention may have to be paid to meaning in the language they hear and see, but the process is natural enough if we do not impede it with overemphasis on structure and form. Third, no one cultural group has an exclusive claim on language or any aspect of it. Pronunciation, word choice, grammar, function, and even purposes of literacy have many acceptable variations within and between cultures. Respecting children's language is remembering that the particular variety individual children bring to school is as much a part of their identity as the teacher's language is to her. It's a matter of respecting the children's expectations about language based on their lived experience. If we fail to understand, for example, that Chipewyan parents do not expect their children to talk before they are 5 years old because they believe that it takes a lifetime to learn their language and that effective learning requires long periods of observation, we run the risk of taking the children's silence as evidence of language delay or as a void that must be filled. If we assume that children who come from non-literate homes do not know about stories, we may well get off on the wrong foot, for there are homes in North America in which the tradition of the story is strongly maintained through oral retelling. Language, and thus learning and school success for all the children who populate our classrooms, is at risk unless we learn to respect the experiences of children and build upon them.

For Further Study

1. Examine three text books commonly used first or second grade for evidence of cultural bias and the possibility of linguistic discontinuity.
2. Read Sanchez (1999) and describe the relevance for teachers of children in kindergarten through grade three.

For Further Reading

Callanan, M., Alba-Speyer, C., & Tenenbaum, H. (December 2000). *Linking home and school through children's questions that followed family science workshops.* Online at: *http://www.crede.ucsc.edu/research/sfc/rb8.shtml.*

Sanchez, S. (1999). *Issues of language and culture impacting the early care of young Latino children.* Online at: *http://www.nccic.org/pubs/sanchez99.html.*

Stone, R. (1999). *Best classroom practices: What award-winning elementary teachers do.* Thousand Oaks, CA: Corwin Press.

Glossary

Alveolar Consonant A consonant articulated on or near the alveolar ridge (e.g., Eng. /t/, /d/, /s/, /z/, /n/, /l/, etc.).

Alveolar Ridge The hard ridge behind the upper front teeth.

Applied Linguistics The sub-discipline of linguistics concerned with real-world language use.

Articulation Disorder The absence of or incorrect production of speech sounds that are developmentally appropriate. These would include regularly occurring simplifications or deviations in an individual's speech from the adult standard, usually one that simplifies the adult phonological pattern.

Assimilation The process by which a sound is influenced by another sound to become more similar. An example of the process historically occurs in the word *assimilation* itself. It is comprised of the Latin prefix *ad-*, the root *simil-*, and the verb suffix *-are*. The *d* of the prefix has become assimilated to the *s* of the initial consonant of the root. In English, the process causes vowels occurring before voiced vowels to be slightly longer than vowels occurring before voiceless consonants.

ASL (American Sign Language) A method used by deaf people to communicate in most English-speaking countries. Based on French sign language, ASL has evolved to a unique language with its own vocabulary and grammar. It is a language related to but distinct from English.

Back Vowel Vowels, for which the location of the back of the tongue at articulation is in the velar area (e.g., /o/, /u/).

Behaviorism A doctrine about human and animal behavior holding that all behavior is observable and can be explained without reference to unobservable mental activity.

Bilingualism The ability to function in an age-appropriate manner in more than one language.

Bound Morpheme A morpheme that never occurs alone, but is attached to other morphemes (e.g., kind*ness*, *un*kind, and all the morphemes in *biology*).

Cognition The process or result of recognizing, interpreting, judging, and reasoning; knowing.

Communication The act of transmitting information, ideas, etc. Communication may involve language but can also occur without language.

Communicative Competence A concept introduced by Dell Hymes, discussed and redefined by many others. The original idea was that to communicate effectively, speakers of a language need more than grammatical knowledge or competence; they also need to know how language is actually used by members of a speech community to accomplish their goals.

Compound Words   Words formed when two existing words are combined to form a different word. *Ballgame, bridegroom,* and *chalkboard* are common examples.

Concept   A general idea that is produced by combining several separate elements into a single entity.

Consonant   Any segment produced by stopping and releasing the air stream (stops), stopping it at one point while it escapes at another (liquids), or a very narrow passage causing friction (fricatives).

Consonant Cluster   A grouping of two or more consonants as in *next* /...kst/.

Cross-Sectional Data   A sampling technique that uses information collected from a number of different populations simultaneously. For example, a researcher interested in children's vocabulary growth in elementary school might test children from first, third, and fifth grades simultaneously rather than measure vocabulary in the same group of children over a 4-year period.

Cultural Discontinuity   An hypothesis that assumes conflicts, misunderstandings, and ultimately school failure are the result of culturally based differences in the communication styles of minority students' home and the Anglo culture of the school.

Derivational Morpheme   A grammatical morpheme that, when added to another, changes the part of speech or grammatical function of the word. For example, when *–tion* is added to the verb *gestate*, the resulting *gestation* is a noun.

Descriptive Linguistics   A subdiscipline of linguistics that deals with the accurate explanation of how languages are constructed.

Developmental Forms   The frequently imperfect language forms, notably different from adult forms, produced by children as they learn the language. Nonnative learners may also produce developmental forms that differ from those used by native speakers.

Diphthong   Syllable nuclei showing a marked glide from one vowel to another, usually a steady vowel plus a glide (e.g., /ou/ in house, /oi/ in toy).

Discourse Analysis   The analysis of language beyond the sentence taking into account context, gender of the speakers, etc.

Displacement   (as a characteristic of human language) The ability to convey a meaning that transcends the immediate context of space and time.

Domain-General Theories of Language Acquisition   The notion that language is learned in ways that are similar to the ways in which other cognitive skills are learned.

Domain-Specific Theories of Language Acquisition   The notion that language is learned and represented in ways that are distinct from the ways in which other cognitive skills are learned and represented.

ESL   English as a second language.

***Fis* Phenomenon**   The difference between what children are able to produce and what they can understand, the latter usually being greater than the former.

Fluency Disorder   The intrusion or repetition of sounds, syllables, and words; prolongations of sounds; avoidance of words; silent blocks; or inappropriate inhalation, exhalation, or phonation patterns. These patterns may also be accompanied by facial and body movements associated with the effort to speak.

Fricative   A consonant produced when the air released by an articulator passes through a narrow passage with audible friction (e.g., /f/, /s/, /β/, /ð/, etc.).

Front Vowel   A vowel for which the point of articulation of the back of the tongue is forward in the mouth as in /I/ or /ɛ/.

Glide   Also called a semivowel. Segments like English /w/ and /y/.

High Vowels   Vowels articulated with the back of the tongue high in the mouth.

Historical Linguistics   The study of not only the history of languages and how languages change, but how languages are related to one another.

Iconic Symbols   (or messages) Symbols that bear some physical resemblance to the meaning they are meant to convey. For example, the system of counting that uses I, II, III, IIII to represent numbers one through four is more iconic than the more symbolic 1, 2, 3, 4.

Idioms   A construction whose meaning cannot be deduced from the meanings of its constituents. Examples include *off the wall, fly off the handle,* and *go bananas.*

Inflectional Morpheme   A bound morpheme used to indicate the grammatical function of a word (e.g., *-'s* to indicate the possessive as in boy's, or *-s* or *-es* to indicate the plural).

Interlanguage Hypothesis   The proposition, first put forth by Selinker (1972), that there exists a system somewhere between the native language and the language being learned that is distinct from either and resulting from a learner's attempted production of the target language.

Intonation   The system of levels (rising and falling) and variations in pitch sequences within speech.

Language Disorder   A breakdown in communication as characterized by problems in expressing needs, ideas, or information that may be accompanied by problems in understanding.

Linguistics   The scientific study of human language.

Liquid   Name given to various /r/ and /l/ sounds.

Longitudinal Data   Information gathered on the same group of people (subjects) over an extended period of time.

Low Vowel   A vowel for which the location of the back of the tongue at articulation is low in the mouth, or farther away from the velum than for other vowels (e.g., /æ/ or /a/).

Metalinguistic Awareness   The process of thinking about and reflecting on the nature and functions of language.

Metathesis   The transposition of letters or sounds such as /æks/ for *ask*.

Mid-vowels   Vowels that are articulated with the back of the tongue in a mid, or intermediate position (e.g., /ə/, /schwa/, /e/, /e:/, /o:/).

Minimal Pair   A grouping of two words that differentiate in only one phoneme (e.g., pail–mail, bush–push, run–bun, wave–wade, ripe–ride, etc.).

MLU   (mean length of utterance) A basic measure of children's language development, first proposed by Roger Brown. Originally measured as the average number of words in each utterance within a speech sample, MLU is now usually measured in terms of morphemes (units of meaning) rather than words.

Morpheme   The smallest unit of meaning. Any word or part of a word that conveys meaning and cannot be further divided into smaller meaningful elements.

Morphology   The study of forms of language, especially the different forms used in word formation.

Nasal   A class of consonants in which air is blocked from the oral cavity and flows through the nasal passage (e.g., /m/, /n/).

Neurolinguistics   A branch of neuropsychology dealing with language.

Phoneme   The smallest significant unit of sound.

Phonetics   A branch of linguistics dealing with the analysis, description, and classification of speech sounds.

Phonics   A system of teaching reading that stresses the correspondences between printed letters (graphemes) and the sound system (phonemes).

Phonological Processes   The process by which a single sound, or target, undergoes a change in a specified context. These processes include assimilation, dissimilation, reduplication, and metathesis.

Phonology   The branch of linguistics concerned with the structural relationships between segments. The study of phonetics and phonemics together in the evolution of speech sounds.

Pragmatics   The study of the aspects of meaning and language use that are dependent on the speaker, the addressee, and other features of the context of utterance.

Productivity   (of language) The property of human language that allows novel and unique utterances to be produced.

Psycholinguistics   The study of the mental faculties involved in the perception, production, and acquisition of language.

Recursion or Recursiveness   A process that can repeat itself indefinitely. The English sentence demonstrates this ability through the embedding elements within clauses (The widow left early; the widow from Chicago left early; the widow from Chicago with three children left early...) and by appending elements (The widow left early and bought a car; the widow left early, bought a car, and robbed a bank).

Reduplication   A morphological process in which a root, stem, or part of it is repeated or a phonological process by which a sound segment is repeated. A child's pronunciation of "Kitty" as /kiki/ is an example of the latter.

Semantic Derogation   The process by which words referring to women are demeaned or acquire sexual connotations.

Semanticity   (as a property of language)

Semantics   The study of meaning of linguistic units or expressions.

Semilingualism   A controversial term used to describe people whose two languages are at a low level of development.

Semi vowel   A speech sound (such as /y/, /w/, or /r/) that has the articulation of a vowel but is shorter in duration and is treated as a consonant in syllables.

Social Interaction Theory A theory of language acquistion that holds that human speech emerged and its forms have their bases in the the social role that language plays in human interaction.

Sociolinguistics The study of language in its social contexts and the study of social life through language.

Stop Segments produced by a complete blockage of the air flow at some point in its passage (e.g., /p/, /t/, /k/, /b/, /d/, /g/).

Stress An increase in the activity of the vocal apparatus of a speaker.

Successive Bilingualism (also called sequential bilingualism) The acquisition of a second language after the first is deemed to be established.

Suffix An affix that is attached to the end of a root or stem.

Syllable A vowel and the consonants that cluster around it.

Syntax The study of how morphemes are combined to form sentences.

Tense A grammatical marking on the verb that may refer to the time of the event or state denoted by the verb in relation to some other temporal reference point.

Theoretical Linguistics The branch of linguistics concerned with philosophical issues such as the essence of language, the relationship between language and formal logic, and the existence and nature of universal language.

Vocalization Either the process of making a voiceless sound voiced or the conversion to a vowel.

Voice Disorder The absence of voice or presence of abnormal quality, pitch, resonance, loudness, or duration.

Voiced A sound segment produced with accompanying vibration of the vocal cords.

Vowel A voiced segment characterized by generalized friction of the air passing in a continuous stream through the pharynx and opened mouth, with relatively no narrowing or other obstruction of the speech organs.

Bibliography

Aaron, I. E., Chall, J. S., Durkin, D., Goodman, K., & Strickland, D. (1990a, January). The past, present, and future of literacy education: Comments from a panel of distinguished educators, Part I. *The Reading Teacher*, pp. 302–311.

Aaron, I. E., Chall, J. S., Durkin, D., Goodman, K., & Strickland, D. (1990b, February). The past, present, and future of literacy education: Comments from a panel of distinguished educators, Part II. *The Reading Teacher*, pp. 302–311.

Abudarham, S. (1980). The problems of assessing the linguistic potential of children with dual language systems and their implications for the formulation of a differential diagnosis. In F. M. Jones (Ed.), *Language disability in children*. MTP Press Ltd.

Allen, P., Swain, M., & Harley, B. (1988). Analytic and experiential aspects of core French and immersion classrooms. *Bulletin of the Canadian Association of Applied Linguistics, 10*, 59–68.

Andersen, R. W. (1981). *New dimensions in second language acquisition research*. Rowley, MA: Newbury House.

Anderson, A. B., & Stokes, S. J. (1984). Social and institutional influences on the development and practice of literacy. In H. Goelman, A. Oberg, & F. Smith (Eds.), *Awakening to Literacy* (pp. 24–37). Portsmouth, NH: Heinemann Educational Books.

Anson, C. M. (1999). Distant Voices: Teaching and writing in a culture of technology. *College English, 61*(3)(January 1999): 63–74. Online at: <*http://www.ncte. org/ce/jan99/anson.html*>.

Applebee, A. N., Langer, J. S., & Mullis, I. V. S. (1987). *Learning to be literate in America*. Princeton, NJ: Educational Testing Service.

Arunkumar, R., Midgley, C., & Urdan, T. (1999). Perceiving high or low home-school dissonance: Longitudinal effects on adolescent emotional and academic well-being. *Journal of Research on Adolescence, 9* (4), 411–466.

Ashworth, M. (1985). *Beyond methodology, second language teaching and the community.* Cambridge: Cambridge University Press.

Ashworth, M. (1988). *Blessed with bilingual brains.* Vancouver, BC: Pacific Educational Press.

Asselin, M., Pelland, N., & Shapiro, J. (1991). *Storyworlds, linking minds and imagination through literature.* Markham, ON: Pippin Publishing.

Asuncion-Lande, N. C. (1998). English as the dominant language for intercultural communication: prospects for the next century. In K. S. Sitaram & M. H. Posser (Eds.), *Civic discourse, multiculturalism, cultural diversity and global communication* (pp. 67–81). Stamford, CT: Ablex.

Atkinson, R. C., & Shiffrin, R. M. (1968). Human memory: A proposed system and its control processes. In K. W. Spence & J. T. Spence (Eds.), *Advances in child development and behavior.* New York: Academic Press.

Atkinson-King, K. (1973). *Children's acquisition of phonological stress contrasts.* (UCLA Working Papers in Phonetics, 25). Los Angeles: University of California at Los Angeles.

Bailey, V. H. (1994). *Identifying cues to cultural filters in symbolic behaviors and pragmatic language of Navajo children.* University of New Mexico: Ph. D. Dissertation.

Baker, L., & Brown, A. L. (1984). Metacognitive skills and reading. In P. D. Pearson (Ed.), *Handbook of reading research, Part 2.* New York: Longman.

Baker, N., & Nelson, K. (1985). Recasting and related conversational techniques for triggering syntactic advances by young children. *First Language, 5,* 3–22.

Barik, H. C., & Swain, M. (1974). English-French bilingual education in the early grades: The Elgin study. *Modern Language Journal, 58,* 392–403.

Barik, H. C., & Swain, M. (1975). Three-year evaluation of a large scale early grade French immersion program: The Ottawa study. *Language Learning, 25,* 1–30.

Barik, H. C., Swain, M., & Guadino, V. (1976). A Canadian experiment in bilingual education in the senior grades: The Peel study through grade two. *International Review of Applied Psychology, 25,* 99–113.

Barke, E. M., & Parry-Williams, D. E. (1938). A further study of the comparative intelligence of children in certain bilingual and monoglot schools in south Wales. *British Journal of Educational Psychology, 8,* 63.

Barnes, D. (1995). Talking and learning in classrooms: An introduction. *Primary Voices, 3*(1), 2–7.

Barnes, S., Gutfreund, M., Satterly, D., & Wells, G. (1983). Characteristics of adult speech which predict children's language development. *Journal of Child Language, 10,* 65–84.

Barrett, M. (Ed.). (1999a). *The development of language.* Hove, Sussex: Psychology Press.

Barrett, M. (1999b). An introduction to the nature of language and to the cenral themes and issues in the study of language development. In M. Barrett (Ed.), *The development of language.* Hove, Sussex: Psychology Press.

Basser, L. S. (1962). Hemiplegia of early onset and the faculty of speech with special reference to the effects of hemispherectomy. *Brain, 85,* 427–460.

Bates, E. (1976). *Language and context: Studies in the acquisition of pragmatics.* New York: Academic Press.

Bates, E. (1979). *The emergence of symbols: Cognition and communication in infancy.* New York: Academic Press.

Bates, E., Benigni, L., Bretherton, I., Camaioni, L., & Volterra, V. (1979). *The emergence of symbols: Cognition and communication in infancy.* New York: Academic Press.

Bates, E., & MacWhinney, B. (1987). Competition, variation, and language learning. In MacWhinney (Ed.), *Mechanisms of language acquisition.* Hillsdale, NJ: Lawrence Erlbaum.

Bates, E., & Snyder, L. (1985). The cognitive hypothesis in language development. In I. Uzgiris & J. M. Hunt (Eds.), *Research with scales of psychological development in infancy.* Champaign-Urbana, IL: University of Illinois Press.

Bear, D. R., Templeton, S., Invernizzi, M., & Johnston, F. (1996). *Words their way.* Upper Saddle River, NJ: Merrill/Prentice Hall.

Beardsmore, H. B., & Kohls, J. (1988). Immediate pertinence in the acquisition of multilingual proficiency: The European schools. *Canadian Modern Language Review, 44,* 680–701.

Beatty, R. (1983). Windyfoggery and bureaucratese. *International Review of Applied Linguistics, 62,* 53–66.

Benton, R. (1964). *Research into the English language difficulties of Maori school children, 1963–1964.* Wellington, New Zealand: Maori Education Foundation.

Bereiter, C., & Scardamalia, M. (1982). From conversation to composition: The role of instruction in a developmental process. In R. Glaser (Ed.), *Advances in instructional psychology.* Hillsdale, NJ: Lawrence Erlbaum.

Berger, J. (1991, January 5). Fernandez proposes placing warranties on graduates in '92. *The New York Times,* p. A1.

Berko, J. (1958). The child's learning of English morphology. *Word, 14,* 150–117.

Berko, J., & Brown, R. (1960). Psycholinguistic research methods. In Paul H. Mussen (Ed.), *Handbook of research methods in child development* (pp. 517–557). New York: John Wiley & Sons.

Berko-Gleason, J. (1993) (Ed.). *The development of language,* (3rd ed.) New York: MacMillan Publishing.

Berko-Gleason, J., & Greif, E. (1983). Men's speech to young children In B. Thorne, C. Kramerae, & N. Henley (Eds.), *Language, gender, and society.* Rowley, MA: Newbury House.

Berman, R. A. (1979). The re-emergence of a bilingual: A case study of a Hebrew-English speaking child. (UCLA Working Papers on Bilingualism, 19). Los Angeles: University of California at Los Angeles.

Berns, M. (1990). Why language teaching needs the sociolinguist. *Canadian Modern Language Review, 46,* 339–353.

Bever, T. G. (1972). Perceptions, thoughts and language. In J. B. Carroll & R. O. Freedle (Eds.), *Language, comprehension and the acquisition of knowledge.* Washington, DC: John Wiley & Sons.

Beveridge, M. (Ed.) (1982). *Children thinking through language.* London: Edward Arnold.

Beveridge, M., & Brierley, C. (1982). Classroom constructs: An interpretive approach to young children's language. In M. Beveridge (Ed.), *Children thinking through language.* London: Edward Arnold.

Bialystok, E. (1987). Words as things: Development of word concept by bilingual children. *Studies in Second Language Acquisition, 9,* 133–140.

Bird, L. (1991a). Joyful literacy at Fair Oaks school. In K. S. Goodman, L. B. Bird, & Y. M. Goodman (Eds.), *The whole language catalog* (pp. 92–93). Santa Rosa, CA: American School Publishers.

Bird, L. (1991b). Classroom demonstrations. In K. S. Goodman, L. B. Bird, & Y. M. Goodman (Eds.), *The whole language catalog* (p. 93). Santa Rosa, CA: American School Publishers.

Bissex, G. L. (1984). The child as teacher. In H. Goelman, A. Oberg, & F. Smith, (Eds.), *Awakening to literacy* (pp. 87–101). Portsmouth, NH: Heinemann Educational Books.

Blakeslee, T. R. (1980). *The right brain.* New York: Berkley.

Block, E. (1986). The comprehension strategies of second language learners. *TESOL Quarterly, 2,* 463–491.

Block, E., & Kessel, F. (1980). Determinants of the acquisition order of grammatical morphemes: A reanalysis and reinterpretation. *Journal of Child Language, 7,* 181–189.

Bloom, L. (1973). *One word at a time: The use of single-word utterances before syntax.* The Hague: Mouton.

Bloom, L., & Lahey, M. (1978). *Language development and language disorders.* New York: John Wiley & Sons.

Bloom, L., Lahey, M., Hood, L., Lifter, K., & Fiess, K. (1980). Complex sentences; acquisition of syntactic connectives and the semantic relations they encode. *Journal of Child Language, 7,* 235–261.

Bloomfield, L. (1933). *Language.* New York: Holt, Rinehart, & Winston.

Bohannon, J. N., (1993). Theoretical approaches to language acquisition. In J. Berko-Gleason, *The development of language* (3rd ed.). Upper Saddle River, NJ: Merrill/Prentice Hall.

Bohannon, J. N., & Stanowicz, L. (1988). The issue of negative evidence: Adult responses to children's language errors. *Developmental Psychology, 24*(5), 684–689.

Bohannon, J. N., & Warren-Leubecker, A. W. (1989). Theoretical approaches to language acquisition. In J. B. Gleason (Ed.), *The development of language* (2nd ed.). Upper Saddle River, NJ: Merrill/Prentice Hall.

Bolinger, D. (1980). *Language, the loaded weapon: The use and abuse of language today.* London: Longman.

Bond, Z. S., Eddey, J. E., & Bermejo, J. J. (1980). VO't del Espanol to English: comparison of a language-disordered and normal child. *Journal of Phonetics, 8,* 287–291.

Bonvillain, N. (1997). *Language, culture, and communication: The meaning of messages.* Upper Saddle River, NJ: Prentice-Hall.

Bowen, J. D., Madsen, H., & Hilferty, A. (1985). *TESOL techniques and procedures.* Rowley, MA: Newbury House.

Bowerman, M. (1981). The child's expression of meaning: Expanding relationships among lexicon, syntax, and morphology. In H. Winitz (Ed.), *Native language and foreign language acquisition.* New York: The New York Academy of Sciences.

Bowey, J. A., & Francis, J. (1991). Phonological analysis as a function of age and exposure to reading instruction. *Applied Psycholinguistics, 12,* 91–121.

Bowey, J. A., & Hansen, J. (1994). The development of orthographic rimes as units of word recognition. *Journal of Experimental Child Psychology, 58,* 465–488.

Bowlby, J. (1960). Grief and mourning in infancy and early childhood. *Psychoanalytic Study of the Child, 15,* 9–52.

Bradley, L., & Bryant, P. E. (1983, February). Categorizing sounds and learning to read—a causal connection. *Nature,* 419–421.

Braine, M. D. S. (1963). The ontogeny of English phrase structures: The first phase. *Language, 39,* 1–13.

Braine, M. D. S. (1971a). On two types of models of internalization of grammars. In D. I. Slobin (Ed.), *The ontogenesis of grammar.* New York: Academic Press.

Braine, M. D. S. (1971b). The acquisition of language in infant and child. In C. E. Reed (Ed.), *The learning of language.* Upper Saddle River, NJ: Merrill/Prentice Hall.

Braine, M. D. S. (1974). On what might constitute a learnable phonology. *Language, 50,* 270–299.

Braine, M. D. S. (1976). Children's first word combinations. *Monographs of the Society for Research in Child Development, 41* (Serial No. 164).

Brannon, J. (1968). Linguistic word classes in the spoken language of normal, hard-of-hearing and deaf children. *Journal of Speech and Hearing Research, 11,* 279–287.

Brent Palmer, C. (1979). A sociolinguistic assessment of the notion "immigrant semi-lingualism" from a social conflict perspective. *Working Papers on Bilingualism, 17,* 137–180.

Britsch, S. (1989). The contribution of the preschool to a Native American community. *Language Arts, 66*(1), 29–43.

Britton, J. (1967). *Talking and writing.* London: Methuen & Company.

Britton, J. (1970). *Language and learning.* Harmondsworth, UK: Penguin.

Brown, H. D. (1980). *Principles of language learning and teaching.* Upper Saddle River, NJ: Merrill/Prentice Hall.

Brown, R. (1973). *A first language.* Cambridge, MA: Harvard University Press.

Bruce, B. (1998). Mixing old technologies with new. *Journal of Adolescent & Adult Literacy, 42,* 136–140. Retrieved from Reading Online at *http://www.readingonline.org/electronic/elec_index.asp?HREF=/electronic/jaal/Oct_Column.html*

Bruck, M., Lambert, W., & Tucker, G. R. (1975). *Assessing functional bilingualism within a bilingual program: The St. Lambert project at grade eight.* Paper presented at TESOL Convention.

Bruner, J. S. (1973). Organization of early skilled action. *Child Development, 44,* 1–11.

Bruner, J. S. (1983). *Child's talk.* New York: Norton Press.

Bruner, J. S. (1984). Language, mind, and reading. In H. Goelman, A. Oberg, & F. Smith (Eds.), *Awakening to literacy* (pp. 193–200). Portsmouth, NH: Heinemann Educational Books.

Bruner, J. S. (1986). *Actual minds, possible worlds.* Cambridge, MA: Harvard University Press.

Bryant, P., MacLean, M., & Bradley, L. (1990). Rhyme, language, and children's reading. *Applied Psycholinguistics, 11,* 239–252.

Bryant, P., MacLean, M., Bradley, L. L., & Crossland, J. (1990). Rhyme and alliteration, phoneme detection, and learning to read. *Developmental Psychology, 26,* 429–438.

Burns, G. E., & Olson, C. P. (1989). Planning and professionalizing other FSL programs. *Canadian Modern Language Review, 45,* 502–516.

Burt, M. K., Dulay, H. C., & Hernandez-Chavez, E. (1975). *Bilingual syntax measure.* New York: Harcourt Brace Jovanovitch.

Cairns, H. S., & Hsu, J. R. (1978). Who, why, when and how: A developmental study. *Journal of Child Language, 5,* 477–488.

Calkins, L. M. (1983). *Lessons from a child: On the teaching and learning of writing.* Portsmouth, NH: Heinemann Educational Books.

Calkins, L. M. (1985). Learning to think through writing. In A. Jaggar & M. T. Smith-Burke (Eds.), *Observing the language learner.* Champaign-Urbana, IL: NCTE.

Campbell, C., & Friend, R. (1998). Deaf culture, pluralism and the field of communication. In K. S. Sitaram & M. H. Prosser, (Eds.), *Civic discourse, multiculturalism, cultural diversity and global communication* (pp. 429–440). Stamford, CT: Ablex.

Caplan, D. (1987). *Neurolinguistics and linguistic aphasiology.* Cambridge, UK: Cambridge University Press.

Caplan, D. (1995). Language and the brain. *The Harvard Mahoney Neuroscience Institute Letter, 4* (4). Online at: *http://www.med.harvard.edu/publications/On_The_Brain/Volume4/Number4/index.html*

Carmichael, L., Hogan, H. P., & Walter, A. A. (1932): An experimental study of the effect of language on visually perceived form. *Journal of Experimental Psychology, 15,* 73–86.

Carrell, P. (1983a). Background knowledge in second language comprehension. *Language, Learning, and Communication, 35,* 183–200.

Carroll, J. B. (Ed.) (1956). *Selected Writings of Benjamin Lee Whorf, Language, Thought and Reality.* Cambridge, Massachusetts: MIT Press

Carrow, Sister M. A. (1957). Linguistic functioning of bilingual and monolingual children. *Journal of Speech and Hearing Disorders, 22,* 371.

Carter, C. (Ed.). (1982). *Non-native and nonstandard dialect students.* Champaign-Urbana, IL: NCTE.

Case, R. (1980). *Intellectual development in infancy: A neo-Piagetian interpretation.* Paper presented at the International Conference for Infant Studies, New Haven, CT.

Cazden, C. (1968). The acquisition of noun and verb inflections. *Child Development, 39,* 433–448.

Cazden, C. (1987). English for academic purposes: The student-talk register. *English Education, 19*(1), 31–44.

Celis, III, W. (1990, November 22). Growing number of parents are opting to teach children at home. *The New York Times*, p. A1.

Chafe, W. (1982). Integration and involvement in speaking, writing, and oral literature. In D. Tannen (Ed.), *Spoken and written language*. Norwood, NJ: Ablex.

Chen, G. M., & Starosta, W. J. (1998). *Foundations of intercultural communication*. Boston: Allyn and Bacon.

Chen H.-C., & Leung, Y. S. (1989). Patterns of lexical processing in a nonnative language. *Journal of Experimental Psychology, Learning, Memory, and Cognition, 15*(2), 316–325.

Cheshire, J. (1982). Dialect features and linguistic conflict in schools. *Educational Review, 34*, 53–67.

Chisolm, I. M. (1994). Preparing teachers for multicultural classrooms. *Journal of Educational Issues of Language Minority Students, 14* (Winter), 43–68. Online at *http://www.ncbe.gwu.edu/miscpubs/jeilms/vol14/chisholm.htm*

Chomsky, N. (1965). *Aspects of the theory of syntax*. Cambridge, MA: MIT Press.

Chomsky, N. (1968). *Language and mind*. New York: Harcourt, Brace, Jovanovitch.

Chomsky, N. (1975). *Reflections on language*. New York: Pantheon.

Chomsky, N. (1980). *Rules and explanations*. New York: Columbia University Press.

Chow, M. (1986). Measuring the growth of writing in the kindergarten and grade one years: How are the ESL children doing? *TESL Canada Journal, 4*, 35–47.

Christian, D. (1996). Two-way immersion education: Students learning through two languages. *The Modern Language Journal, 80*(1), 66–76.

Churchland, P. M. (1995). *The engine of reason, the seat of the soul: A philosophical journey into the brain*. Cambridge, MA: MIT Press.

Clark, E. V. (1977). Strategies and the mapping problem in first language acquisition. In J. MacNamara (Ed.), *Language learning and thought*. New York: Academic Press.

Clark, M. M. (1984). Literacy at home and at school: Insights from a study of young fluent readers. In H. Goelman, A. Oberg, & F. Smith (Eds.), *Awakening to literacy*. Portsmouth, NH: Heinemann Educational Books.

Clarke, M. A., & Silberstein, S. (1979). Toward a realization of psycholinguistic principles in the ESL reading class. In R. Mackay, B. Barkman & R. R. Jordan (Eds.), *Reading in a second language: Hypotheses, organization, and practice*. Rowley, MA: Newbury House.

Clay, M. M. (1973). *Reading: The patterning of complex behavior*. Auckland, NZ: Heinemann Educational Books.

Clyde, J. (1990). A natural curriculum. In H. Mills & J. A. Clyde (Eds.), *Portraits of whole language classrooms* (chap. 2). Portsmouth, NH: Heinemann Educational Books.

Clyne, M. (1985). Development of writing skills in young second language learners. *International Review of Applied Linguistics, 67–68*, 9–24.

Coady, J. (1979). A psycholinguistic model of the ESL reader. In R. Mackay, B. Barkman, & R. R. Jordon (Eds.), *Reading in a second language: Hypotheses, organization, and practice*. Rowley, MA: Newbury House.

Cohen, R. (1991). *Negotiating Across Cultures: Communication Obstacles in International Diplomacy.* Washington, D.C.: United States Institute of Peace Press.

Cole, P. G., & Mengler, E. D. (1994). Phonemic processing of children with language deficits; which tasks best discriminate children with learning disabilities from average readers. *Reading Psychology: An International Quarterly, 15,* 223–243.

Comber, B. (2000). What *really* counts in early literacy lessons. *Language Arts, 78* (1), 39–49.

Commins, N. L. (1989). Language and affect: Bilingual students at home and at school. *Language Arts, 66*(1), 29–43.

Connors, K., Menard, N., & Singh, R. (1978). Testing linguistic and functional competence in immersion programs. In M. Paradis (Ed.), *Aspects of bilingualism.* Columbia, SC: Hornbeam.

Content, A., Kolinsky, R., Morais, J., & Bertelson, P. (1986). Phonetic segmentation in prereaders: Effect of corrective information. *Journal of Experimental Child Psychology 42,* 49–72.

Cook, V. J. (1985). Universal grammar and second language learning. *Journal of Applied Linguistics, 6,* 2–18.

Coombs, N. (1995 March/April). Closing the windows on opportunity. *Educom Review, 30*(2), pp. 28–29.

Cooper, C. R., & Odell L. (Eds.). (1999). *Evaluating writing, the role of teachers' knowledge and bout text, learning, and culture.* Urbana, IL: National Council of Teachers of English.

Corrigan, R. (1978). Language development as related to stage six object permanence development. *Journal of Child Language, 5,* 173–190.

Cotton, E. G. (1978). Noun-pronoun pleonasms: The role of age and situation. *Journal of Child Language, 5,* 489–499.

Crago, M. B. (1990). Development of communicative competence in Inuit children: Implications for speech-language pathology. *Journal of Childhood Communication Disorders, 13*(1), 73–83.

Crago, M. B. (1992). Communicative interaction and second language acquisition: An Inuit example. *TESOL Quarterly, 26*(3), 487–505.

Crago, M. B., & Allen, S. E. M. (1995). Morphemes gone askew: Linguistic impairment in Inuktitut. *McGill Working Papers in Linguistics, 10,* 206–215.

Crago, M. B., Annahatak, B., & Ningiuruvik, L. (1993). Changing patterns of language socialization in Inuit homes. *Anthropology and Education Quarterly, 24*(3), 205–223.

Crystal, D. (1976). *Child language, learning and linguistics.* London: Edward Arnold.

Crystal, D. (1987). *The Cambridge encyclopedia of language.* Cambridge, UK: Cambridge University Press.

Crystal, D. (1993). *The Cambridge factfinder* (2nd ed.). Cambridge, UK: Cambridge University Press.

Cumine, V., Leach, J., & Stevenson, G. (1998). *Asperger syndrome, a practical guide for teachers.* London: David Fulton.

Cummins, J. (1978). Educational implications of mother tongue maintenance in minority language groups. *The Canadian Modern Language Review, 34,* 3.

Cummins, J. (1979a). Linguistic interdependence and the educational development of bilingual children. *Review of Educational Research, 49*, 222–251.

Cummins, J. (1979b). Cognitive academic language proficiency, linguistic interdependence, the optimum age question and some other matters. *Working Papers on Bilingualism, 19*, 197–205.

Cummins, J. (1980). The cross-lingual dimensions of language proficiency: Implications for bilingual education and the optimal age issue. *TESOL Quarterly, 14*, 25–60.

Cummins, J. (1984). Wanted: A theoretical framework for relating language proficiency to academic achievement among bilingual students. In C. Rivera (Ed.), *Language proficiency and academic achievement.* Clevedon, UK Multilingual Matters.

Cummins, J. (1988). From multicultural to antiracist education: An analysis of programmes and policies in Ontario. In T. Skutnabb-Kangas & J. Cummins (Eds.), *Minority education: From shame to struggle.* Clevedon, UK: Multilingual Matters.

Cunningham, A. E. (1990). Explicit versus implicit instruction in phonemic awareness. *Journal of Experimental Child Psychology, 50*, 429–444.

Cunningham, A. E., & Stanovich, K. E. (1991). Tracking the unique effects of print exposure in children: Associations with vocabulary, general knowledge, and spelling. *Journal of Educational Psychology, 83*(2), 264–274.

Curtiss, S. (1977). *Genie: A psycholinguistic study of a modern-day "wild child."* New York: Academic Press.

Curtiss, S. (1981). Dissociations between language and cognition: Cases and implications. *Journal of Autism and Developmental Disorders, 11*, 15–30.

Curtiss, S., & Yamada, J. (1978). *Language = cognition.* Paper presented at the Third Annual Boston University Conference on Language Development, Boston, MA.

Curtiss, S., Yamada, J., & Fromkin, V. (1979). How independent is language? On the question of formal parallels between action and grammar. *UCLA Working Papers in Cognitive Linguistics, 1*, 131–157.

Cuvo, A. J. (1975). Developmental differences in rehearsal and free recall. *Journal of Experimental Child Psychology, 19*, 65–78.

Dale, P. S. (1976). *Language development: Structure and function* (2nd ed). New York: Holt, Rinehart, & Winston.

Dalrymple, K. S. (1989). "Well, what about his skills?" Evaluation of whole language in the middle school. In K. S. Goodman, Y. M. Goodman, & W. J. Hood (Eds.), *The whole language evaluation book* (chap. 10). Portsmouth, NH: Heinemann Educational Books.

Danesi, M. (1988a). Neurological, bimodality and theories of language teaching. *Studies in Second Language Acquisition, 10*, 13–31.

Danesi, M. (1988b). Neurobiological differentiation of primary and secondary language acquisition. *Studies in Second Language Acquisition, 10*, 303–337.

d'Anglejan, A. (1978). Language learning in and out of classrooms. In J. C. Richards, (Ed.), *Understanding second and foreign language learning.* Rowley, MA: Newbury House.

Das, J. P. (1980). On cognitive competence and incompetence: A cross-cultural perspective. *Mental Retardation, 8*(2), 81–95.

Davies, A. (1977). *Language and learning in early childhood*. London: Heinemann Educational Books.

Davies, A., Criper, C., & Howatt, A. P. R. (Eds.). (1984). *Interlanguage*. Edinburgh: Edinburgh University Press.

Davis, K. (1975). Severe social isolation. In S. Rogers (Ed.), *Children and language*. London: Oxford University Press.

Davis, P. S. (1991, April). Parents writing with students. *English Journal*, 62–64.

DeFries, J. C., Olson, R. K., Pennington, B. F., & Smith, S. D. (1991). Colorado reading project: An update. In D. Duane & D. Gray (Eds.), *The reading brain: The biological basis of dyslexia* (pp. 58–87). Parkton, MD: York Press.

deHirsch, K., Jansky, J., & Langford, W. (1966). *Predicting reading failure*. New York: Harper & Row.

De Keyser, R. M. (1986). Individual differences in first language acquisition and some educational implications. *International Review of Applied Linguistics, 73*, 1–26.

Demetras, M., Post, K., & Snow, C. (1986). Feedback to first language learners: The role of repetitions and clarification questions. *Journal of Child Language, 13*, 275–292.

Demuth, K., & Fee, E. J. (1995). *Minimal words in early phonological development*. Manuscript. Brown University, Providence, RI and Dalhousie University, Halifax, Nova Scotia.

Derwing, B. L. (1977). Is the child really a "little linguist"? In J. Macnamara (Ed.), *Language learning and thought*. New York: Academic Press.

Derwing, B. L., & Baker, W. J. (1977). The psychological basis for morphological rules. In J. MacNamara (Ed.), *Language learning and thought*. New York: Academic Press.

deVilliers, J. G., & deVilliers, P. A. (1973). A cross-sectional study of the acquisition of grammatical morphemes in child speech. *Journal of Psycholinguistic Research, 2*, 267–278.

Deyhle, D., & Swisher, K. (1997). Research in American Indian and Alaska Native education: From assimilation to self-determination. In M.W. Apple (Ed.), *Review of Research in Education, 22*, (pp. 113–194). Washington, DC: American Educational Research Association. Retrieved from *http://www.indianeduresearch.net/Anchor-Deyhl-44091*

Dickinson, D., & Snow, C. E. (1987). Interrelationships among prereading and oral language skills in kindergartners from two social classes. *Early Childhood Research Quarterly, 1*, 1–26.

Dickinson, D., Wolf, M., & Stotsky, S. (1993). Words move: The interwoven development of oral and written language. In J. B. Gleason (Ed.), *The development of language* (3rd ed.). Upper Saddle River, NJ: Merrill/Prentice Hall.

Dillon, D. (1980). Teaching about language itself. In G. S. Pinnell (Ed.), *Discovering language with children*. Champaign-Urbana, IL: NCTE.

Dillon, D. (1989). Editorial. *Language Arts, 66*(1), 7–9.

Dirven, R., & Verspoor, M. (1998). *Cognitive exploration of language and linguistics*. Amsterdam: John Benjamins Publishing Co.

Doebler, L. K., & Mardis, L. J. (1980). Effects of a bilingual education program for Native American children. *NABE Journal, 5*(2), 23–28.

Donaldson, M. (1978). *Children's minds.* Glasgow: Fontana/Collins.

Donaldson, M. (1984). Speech and writing and modes of learning. In H. Goelman, A. Oberg, & F. Smith (Eds.), *Awakening to literacy.* Portsmouth, NH: Heinemann Educational Books.

Drasgpw. E. (1993). Bilingual/bicultural deaf education: An overview. *Sign Language Studies, 80,* 243–265.

Dressman, M. (2000). Theory *into* practice?: Reading against the grain of good practice narratives. *Language Arts, 78* (1), 50–59.

Dudley-Marling, C., & Fine, E. (1997). Politics of whole language. *Reading and Writing Quarterly, 14,* 247–260.

Dulay, H., & Burt, M. K. (1974). Natural sequences in child second language acquisition. *Language Learning, 24,* 37–53.

Dulay, H., Burt, M. K., & Krashen, S. D. (1982). *Language two.* New York: Oxford University Press.

Dunn, L., & Dunn, L. (1981). *Peabody Picture Vocabulary Test-Revised (PPVT-R).* Circle Pines, MN: American Guidance Service.

Durgunoglu, A. Y. (1998). Acquiring literacy in English and Spanish in the United States. In A. Y. Durgunoglu and L. Verhoeven (Eds.), *Literacy development in a multilingual context: Cross-cultural perspectives* (pp. 135–145) Mahwah, NJ: Lawrence Erlbaum Assoc.

Durgunoglu, A. Y., & Verhoeven L. (Eds.). (1998). *Literacy development in a multilingual context: Cross-cultural perspectives.* Mahwah, NJ: Lawrence Erlbaum Associates.

Durkin, D. (1966). *Children who read early.* New York: Teachers College Press.

Eagan, R., & Cashion, M. (1988). Second year report of a longitudinal study of spontaneous reading in English by students in early French immersion classes. *Canadian Modern Language Review, 33,* 523–535.

Early Literacy Advisor. (2002). *Early Literacy Development.* Retrieved from *http://www.mcrel.org/resources/literacy/ela/development.asp*

Edelsky, C. (1977). Acquisition of an aspect of communicative competence: Learning what it means to talk like a lady. In S. Ervin-Tripp & C. Mitchell Kernan (Eds.), *Child Discourse* (pp. 225–243). New York: Academic Press.

Edelsky, C. (1982). Writing in a bilingual program: The relation of L1 and L2 texts. *TESOL Quarterly, 6,* 211–228.

Edelsky, C. (1986). *Writing in a bilingual program: Habia una vez.* Norwood, NJ: Ablex.

Edelsky, C., Altwerger, B., Barkin, F., Flores, B., Hudelson, S., & Jilbert, K. (1983). Semilingualism and language deficit. *Applied Linguistics 4*(1), 1–22.

Ehrenreich, B. (1981). The politics of talking in couples. *Ms., 5,* 43–55, 86–89.

Ehri, L. C., & Wilce, L. S. (1987). Does learning to spell help beginners learn to read words? *Reading Research Quarterly, 22*(1), 47–65.

Eilers, R. E., Gavin, W. J., & Wilson, W. R. (1979). Linguistic experience and phonemic perception in infancy: A crosslinguistic study. *Child Development, 50,* 14–18.

Eimas, P. D., Siqueland, E. R., Jusczyk, P., & Vigorito, J. (1971). Speech perception in infants. *Science, 171,* 303–306.

Einstein, Albert. (1954). *Ideas and Opinions.* New York: Bonanza Books.

Elliot, A. J. (1981). *Child language.* Cambridge, UK: Cambridge University Press.

Ellis, R. (1985). *Understanding second language acquisition.* Oxford: Oxford University Press.

Engel, W. von R. (1965). Del bilinguismo infantile. *Archivio Glottologico Italiano, 50,* 175–180.

Engel, W. von R. (1966). Linguaggio attivo e linguaggio passivo. *Orientamenti Pedagogici, 13,* 893–894.

Erikson, E. H. (1959). Identify and the life cycle: Selected papers. *Psychological Issues, 1,* 1–171.

Ervin-Tripp, S. (1981). Social process in first- and second-language learning. In H. Winitz (Ed.), *Native language and foreign language acquisition.* New York: The New York Academy of Sciences.

Ervin-Tripp, S., & Gordon, D. (1986). The development of requests. In R. Schiefelbusch (Ed.), *Language competence: Assessment and intervention.* San Diego, CA: College-Hill Press.

Fagan, W. T., & Hayden, H. M. (1988). Writing processes in French and English of fifth grade French immersion students. *Canadian Modern Language Review, 44,* 653–668.

Fanselow, J. (1987). *Breaking rules: Generating and exploring alternatives in language teaching.* White Plains, NY: Longman.

Ferguson, C., & Farwell, C. (1975). Words and sounds in early language acquisition: English initial consonants in the first 50 words. *Language, 51,* 431–491.

Ferguson, C., & Garnica, O. (1975). Theories of phonological development. In E. Lenneberg & E. Lenneberg (Eds.), *Foundations of language development.* UNESCO: NY.

Ferguson, C., & Slobin, D. (Eds.). (1973). *Studies of child language development.* New York: Holt, Rinehart, & Winston.

Ferreiro, E. (1984). The underlying logic of literacy development. In H. Goelman, A. Oberg, & F. Smith (Eds.), *Awakening to literacy.* Portsmouth, NH: Heinemann Educational Books.

Ferreiro, E., & Teberosky, A. (Translated by Karen Goodman Castro) (1982). *Literacy before schooling.* Portsmouth, NH: Heinemann Educational Books.

Field, T., Woodson, R., Greenberg, R., & Cohen, D. (1982). Discrimination and imitation of facial expressions by neonates. *Science, 218,* 179–181.

Finn, C. E., Jr. (1991, May 27). Accounting for results. *National Review,* pp. 38–41, 61.

Fisher, C. J., & Terry, C. A. (1990). *Children's language and the language arts.* Boston: Allyn & Bacon.

Fishman, J., Cooper, R. L., & Ma, R. (1975). *Bilingualism in the barrio. Language Science Monographs,* (Vol. 7). Bloomington, IN: Indiana University Press.

Fitch, S. (2000). Grand LaPierre, Newfoundland. *Language Arts, 77,* (5), 438–439.

Fletcher, P., & Garman, M. (Eds.). (1979). *Language acquisition.* Cambridge, UK: Cambridge University Press.

Flower, L., & Hayes, J. R. (1981). A cognitive process theory of writing. *College Composition and Communication, 32,* 365–387.

Foley, K. S., Harley, B., & d'Anglejan, A. (1988). Research in core French: A bibliographic review. *Canadian Modern Language Review, 44*, 593–618.

Foorman, B., Francis, D., & Fletcher, J. (1997, March 18). Breaking the alphabetic code. *The Globe and Mail*, Toronto, Canada.

Forrest, D. L., & Walker, T. G. (1979, March). Cognitive and metacognitive aspects of reading. Paper presented at the meeting of the Society for Research in Child Development, San Francisco.

Foster, J. C. (1991, February). The role of accountability in Kentucky's education reform act of 1990. *Educational Leadership*, pp. 34–36.

Foster, M. (1982). Indigenous languages: Present and future. *Language and Society, 7*, 7–14. Ottawa, Canada: Commissioner of Official Languages.

Fowlie, Gary. (1996, May 17). Pulling weeds from the kindergarten. *The Globe and Mail*, p. A22.

Franklin, E., & Thompson, J. (1994). Describing students' collected works: Understanding American Indian children. *TESOL Quarterly, 28*(3), 489–506.

Freedman, D. G. (1979, January). Ethnic differences in babies. *Human Nature Magazine*, pp. 36–43.

Froese, V. (Ed.). (1990). *Whole-language practice and theory.* Scarborough, ON: Prentice-Hall Canada, Inc.

Fromkin, V. & Rodman, R. (1988). *An introduction to language* (4th ed.). New York: Holt, Rinehart and Winston, Inc.

Gagne, R. M. (1965). *The conditions of learning.* New York: Holt, Rinehart, & Winston.

Galloway, L. (1981). Bilingualism: Neuropsychological considerations. *Journal of Research and Development in Education, 15*, 12–28.

Gantt-Gentry, C., White, H., & Randolph, M. (1994). Laterality effects in Cherokee and anglo children. *The Journal of Genetic Psychology, 155*(1), 123–124.

Gardner, B. T., & Gardner, R. A. (1975). Evidence for sentence constituents in the early utterances of child and chimpanzee. *Journal of Experimental Psychology, 104*, 244–262.

Gardner, H. (1983). *Frames of Mind.* New York: Basic Books.

Gardner, H. (1993). *Multiple intelligences: The theory in practice.* New York: Basic Books.

Gardner, H. (1997). *Extraordinary minds: Portraits of exceptional individuals and an examination of our extraordinariness.* New York: BasicBooks.

Gardner, H. (1999). *Intelligence reframed.* New York: Basic Books.

Gardner, H., Kornhaber, M., & Wake, W. (1996). *Intelligence: Multiple perspectives.* Fort Worth, TX: Harcourt Brace.

Garnica, O. K. (1973). The development of phonemic speech perception. In T. E. Moore (Ed.), *Cognitive development and the acquisition of language.* New York: Academic Press.

Garnica, O. K., & Herbert, R. K. (1979). Some phonological errors in second language learning: Interference doesn't tell it all. *International Journal of Psycholinguistics, 6*, 5–19.

Gary, J. O. (1975). Delayed oral practice in initial stages of second language learning. In M. Burt & H. Dulay (Eds.), 1975, *New directions in second language learning, teaching, and bilingual education* (pp. 89–95). Washington, DC: TESOL.

Gass, S. (1984). A review of interlanguage syntax: Language transfer and language universals. *Language Learning, 34,* 115–132.

Gathercole, S. E., Willis, C., & Baddeley, A. D. (1991). Differentiating phonological memory and awareness of rhyme: Reading and vocabulary development in children. *British Journal of Psychology, 82,* 387–406.

Gay, G. (1993). Building cultural bridges: A bold proposal for teacher education. *Education and Urban Society, 25* (3), 284–299.

Genesee, F. (1983). Bilingula education of majority-language children: The immersion experiments in review. *Applied Psycholinguistics, 4,* 1–46.

Genesee, F., & Lambert, W. E. (1983). Trilingual education for majority-language children. *Child Development, 54,* 105–114.

Genesee, F., Tucker, G. R., & Lambert, W. E. (1976). Communication skills of bilingual children. *Child Development, 46,* 1010–1014.

Gesi Blanchard, A. T. (1998). Transfer effects of first language proficiency on second language reading. In A. F. Healy and L. E. Bourne, (Eds.). *Foreign Language Learning, Psycholingustic studies on training and retention.* pp. 291–314, Mahwah, NJ: Lawrence Erlbaum Associates.

Geva, E., & Wade-Woolley, L. (1998). Component processes in becoming English-Hebrew Biliterate. In A. Y. Durgunoglu & L. Verhoeven (Eds.), *Literacy development in a multilingual context: Cross-cultural perspectives* (pp. 85–109). Mahwah, NJ: Lawrence Erlbaum Associates.

Gibson, E. J., & Levin, H. (1975). *The psychology of reading.* Cambridge, MA: MIT Press.

Giles, H., Bourhis, R., & Taylor, D. (1977). Toward a theory of language in ethnic group relations. In H. Giles (Ed.), *Language ethnicity and intergroup relations.* New York: Academic Press.

Giles, H., & Byrne, J. (1982). An intergroup approach to second language acquisition. *Journal of Multilingual and Multicultural Development, 3,* 17–40.

Glaser, T. (1998). U.S.–China Miscommunication [Summary of *Negotiating across cultures: Communication obstacles in international diplomacy,* p. 126, by R. Cohen]. Retrieved from *http://www.colorado.edu/conflict/peace/example/cohe7521.htm*

Glass, L. (1992). *He says, she says: Closing the communication gap between the sexes.* New York: Putnam.

Gleason, J. B. (Ed.). (1989). *The development of language* (2nd ed.). Upper Saddle River, NJ; Merrill/Prentice Hall.

Gleitman, L., & Wanner, E. (1982). Language acquisition: The state of the state of the art. In E. Wanner & L. Gleitman (Eds.), *Language acquisition: The state of the art.* Cambridge, UK: Cambridge University Press.

Glucksberg, S., & Danks, J. H. (1975). *Experimental psycholinguistics: An introduction.* New York: John Wiley & Sons.

Godby, C. J., Wallace, R., & Jolley, C. (1982). *Language files: Materials for an introduction to language.* Reynoldsburg, OH: Advocate Publishing Group.

Goelman, H., Oberg, A., & Smith, F. (Eds.). (1984). *Awakening to literacy.* Portsmouth, NH: Heinemann Educational Books.

Goldberg, E., & Costa, L. D. (1981). Hemisphere differences in the acquisition and use of descriptive systems. *Brain and Language, 14,* 144–173.

Golinkoff, R. (1983). The preverbal negotiation of failed messages: Insights into the transition period. In R. Golinkoff (Ed.), *The transition from preverbal to verbal communication.* Hillsdale, NJ: Lawrence Erlbaum.

Gonzalez, V. (Ed.). (1998). *Language and cognitive development in second language learning, educational implications for children and adults.* Boston: Allyn and Bacon.

Gonzalez, V., & Riojas-Clark, E. (1998). Folkloric and historical views of giftedness in language-minority children. In V. Gonzalez (Ed.), *Language and cognitive development on second language learning, educational implications for children and adults* (pp. 1–18). Boston: Allyn and Bacon.

Gonzalez, V., & Schallert, D.L. (1998). An integrative analysis of the cognitive development of bilingual and bicultural children and adults. In V. Gonzalez (Ed.), *Language and cognitive development in second language learning, educational implications for children and adults* (pp. 19–55). Boston: Allyn and Bacon.

Goodman, G. (1989). Worlds within worlds: Reflections on an encounter with parents. *Language Arts, 66*(1), 14–20.

Goodman, K. S. (1967). Reading: A psycholinguistic guessing game. *Journal of the Reading Specialist, 32,* 34–41.

Goodman, K. S., Bird, L. B., & Goodman, Y. M. (1991). *The whole language catalog.* Santa Rosa, CA: American School Publishers (Macmillan).

Goodman, K. S., Goodman, Y. M., & Hood, W. J. (Eds.). (1989). *The whole language evaluation book.* Portsmouth, NH: Heinemann Educational Books.

Goodman, Y. (1984). The development of initial literacy. In H. Goelman, A. Oberg, & F. Smith (Eds.), *Awakening to literacy.* Portsmouth, NH: Heinemann Educational Books.

Goodman, Y. M. (1986). Children coming to know literacy. In W. H. Teale & E. Sulzby (Eds.), *Emergent literacy: Writing and reading.* Norwood, NJ: Ablex.

Goswami, U. (1993). Toward an interactive analogy model of reading development: decoding vowel grapheres in beginning reading. *Journal of Experimental Child Psychology, 56,* 443–475.

Goswami, U., & Bryant, P. E. (1990). *Phonological skills and learning to read.* Hillside, NJ: Lawrence Erlbaum.

Grabo, R. P. (1931). *A study of the comparative vocabularies of junior high school pupils from English and Italian speaking homes* (Bulletin No. 13). Washington, DC: US Office of Education.

Graham, A. (1975). The making of a nonsexist dictionary. In B. Thorne & N. Henley (Eds.), *Language and sex: Difference and dominance.* Rowley, MA: Newbury House.

Graham, L., & House, A. S. (1971). Phonological oppositions in children: A perceptual study. *Journal of the Acoustical Society of America, 49,* 559–569.

Graves, D. (1977). *Balance the basics: Let them write.* New York: The Ford Foundation.

Graves, D. (1983). *Writing teachers and children at work.* Portsmouth, NH: Heinemann Educational Books.

Greenberg, J. H. (1966). *Language universals: With special reference to feature hierarchies.* The Hague: Mouton.

Gregg, K. R. (1984). Krashen's monitor and Occam's razor. *Applied Linguistics, 5,* 79–100.

Griffin, M. L. (2001). Social contexts of beginning reading. *Language Arts, 78* (4), 371–378.

Grosjean, F. (1992). The bilingual and the bicultural person in the hearing and the deaf world. *Sign Language Studies, 77,* 307–320.

Grunwell, P. (1982). *Clinical phonology.* London: Croom Helm.

Gunderson, L. (1990). Reading and language development. In V. Froese (Ed.), *Whole-language practice and theory.* Scarborough, ON: Prentice-Hall Canada, Inc.

Gunderson, L. (1991). *ESL literacy instruction, a guidebook to theory and practice.* Upper Saddle River, NJ: Merrill/Prentice Hall.

Halliday, M. A. K. (1975). *Learning how to mean.* London: Edward Arnold.

Halliday, M. A. K. (1976). *System and function in language.* London: Oxford University Press.

Halliday, M. A. K. (1978). *Language as a social semiotic: The social interpretation of language and meaning.* Baltimore, MD: University Park Press.

Halliday, M. A. K. (1985). It's a fixed word order language is English. *International Review of Applied Linguistics, 67–68,* 91–116.

Hammermeister, F. (1972). Reading achievement in deaf adults. *American Annals of the Deaf, 116,* 25–28.

Hansen, J. (1983). First grade writers who pursue reading. In P. L. Stock (Ed.), *Forum: Essays on theory and practice in the teaching of writing* (pp. 155–162). Upper Montclair, NJ: Boynton-Cook.

Harding, C. G., & Golinkoff, R. M. (1979). The origins of intentional vocalizations in prelinguistic infants. *Child Development, 50,* 338–340.

Harlin, R., Lipa, S. E., & Lonberger, R. (1991). *The whole language journey.* Markham, ON: Pippin Publishing.

Harris, G. A. (1985, September). Considerations in assessing English language performance of Native American children. *Topics in Language Disorders,* 42–52.

Harste, J. C., Woodward, V. A., & Burke, C. (1984). *Language stories and literacy lessons.* Portsmouth, NH: Heinemann Educational Books.

Hatch, E. (1978a). *Second language acquisition.* Rowley, MA: Newbury House.

Hatch, E. (1978b). Acquisition of syntax in a second language. In J. Richards (Ed.), *Understanding second and foreign language learning: Issues and approaches.* Rowley, MA: Newbury House.

Hatch, E. (1978c). Discourse analysis and second language acquisition. In E. Hatch (Ed.), *Second language acquisition research.* New York: Academic Press.

Hatch, E. (1978d). Discourse analysis, speech acts and second language acquisition. In W. Ritchie (Ed.), *Second language acquisition research.* New York: Academic Press.

Hatch, E. M. (1983). *Psycholinguistics.* Rowley, MA: Newbury House.

Haugen, E. (1956). *Bilingualism in the Americas.* Tuscaloosa, AL: University of Alabama Press.

Haussler, M. M., Tompkins, C., & Jeanne, L. M. (1987). Young Hopi writers and readers. *NABE Journal,* 83–93.

Hayes, C. W., Ornstein, J., & Gage, W. W. (1987). *The ABC's of languages and linguistics.* Lincolnwood, IL: The National Textbook Company.

Healy, A. F., & Bournĕe, L. E. Jr. (Eds.). (1998). *Foreign language learning, Psycholinguistic studies on training and retention.* Mahwah, NJ: Lawrence Erlbaum Associates.

Heath, S. B. (1978). *Teacher talk: Language in the classroom.* Washington, DC: Center for Applied Linguistics.

Heath, S. B. (1983). Research currents: A lot of talk about nothing. *Language Arts, 60* (8).

Heath, S. B. (1983). *Ways with words: Language, life, and work in communities and classrooms.* Cambridge, UK: Cambridge University Press.

Heath, S. B. (1986). Separating 'things of imagination' from life: Learning to read and write. In W. H. Teale & E. Sulzby (Eds.), *Emergent literacy: Writing and reading.* Norwood, NJ: Ablex.

Heath, S. B., & Thomas, C. (1984). The achievement of preschool literacy for mother and child. In H. Goelman, A. Oberg, & F. Smith (Eds.), *Awakening to literacy.* Portsmouth, NH: Heinemann Educational Books.

Heatherington, M. E. (1980). *How language works.* Cambridge, MA: Winthrop.

Hersov, L. A., Berger, M., & Nicol, A. R. (Eds.). (1980). *Language and language disorders in childhood.* Oxford: Pergamon Press.

Hickman, J., & Kimberley, K. (Eds.). (1988). *Teachers, language and learning.* London: Routledge.

Hills, E. C. (1914). The speech of a child two years of age. *Dialect Notes, 4,* 84–100.

Hinkel, E. (Ed.). (1999). *Culture in second language teaching and learning.* New York: Cambridge University Press.

Hirsh-Pasek, K., Treiman, R., & Schneiderman, M. (1984). Brown and Hanlon revisited: Mothers' sensitivity to ungrammatical forms. *Journal of Child Language, 11,* 81–88.

Hoff-Ginsberg, E. (1986). Function and structure in maternal speech: Their relation to the child's development of syntax. *Developmental Psychology, 22,* 155–163.

Hofstadter, R. (1963). *Anti-Intellectualism in American life.* New York: Alfred A. Knopf.

Hofstede, G. (1980). *Culture's consequences: International differences in work-related values.* Beverly Hills: Sage.

Holm, A., & Holm, W. (1990). Rock Point, a Navajo way to go to school: A valediction, *Annals, AAPSS, 508,* 170–184.

Holt, J. (1967). *How children learn.* New York: Merloyd Lawrence (Dell).

Holt, J. (1983). *How children learn* (Rev. ed.). New York: Merloyd Lawrence (Dell).

Holt, J. (1989). *Learning all the time.* Reading, MA: Addison-Wesley.

Honeyĝhan, G. (2000). Rhythm of the Caribbean: Connecting oral history and literacy. *Language Arts, 77 (5),* 406–413.

Horgan, D. (1978). The development of the full passive. *Journal of Child Language, 5,* 65–80.

Hoyle, S. M., & Adĝer, C. T. (Eds.). (1998). *Kids talk: Strategic language use in later childhood.* New York: Oxford University Press.

Huang, H. S., & Hanley, J. R. (1995). Phonological awareness and visual skills in learning to read Chinese and English. *Cognition, 54,* 73–98.

Hulit, L. M., & Howard, M. R. (1986). *Born to talk.* Upper Saddle River, NJ: Merrill/Prentice Hall.

Hulit, L.M. & Howard, M. R. (1993). *Born to talk: An introduction to speech and language development.* New York: Macmillan.

Hurtado, A., & Rodriguez, R. (1989). Language as a social problem: The repression of Spanish in south Texas. *Journal of Multilingual and Multicultural Development, 10*(5), 401–419.

Hutchings, M. (1986). What teachers are demonstrating. In J. Newman (Ed.), *Whole language theory in use.* Portsmouth, NH: Heinemann Educational Books.

Ingram, D. (1974). Phonological rules in young children. *Journal of Child Language, 1,* 49–64.

Ingram, D. (1976). *Phonological disability in children.* New York: Elsevier.

Ingram, D. (1979). Phonological patterns in the speech of young children. In P. Fletcher & M. Garman (Eds.), *Language acquisition.* Cambridge, UK: Cambridge University Press.

Ingram, D. (1989). *First language acquisition, method, description and explanation.* Cambridge, UK: Cambridge University Press.

Itoh, H., & Hatch, E. (1978). Second language acquisition: A case study. In E. Hatch (Ed.), *Second language acquisition.* Rowley, MA: Newbury House.

Jacob, E. (1984). Learning literacy through play: Puerto Rican kindergarten children. In H. Goelman, A. Oberg, & F. Smith (Eds.), *Awakening to literacy.* Portsmouth, NH: Heinemann Educational Books.

Jagger, A. (1980). Allowing for language differences. In G. S. Pinnell (Ed.), *Discovering language with children.* Champaign-Urbana, IL: NCTE.

Jago, C. (1989). Whose book is it anyway? *Language Arts, 66*(1), 29–43.

Jakobsen, R. (1941). *Kindersprache, Aphasie und Allgemeine Lautesetze.* Uppsala: Almquist and Wiksell.

Jakobson, R. (1968). *Child language, aphasia, and phonological universals* (A. Keiler, Trans.). The Hague: Mouton.

Jakobson, R., & Halle, M. (1956). *Fundamentals of language.* The Hague: Mouton.

Johnson, C., & Lancaster, P. (1998). The development of more than one phonology: A case study of a Norwegian-English bilingual child. *International Journal of Bilingualism (Special Issue), 2 (3).*

Johnson, D. (1990, November 4). Indian rootlessness. *The New York Times,* Sec. 4A, p. 27.

Johnson, J. M., Watkins, R. V., & Rice, M. L. (1992). Bimodal bilingual language development in a hearing child of deaf parents. *Applied Psycholinguistics 13, (1),* 31–52.

Johnston, R. S., & Rugg, M. D. (1989). Rhyme judgment ability in good and poor readers. *Language and Education, 3*(4), 223–232.

Jones, M. L., & Quigley, S. P. (1979). The acquisition of question formation in spoken English and American Sign Language by two hearing children of deaf parents. *Journal of speech and hearing disorders,* XLIV, 196–208.

Just, M. A., & Carpenter, P. A. (1987). *The psychology of reading and language comprehension.* Newton, MA: Allyn & Bacon.

Kasten, W. C. (1987). Medicine men, Bethlehem, and Pacman: Writing in a cultural content. *Anthropology and Education Quarterly, 18,* 116–125.

Kasten, W. C. (1992). Bridging the horizon: American Indian beliefs and whole language learning. *Anthropology and Education Quarterly, 23,* 108–119.

Kavanagh, J. F., & Mattingly, I. G. (1972). *Language by ear and by eye.* Cambridge, MA: MIT Press.

Kellerman, E. (1979). Transfer and non-transfer: Where we are now? *Studies in Second Language Acquisition, 2,* 37–57.

Kellerman, E. (1984). The empirical evidence for the influence of the L1 interlanguage. In A. Davies, C. Criper, & A. P. R. Howatt (Eds.), *Interlanguage.* Edinburgh: Edinburgh University Press.

Kelso, E. B. (2000). Talking to write: a mother and son at home. *Language Arts, 77* (5), 414–419.

Kerr, A. (1984). Language and the education of immigrants' children in Sweden. In C. Kennedy (Ed.), *Language planning and language education.* London: George Allen and Unwin.

Kessler, C. (1971). *The acquisition of syntax in bilingual children.* Washington, DC: Georgetown University Press.

Khubchandani, L. M. (1978). Multilingual education in India. In B. Spolsky & R. L. Cooper (Eds.), *Case studies in bilingual education.* Rowley, MA: Newbury House.

Kim, H. (1997). *Diversity among Asian American high school students.* Princeton, NJ: Educational Testing Service.

Kinsbourne, M. (1981). Neuropsychological aspects of bilingualism. In H. Winitz (Ed.), *Native language and foreign language acquisition.* New York: The New York Academy of Sciences.

Kiparsky, P., & Menn, L. (1977). On the acquisition of phonology. In J. MacNamara (Ed.), Language learning and thought. New York: Academic Press.

Kirtley, C., Bryant, P., MacLean, M., & Bradley, L. (1989). Rhyme, rime, and the onset of reading. *Journal of Experimental Child Psychology, 48,* 224–245.

Kleinfeld, J. (1985). *Alaska's small rural high schools: Are they working?* (Abridged ed.). (ED 264989). Fairbanks: University of Alaska Center for Cross-Cultural Studies.

Kornfeld, J. (1971). Theoretical issues in child phonology. *PCLS,* Seventh Regional Meeting, 454–468.

Kossan, N. (1981). Developmental differences in concept acquisition strategies. *Child Development, 52,* 290–298.

Kowal, K. H. (1998). *Rhetorical implications of linguistic relativity, theory and application to Chinese and Taiwanese interlanguages.* New York: Peter Lang.

Krashen, S. D. (1973). Lateralization, language learning, and the critical period: Some new evidence. *Language Learning, 23,* 63–74.

Krashen, S. D. (1977a). The monitor model for second language performance. In M. Burt, H. Dulay, & M. Finocchiaro, (Eds.), *Viewpoints on English as a second language.* New York: Regents.

Krashen, S. D. (1977b). Some issues relating to the monitor model. In H. Brown, C. Yorio, & R. Crymes (Eds.), *On TESOL '77.* Washington, DC: TESOL.

Krashen, S. D. (1978). Individual variation in the use of the monitor. In W. Ritchie (Ed.), *Second language acquisition research*. New York: Academic Press.

Krashen, S. D. (1979). A response to McLaughlin, 'The monitor model: Some methodological considerations.' *Language Learning, 29*, 151–167.

Krashen, S. D. (1981). *Second language acquisition and second language learning.* Oxford: Pergamon Press.

Krashen, S. D. (1982). *Principles and practices of second language acquisition.* Oxford: Pergamon Press.

Krashen, S. D. (1985). *The input hypothesis: Issues and implications.* London: Longman.

Kress, G. (2000). *Early spelling; between convention and creativity.* London: Routledge.

Kuczaj, S. A. (1999). The world of words: thoughts on the development of a lexicon. In M. Barrett (Ed.), *The development of language.* Hove, Sussex: Psychology Press.

Kuschner, D. (1989). From the personal world of childhood to the public world of school. *Language Arts, 66*(1), 44–49.

Labov, W. (1972). *Sociolinguistic patterns.* Philadelphia: University of Pennsylvania Press.

Labov, W. (1982). Objectivity and commitment in linguistic science; The case of the Black English trial in Ann Arbor. *Language in Society, 11*, 165–201.

Lake, D. T. (1989). Computers in the classroom: Teaching writing in the 1990s. *English Journal, 78*(7), 73–74.

Lalonde, R. N., Lee, P. A., & Gardner, R. C., (1987). The common view of the good language learner: An investigation of teachers' beliefs. *Canadian Modern Language Review, 44*, 16–34.

Lamendella, J. (1979). The neurofunctional basis of pattern practice. *TESOL Quarterly, 13*, 5–19.

Lanauze, M., & Snow, C. (1989). The relation between first- and second-language writing skills: Evidence from Puerto Rican elementary school children in bilingual programs. *Linguistics and Education, 1*, 323–339.

Language Files (4th ed.) (1988). Columbus, OH: The Ohio State University Department of Linguistics.

Lantolf, J. P. (1999). Second culture acquisition, cognitive considerations. In E. Hinkel, (Ed.), *Culture in second language teaching and learning* (pp. 28–46). New York: Cambridge University Press.

Lanza, E. (1997). *Language mixing in infant bilingualism, a sociolinguistic perspective.* Oxford: Clarendon Press.

Laosa, L. M. (1975). Bilingualism in three United States Hispanic Groups: Contextual use of language by children and adults in their families. *Journal of Educational Psychology, 67*(5), 617–627.

Larsen-Freeman, D. (1983). Second language acquisition: Getting the whole picture. In K. M. Bailey, M. H. Long, & S. Peck (Eds.), *Second language acquisition studies.* Rowley, MA: Newbury House.

Larsen-Freeman, D., & Long, M. (1991). *An introduction to second language acquisition research.* New York: Longman.

Lasky, R. E., Syrdal-Lasky, A., & Klein, R. E. (1975). VOT discrimination by four to six and a half month old infants from Spanish environments. *Journal of Experimental Child Psychology 20*, 215–225.

Leichter, H. J. (1984). Families as environments for literacy. In H. Goelman, A. Oberg, & F. Smith (Eds.), *Awakening to literacy*. Portsmouth, NH: Heinemann Educational Books.

Lenneberg, E. (1967). *Biological foundations of language*. New York: John Wiley & Sons.

Leong, C.K., & R.M. Joshi (Eds.). (1997). *Cross-language studies of learning to read and spell*. London: Kluwer Academic Publishers.

Leopold, W. F. (1939). *Speech development of a bilingual child: A linguist's record* (Vol. 1). Evanston, IL: Northwestern University Press.

Leopold, W. F. (1947). *Vocabulary growth in the first two years* (Vol. 2). Evanston, IL: Northwestern University Press.

Leopold, W. F. (1948). Semantic learning in infant language. *Word, 4*, 173–180.

Leopold, W. F. (1949a). Sound learning in the first two years. (Vol. 3). Evanston, IL: Northwestern University Press.

Leopold, W. F. (1949b). *Grammar and general problems in the first two years.* (Vol. 4). Evanston, IL: Northwestern University Press.

Letts, C. A. (1991). Early second language acquisition: A comparison of the linguistic output of a pre-school child acquiring English as a second language with that of a monolingual peer. *British Journal of Disorders of Communication, 26*, 219–234.

Leung, C. (1989). The multilingual classroom: The case for minority pupils. *Journal of Multilingual and Multicultural Development, 10,*(6), 461–472.

Levelt, W. J. M. (1978). Skill theory and language teaching. *Studies in second language acquisition, 1*, 53–70.

Levinson, S. C. (1997). From outer to inner space: linguistic categories and non-linguistic thinking. In J. Nuyts & E. Pederson (Eds.), *Language and conceptualization*. Cambridge, UK: Cambridge University Press.

Lewis, M., & Rosenblum, L. A. (Eds.). (1977). *Interaction, conversation, and the development of language*. New York: John Wiley & Sons.

Liberman, I. Y., Shankweiler, D., Fischer, F. W., & Carter, B. (1974). Explicit syllable and phoneme, segmentation in the young child. *Journal of Experimental Child Psychology, 18*, 201–212.

Lieven, E. V. M. (1982). Context, process and progress in young children's speech. In M. Beveridge (Ed.), *Children thinking through language*. London: Edward Arnold.

Limber, J. (1973). The genesis of complex sentences. In T. E. Moore (Ed.), *Cognitive development and the acquisition of language*. New York: Academic Press.

Lindfors, J. W. (1987). *Children's language and learning*. Upper Saddle River, NJ: Merrill/Prentice Hall.

Lindsay, A. (1992). Oral narrative discourse style of first nations children and the language of schooling. *Reflections on Canadian Literacy, 10*(4), 205–209.

Lipka, J., & McCarty, T. L. (1994). Changing the culture of schooling: Navajo and Yup'ik cases. *Anthropology and Education Quarterly, 25*(3), 266–284.

Loban, W. D. (1963). *The language of elementary school children*. Champaign-Urbana, IL: NCTE.

Loftus, E. F., Miller, D. G., & Burns, H. J. (1978). Semantic integration of verbal information into a visual memory. *Journal of Experimental Psychology, 4*, 19–31.

Loftus, E. F., & Palmer, J. C. (1974). Reconstruction of automobile destruction: an example of the interaction between language and memory. *Journal of Verbal Learning and Verbal Behaviour, 13*, 585–589.

Lorenz, K. (1971). *Studies in animal behavior.* Cambridge, MA: Harvard University Press.

Lundberg, I., Frost, J., & Petersen, O. (1988). Effects of an extensive program for stimulating phonological awareness in preschool children. *Reading Research Quarterly, XXIII/3*, 263–284.

Luria, A. R., & Yudovich, F. I. (1971). *Speech and the development of mental processes in the child.* Middlesex: Penguin Books.

Lynwander, L. (1990, October 7). Pupils get financial incentives. *The New York Times,* Sec. 12, p. 6.

MacGinitie, W. H. (1991, March). Reading instruction: Plus ça change … *Educational leadership,* pp. 55–58.

Mackay, R. (1990). Bridging the gap between practice and research: Inuit students and English instruction. *Bulletin of the Canadian Association of Applied Linguistics, 12*(1), 9–21.

Mackay, R., Barkman, B., & Jordan, R. R. (Eds.). (1979). *Reading in a second language: Hypotheses, organization, and practice.* Rowley, MA: Newbury House.

Macken, M. A. (1979). Developmental reorganization of phonology: A hierarchy of basic units of acquisition. *Lingua, 49*, 11–49.

Macken, M. A., & Barton, D. (1980). The acquisition of the voicing contrast in English: A study of voice onset time in word-initial stop consonants. *Journal of Child Language, 7*, 41–75.

MacNamara, J. (1966). *Bilingualism in primary education.* Edinburgh: Edinburgh University Press.

MacNamara, J. (Ed.). (1977). *Language learning and thought.* New York: Academic Press.

MacNamara, J. (1977). On the relation between language learning and thought. In J. MacNamara (Ed.), *Language learning and thought.* New York: Academic Press.

MacWhinney, B. (Ed.). (1987). *Mechanisms of language acquisition.* Hillsdale, NJ: Lawrence Erlbaum.

MacWhinney, B. (1987). The competition model. In B. MacWhinney (Ed.), *Mechanisms of language acquisition.* Hillsdale, NJ: Lawrence Erlbaum.

Madrid, D., & Torres, I. (1986). An experimental approach to language training in second language acquisition: Focus on negation. *Journal of Applied Behavior Analysis, 19*, 203–208.

Maestas y Moores, J. (1980). Early linguistic environment: Interactions of deaf parents with their infants. *Sign Language Studies, 26*, 1–13.

Maguire, M. H. (1989). Teaching English and French as first languages: Are changes necessary? *Bulletin of the Canadian Association of Applied Linguistics, 11*, 29–50.

Major, D. (1974). *The acquisition of modal auxiliaries in the language of children*. The Hague: Mouton.

Malsheen, B. (1980). Two hypotheses for phonetic clarification in the speech of mothers to children. In G. Yeni-Komshian, J. F. Kavanagh, & C. A. Ferguson (Eds.), *Child phonology, Perception* (Vol. 2) New York: Academic Press.

Maratsos, M., Gudeman, R., Poldi, G., & DeHart, G. (1987). A study in novel word learning: The productivity of the causative. In B. MacWhinney (Ed.), *Mechanisms of language acquisition*. Hillsdale, NJ: Lawrence Erlbaum.

Markman, E. M. (1979). Realizing that you don't understand: Elementary school children's awareness of inconsistencies. *Child Development, 50*, 543–655.

Marler, P. (1970). A comparative approach to vocal learning: Song development in white-crowned sparrows. *Journal of Comparative and Physiological Psychology, 71*, (Pt. 2) 1–25.

Marler, P. (1977). Sensory templates, vocal perception, and development: A comparative view. In M. Lewis & L. A. Rosenblum (Eds.), *Interaction, conversation, and the development of language*. New York: John Wiley & Sons.

Marshall, R., & Tucker, M. (1992). *Thinking for a living*. New York: Basic Books.

Martin-Jones, M. (1986). Review of 'Bilingualism or not: The education of minorities.' *Journal of Multilingual and Multicultural Development, 7*(4), 319–324.

Martin-Jones, M., & Romaine, S. (1986). Semilingualism: A half-baked theory of communicative competence. *Applied Linguistics, 7*(1), 26–38.

Mathes, P. G., & Torgesen, J. K. (2000). A call for equity in reading instruction for all students: A response to Allington and Woodside-Jiron. *Educational Researcher, 29* (6), 4–14.

Mattes, L. J., & Omark, D. R. (1984). *Speech and language assessment for the bilingual handicapped*. San Diego, CA: College-Hill Press.

Mayfield, M. I. (1985, December). Parents, children and reading: Helping Canadian native Indian parents of preschoolers. *The Reading Teacher.*

Mazurkewich, I., & White, L. (1984). The acquisition of the dative alternation: Unlearning overgeneralizations. *Cognition, 16*, 261–283.

McCarty, T. L., Wallace, S., Lynch, R. H., & Benally, A. (1991). Classroom inquiry and Navajo learning styles: A call for reassessment. *Anthropology and Education Quarterly, 22*, 42–59.

McCutchen, D., & Perfetti, C. A. (1982). Coherence and connectedness in the development of discourse production. *Text, 2*, 113–139.

McDermott, R. (1987). Achieving school failure: an anthropological approach to illiteracy and social stratification. In George Spindler (Ed.), *Education and cultural process: Anthropological illiteracy and social stratification*. Prospect Heights, IL: Waveland Press.

McEachern, W. R., & Luther, F. (1989). The relationship between culturally relevant materials and listening comprehension of Canadian native children. *Language, Culture, and Curriculum, 2*(1), 55–60.

McGill, J. (1988). In the history classroom. In J. Hickman & K. Kimberley, (Eds.), *Teachers, language and learning*. London: Routledge.

McLaughlin, B. (1978). *Second language acquisition in childhood*. Hillsdale, NJ: Lawrence Erlbaum.

McLaughlin, B. (1981). Differences and similarities between first and second-language learning. In H. Winitz (Ed.), *Native language and foreign language acquisition*. New York: The New York Academy of Sciences.

McLaughlin, B. (1984). *Second language acquisition in childhood: Preschool children* (Vol. 1) (2nd ed.). Hillsdale, NJ: Lawrence Erlbaum.

McLaughlin, B. (1985). *Second language acquisition in childhood: School-age children* (Vol. 2) (2nd ed.). Hillsdale, NJ: Lawrence Erlbaum.

McLaughlin, B. (1987). *Theories of second language acquisition*. London: Edward Arnold.

McLaughlin, B. (1998). Second language learning revisited: the psycholinguistic perspective. In A. Healy and L. E. Bournğe (Eds.), *Foreign Language Learning, Phycholinguistic studies on training and retention*. Mahwah, pp. 399–411, NJ: Lawrence Erlbaum Associates.

McLaughlin, B., Rossman, T., & McLeod, B. (1983). Second-language learning: An information-processing perspective. *Language Learning, 33*, 135–158.

McLeod, B., & McLaughlin, B. (1986). Restructuring or automaticity? Reading in a second language. *Language Learning, 36*, 109–123.

McMartin, P. (2001). Dick and Jane haven't a hope, the way kids are taught today. *Vancouver Sun, 23* (November), B7.

McNeill, D. (1966) Developmental psycholinguistics. In F. Smith & G. Miller (Eds.), *The genesis of language: A psycholinguistic approach*. Cambridge, MA: MIT Press.

Menn, L. (1971). Phonotactic rules in beginning speech. *Lingua, 26*, 251–255.

Menn, L. (1976). *Pattern, control, and contrast in beginning speech: A case study in the acquisition of word form and function*. Unpublished doctoral dissertation, University of Illinois.

Menn, L. (1983). Development of articulatory, phonetic, and phonological capabilities. In B. Butterworth (Ed.), *Language production* (Vol. 2). London: Academic Press.

Menn, L. (1989). Phonological development: Learning sounds and sound patterns. In J. B. Gleason (Ed.), *The development of language* (2nd ed.). Upper Saddle River, NJ: Merrill/Prentice Hall.

Menyuk, P. (1969). *Sentences children use*. Cambridge, MA: MIT Press.

Menyuk, P. (1971). *The acquisition and development of language*. Upper Saddle River NJ: Merrill/Prentice Hall.

Menyuk, P. (1999). *Reading and linguistic development*. Cambridge, MA: Brookline Books.

Michaels, S., & Cazcen, C. (1987). Teacher/child collaboration as oral preparation for literacy. In B. B. Schieffelin (Ed.), *Acquisition of literacy: Ethnographic perspectives*. Norwood, NJ: Ablex.

Mills, H., & Clyde, J. A. (Eds.). (1990). *Portraits of whole language classrooms*. Portsmouth, NH: Heinemann Educational Books.

Milon, J. P. (1975). Dialect in the TESOL program: If you never knew better. In M. Burt & H. Dulay (Eds.), *New directions in second language learning, teaching, and bilingual education*. Washington, DC: TESOL.

Mitchell, C. A. (1989). Linguistic and cultural aspects of second language acquisition: Investigating literature/literacy as an environmental factor. *Canadian Modern Language Review, 46*, 73–82.

Mitchell, R. & Myles, F. (1998). *Second language learning theories.* London: Arnold.

Mollica, A. (1989). The immersion experience. *Canadian Modern Language Review, 45*, 434.

Moore, T. E. (Ed.). (1973). *Cognitive development and the acquisition of language.* New York: Academic Press.

Morrow, L. M. (1989). *Literacy development in the early years: Helping children read and write.* Upper Saddle River, NJ: Merrill/Prentice Hall.

Moskowitz, A. (1973). On the status of vowel shift in English. In T. E. Moore (Ed.), *Cognitive development and the acquisition of language.* New York: Academic Press.

Moskowitz, B. A. (1980). Idioms in phonology acquisition and phonological change. *Journal of Phonetics, 8*, 69–83.

Murrell, M. (1966). Language acquisition in a trilingual environment: Notes from a case study. *Studia Linguistica, 20*, 9–35.

Myers, D. T. (1964). *Understanding language.* Upper Montclair, NJ: Boynton-Cook.

Nakazina, S. A. (1962). A comparative study of the speech developments of Japanese and American English in childhood (1): A comparison of the developments of voices at the prelinguistic period. *Studia Phonologica, 2*, 27–46.

National Commission on Excellence in Education. (1983). *A nation at risk: The imperative for educational reform.* Washington, DC: U.S. Government Printing Office.

Nelson, K. (1973). Structure and strategy in learning to talk. *Monographs of the Society for Child Development, 38*, 149.

Nelson, K. (1977). The conceptual basis for naming. In J. Macnamara (Ed.), *Language learning and thought.* New York: Academic Press.

Netten, J. E., & Spain, W. H. (1989). Student-teacher interaction patterns in the French immersion classroom: Implications for levels of achievement in French language proficiency. *Canadian Modern Language Review, 45*(3), 485–501.

Newman, J. (Ed.). (1985a). *Whole language theory in use.* Portsmouth, NH: Heinemann Educational Books.

Newman, J. (1985b). Using children's books to teach reading. In J. Newman (Ed.), *Whole language theory in use* (chap. 4). Portsmouth, NH: Heinemann Educational Books.

Newman, J. (1985c). What about reading? In J. Newman (Ed.), *Whole language theory in use* (chap. 9). Portsmouth, NH: Heinemann Educational Books.

Newport, E. (1976). Motherese: The speech of mothers to young children. In N. Castellan, D. Pisoni, & G. Potts (Eds.), *Cognitive theory* (Vol. 2). Hillsdale, NJ: Lawrence Erlbaum.

Nickse, R. S. (1989). *The noises of literacy: An overview of intergenerational and family literacy programs* (ERIC Document Reproduction Service No. ED 308 415). Washington, DC: Office of Educational Research and Improvement.

Nieto, S. (1994). Lessons from students on creating a chance to dream. *Harvard Educational Review, 64*(4), 392–426.

Nieto, S. (2000). *The sociopolitical context of multicultural education*. New York: Longman.

Nova. (1997, March 24). *Secret of a wild child*. New York and Washington, DC: Public Broadcasting Service. Retrieved from *http://www.pbs.org/wgbh/nova/transcripts/2112gchild.html*

Nuyts, J., & Pederson, E. (Eds.). (1997). *Language and conceptualization*. Cambridge, UK: Cambridge University Press.

Obler, L. K., & Gjerlow, K. (1999). *Language and the brain*. Cambridge: Cambridge University Press.

O'Connor, N. M., & Rotatori, A. F. (1987). Culturally diverse special education students. In A. Rotatori, M. M. Banbury, & R. A. Fox, (Eds.), *Issues in special education*. Mountain View, CA: Mayfield Publishing.

Oksaar, E. (1970). Zum Spracherwerb des Kindes in zweisprachiger Umgebung. *Folia Linguistica, 4*, 330–358.

Oldford-Matchim, J. (1995). *Help your child become a better writer*. Clearwater, FL: Global Publishing.

Olson, D. R. (1977). The contexts of language acquisition. *Language learning and thought*. New York: Academic Press.

Olson, D. R. (1984). "See! Jumping!" Some oral language antecedents of literacy. In H. Goelman, A. Oberg, & F. Smith (Eds.), *Awakening to literacy*. Portsmouth, NH: Heinemann Educational Books.

Olson, R. K., & Wise, B. W. (1992). Reading on the computer with orthographic and speech feedback. *Reading and Writing: An Interdisciplinary Journal, 4*, 107–144.

O'Malley, J. M., Chamot, A. U., & Walker, C. (1987). Some applications of cognitive theory to second language acquisition. *Studies in Second Language Acquisition, 9*, 287–306.

Omark, D. R., & Erickson, J. G. (Eds.). (1983). *The bilingual exceptional child*. San Diego, CA: College-Hill Press.

O'Neill, C. (1989). Dialogue and drama: The transformation of events, ideas, and teachers. *Language Arts; 66*(2), 147–159.

Oritz, F. I. (1988). Hispanic-American children's experiences in classrooms: A comparison between Hispanic and Non-Hispanic children. In L. Weis (Ed.), *Class, race and gender in American education*. Albany: SUNY Press.

Over, W. (1998). Contemporary advocacy and intercultural communication. In K. S. Sitaram & M. H. Prosser (Eds.), *Civic discourse: multiculturalism, cultural diversity, and global communication*. pp. 95–107. Stamford, CT: Ablex.

Page, M. M. (1966). We dropped FLES. *Modern Language Journal, 50*, 139–141.

Pan, B. A., & Snow, C. E. (1999). The development of conversational and discourse skills. In M. Barrett (Ed.), *The development of language*. Hove, Sussex: Psychology Press.

Paradis, M. (Ed.). (1978). *Aspects of bilingualism*. Columbia, SC: Hornbeam.

Parlee, M. (1979). Conversational politics. *Psychology Today, 5*, 48–56.

Peal, E., & Lambert, W. (1962). The relation of bilingualism to intelligence. *Psychological Monographs, LXXVI 27*, 1–23.

Pease, D. M., Gleason, J. B., & Pan, B. A. (1989). Gaining meaning: Semantic development. In J. B. Gleason (Ed.), *The development of language*, (2nd ed.). Upper Saddle River, NJ: Merrill/Prentice Hall.

Penfield, W., & Roberts, L. (1959). *Speech and brain mechanisms.* Princeton, NJ: Princeton University Press.

Penner, P. G., & McConnell, R. E. (1980). *Learning language.* Toronto, ON: Gage Publishing Ltd.

Penner, S. (1987). Parental responses to grammatical and ungrammatical child utterances. *Child Development, 58,* 376–384.

Perera, K. (1984). *Children's writing and reading: Analyzing classroom language.* Oxford: Basil Blackwell.

Perfetti, C. A. (1984). *Reading ability.* New York: Oxford University Press.

Perozzi, Joseph A. (1985). A pilot study of language facilitation for bilingual, language-handicapped children: Theoretical and intervention implications. (1985). *Journal of speech and hearing disorders, 50,* 403–406.

Perry, T., & Delpit, L. (Eds.). (1999). *The real ebonics debate; power, language, and the education of African-American children.* Boston: Beacon Press.

Pew Research Center. (1998). *Online newcomers more middle-brow, less work-oriented: The internet news audience goes ordinary.* Retrieved from http://208.240.91.18/tech98sum.htm

Pflaum, S. W. (1986). *The development of language and literacy in young children.* Upper Saddle River, NJ: Merrill/Prentice Hall.

Phillips, C. J., & Birrell, H. V. (1994). Number learning of Asian pupils in English primary schools. *Educational Research, 36*(1), 51–62.

Phinney, M. (1981). Children's interpretation of negation in complex sentences. In S. L. Tavakolian (Ed.), *Language acquisition and linguistic theory.* Cambridge, MA: MIT Press.

Piaget, J. (1955). *The language and thought of the child.* Cleveland, OH: World Publishing.

Piaget, J. (1962). *Play, dreams and imitation in childhood.* New York: Norton.

Piaget, J., & Inhelder, B. (1969). *The psychology of the child.* New York: Basic Books.

Pinker, S. (1984). *Language, learnability and language development.* Cambridge, MA: Harvard University Press.

Pinker, S. (1994). *The language instinct: The new science of language and mind.* London: Penguin.

Pinnell, G. S. (Ed.). (1980). *Discovering language with children.* Champaign-Urbana, IL: NCTE.

Piper, D. (1992). *Language theories and educational practice.* San Francisco: Mellon Research University Press.

Piper, T. (1983). Phonics for ESL learners. *Reading-Canada-Lecture, 2,* 56–62.

Piper, T. (1984a). Phonological processes in the ESL learner. *TESL Canada Journal, 1,* 71–80.

Piper, T. (1984b). Observations on the second language acquisition of the English sound system. *The Canadian Modern Language Review, 40,* 542–551.

Piper, T. (1984c). Successive approximation in second language acquisition. *Canadian Journal of Linguistics, 29*, 2.

Piper, T. (1986a). A tale of two learners. *Canadian Children, 11*(1), 41–60.

Piper, T. (1986b). The role of prior linguistic experience on second language acquisition. *Reading-Canada-Lecture, 4*, 68–81.

Piper, T. (1986c). Learning about language learning. *Language Arts, 65*, 466–471.

Piper, T. (1987). On the difference between L1 and L2 acquisition of phonology. *Canadian Journal of Linguistics, 32*, 245–259.

Piper, T., & McEachern, W. R. (1988). Content bias in cloze as a general language indicator. *English Quarterly, 1*, 41–48.

Pisoni & Potts, G. (Eds.), *Cognitive theory* (Vol. 2). Hillsdale, NJ: Lawrence Erlbaum.

Porter, J. (1977): A cross-sectional study of morpheme acquisition in first language learners. *Language Learning, 27*(1), 47–62.

Potter, G. (1989). Parent participation in language arts programs. *Language Arts, 66*(1), 29–43.

Power, D., & Quigley, S. (1973). Deaf children's acquisition of the passive voice. *Journal of Speech and Hearing Research, 25*(16), 5–11.

Premack, A. J. (1976). *Why chimps can read.* New York: Harper & Row.

Premack, D., & Premack, A. J. (1983). *The mind of an ape.* New York Norton.

Priest, G. E. (1985). Aboriginal languages in Canada. *Language and Society, 15,* 13–19. Ottawa, ON: Commissioner of Official Languages.

Prinz, P. M., & Prinz, E. A. (1979). Simultaneous acquisition of ASL and spoken English in a hearing child of a deaf mother and hearing father: Phase I: Early lexical development. *Sign Language Studies, 25*, 283–296.

Prinz, P. M., & Prinz, E. A. (1981). Acquisition of ASL and spoken English by a hearing child of a deaf mother and a hearing father: Phase II, early combinatorial patterns. *Sign Language Studies, 30*, 78–88.

Prior, M. (1996). *Understanding specific learning difficulties.* Hove, UK: Psychology Press.

Pyles, T., & Algeo, J. (1970). *English: An introduction to language.* New York: Harcourt, Brace, & World.

Quigley, S., Montanelli, D., & Wilbur, R. B. (1976). Some aspects of the verb system in the language of deaf students. *Journal of Speech and Hearing Research, 19*, 536–550.

Quigley, S., Smith, N., & Wilbur, R. B. (1974). Comprehension of relativized sentences by deaf students. *Journal of Speech and Hearing Research, 17*, 325–341.

Quigley, S., Wilbur, R. B. & Montanelli, D. (1974). Question formation in the language of deaf students. *Journal of Speech and Hearing Research, 17*, 699–713.

Quigley, S., Wilbur, R. B., & Montanelli, D. (1976). Complement structures in the language of deaf students. *Journal of Speech and Hearing Research, 19*, 448–457.

Raffler, E. W. von (1973). The development from sound to phoneme in child language. In C. A. Ferguson & D. Slobin (Eds.), *Studies of child language development.* New York: Holt, Rinehart, & Winston.

Rasinski, T. V., & Fredericks, A. D. (1989, December). What do parents think about reading in the schools? *The Reading Teacher,* pp. 262–263.

Ratner, N. B. (1989). Atypical language development. In J. B. Gleason (Ed.), *The development of language*, (2nd ed.). Upper Saddle River, NJ: Merrill/Prentice Hall.

Ratner, N. B. (1993). Atypical language development. In J. Berko-Gleason (Ed.), *The development of language*, (3rd ed.). Upper Saddle River, NJ: Merrill/Prentice Hall.

Reddy, V. (1999). Prelinguistic communication. In Barrett, M. (Ed.). *The development of language*. Hove, UK: Psychology Press.

Reich, P. A. (1986). *Language development*. Upper Saddle River, NJ: Merrill/Prentice Hall.

Resnick, D. P., & Resnick, L. B. (1985). Standards, curriculum, and performance: A historical and comparative perspective. *Educational Researcher, 14*(4), 5–21.

Reuters. (1998, February 14). *For want of vocal cords: Talking: Not just for humans anymore?* Retrieved from *http://www.geocities.com/RainForest/Vines/4451/ForWant OfVocalCords.html*

Richards, J. (Ed.). (1978). *Understanding second and foreign language learning: Issues and approaches.* Rowley, MA: Newbury House.

Richards, J., Platt, J., & Weber, H. (1985). *Longman dictionary of applied linguistics.* London: Longman.

Richards, J. C., & Rodgers, T. S. (1986). *Approaches and methods in language teaching.* Cambridge, UK: Cambridge University Press.

Ridley, L. (1990a, May). Enacting change in elementary school programs: Implementing a whole language perspective. *The Reading Teacher*, pp. 640–646.

Ridley, L. (1990b). Whole language in the ESL classroom. In H. Mills & J. A. Clyde (Eds.). *Portraits of whole language classrooms* (chap. 11). Portsmouth, NH: Heinemann Educational Books.

Rigg, P., & Allen, V. G. (Eds.). (1989). *When they don't all speak English.* Champaign-Urbana, IL: NCTE.

Ritchie, W. (Ed.). (1978). *Second language acquisition research.* New York: Academic Press.

Rodríguez- Rodríguez, A. L. (1998). How global is global? A critical look at the language and ideology of globalization. In K. S. Sitaram & M. H. Prosser, (Eds.), *Civic discourse: Multiculturalism, cultural diversity, and global communication* (pp. 83–93). Stamford, CT: Ablex Publishing Corporation.

Roeper, T., Lapointe, S., Bing, J., & Tavakolian, S. (1981). A lexical approach to language acquisition. In S. L. Tavakolian (Ed.), *Language acquisition and linguistic theory.* Cambridge, MA: MIT Press.

Rogers, S. (Ed.). (1975). *Children and language.* London: Oxford University Press.

Roller, C. (1989). Classroom interaction patterns: Reflections of a stratified society. *Language Arts, 66*(5), 492–500.

Romney, J. C., Romney, D. M., & Braun, C. (1989). The effects of reading aloud in French to immersion children on second language acquisition. *Canadian Modern Language Review, 45,* 530–538.

Rondal, J. A. (1980). Fathers' and mothers' speech in early language development. *Journal of Child Language, 7,* 353–369.

Ronjat, J. (1913). *Le développement du langage observé chez un enfant bilingue.* Paris: Champion.

Rosch, E., & Mervis, C. B. (1975). Family resemblances: Studies in the internal structure of categories. *Cognitive Psychology, 8,* 382–439.

Rosch, E., Mervis, C. B., Gray, W. D., Johnson, D. M., & Boyes-Braem, P. (1976). Basic objects in natural categories. *Cognitive Psychology, 8,* 382–439.

Rosier, P., & Farella, M. (1976). Bilingual education at Rock Point—some early results. *TESOL Quarterly, 10*(4), 379–388.

Roth, F. P., & Davidge, N. S. (1985). Are early verbal communicative intentions universal? A preliminary investigation. *Journal of Psycholinguistic Research, 14*(4), 351–363.

Ruke-Dravina, V. (1965). The process of acquisition of apical /r/ and uvular /r/ in the speech of children. *Linguistics, 17,* 56–68.

Ruke-Dravina, V. (1967). *Mehrsprachigkeit im Vorschulalter.* Lund: Gleerup.

Sachs, J. (1989). Communication development in infancy. In J. B. Gleason (Ed.), *The development of language* (2nd ed.). Upper Saddle River, NJ: Merrill/Prentice Hall.

Saer, D. J. (1922). An enquiry into the effects of bilingualism upon the intelligence of young children. *Journal of Experimental Pedagogy, 6.*

Samovar, L. A., Porter, R. E., & Stefani, S. L. A. (1998). *Communication between cultures* (3rd ed.). Belmont, CA: Wadsworth Publishing Co.

Savage-Rumbaugh, E.S., Shaker, S., & Taylor, T. (1998). *Apes, language and the human mind.* Oxford: Oxford University Press.

Saville-Troike, M. (1980). Discovering what children know about language. In G. S. Pinnell (Ed.), *Discovering language with children.* Champaign-Urbana, IL: NCTE.

Schacter, F. F., Kirshner, K., Klips, B., Friedrickes, M., & Sanders, K. (1974). Everyday preschool interpersonal speech usage: Methodological development and sociolinguistic studies. In *Monographs of the Society for Research and Child Development.* Chicago: University of Chicago.

Schickedanz, J. D., York, M. E., Stewart, I. S., & White, D. (1990). *Strategies for teaching young children* (3rd ed.). Upper Saddle River, NJ: Merrill/Prentice Hall.

Schieffelin, B. B., & Cochran-Smith, M. (1984). Learning to read culturally: Literacy before schooling. In H. Goelman, A. Oberg, & F. Smith (Eds.), *Awakening to literacy.* Portsmouth, NH: Heinemann Educational Books.

Schieffelin, B. B., & Ochs, E. (1983). A cultural perspective on the transition from prelinguistic to linguistic communication. In R. M. Golinkoff (Ed.), *The transition from preverbal to verbal communication.* Hillsdale, NJ: Lawrence Erlbaum.

Schiff, N. B., & Ventry, I. M. (1976). Communication problems in hearing children of deaf parents. *Journal of Speech and Hearing Disorders, XLI,* 348–358.

Schlesinger, I. M. (1977). The role of cognitive development and linguistic input in language acquisition. *Child Language, 4,* 153–169.

Schumann, J. (1978a). *The pidginization process: A model for second language acquisition.* Rowley, MA: Newbury House.

Schumann, J. (1978b). Social and psychological factors in second language acquisition. In J. Richards (Ed.), *Understanding second and foreign language learning: Issues and approaches.* Rowley, MA: Newbury House.

Schumann, J. (1978c). The acculturation model for second language acquisition. In R. Gingras (Ed.), *Second language acquisition and foreign language teaching.* Arlington, VA: Center for Applied Linguistics.

Schumann, J. (1981a). Discussion of "Two perspectives on pidginization as second language acquisition." In R. Anderson (Ed.), *New dimensions in second language acquisition research.* Rowley, MA: Newbury House.

Schumann, J. (1981b). Reaction to Gilbert's discussion of Andersen's paper. In R. Andersen (Ed.), *New dimensions in second language acquisition research.* Rowley, MA: Newbury House.

Schumann, J. (1982). Simplification, transfer and relexification as aspects of pidginization and early second language acquisition. *Language Learning, 32,* 337–366.

Scollon, R., & Scollon, S. (1983). *Narrative, literacy and face in interethnic communication.* Norwood, NJ: Ablex.

Scovel, T. (1982). Questions concerning the application of neurolinguistic research to second language learning/teaching. *TESOL Quarterly, 16,* 323–331.

Scoville, R. (1983). Development of the intention to communicate: The eye of the beholder. In L. Feagans, C. Garvey, & R. Golinkoff (Eds.), *The origins and growth of communication.* Norwood, NJ: Ablex.

Segalowitz, N. (1986). Skilled reading in the second language. In J. Vaid (Ed.), *Language processing in bilinguals: Psycholinguistic and neuropsychological perspectives.* Hillsdale, NJ: Lawrence Erlbaum.

Selinker, L. (1972). Interlanguage. *International Review of Applied Linguistics X,* 209–230.

Selinker, L., & Lamendella, J. (1976). Two perspectives on fossilization in interlanguage learning. *Interlanguage Studies Bulletin, 3,* 144–191.

Selinker, L., Swain, M., & Dumas, G. (1975). The interlanguage hypothesis extended to children. *Language Learning, 25,* 139–191.

Serebrin, W. (1985). Andrew and Molly, writers and context in concert. In J. Newman (Ed.), *Whole language theory in use.* Portsmouth, NH: Heinemann Educational Books.

Seymour, P. H. K., & Elder, L. (1986). Beginning reading without phonology. *Cognitive Neuropsychology, 3,* 1–36.

Shacter, F. F., Kirshner, K., Klips, B., Friedrickes, M., & Sanders, K. (1974). Everyday preschool interpersonal speech usage: Methodological development and sociolinguistic studies. In *Monographs of the Society for Research and Child Development.* Chicago: University of Chicago Press.

Shafer, R. E., Staab, C., & Smith, K. (1983). *Language functions and school success.* Glenview, IL: Scott, Foresman & Co.

Shapiro, J. (1990). Research perspectives on whole language. In V. Froese (Ed.), *Whole-language practice and theory* (pp. 268–305). Scarborough, ON: Prentice-Hall Canada, Inc.

Shvachkin, N. (1973). The development of phonemic speech perception in early childhood. In C. A. Ferguson & D. I. Slobin (Eds.), *Studies of child language development.* New York: Holt, Rinehart, & Winston.

Siegler, R. S. (1986). *Children's thinking.* (1st ed.). Upper Saddle River, NJ: Merrill/Prentice Hall.

Siegler, R. S. (1991). *Children's thinking* (2nd ed.). Upper Saddle River, NJ: Merrill/Prentice Hall.

Sinclair, H. (1977). The cognitive basis of the comprehension and production of relational terminology. *Journal of Experimental Child Psychology, 24,* 40–52.

Sitaram, K.S., & Prosser, M. H. (Eds.). (1998). *Civic discourse: multiculturalism, cultural diversity, and global communication.* Stamford, CT: Ablex.

Skinner, B. F. (1957). *Verbal behavior.* Upper Saddle River, NJ: Merrill/Prentice Hall.

Skuktnabb-Kangas, T. (1984). *Bilingualism or not: The education of minorities.* Clevedon, UK: Multilingual Matters Ltd.

Slobin, D. (1966). Comments on developmental psycholinguistics. In F. Smith & G. Miller (Eds.), *The genesis of language: A psycholinguistic approach.* Cambridge, MA: MIT Press.

Slobin, D. (1971). *Psycholinguistics.* Glenview, IL: Scott, Foresman & Company.

Slobin, D. (1973). Cognitive prerequisites for the acquisition of grammar. In C. A. Ferguson & D. I. Slobin (Eds.), *Studies of child language development.* New York: Holt, Rinehart, & Winston.

Slobin, D. (1979). *Psycholinguistics* (2nd ed.). Glenview, IL: Scott, Foresman & Company.

Slobin, D. (1982). Universal and particular in the acquisition of language. In E. Wanner & L. Gleitman (Eds.), *Language acquisition: The state of the art.* Cambridge, UK: Cambridge University Press.

Slobin, D. (Ed.). (1985). *The cross-linguistic study of language acquisition: The data.* (Vol. 1). Hillsdale, NJ: Lawrence Erlbaum.

Slobin, D., Dasinger, L., Aylin, K., & Toupin, C. (1993). Native language reacquisition in early childhood. *Proceedings of the twenty-fourth annual child language research forum.* San Francisco: Center for the Study of Language and Information, 179–196.

Smith, C. (1991). Family literacy: The most important literacy. *The Reading Teacher, 44*(9), 700–701.

Smith, E. B., Goodman, K. S., & Meredith, R. (1976). *Language and thinking in school* (2nd ed.). New York: Holt, Rinehart, & Winston.

Smith, F. (1975). *Comprehension and learning: A conceptual framework for teachers.* New York: Holt, Rinehart, & Winston.

Smith, F. (1983). *Essays into literacy.* Portsmouth, NH: Heinemann Educational Books.

Smith, F. (1984). The creative achievement of literacy. In H. Goelman, A. Oberg, & F. Smith (Eds.), *Awakening to literacy.* Portsmouth, NH: Heinemann Educational Books.

Smith, F. (1985). *Reading without nonsense* (2nd ed.). New York: Teachers College Press.

Smith, F. (1988). *Joining the literacy club: Further essays into education.* Portsmouth, NH: Heinemann Educational Books.

Smith, F., & Miller, G. (Eds.). (1966). *The genesis of language: A psycholinguistic approach.* Cambridge, MA: MIT Press.

Smith, M. E. (1933). A study of the speech of bilingual children in Hawaii. *Psychological Bulletin, 30.*

Smith, M. E. (1935). A study of the speech of eight bilingual children of the same family. *Child Development, 6,* 19–25.

Smith, N. V. (1973). *The acquisition of phonology: A case study.* London: Cambridge University Press.

Smolkin, L. B., & Suina, J. H. (1996). Lost in language and language lost: Considering native language in classrooms. *Language Arts, 73,* 166–172.

Snow, C. (1972). Mother's speech to children learning language. *Child Development, 43,* 549–565.

Snow, C. (1979). The role of social interaction in language acquisition. In W. A. Collins (Ed.), *Minnesota symposia on child psychology* (Vol. 12). Hillsdale, NJ: Lawrence Erlbaum.

Snow, C., & Ninio, A. (1986). The contracts of literacy: What children learn from learning to read books. In W. H. Teale & E. Sulzby (Eds.), *Emergent literacy: Writing and reading.* Norwood, NJ: Ablex.

Snowling, M. J., Hulme, C., Smith, A., & Thomas, J. (1994). The effects of phonetic similarity and list length on children's sound categorization performance. *Journal of Experimental Child Psychology, 58,* 160–180.

Snowling, M. J., Stackhouse, J., & Rack, J. (1986). Phonological dyslexia and dysgraphia— a developmental analysis. *Cognitive Neuropsychology, 3*(3), 309–339.

Snyder, G. (1990). Parents, teachers, children and whole-language. In V. Froese (Ed.). *Whole-language practice and theory.* Scarborough, ON: Prentice-Hall Canada, Inc.

Soldier, L. L. (1985). The whys and wherefores of native American bilingual education. *The Urban Review, 17*(4), 225–232.

Soudek, L. I. (1981). Two languages in one brain: Recent work in neurolinguistics and its implications for second-language learning. *English Language Teaching Journal, 35,* 219–224.

Spolsky, B. (1978). *Educational linguistics.* Rowley, MA: Newbury House.

Spolsky, B. (1985). Formulating a theory of second language learning. *Studies in Second Language Acquisition, 7,* 269–288.

Spolsky, B., & Cooper, R. L. (Eds.). (1978). *Case studies in bilingual education.* Rowley, MA: Newbury House.

St. Germaine, R. (1995). *Dropout rates among American Indian and Alaska native students: beyond cultural discontinuity.* Doc. 388492. New York: ERIC/Cress Publications.

St. Germaine, R. (1995a). Bureau schools adopt Goals 2000. *Journal of American Indian Education, 35* (1), 38–43.

St. Germaine, R. (1995b). BIA schools complete first step of reform effort. *Journal of American Indian Education, 35* (1), 30–38.

Staab, C. (1990). Talk in whole-language classrooms. In V. Froese (Ed.), *Whole-language practice and theory* (chap. 2). Scarborough, ON: Prentice-Hall Canada, Inc.

Staab, C. (1991). Teachers' practices with regard to oral language. *Alberta Journal of Educational Research, 37*(1), 31–48.

Stampe, D. (1979). *A dissertation on natural phonology*, J. E. Hankamer (Ed.). New York: Garland Publishing Company.

Steiner-Khamsi, G. (1990). Community languages and anti-racist education: The open battlefield. *Educational Studies, 16*(1), 33–47.

Stephens, D., Huntsman, R., O'Neill, K., Story, J., Watson, V., & Toomes, J. (1990). We call it good teaching. In H. Mills & J. A. Clyde (Eds.), *Portraits of whole language classrooms* (chap. 15). Portsmouth, NH: Heinemann Educational Books.

Stern, D., Beebe, B., Jaffe, J., & Bennett, S. (1977). The infant's stimulus world during social interaction: A study of caregiver behaviors with particular reference to repetition and timing. In H. Schaffer (Ed.), *Studies in mother-infant interaction*. New York: Academic Press.

Stevick, E. W. (1990). *Humanism in language teaching.* Oxford, UK: Oxford University Press.

Strickland, D. S. (1994). Educating African American learners at risk: Finding a better way. *Language Arts, 71*(5), 328–336.

Strickland, D. S., & Morrow, L. M. (Eds.). (1989). *Emerging literacy: Young children learn to read and write.* Newark, DE: The International Reading Association.

Strickland, R. G. (1962). The language of elementary school children: Its relationship to the language of reading textbooks and the quality of reading of selected children. *Bulletin of the School of Education, 38*(4). Bloomington, IN: University of Indiana.

Stringer, D., Bruce, D., & Oates, J. (1973). *Generative linguistics: An introduction to the work of Noam Chomsky; Language acquisition: Language and cognition.* Milton Keynes, UK: The Open University Press.

Stuart, M., & Coltheart, M. (1988). Does reading develop in a sequence of stages? *Cognition, 30,* 139–181.

Stubbs, M. (1986). *Educational linguistics.* Oxford, UK: Basil Blackwell.

Sullivan, M. W., Rovee-Collier, C. K., & Tynes, D. M. (1979). A conditioning analysis of infant long-term memory. *Child Development, 50,* 152–162.

Swain, M. (1974). French immersion programs across Canada: Research findings. *Canadian Modern Language Review, 31,* 117–129.

Swain, M. (1976). Bibliography: Research on immersion education for the majority child. *Canadian Modern Language Review, 32,* 592–596.

Swain, M. (1978). French immersion: Early, late or partial? *Canadian Modern Language Review, 34,* 557–585.

Swain, M. (1979). Bilingual education: Research and its implications. In C. Yorio, K. Perkins, & J. Schachter (Eds.), *On TESOL 1979: The learner in focus.* Washington, DC: TESOL.

Swain, M., Barik, H., & Nwanunobi, E. (1973). *Bilingual education project: Evaluation of Elgin County Board of Education partial immersion program for grades one, two and three.* Unpublished Paper. Toronto, ON: Ontario Institute for Studies in Education.

Swain, M., & Lapkin, S. (1982). *Evaluating bilingual education: A Canadian case study.* Clevedon, UK: Multilingual Matters.

Swacher, M. (1975). The sex of the speaker as a sociolinguistic variable. In B. Thorne & N. Henley (Eds.), *Language and sex: Difference and dominance*. Rowley, MA: Newbury House.

Swinburne, A. C. (1887). March: An Ode. *Swinburne's Collected Poetical Works*, vols. 1–2 London: William Heinemann, I, 465–69.

Swisher, K., & Hoisch, M. (1992). Dropping out among American Indians and Alaska Natives: A review of studies. *Journal of American Indian Education, 31*(2), 3–23.

Tabors, P. O. (1997). *One child, two languages, a guide for preschool educators of children learning English as a second language*. Baltimore: Paul H. Brookes.

Tabouret-Keller, A. (1962). L'acquisition du language parle chez un petit enfant en milieu bilingue. *Problemes de Psycholinguistique, 8*, 205–219.

Tager-Flusberg, H. (1989). Putting words together: Morphology and syntax in the preschool years. In J. B. Gleason (Ed.), *The development of language*, (2nd ed.). Upper Saddle River, NJ: Merrill/Prentice Hall.

Tardif, C., & Weber, S. (1987). French immersion research: A call for new perspectives. *Canadian Modern Language Review, 44*, 67–78.

Tarone, E. (1982). Systematicity and attention in interlanguage. *Language Learning, 30*, 417–431.

Tartter, V. C. (1998). *Language processing in atypical populations*. London: SAGE Publications.

Tavakolian, S. L. (Ed.). (1981). *Language acquisition and linguistic theory*. Cambridge, MA: MIT Press.

Taylor, D. M., Wright, S. C., Ruggiero, K. M., & Aitchison, M. C. (1993). Language perceptions among the Inuit of arctic Quebec: The future role of the heritage language. *Journal of Language and Social Psychology, 12*(3), 195–206.

Taylor, I. (1998). Learning to read in Chinese, Korean, and Japanese. In A. Y. Durğunoğlu & L. Verhoeven (Eds.), *Literacy development in a multilingual context cross-cultural perspectives* (pp. 225–248). Mahwah, NJ: Lawrence Erlbaum Associates.

Teale, W. H. (1986). Home background and young children's literacy development. In W. H. Teale & E. Sulzby (Eds.), *Emergent literacy: Writing and reading*. Norwood, NJ: Ablex.

Teale, W. H., & Sulzby, E. (Eds.). (1986). *Emergent literacy: writing and reading*. Norwood, NJ: Ablex Publishing.

Teitelbaum, H., & Hiller, R. J. (1977). The legal perspective. In *Bilingual education: Current perspectives (Law), 3*, (pp. 1–64). Arlington, VA: Center for Applied Linguistics.

Temple, C., & Gillet, J. W. (1989). *Language arts: Learning processes and teaching practices*. Glenview, IL: Scott, Foresman, & Company.

Templin, M. C. (1957). *Certain language skills in children: Their development and interrelationships*. (Institute of Child Welfare Monograph 26). Minneapolis, MN: University of Minnesota Press.

Terrace, H. S. (1980). *Nim: A chimpanzee who learned sign language*. New York: Knopf.

Thomas, L., and Waering, S. (Eds.). (1999). *Language, society and power.* London: Routledge.

Tierney, R. J. (1983). Writer-reader transactions: Defining the dimensions of negotiation. In P. L. Stock (Ed.), *Forum: Essays on theory and practice in the teaching of writing* (pp. 147–151). Upper Montclair, NJ: Boynton-Cook.

Tierney, R. J., & Pearson, P. D. (1984). Toward a composing model of reading. In J. M. Jensen (Ed.), *Composing and comprehending.* Champaign-Urbana, IL: NCRE/ERIC.

Titone, R., & Danesi, M. (1985). *Applied psycholinguistics: An introduction to the psychology of language learning and teaching.* Toronto, ON: University of Toronto Press.

Tittle, C. E. (1973). Women and educational testing. *Phi Delta Kappan, 55*(2), 118–119.

Torrey, J. W. (1973). Learning to read without a teacher: A case study. In F. Smith (Ed.), *Psycholinguistics and reading.* New York: Holt, Rinehart, & Winston.

Totten, G. O. (1960). Bringing up children bilingually. *American Scandinavian Review, 48,* 42–50.

Tough, J. (1977). *The development of meaning.* London: Allen & Unwin.

Tough, J. (1979). *Talk for teaching and learning.* London: Ward Lock Educational.

Toukomaa, P., & Skutnabb-Kangas, T. (1977). *The intensive teaching of the mother tongue to migrant children of pre-school age and children in the lower level of comprehensive school.* Helsinki: The Finnish National Commission for UNESCO.

Treiman, R. (1985). Onsets and rimes as units of spoken syllables: Evidence from children.

Treiman, R., & Zukowski, A. (1988). Units in reading and spelling. *Journal of Memory and Language, 27,* 466–477.

Triandis, H. C. (1972). *The analysis of subjective culture.* New York: Wiley.

Trybus, R., & Karchmer, M. (1977). School achievement scores of hearing impaired children: National data on achievement status and growth patterns. *American Annals of the Deaf, 122,* 62–69.

Tucker, G. R., & Gray, T. C. (1980). The pursuit of equal opportunity. *Language and Society, 2,* 5–8.

Tulving, E. (1983). *Elements of episodic memory.* New York: Oxford University Press.

Vaid, J. (Ed.). (1986). *Language processing in bilinguals: Psycholinguistic and neuropsychological perspectives.* Hillsdale, NJ: Lawrence Erlbaum.

Valian, V., Winzemer, J., & Erreich, A. (1981). A 'little linguist' model of syntax learning. In S. L. Tavakolian (Ed.), *Language acquisition and linguistic theory.* Cambridge, MA: MIT Press.

Van Buren, P. (1975). Semantics and language teaching. In J. P. B. Allen & S. P. Corder (Eds.), *The Edinburgh course in applied linguistics: Papers in applied linguistics* (Vol. 2). London: Oxford University Press.

Van Keulen, J. E., Weddington, G. T., & DeBose, C. E. (1998). *Speech, language, learning, and the African American child.* Boston: Allyn and Bacon.

Van Lawick-Goodall, J. (1971). *In the shadow of man.* Boston: Houghton Mifflin.

Velten, H. V. (1943). The growth of phonetic and lexical pattern in infant language. *Language, 19,* 281–292.

Vihman, M. M., & McLaughlin, B. (1982). Bilingualism and second language acquisition in preschool children. In C. J. Brainerd, & M. Pressley (Eds.), *Progress in cognitive development research: Verbal processes in children*. Berlin: Springer Verlag.

Vocolo, J. M. (1967). The effect of foreign language study in the elementary school upon achievement in the same language in high school. *Modern Language Journal, 51*, 463–469.

Volk, D. (1999). "The teaching and the enjoyment and being together...": Sibling teaching in the family of a Puerto Rican kindergartner. *Early Childhood Research Quarterly, 14* (1), 5–34.

Vorih, L., & Rosier, P. (1978). Rock Point community school: An example of a Navajo-English bilingual elementary school program. *TESOL Quarterly, 12*(3), 263–269.

Voss, M. M. (1988). "Make way for applesauce": The literate world of a three year old. *Language Arts, 65*(3), 272–278.

Vygotsky, L. S. (1962). *Thought and language*. Cambridge, MA: MIT Press.

Waering, S. (1999a). Language and gender. In L. Thomas & S. Waering (Eds.), *Language, society and power*. London: Routledge.

Waering, S. (1999b). What is language and what does it do? In L. Thomas & S. Waering (Eds.), *Language, society and power*. London: Routledge.

Wagner, R. K., & Torgesen, J. K. (1987). The nature of phonological processing and its causal role in the acquisition of reading skills. *Psychological Bulletin, 101*(2), 192–212.

Walkerdine, V. (1982). From context to text: A psychosomatic approach to abstract thought. In M. Beveridge (Ed.), *Children thinking through language*. London: Edward Arnold.

Wan, G. (2000). A Chinese girl's storybook experience at home. *Language Arts, 77*, (5), 398–405.

Ward, A. (1990). Communicative inequality: The participation of native Indian and non-native children in instructional dialogue in a cross-cultural kindergarten class. *Reflections on Canadian Literacy, 8*(1), 22–28.

Wardhaugh, R. (1998). *An introduction to sociolinguistics*. Malden, MA: Blackwell.

Warren-Leubecker, A. W., & Bohannon, J. N. (1989). Pragmatics: Language in social contexts. In J. Gleason (Ed.), *The development of language*, (2nd ed.). Upper Saddle River, NJ: Merrill/Prentice Hall.

Waterhouse, L. H. (1986). Problems in facing the nature/nurture question in child language acquisition. *Language Sciences, 8*(2), 153–168.

Wells, A. S. (1991, January 6). In the market for a public school? *The New York Times*, Sec. 4A, p. 6.

Wells, G. (1986). *The meaning makers: Children learning language and using language to learn*. Portsmouth, NH: Heinemann Educational Books.

Westby, C. E., & Roman, R. (1995, August). Finding the balance: Learning to live in two worlds. *Topics in Language Disorders*, 68–88.

Wexler, K. (1982). A principle theory for language acquisition. In E. Wanner & L. Gleitman (Eds.), *Language acquisition: The state of the art*. Cambridge, UK: Cambridge University Press.

Whitaker, H. A., Bub, D., & Leventer, S. (1981). Neurolinguistic aspects of language acquisition and bilingualism. In H. Winitz (Ed.), *Native language and foreign language acquisition*. New York: The New York Academy of Sciences.

White, R. W. (1960). Competence and the psychosexual stages of development. In M. Jones (Ed.), *Nebraska symposium on motivation* (pp. 97–141). Lincoln, NE: University of Nebraska Press.

Whitehurst, G., & Vasta, R. (1975). Is language acquired through imitation? *Journal of Psycholinguistic Research, 4,* 37–59.

Whitney, P. (1998). *The Psychology of language.* New York: Houghton Mifflin.

Whorf, B. L. (1975). The organization of reality. In S. Rogers (Ed.), *Children and language.* London: Oxford University Press.

Wieczkiewicz, H. C. (1979, May). A phonic reading program for Navajo students. *Journal of American Indian Education,* 20–27.

Wiggins, G. (1991, February). Standards, not standardization: Evoking quality student work. *Educational Leadership,* pp. 18–25.

Wilbur, R. B., Montanelli, D., & Quigley, S. (1976). Pronominalization in the language of deaf students. *Journal of Speech and Hearing Research, 19,* 120–140.

Wilkerson, I. (1990, November 4). Blacks look to basics. *The New York Times,* Sec. 4A, p. 26.

Willis, F., & Williams, S. (1976). Simultaneous talking in conversation and the sex of speakers. *Perceptual and motor skills, 43,* 1067–1070.

Wilson, P. (1991). Trauma of Sioux Indian high school students. *Anthropology & Education Quarterly, 22*(4), 367–383.

Wimmer, H., Landerl, K., & Schneider, W. (1994). The role of rhyme awareness in learning to read a regular orthography. *British Journal of Developmental Psychology, 12,* 469–484.

Winitz, H. (Ed.). (1981). *Native language and foreign language acquisition.* New York: The New York Academy of Sciences.

Winter, M., & Rouse, J. (1990, February). Fostering intergenerational literacy: The Missouri parents as teachers program. *The Reading Teacher,* pp. 382–386.

Wiss, C. (1989). Early French immersion programs may not be suitable for every child. *Canadian Modern Language Review, 45,* 517–529.

Wode, H. (1980). Operating principles and 'universals' in L1, L2 and FLT. In D. Nehls (Ed.), *Studies in language acquisition.* Heidelberg: Julius Groos.

Wolf, D., Moreton, J., & Camp, L. (1994). Children's acquisition of different kinds of narrative discourse: genres and lines of talk. In J. Sokolov & C. Snow (Eds.), *Handbook of research in language development using CHILDES* (pp. 286–323), Hillsdale, NJ: Lawrence Erlbaum Associates, Inc.

Wootten, J., Merkin, S., Hood, L., & Bloom, L. (1979, March). *Wh-questions: Linguistic evidence to explain the sequence of acquisition.* Paper presented at the biennial meeting of the Society for Research in Child Development, San Francisco.

Wright, T. (1987). *Roles of teachers and learners.* Oxford: Oxford University Press.

Yamada, J. (1981, August). On the independence of language and cognition: Evidence from a hyperlinguistic retarded adolescent. Paper presented at the International Congress of Child Language, University of British Columbia, Vancouver.

Yardley, A. (1973). *Young children thinking.* London: Evans Brothers.

Yopp, H. K. (1988). The validity and reliability of phonemic awareness tests. *Reading Research Quarterly, 23,* 159–177.

Yule, G. (1985). *The study of language.* Cambridge, UK: Cambridge University Press.

Zakaluk, B. L., & Sealey, D. B. (1988). Teaching reading to Cree-speaking children: Instructional implications from an interactive model of reading. *Reading-Canada-Lecture, 6*(2), 93–99.

Zappert, L. T., & Cruz, B. R. (1977). *Bilingual education: An appraisal of empirical research.* Berkeley, CA: Bay Area Bilingual Education League/Lau Berkeley Unified School District.

Zareba, A. (1953). Jezyk polski w szwecji. *Jezyk Polski, 33,* 29–31, 98–111.

Zentella, A. C. (1997). *Growing up bilingual, Puerto Rican children in New York.* Oxford: Blackwell.

Zutell, J. (1980). Learning language at home and at school. In G. S. Pinnell (Ed.), *Discovering language with children.* Champaign-Urbana, IL: NCTE.

Name Index

Subject Index